STUDIA TRADITIONIS THEOLOGIAE
EXPLORATIONS IN EARLY AND MEDIEVAL THEOLOGY

Theology continually engages with its past: the people, experience, Scriptures, liturgy, learning and customs of Christians. The past is preserved, rejected, modified; but the legacy steadily evolves as Christians are never indifferent to history. Even when engaging the future, theology looks backwards: the next generation's training includes inheriting a canon of Scripture, doctrine, and controversy; while adapting the past is central in every confrontation with a modernity.

This is the dynamic realm of tradition, and this series' focus. Whether examining people, texts, or periods, its volumes are concerned with how the past evolved in the past, and the interplay of theology, culture, and tradition.

STUDIA TRADITIONIS THEOLOGIAE

EXPLORATIONS IN EARLY AND MEDIEVAL THEOLOGY

51

Series Editor: Thomas O'Loughlin,
Professor of Historical Theology
in the University of Nottingham

EDITORIAL BOARD

Director
Prof. Thomas O'Loughlin

Board Members
Dr Andreas Andreopoulos, Dr Nicholas Baker-Brian, Dr Augustine
Casiday, Dr Mary B. Cunningham, Dr Juliette Day, Prof. Johannes
Hoff, Prof. Paul Middleton, Prof. Simon Oliver, Prof. Andrew Prescott,
Dr Patricia Rumsey, Prof. Jonathan Wooding, Dr Holger Zellentin

"The Letter Killeth"

Redeeming Time in Augustine's Understanding of the Authority of Scripture

LAL DINGLUAIA

BREPOLS

Cover illustration:
Tabula Peutingeriana © ÖNB Vienna Cod. 324, Segm. VIII + IX

©© 2022, Brepols Publishers n. v., Turnhout, Belgium.

All rights reserved. No part of this publication may be reproduced, stored in a retrieval system, or transmitted, in any form or by any means, electronic, mechanical, photocopying, recording, or otherwise without the prior permission of the publisher.

D/2022/0095/174
ISBN 978-2-503-60116-8
eISBN 978-2-503-60117-5
DOI 10.1484/M.STT-EB.5.130571

ISSN 2294–3617
eISSN 2566–0160

Printed in the EU on acid-free paper.

Table of Contents

Preface   9

Abbreviations   11
1. Abbreviations for Biblical Materials   11
2. Other abbreviations   11
3. References to the works of Augustine   13

Introduction   15
Timeless Word and Words in Time   16
Methodological Considerations   20
Outline of the Work   27

Chapter 1: "… Nisi me catholicae ecclesiae conmoueret auctoritas"   29
Authority, Tradition and Time
1. Authority in Common Parlance Today   29
2. Authority in Antiquity   33
3. Tension of "the Time" in *Aureum Saeculum* and *Consummatio Saeculi*   36
4. *Trado* and the Adaptation of *Auctoritas* in the Early Church   40
5. After *Tempora Christiana*: Devolution of Traditions and Authority   43
Concluding Remarks   45

Chapter 2: "Si quam dubitationem attulerit latinorum interpretum infinita uarietas"   47
Physical Evolution of the Scriptures and its Theological Implications
1. *Vetus Latina* — A Brief Sketch of Augustine's "Common Edition" of the Scriptures   48
2. The Septuagint, *Vetus Latina* and *Hebraica Veritas*   50
3. The *Vetus Latina* and Traditions of the Church Regarding the Septuagint   53
4. Emergence of the "New Testament" and the Notion of a "Complete Canon"   55
Concluding Remarks   61

Chapter 3: "Our Hearts are Restless until they Rest in You"   63
The Longing for the Fullness of Time in the Confessiones
1. The Ambivalence of Authorities in Augustine   63
2. Augustine's Tryst with the Authority of Scripture   65
3. Discerning the Principle behind the Authority of Scripture   69

    4. Implications of Ambrose's Principle in Augustine's Reading of the Scriptures   71
Concluding Remarks   77

Chapter 4: "Exercet autem hoc tempore et purgat"   79
Discerning the Signs of the Time in the De doctrina Christiana
1. Tyconius and the Socio-Political and Religious Context of the "Donatist" Controversy   80
2. Discerning the Underlying Theological Issue in the "Complex" Donatist Controversy   84
3. Engaging Tyconius's *Liber Regularum* in the *De doctrina Christiana*   86
4. Fitting Tyconius's *Liber Regularum* into Augustine's Wider Exegetical Concerns   92
Concluding Remarks   94

Chapter 5: "Instead of doing what I had asked you, you thought up a new argument"   97
The Emergence of Paul in the Correspondence between Augustine and Jerome
1. The "Great Prefaces" to the Correspondence   98
2. Jerome and the Notions of Authority in the Correspondence   102
3. Augustine and the Notion of Scriptural Authority in the Correspondence   107
4. From *Signa* to *Res* in the "New Argument"   109
5. Humility, *Caritas* and Authority   113
Concluding Remarks   115

Chapter 6: "Ea ipsa est simplex fides, qua credimus"   117
Retrieving Paul Through the Book of Genesis
1. "Paul" of the Manicheans   118
2. Augustine's Early Responses to the Manicheans   123
3. Retrieving Paul through the Book of *Genesis*   128
Concluding Remarks   140

Chapter 7: "There we shall rest and see"   143
Beyond "Time" and "the Authority of Scripture" in the De Civitate Dei
1. "Rome" as an Ideological Construct   144
2. "Eternal Rome" in the "Collective" and "Personal" Memories: Reading *Confessiones* as a Subversive Literary Device   147
3. Of Heroes and Martyrs, Guardians and Sanctuaries: Interrogating Rome via Milan   152
4. What is Time? Discerning the Authority of Scripture in the *De civitate Dei*   158
Concluding Remarks   166

Chapter 8: Not "Perfection" but "Progress towards the Better" 169
The Retractationes *as the Epitome of* Crede ut Intellegas
1. The Indispensability of the Scriptures 171
2. The Human Aspects of the Scriptures 172
3. *Retractationes* as the Epitome of *Crede ut Intellegas* — The Theological Basis and Implications of "Progress towards the Better" in Augustine's Scriptural Odyssey 173
4. Beyond Time, Beyond "the Authority of Scripture" 177
Conclusions 177

Bibliography 181
1. Ancient Sources 181
2. Modern Authors 184

Indices 203
1. Index of Scriptures 203
2. Index of the Works of Augustine 206
3. Index of Other Ancient Authors 212
4. Index of Modern Authors 214

Preface

This book re-examines the notion of "the authority of Scripture", epitomized in the watchword of the Protestant Reformation *Sola Scriptura*, by drawing upon the insights of Augustine of Hippo. Augustine, who considerably resorted to the Scriptures in his writings, has played a uniquely important role in the formation of Christian theology; and the Reformation of the Sixteenth Century represented, theologically, a revival of Augustine's thought and has left its mark on the Protestant churches while scriptural authority has been the hallmark and the cornerstone of Protestant theology.

The principle of *Sola Scriptura* may be fairly represented by the Confession of Faith of the Presbyterian Church of India which asserts, "The Scriptures of the Old and New Testaments are the Word of God and the only infallible rule of faith and duty". Yet, such an innovative and dynamic notion as "the authority of Scripture", when it has been condensed into a statement of faith, can became a stagnant and disputed concept as it has been passed on to later generations. Being a product of specific contexts, challenges and issues, a rigid confession of faith can get distorted from, and even lead to the negation of, the underlying principles it seeks to express.

On the one hand, these distortions can be represented by a form of bibliolatry that has been perpetuated by the "fundamentalist" mindset. On the other end of the spectrum, Scripture can be considered as nothing more than a collection of ancient, outdated documents. And somewhere in between, there are those who hold Scripture as the crucial documents of a faith communities but who seek their value in some *Urtext* — thereby spawning the quest for an original or the earliest version of a text, to which later versions can be compared before one arrives at the true meaning of the text. As extensive as they are, all these positions partly share, or react against, the assumption that the authority of Scripture equates with the authority of stable texts which were mass-produced as the Bible.

For Augustine, the authority of Scripture is not propositional but relational, rooted in the incarnation of the Word of God. By infusing Augustine's insight, particularly his awareness of a tension in "Christocentric" time, this book argues that the authority of Scripture is not "solely" the authority of "the Book" but is related to more complicated sources of authority that are linked to this specific notion of time. Discerning the significance of these intricacies along with the "fluidity" of Scripture in early Christianity, this book emphasizes how the various theological expressions of the tension inherent in time are something that shaped Augustine in the depth of his thought. In other words, this book affirms that Augustine's concept of the authority of Scripture was embedded in his awareness of time and tries to tease out the full implications of this insight.

In writing this book, which is the outcome of my doctoral dissertation in the University of Nottingham, I express my sincere gratitude to Professor Thomas O'Loughlin, my supervisor. Tom has been very patient in pointing to the *res* behind the *signa* with his finger but many a times, my eyesight was too weak to even see his finger. Without his help and encouragement, this book will not come to fruition. I also wish to thank Professors Lewis Ayres and Alison Milbank, who examined my doctoral dissertation, for their valuable feedback and suggestions.

I am very grateful to the Research and Capacity Development of the Council for World Mission, and the Women's Department of the Eglwys Bresbyteraidd Cymru (The Presbyterian Church of Wales), for their financial support towards my studies. I also thank the Theological Education Board of the Presbyterian Church of India, Mizoram Synod, for giving me study leave and supporting me in various capacities.

I also express my appreciation to Dr Lalthansangi Ralte, for her proof reading; to Mike Cook, for his insightful comments; and to Revd Dr Phillip Brown, for the invaluable materials of Augustine's works in Latin. I am indebted to friends and families in India and the UK, particularly members of St Barnabas Church at Lenton Abbey in Nottingham and to my friends in UK Zofate, whose encouragement and unceasing prayers gave me strength in such an uncertain time.

And through it all, my wife Achhani (Lalchhanhimi Ralte) and my children, Calvin, Caleb, and Clement were beside me, sharing the burden of my studies. I thank them all for their patience and love, and I dedicated this book to them.

My deepest gratitude to God for his abounding grace!

Abbreviations

1. Abbreviations for Biblical Materials

Gen	Genesis
Ps	Psalms
Prov	Proverbs
Is	Isaiah
Dan	Daniel
Mt	Matthew
Mk	Mark
Lk	Luke
Jn	John
Act	Acts of the Apostles
Rom	Romans
1 Cor	1 Corinthians
2 Cor	2 Corinthians
Gal	Galatians
Eph	Ephesians
Phil	Philippians
Col	Colossians
1 Thes	1 Thessalonians
1 Tim	1 Timothy
2 Tim	2 Timothy
Tit	Titus
Jas	James
1 Pet	1 Peter
Apoc [Rev]	Apocalypse [Revelation]

2. Other abbreviations

ABD	*Anchor Bible Dictionary*
AJP	*American Journal of Philology*
AL	*Augustinus-Lexikon*
AS	*Augustinian Studies*
ATA	*Augustine through the Ages: An Encyclopedia*
CCSL	*Corpus Christianorum, Series Latina*
CH	*Church History*

CMC	*Cologne Mani Codex*
CR	*Corpus Reformatorum*
CSEL	*Corpus Scriptorum Ecclesiasticorum Latinorum*
DRev	*Downside Review*
ET	Encyclopedia of Time: Science, Philosophy, Theology and Culture
FOTC	Fathers of the Church
HI	*Hieronymus*
Historia	*Historia: Zeitschrift für Alte Geschichte*
HPT	*History of Political Thought*
HSCP	*Harvard Studies in Classical Philology*
ICS	*Illinois Classical Studies*
IJPS	*International Journal of Philosophical Studies*
JAAR	*Journal of the American Academy of Religion*
JECS	*Journal of Early Christian Studies*
JEH	*Journal of Ecclesiastical History*
JHI	*Journal of the History of Ideas*
JSAH	*Journal of the Society of Architectural Historians*
JTS	*Journal of Theological Studies*
LCL	*Loeb Classical Library*
LR	*Liber Regularum*
LXX	*Septuagint*
MSch	*Modern Schoolman*
MT	Masoretic Text
NCHB	The New Cambridge History of the Bible
NPNF	*Nicene and Post-Nicene Fathers*
OGHRA	The Oxford Guide to the Historical Reception of Augustine
PG	*Patrologia Graeca*
PL	*Patrologia Latina*
PEW	*Philosophy East and West*
RA	*Recherches Augustiniennes et Patristiques*
RB	*Revue Bénédictine*
RC	*Religion Compass*
REA	*Revue d'Etudes Augustiniennes et Patristiques*
RGDA	*Res Gestae Divi Augusti*
Rev.Politics	*Review of Politics*
RTAM	*Recherches de théologie ancienne et médiévale*
SBLGNT	*Society of Biblical Literature Greek New Testament*
SP	*Studia Patristica*
TAPA	*Transactions of the American Philological Association*
TDNT	*Theological Dictionary of the New Testament*
TDOT	*Theological Dictionary of the Old Testament*
VC	*Vigiliae Christianae*
VL	*Vetus Latina*
WSA	*The Works of Saint Augustine*
ZAC	*Zeitschrift für Antikes Christentum*

3. References to the works of Augustine

The referencing system throughout this work for Augustine is from H. J. Frede, *Kirchenschriftsteller: Verzeichnis und Sigel* (Vetus Latina: Die Reste der Altlateinischen Bibel 1/1, Freiburg, 1995).

Ad	*Contra Adimantum*
2 an	*de duabus animabus*
cf	*Confessiones*
ci	*De ciuitate Dei*
do	*De doctrina Christiana*
ench	*Enchiridion ad Laurentium, seu de fide, spe et caritate*
ep	*Epistulae*
Ev	*De consensu euangelistarum*
Fau	*Contra Faustum Manichaeum*
Fel	*Contra Felicem Manichaeum*
Fo	*Contra Fortunatum Manichaeum disputatio*
fu	*Contra epistulam Manichaei quam uocant fundamenti*
Gal	*Epistulae ad Galatas expositionis*
gest	*De gestis Pelagii*
Gn im	*De Genesi ad litteram imperfectus*
Gn li	*De Genesi ad litteram*
Gn Ma	*De Genesi contra Manichaeos*
Gn q	*Quaestionum in Heptateuchum*
hae	*De haeresibus ad Quoduultdeum*
Jo	*In Iohannis euangelium tractatus*
Jul	*Contra Iulianum*
Jul im	*Contra Iulianum opus imperfectum*
lib	*De libero arbitrio*
men	*De mendacio*
mor	*De moribus ecclesiae Catholicae et de moribus Manicheorum*
Par	*Contra epistulam Parmeniani*
pec	*De peccatorum meritis et remissione et de baptismo paruulorum ad Marcellinum*
Pel	*Contra duas epistulas Pelagianorum*
Pet	*Contra litteras Petiliani*
pers	*De dono perseuerantiae*
Ps	*Enarrationes in Psalmos*
q	*De diuersis quaestionibus octoginta tribus*
q Si	*Ad Simplicianum de diuersis quaestionibus*
re	*Retractationes*
rel	*De uera religione*
Rm	*Expositio quarundam propositionum ex epistola ad Romanos*
Rm in	*Epistolae ad Romanos inchoata expositio*
s	*Sermones*
s Den	*Sermones M. Denis*

s Dol	*Sermones Dolbeau*
sp	*De Spiritu et littera*
sy	*De fide et symbolo*
vit	*De Beata uita*

Introduction

bene uiuamus, et bona sunt tempora. nos sumus tempora: quales sumus, talia sunt tempora.[1] This exhortation by Bishop Augustine to his congregants, made around 410[2] when the sack of Rome cast a shadow of fear and uncertainty over the Roman empire, shows that even in the most challenging circumstance, the experience of time is always momentous and stimulating to Augustine's theological reflection.

Indeed, Augustine seems to be fascinated by time. His extensive meditation on time in *Confessiones* Book 11 shows that he persistently pondered the question, "what is time?" While Augustine's insights on the subject still influenced many thinkers even today, they often extrapolate his treatment of time from its original context, which was an exegesis of the opening passages of Genesis, and considered it separately from all his other works.[3] For Augustine, time was interconnected with other themes like nature and human history, body and soul, good and evil which can fall under the wider scope of creations.[4] His entire theological narrative would probably crumble like a weak structure if we were to wipe off and detach his notion of time from it. And delving into his understanding of time can open the door to other aspects of his thought. In other words, "time" is the starting point that can take us "back in time" to Augustine.

But then, time is a complicated subject in Augustine. According to John M. Quinn, there are four related senses of "time" in Augustine: psychological, physical, moral and historical time. Psychological time is a theoretical inquiry concerning the existence, nature and value of time.[5] This psychic time has its correlates in the physical world, particularly with motion in the celestial realm. The measurable aspect

---

1   "Let us live good lives, and the times are good. We ourselves are the times. Whatever we are like, that's what the times are like" s 80.8 (PL 38.498; Hill 355–56).
2   Unless otherwise stated, all dates/centuries are CE. All the dating of Augustine's works according to Frede (1995).
3   Pasquale (2013), 1814; According to Jean-Luc Marion, "it is only once the question of time is put back into its theological setting, that is, creation ..., that the analysis of time properly speaking really begins". Marion (2012), 202. But on how "a certain justification can be found" for this extrapolation in "Augustine's own reasoning", see Ricoeur (1984), 5; see also Brachtendorf (2012) for an overview of Augustine's influence on phenomenology and philosophy of language. See Ganssle (2002) for philosophical explorations into the nature of God and God's relation to time.
4   See Christian (1955), 315. In other words, time as a "creature" (see cf 11.14.17; ci 11.6) does not basically depend on human consciousness.
5   Quinn (1999), 832–33. Accordingly, time is a phenomenon of human consciousness. But Sorabji remarked that "Augustine's psychological account of time is not ... taken up by his immediate successors, nor even by himself in later writings". Sorabji (1983), 30.

of movement according to before and after which is rooted in mutability is physical time.[6] Moral time can denote the time-boundedness of our human life marked by suffering and trouble due to "the Fall". Historical time is concretely connected with the human predicament as socially lived in the past. While psychological and physical time are analysed by reason alone, moral and historical time fundamentally depends on supernatural faith.[7]

Although we can discern these four senses of time, they were not mutually exclusive, basically sharing the common essence of temporality and mutability. In contradistinction to time which is "relative to changing things and exists where such things exist" is eternity.[8] Eternity is the realm beyond time that belongs to God who is without temporal beginning or end.[9] Against this backdrop of God's eternity, can Augustine's notion of time shed a light on his understanding of the authority of Scripture?

Timeless Word and Words in Time

In the overall scheme of things which transcends time, Scripture is a "temporal dispensation" (*dispensatio temporalis*) with a transitory role that can be akin to the advent of Christ in the flesh.[10] From this aspect, the words of Scripture were words uttered in time (*tempus facta uerba*) and sounding in time (*uerba temporaliter sonantia*) that fled and pass away (*fugiunt et praetereunt*) while only Christ is the eternal Word of God (*aeternum uerbum tuum*) that remains forever (*manet in aeternum*).[11] Besides, Augustine was aware that the questions which Scripture raised to the probing mind converged eventually in the incomprehensible mystery of God.[12] Therefore, Scripture is contingent in the overall scheme of things.

---

6 Quinn (1999), 835. See cf 11.23.30; ci 12.16 for Augustine's own account.
7 Quinn (1999), 832–38; see also Quinn (1992) for a more thorough treatment of "times" in Augustine.
8 Christian (1955), 318.
9 According to Augustine, *quod tempus sine aliqua mobili mutabilitate non est, in aeternitate autem nulla mutatio est*. ci 11.6 (CCSL 48.326). So, eternity expressed "the qualitative difference between divine and created being". O'Daly (1986–1994a), 159. But Heidegger asserted that "philosophy will never have eternity and, accordingly, we will never be able to employ eternity methodologically as a possible respect in which to discuss time" (*wird die Philosophie die Ewigkeit nie haben und diese sonach nie als mogliche Hinsicht flir die Diskussion del' Zeit in methodischen Gebrauch genommen werden konnen*). Heidegger (1924), 1. Regarding the idea of eternity as "timelessness" and "everlastingness" and its implication for theology, see Filice (2009), 437–41. Regarding "Atemporal, Semipiternal, or Omnitemporal", see DeWeese (2002), 49–61.
10 See do 1.38.81–39.85; also rel 7.13; sy 4.8.
11 cf 11.6.8; in this regard, Cameron's quotation of Bochet's observation is remarkable: "In the Augustinian optic, one goes to the eternal by the temporal, more than one finds the eternal within the temporal … Scripture is only a mediation, necessary, to be sure, but only provisional. It stands at the service of this interior teaching, which, in return, gives an inexhaustible fecundity to reading it". Cameron (2012a), 209.
12 Fiedrowicz (2006), 16. On the rhetorical question how God was always the Creator and always Lord (*semper creator, semper dominus*) if created beings does not always exist to serve God, he asserted that they were perilous questions one should abstain from and discouraged the notion that one is

Then again, in this temporal realm, Scripture sheds light on the meaning of history whose rationale can be apprehended with faith. Here, Augustine's concept of the authority of Scripture was intertwined with his notion of an historical time which is the realm where divine revelation discloses the meaning of sacred history.[13] This perception radically differs from the Neoplatonic notion of time[14] that is a shadowy process in which there can be no decisively novel events. Following their concept of reincarnation of the soul and divine immutability, the flux of history is a mere reflection of timeless forms. For the Stoic too, the history of the world consists of perpetually recurring cycles of events.[15] The Manicheans,[16] being an offshoot of the Gnostic movement,[17] also shared their devaluation of time and material reality.[18] And their teaching is not compatible with the notion of an incarnation that centred upon the decisiveness of the crucifixion of Christ.[19] However, Augustine sees history

---

capable of understanding everything: *quaestionum periculis debeant temperare ... ad omnia se idoneos arbitrentur potiusque intellegant*. ci 12.16 (CCSL 48.372). Regarding the soul's origin: *nec tunc sciebam nec adhuc scio*. re 1.1.3 (CCSL 57.10).

13 For Markus, the conception of "sacred history" makes explicit what is implicit in Augustine's view and is closely related but not exactly identical with *Heilsgeschichte*. "'Sacred history' is defined by the special character of the record". Markus (1970), 231. As Gilson remarked, "Even though understanding is supernatural in origin and nature, it produces effects observable in the natural order. By its light, knowledge of some things becomes accessible to reason which reason unaided could not have attained". See Gilson (1967), 187. But on how sacred history, in which "the individual fits into the pattern of a larger and objectively planned arrangement of reality", may differ from the existentialists' idea of 'historicity', "meaning no more than the present decision of an individual free will", see Danielou (1958), 8.

14 But see Sorabji who asserted that there was cross-fertilization between Platonists and Christians on the subject of time. "On some aspects of it they were violently opposed, while on others they came surprisingly close together". Sorabji (1983), 2. On the fallacy of the simple distinction that the Greek had a "circular" conception of time, as opposed to the "linear" or teleological conception, see Feeney (2007), 3.

15 Christian (1955), 323–24; Quinn (1999), 837. See ci 12.10–14 for Augustine's own reproduction.

16 Coyle remarked that "Manichaeism", who refers to themselves as the "Religion of Light", is a word coined by its adversaries from the name of the movement's founder, Mani. See Coyle (2009), 308.

17 Considering how they draw upon elements from Zoroastrianism, Buddhism and Christianity, Bonner regarded Manichaeism as the last and the greatest manifestation of Gnosticism. See Bonner (1986), 161.

18 But according to Mirecki and BeDuhn, "The Manichaean response to the world was more complex than simple rejection. Mani considered all of human history moving toward the same goal his religion envisioned, and so Manichaeans look what was useful from surrounding cultures and made it their own". Mirecki and BeDuhn (2001), 2.

19 Bonner remarked that the "very suggestion of the Incarnation was unthinkable" for the Manicheans "since it involved the descent of the pure Spirit of God into the foul prison of the flesh". Bonner (1986), 167. Henrichs also asserts that in the eyes of the Manicheans, "the real crucifixion of Christ was not a one-time event but the ongoing suffering of Light imprisoned in Matter. St Augustine quotes similar Manichaean legends but scholars were inclined to think that he had made them up in order to ridicule the creed to which he himself once belonged. The *Cologne Codex* proves that they are genuinely Manichaean". Henrichs (1979), 340.

as a drama of salvation with a beginning, a middle and an end. This linear narrative implies a process within which genuinely novel and decisive events can and do occur.[20]

Although Augustine's notion of historical time, which privileged the scriptural canon as the crucible of sacred history, was best explicated in the *De civitate Dei* which he had written during 412–426, the concept — rooted deeply in his meditations on the opening passages of Genesis — was accumulated over a long period of time. As early as 388/89, Augustine wrote the *De Genesi contra Manichaeos* in which he asserted that "these seven days furnish us with a miniature symbolic picture of the entire span of world history from start to finish".[21] "History" in his *De Genesi ad litteram imperfectus liber*, "is when things done by God or man are recounted" and in the more detailed *De Genesi ad litteram*, history is "the account of events that actually happened".[22] Though Augustine favoured an allegorical reading during his earlier works on Genesis, his notion of "historical time" guided his later reading, which in turn conveyed his notion of the authority of Scripture. As O'Loughlin succinctly remarked, it was important to Augustine's "whole theology that Gen 1–6 be a factual historical account and so every possible challenge had to be taken up".[23]

Beyond Genesis, this rationale was probably most obvious in Augustine's defence of the story of the prophet Jonah that was often bitterly jeered at by unbelievers.[24] Defending the factuality of the miraculous nature of the story, he asserted, "Human speech is wont to express itself by words, but divine power by deeds ... divine eloquence becomes, in a sense, more beautiful by miraculous deeds, which have an appropriate meaning".[25] The *facta* of history became a *uerba* — events become God's communication to humankind[26] — but one needs to believe in order to understand the meaning: "For, there are numberless difficulties which cannot be settled before one accepts the faith".[27]

Of course, there was a time when Augustine "will be sceptical" to maintain that the Scriptures shed light on the meaning of history which can be comprehended only with faith. Burns asserts that after reading Cicero's *Hortensius*, "Augustine had sought to understand rather than to believe" and subsequent events were the outcome of this desire.[28] Disappointed by the crudeness of, and impropriety in, the Scriptures,

---

20 Christian (1955), 323–28; Quinn (1999), 837.
21 Gn Ma 2.1.1 (Hill 69).
22 Gn im 2.5 (Hill 116); Gn li 8.1.2 (Hill 347).
23 O'Loughlin (1995), 209. In Augustine's words: *Nunc autem defendenda mihi uidetur historia.* ci 15.8 (CCSL 48.462).
24 *multo cachinno a paganis grauiter inrisum animaduerti.* In reply, Augustine argued, *omnia diuina miracula credenda non sint aut, hoc cur non credatur, causa nulla sit.* ep 102.30–31 (CSEL 34.2.570); cf. ci 1.14.
25 *Nam sicut humana consuetudo uerbis ita divina potentia etiam factis loquitor et ... ita in factis mirabilibus congruenter aliquid significantibus quodam modo luculentior est divina eloquentia.* ep 102.33 (CSEL 34.2.573; Parsons 172–73).
26 Markus (1970), 196.
27 *Sunt enim innumerabiles, quae non sunt finiendae ante fidem.* ep 102.38 (CSEL 34.2.578; Parsons 176–77).
28 Burns (1990), 376, cf. 384 n. 30. Beduhn asserts the Manichaeans "positioned themselves as the proponents of reason in the face of dogmatic authority, taking up the language, if not the actual positions, of scepticism as it was propounded in the literature of the Pyrrhonic and Academic schools". See BeDuhn (2009), 2–3.

particularly the Old Testament and its characters, Augustine joined the Manicheans. Drawing from *De beata uita* 1.4 and *De utilitate credendi* 1.2, TeSelle asserted that "the type of Christianity ... which stressed reverence for divine authority at the expense of rational enquiry" deterred Augustine while the Manichean's claim "to lead men to God through reason alone" appealed to him.[29]

But, ten years after Augustine negated and abhorred the Scriptures, he was still disappointed in the rational enquiry undertaken, particularly with Faustus the Manichean and the Academics.[30] While in this state of mind, Augustine listened to the preaching of Bishop Ambrose in Milan, whose "spiritual" reading gradually dispelled his misgiving upon the Scriptures.

Once he renounced the Manicheans, Augustine made much effort to defend and explicate the Scriptures, particularly the creation narratives of the book of Genesis which negated the Manichean dualistic cosmogony. According to Torchia, in the doctrine of *creatio ex nihilo*, Augustine "found the origin of the intimate causal relationship between God and the rest of reality";[31] Cameron considered Augustine's early exposition of Genesis 2:5–6 in *De Genesi contra Manichaeos* as "The classic source for Augustine's understanding of the need for Scripture".[32] Behind Augustine's assertion that "Scripture" is essential to fallen humanity, we therefore see the basis of "authority" that would eventually take a definite shape in his accounts.[33] For Augustine, authority is not an abstract quality but emerges from humanity's need in the status of reality as created and formed. It is this exploration which is the kernel of this work.

We shall see that over the "allegorical" reading he adopted against the Manicheans in the initial stage, Augustine gradually appropriated a "literal" approach in his reading of Genesis narratives and the Scriptures as a whole, thereby attaching greater significance to "historical time" in his evolving notion of the authority of Scripture. Hence, Augustine's view of Scripture is reflected in the way he actually uses it in exegesis and his understanding of the authority of Scripture and his scriptural interpretation mutually determine each other.

---

29 TeSelle (1970), 27. According to Teske, "The African church seems to have preserved the anti-intellectual spirit of Tertullian famous for his claim to believe precisely because it is absurd". Teske (2009), 112.
30 cf 5.7.13; 6.11.18.
31 Torchia (1999), 65. We will see more of *creatio ex nihilo* later in chapter three.
32 Cameron (2012a), 202. According to Augustine: *quae dum tractando exprimuntur bene intellegentibus tamquam imber ueritatis infunditur. sed hoc nondum erat antequam anima peccaret ... irrigabat eam fonte interiore loquens in intellectu eius, ut non extrinsecus uerba exciperet tamquam de supradictis nubibus pluuiam, sed fonte suo, hoc est de intimis suis manante ueritate satiaretur*. Gn Ma 2.5 (CSEL 91.123).
33 On the shifts in "emphasis from the intellect to the affections" in Augustine's scriptural interpretation and how "Everything is set in motion because of the situation of fallen humanity", see TeSelle (2002a), 23–32. J. van Oort even asserted that "It is through Augustine that western Christianity developed a doctrine of Scripture's infallibility; but this concept (and its basis in the idea of a fixed canon of biblical writings) was clearly also nourished by his anti-Manichean feelings". van Oort (2012), 199.

Methodological Considerations

Augustine was a prolific writer who extensively quoted from, and interpreted, the Scriptures. Of the surviving five million words that he had produced,[34] at least two-thirds are "either commentaries or sermons on scriptural texts".[35] So, it is easy to assume that one can simply understand Augustine's perspective on the Scriptures, particularly through reading his major writings. But Augustine maintained that in the process of reading, "casual readers are misled by problems and ambiguities of many kinds, mistaking one thing for another".[36] Indeed, we can see "both continuity and dynamic movement" in Augustine's notion on the Scriptures[37] and not a static concept. So, in considering Augustine's dynamic "doctrine" of the Scriptures, although it is tempting to eagerly collect statements from his writings that speak very highly about the Scriptures, one also needs to acknowledge the "truly human aspect of Scripture" where he definitely asserts "the human agency in the writing and translating Scripture".[38]

Similarly, looking at Augustine's understanding of authorities, especially that of the authority of Scripture, one need to be self-aware of our modern preoccupations, so as not to impose and assert our assumptions — whether they are doctrinal and theological, philosophical and psychological, social and political, cultural and religious conjectures — on Augustine.[39] But then again, it is because we believe that Augustine's *cor inquietum*[40] — the "restless heart" — can be correlated to our modern existential angst which still makes his writings relevant. So, in acknowledging the dialectic between the perpetuity of Augustine's insights with its rootedness in his own specific context, we will try to explore Augustine's vision of the authority of Scripture.

Instead of doing a selective reading of Augustine's works alone, we will also look at his interlocutors because one understands Augustine more the better one takes his dialogue partners into consideration. We will try to locate the enigma of "time" — the tension between the already and the not yet — in his narratives and argue that the various expressions of this "tension" is something that shaped Augustine unconsciously, as much as it is something that he consciously reacted to. His attempt to come to terms with this tension in time, the dialectic of the already and the not yet in which he perceived the incarnation of Christ as the pivotal event, should be

---

34 O'Donnell (2001), 16. Cameron noted out that according to one estimate, there are some 45,000 references to the Scriptures in Augustine's writings. Costello asserted that due to Augustine's extensive use of the Scriptures, "one could reconstruct from his works alone more than two-thirds of the Bible". See Cameron (2012a), 200; Costello (1930), xi.
35 Harrison (2005), 76.
36 do 2.7.10 (Green 61).
37 Cameron (2012a), 201.
38 Toom (2013), 81.
39 In other words, one must be wary of Gadamer's observation when reading Augustine: "A person who is trying to understand a text is always projecting. He projects a meaning for the text as a whole as soon as some initial meaning emerges in the text". Gadamer (2004), 269.
40 cf 1.1.1; cf. cf 11.29.39 where he expressed similar feeling: *at ego in tempora dissilui, quorum ordinem nescio* (CCSL 27.215).

employed as a hermeneutical key to see Augustine's understanding of the Scriptures and scriptural authority.

This insight represents a profound "methodological shift" from any "selective" reading of Augustine, and from the perspective of systematic theology.[41] Our struggle is to read Augustine accurately and in his own terms, rather than to look at him from a distance through the "binoculars" of a systematic theologian. Our desire is to get closer to Augustine and to "converse" with him and take into account Augustine's interlocutors in their specific contexts. In my attempt to do this, I realized that in order to comprehend Augustine's complex and dynamic understanding of "the authority of Scripture", I also needed to "redeem" his notion of time.

The phenomenon of time that enthrals the human mind is both pervasive and elusive, with manifold factors determining our orientation to, and discernment of, time.[42] Recounting how a "cyclical" notion of time, dominant[43] in the pre-Christian era, has been largely eclipsed by a "linear" notion of time, John Hassard asserts that this "unilinear image" is later fused with the image of time as a valuable commodity. "Whereas in modern theology linear-time has as its conclusion the promise of eternity, in the mundane, secular activities of industrialism temporal units are finite."[44] Though "time seems a central property to the objects and events of the everyday living world" now, Sean Enda Power highlights how theorists "have often argued for counter-intuitive ideas of time." While some argue that time is unreal, or that we cannot know about time itself, others argue that our beliefs about time are contradictory, or that time is really nothing like time as we think of or encounter it.[45] Observing that "Perspectives on time range from subatomic particles to cosmic evolution", H. James Birx maintains that one must "embrace both evolutionary biology and relativity physics" to grasp the modern perception and appreciation of time.[46] Considering how "contemporary time studies" make a distinction between time as it is in itself, i.e., the scientific image of time, and time as we humans perceive and experience it, i.e., the manifest images of time, Heather Dyke and Adrian Bardon assert that one goal of the philosophy of time is to resolve the tensions between these two images.[47]

41　This simply denoted my theological orientation that "pre-determined" my reading of Augustine. For brief definitions, scopes, and criticisms of "systematic theology", see Thiselton (2015), 1–6; McGrath (2013), 67; on how a collection of writings attributed to Dionysius the Areopagite "had to be taken as the first corpus of systematic theology, composed in Apostolic times", see Perczel (2015), 212; but on how "Systematic theology was the invention of the early twelfth century", see Colish (2006), 138.

42　The "indeterminacy" which makes "time studies today" still relevant has been stated thus: "If concepts of time are historically situated, mutating as societies and their science, economics, values, language, and institutions change, then it is logical to ask what are our own twenty-first-century concepts of time." Burges, Elias (2016), 2.

43　We must note that the "Greek philosophers were not unanimous" regarding a cyclical notion of time and that "the Greeks repeatedly changed their views about time." See Momigliano (1977), 185–87; also n. 14 above.

44　Hassard (1990), 11–12.

45　Power (2021), 1–2.

46　Birx (2009), xxix.

47　Dyke, Bardon (2013), 1–2.

In this regard, Augustine's notion of time is still a subject of immense interest.[48] As John M. Quinn asserted, Augustine "ordinarily speaks of times rather than time" and he specified the "four faces" of time, viz., psychological, physical, moral and historical, in Augustine's writings.[49] A brief literature review reveals that the scholarly receptions of Augustine's "four faces" of time can roughly be classified into "subjective-philosophical" and "objective-historical" categories. Those in the former category tend to engage more with the *Confessiones* while those in the latter category tend to reflect more upon *De civitate Dei*, even though Augustine's treatment of "times" is far from being confined within these two books alone, as we have already pointed out in the previous section.

While we see no consensus among scholars who delved more into the subjective-philosophical aspect of time in Augustine's thought, we can at least assert the significance of the *Confessiones*, particularly Book 11, in determining their approaches. According to Joan Stambaugh "It has almost become a hallowed tradition when one speaks on the problem of time to quote Augustine who stated that if you did not ask him what time was, he knew; but if you did ask him, he no longer knew."[50] This observation has been espoused by Lyotard in his reading of Augustine's meditation on time in the *Confessiones*. Asserting that the "prose of the world gives place to...the phenomenology of internal time", Lyotard maintained that "The whole of modern, existential thought on temporality ensues from this meditation".[51] Examining the works of modern philosophers like Husserl, Heidegger and other "phenomenologists",[52] David van Dusen observed that they have "unmixed praise for Confessions XI".[53] Insisting that these philosophers tend to focus on the issues of "language, textuality, and narrative", and "memory, temporality, and the metaphysics of presence", Andrea Nightingale asserted that they had neglected Augustine's view of temporal human embodiment. However, he too insists that Augustine's discourses on the body cannot be investigated without examining Augustine's theory of time as set forth in Book 11 of the *Confessiones*.[54]

Others "situate" Augustine in the philosophical traditions of his day and focus more on who could have inspired him while also discerning where Augustine's

---

48 As Timothy George noted, "Augustine's discussion of time and eternity continues to resonate, not only among theologians such as Karl Barth, Jürgen Moltmann, Colin Gunton, Robert Jensen, and many others, but also among philosophers and postmodernist thinkers including Martin Heidegger, Jean François Lyotard, and Paul Ricoeur." George (2005), 27–28.
49 Quinn (1999), 832-33. Modern sociologists usually take one of two courses when defining the nature of time: i.e., to (a) describe differences between concepts of 'social-time' and 'clock-time' or (b) decode metaphors of time-patterning (e.g., procedural, mechanical, linear, cyclic, dialectical). See Hassard (1990), 6.
50 Stambaugh (1974), 129.
51 Lyotard (2000), 73–74.
52 "To study time from a phenomenological point of view is to attempt to understand time not in terms of physics or mathematics, but solely to describe it in nonempirical, philosophical terms." Anderson (2009), 1297.
53 van Dusen (2014), 11.
54 Nightingale (2011), 2, 7.

originality lies. Richard Sorabji explored different theories of time in antiquity and the dynamics of fusion and tension between the Platonist's and the Christian's view of time. Sorabji was primarily interested in locating Augustine within the philosophical traditions of his day and seeing how Augustine adapted them for his Christian purposes.[55] Relying upon his examination of Augustine's notion of time in Book 11 of the *Confessiones*, John F. Callahan explored how Plato, Aristotle, Plotinus and Augustine consider the question of time from entirely different perspectives.[56] Roland J. Teske also explored how Augustine resolved three paradoxes concerning time in Book 11 of the *Confessiones*, and argued that Augustine's resolution to these paradoxes "is tied" to what he learned from Plotinus.[57] In a more general sense, Adrian Bardon categorized theories about the nature of time over the centuries under idealism, realism, and relationism. Also relying upon his reading of the *Confessiones*, he asserts that Augustine is a "temporal idealist" for whom "time is a merely subjective matter, and nothing in reality corresponds to it."[58]

From this overview of scholarly opinions, we can assert that Augustine's notion of time that he expressed in the *Confessiones* still draws immense interest, particularly for those whose responses could fall under the subjective-philosophical category. Yet, Augustine's notion of time, however insightful and intriguing it may prove to be, will lose its potential if one focuses only on his philosophical questions without subscribing to his "Christian vision". Augustine meditates on time as he attempts to reconcile his sense of temporality[59] with a time-transcending God whose will however transpires in the temporal realm, most perceptibly in the incarnation of the Eternal Word. As the Timeless Word addressed Augustine "in time", time assumed a deeper sense that comprised a creative tension and this, in turn, enabled him to tease out the deeper meaning of Scripture in a hermeneutic circle.

In *De civitate Dei*, Augustine's reflection on "time" takes a more definite direction as he employs his "subjective-philosophical" view of time at the service of his exposition of the Scriptures while also corroborating his "objective-historical" view of time.[60] In assessing this work, some scholars focused on Augustine's historical experience and how his objective-historical scheme unfolds throughout the books. Others focused upon his "external" sources and enquired whether Augustine quoted these historical and philosophical sources verbatim or recollect them from memory. But *De civitate Dei* covers several interrelated issues over a period of time that cannot be confined to his philosophical and historical context. J. O'Meara offered an assessment upon the various

---

55 See Sorabji (1983), 2, 163–72.
56 Callahan (1948), 149, 188.
57 Teske (1996), 1.
58 Bardon (2013), 6–7, 24–26. On the argument that for Augustine, time is only in the mind and not mind-independent, and the possible objections to Augustine's position, see Power (2021), 150–82.
59 Stressing the significance of Augustine's "primordial discovery of temporality", Pranger even asserts that "the created and temporal status of the world had been his great discovery in his search for wisdom." Pranger (2006), 114.
60 For O'Meara, *De civitate Dei* "is no more purely theoretical than it is purely theological." O'Meara (1961), viii–ix.

readings of this work by different scholars which ranged from being a philosophy of history, a theology of history, a political theory, a work dominated by Platonic idealism and a Christian apologetic.[61] More recently, *A Critical Guide* to the book asserts that "Augustine's *City of God* has profoundly influenced the course of Western political philosophy" and that the essays within were meant to deepen "our understanding of Augustine's most influential work and provide a rich overview of Augustinian political theology and its philosophical implications."[62] Relating the numerous themes present in *De civitate Dei*, John Cavadini asserts that the work "is a brilliant weaving of philosophy, biblical theology, political thought, and Christian pastoral concerns."[63]

While scholars differed in their approaches to, and assessments of, Augustine's myriad themes, D. V. Meconi contends that "It is the presence of God in human history that interests Augustine, and this is the goal of the [work]: to help to clarify the relationship between those events which occur in time and those eternal verities which alone can give the human condition ultimate meaning."[64] Written amidst the upheavals after the sack of Rome, Augustine deconstructed the ideology inherent in the history of "the City of Rome" and offered an alternative vision of "the City of God" based on Scripture. His fundamental theological proposition is that human history actually reveals the presence of two contrasting cities created by two kinds of loves. Starting with the history of the Roman empire, he draws parallels between the origin of the city of Rome and the scriptural account of a city that Cain found (ci 15.1). The strife between Remus and Romulus represented natural human tendency while the hostility of Cain upon Abel is a spiritual representation of the contrast between these two cities (ci 25.23). Thus, we can see Augustine's historical vision blended with his theological conviction[65] during what would otherwise have been an elusive,[66] uncertain time as he probed "the origin and progress and merited ends of the two cities", and how both "are in this present world mixed together and, in a certain sense, entangled with one another" (ci 11.1).

The notion of time as an objective linear entity — with a beginning, a middle[67] and an end — that Augustine advocated explicitly in the *De civitate Dei*[68] still "impinges"

---

61 O'Meara (1961). On how the "grids" that O'Meara outlined were still relevant, see Meconi (2021), 1–18.
62 Wetzel (2012), i.
63 Meconi (2021), 17.
64 Meconi (2021), 21.
65 On the significance of "theological, temporal determinations which lay transverse to 'empirical' findings" through which Augustine can "develop an 'enduring answer' to every historical situation" see Koselleck (1985), 99.
66 Timothy George astutely stated the "elusiveness" of time in Augustine's mind thus: "Augustine is forever confessing his ignorance and lack of understanding about so deep a mystery. The appropriate mood [for approaching the question of time] is interrogative, or at best subjunctive; not declarative, much less imperative." George (2005), 30.
67 Danielou remarked that "It is a further peculiarity of the Christian outlook on history that the centre of interest is neither at the beginning, as it was for the Greeks, nor at the end, as it is in evolutionary theories, but in the middle." Danielou (1958), 10.
68 C. S. Smith and L. Hung even asserted that the Christian notion of time as linear was first mentioned by Augustine "in his seminal *City of God*, written during the 5th century." Smith, Hung (2009), 87. Augustine's innovative venture has been reflected in an insightful observation that Momigliano made: "St. Augustine is a valid witness only for himself - or perhaps for those pagan philosophers whom he

upon our understanding of time.[69] More significantly, Augustine's systematic rendition of a linear time which located him, the church, and the universal members of the heavenly city, entangled and straining under the tension of the "already and not yet"-ness of time, is a window through which his notion of scriptural authority has been exhibited. Given that Augustine's dynamic understanding of the authority of Scripture has never been extensively examined in the light of his awareness of time, specifically as the "already and not yet", this book is an attempt to do just that.

This approach will also be a fundamental departure from the "modern" understanding of the "authority of Scripture" as epitomized in the watchword of the Protestant Reformation *sola scriptura*. While the significances of the principle that *sola scriptura* entailed in the sixteenth century cannot be denied,[70] divergent understandings and interpretations thereafter[71] also make this concept contentious and largely contorted. Abusing the *sola* principle has various outcomes in different Christian "camps", ranging from bibliolatry and negation of church traditions[72] to schism and outright denial of the authority of Scripture.[73] Specifying how these discords[74] can relatively be the consequences of assuming that the "authority of Scripture" amounts to the

---

knew. His dilemma does not necessarily correspond to what ordinary Jews, Greeks, and Christians felt in the fifth century A.D. - it is even less valid for what ordinary Jews and Greeks felt about time, say, in the fifth century B.C." Momigliano, (1977), 184.

69 According to R. Lamb, "This view has long predominated in Western thinking, and any alternate view is discounted as ill-informed and without substance. It is fundamental to nearly all Western worldviews, including those found in the contemporary physical and social sciences. It is integral to concepts as basic as growth, evolution, and cause and effect." Lamb (2009), 1273.

70 Paul L. Allen noted that this principle emerged "from the strain of a medieval theological practice that had grown diffuse … a methodological emphasis that stems from medieval Augustinianism." Allen (2012), 118. Identifying the profound effect of this principle on Christian theology, R. Ward Holder remarked that "thinkers now had a tool that logically made the knowledge of one book, the Bible, more important than the knowledge of all other sacred books put together." Holder (2012), 44.

71 Van den Belt argued that *sola scriptura* is not very adequate to express the orthodox Protestant view of the authority of Scripture. Maintaining that the term *sola scriptura*, together with *sola fide*, and *sola gratia* "emerged only in Scholarship shortly before the 1917 commemoration of the Reformation", he asserted that "It is misguiding to define the core of the Reformation itself from the point of later polemics." van den Belt (2018), 38–41.

72 According to Paddison, "Fundamentalism and historical criticism both presume that the church and the church's teaching is an obstacle, not an aid, to reading Scripture well." Paddison (2009), 66–67. R. Jenson even argued that "The slogan *sola Scriptura*, if by that it meant 'apart from creed, teaching office, or authoritative liturgy,' is an oxymoron." Jenson (1997), 28.

73 Herman Bavinck asserted that "*Sola scriptura* does not only lead to reformation, but also to disintegration of the church." See van den Belt (2008), 253. On the assertion that many modern evangelicals either used it "to justify endless schism" or "to justify every manner of false doctrine", that in turn left many "increasingly frustrated" with the doctrine of *sola scriptura*, see Mathison (2001), 14.

74 The "discords" in both extremes may be represented by the fundamentalists and liberalists' "camps". Reflecting upon the issue of scriptural authority from a "Chalcedonian perspective", Allen Verhey observed that fundamentalism "identifies and confuses the human words of scripture with the divine word" while liberalism "divides the two and contrasts the human words with the divine word." Verhey (1986), 58. Specifically in relation to time and scriptural authority, contrasting approaches can be

authority of stable texts which were mass-produced as the Bible,[75] this book instead attempts to see what "authority of Scripture" signified for Augustine in the light of his sense of temporality.

Basically, I draw my methodological stances from the insights of both Oscar Cullman and Hans-Georg Gadamer. Cullman considered the "tension" between the "already and not yet" as essential to the whole message and identity formation of the early Christians.[76] Gadamer's concept of *wirkungsgeschichtliches bewusstsein* stressed the necessity of a "consciousness" or an awareness that our "situatedness" in time limits our horizons, which makes our hermeneutical output provisional while also giving legitimacy to the authority of tradition.[77] While I am not engaging with Cullman and Gadamer,[78] since my primary engagement is with Augustine, I am using their ideas to enlighten my own reading of Augustine that has allowed me to explore his works with new details and greater depth. Similarly, I am not engaging in an extensive literature review of Augustinian scholarship — past and present — since I mainly try to tease out Augustine's concept of the authority of Scripture, which was embedded in his awareness of time.

---

roughly represented by the biblical fundamentalists' insistence on "a strict and literal interpretation of Creation as presented in Genesis" with its corresponding notion of time set against the scientific evolutionists' temporal framework, marked by its perpetuity. See Birx (2009), xxx–xxxi.

75 The mass-production of a uniform text through the widespread use of printing technologies in the early modern period resulted in its ready accessibility. In this regard, H. L. Carrigan asserted that "Because Protestants have encouraged the reading authority of the individual believer, Bible versions have been challenged and the work of translators has been questioned. At stake for such readers is the Bible's inspiration and its infallibility." Carrigan Jr. (2004), 365–67. In chapter two, we will see how the physical nature of the scriptural texts also determines the meaning and theological status ascribed to the texts.

76 In the words of Cullmann, "What is specifically Christian [in a notion of linear time] is rather that tension, and the orientation of all events from the new, decisive incision … It is already the time of the end, and yet is not the end. This tension finds expression in the entire theology of Primitive Christianity … To anyone who does not take clear account of this tension, the entire New Testament is a book with seven seals, for this tension is the silent presupposition that lies behind all that it says". In the "Introductory Chapter to the Third Edition", Cullmann summarized the antithetical stances held by Bultmann and proponents of consistent eschatology: "Both present the incorporation of eschatology into redemptive history as a wrong solution of the delayed *parousia*, as an impossible afterthought". See Cullmann (1962), xvii–xxx, 145–46. For the four scholarly models of eschatology, see chapter one, n. 58 below. On the similarity and divergence of Augustine's "sacred history" from Cullmann's notion of "salvation history", see Markus (1970), 231–32.

77 For Gadamer, *wirkungsgeschichtliches bewusstsein* (historically effected consciousness) "mean at once the consciousness effected in the course of history and determined by history, and the very consciousness of being thus effected and determined … We always find ourselves within a situation, and throwing light on it is a task that is never entirely finish". Regarding tradition, Gadamer maintains that "our finite historical being is marked by the fact that the authority of what has been handed down to us — and not just what is clearly grounded — always has power over our attitudes and behaviour". See Gadamer (2004), xxx, 282, 301–06.

78 It is interesting to note that in *The Oxford Guide to the Historical Reception of Augustine*, there are articles on prominent modern hermeneuticians like Martin Heidegger, Edmund Husserl and Paul Ricoeur but none on Gadamer, although the article on "Hermeneutics" in the same book pointed out that Augustine is "at the heart of Gadamer's hermeneutical philosophy". See Wisse (2013), 1134. This comment clearly highlights the relevance of Gadamer's insights for reading Augustine today.

Outline of the Work

This work can be seen as comprising of four parts. The first part, chapters one and two will deal with the concepts of "authority" and "Scripture" respectively, which developed as separate entities until they eventually converged into a distinctive theological notion as the authority of Scripture. Maintaining that authority is the natural consequence of being in a relationship, we will trace how *auctoritas* was adapted as a theological concept and see how the ability to exert durable influence long after an event actually occurred is fundamental to the whole notion of authority. And we will delineate how Scriptures exerted durable influence over the Christian community when we explore how the physical nature of the scriptural texts also determines the meaning of, and the theological status ascribed to, the texts. We will see that the Christian Scripture has been forged between two divergent notions that the New Testament was "prophetically void" and that the Old Testament was "superseded" by the New Testament. These interacting notions will highlight how the Christian Scriptures documented the enigma of "time" in the formative stage and well into the time of Augustine.

The second part, chapters three and four will deal specifically with *Confessiones* and *De doctrina Christiana*, two important works of Augustine which illustrated his understanding of the authority of Scripture. Starting with his initial negation of the Scriptures which he recounted in his *Confessiones*, we shall see how Augustine evolved into an ardent expositor of the scriptures in the *De doctrina Christiana*. As we look at the changing socio-political and religio-theological background behind these two works, we shall argue that much of the problems and the solutions recounted therein lies with Augustine's own engagement with the enigma of time. We will see how the incarnation of Christ is the pivotal event determining his understanding of the authority of Scripture. We will assert that one of the most significant insights that Augustine draws from Tyconius is the decisiveness of the present as the point where the past and the future collate. Accordingly, in Augustine's "new" reading of Paul, we see how the dialectic of the "already" and the "not yet" was interiorized in the perpetual struggle of the self that is helpless without the grace of God which finds full expression in the incarnation.

The third part, chapters five and six will deal with the development of Augustine's thought over a period of time, particularly as he engaged with Jerome and the Manicheans, and centred upon his reading of the Pauline letters and the book of Genesis. Starting with his correspondence with Jerome, we will see how a "new" reading of Paul emerged in Augustine. As he "thought up a new argument" in the course of the correspondence, Augustine asserted that God's decisive act in the realm of time has been recorded in the Scriptures so that falsification of these accounts would amount to shaking the foundation of scriptural authority. On the question of the imposition of Jewish rituals upon the Gentiles, we will see how the dialectic of the "already" and the "not yet" which preoccupied the early church was still very much an interpretative conundrum during the time of Augustine. In his intertextual reading of Genesis with the epistles of Paul, we will see how Augustine countered the Manichean "attack" on the Scriptures. Against the Manicheans, he maintained that the two testaments of the Scriptures are in perfect harmony. Drawing largely upon Genesis to substantiate his reading of the Pauline epistles, we will see how he negated the Manichean dualism by affirming that all the creations were created by and through the Word of God. The transgression of God's commandment without external coercion but solely through their own free will severed the relationship of human with God. The incarnation of the Word of God in creation to save and restore this broken relationship negated the Manichean docetic Christology and the inbreaking of an eternal God within the realm of time in history affirms that history has definite meaning and specific direction. We will see how it was Augustine's conviction that history is the manifestation of God's salvation within the realm of time which determined his understanding of the nature and authority of Scripture.

The fourth part, chapters seven and eight will deal with how all these theological developments crystallized to take a definite shape in Augustine's narratives. Chapter seven will focus upon the *De civitate Dei* where much of Augustine's arguments were the expression of concepts that developed over time and see how he aligned new developments in his thought with his previous stances in this work. We will see that in the uncertainty of the times surrounding the sack of Rome, Augustine seems to seek meaning and purpose in Scripture whereby he expressed with confidence that history takes it course under the authority of God.

Since Augustine reflected upon the progression of his "scriptural odyssey" and brought his own thoughts to conclusion with the *Retractationes*, we shall conclude our survey of his works with the *Retractationes* in the final chapter. There we shall see how his experience of time as a living, ongoing and creative tension had implications in his approach to Scripture and look at how the two seams of time and the authority of Scripture are finally interwoven in Augustine's mind. In short, this work will interweave the study of two questions central to Augustine: What is time, and what is the authority of Scripture?

CHAPTER 1

"… Nisi me catholicae ecclesiae conmoueret auctoritas"

Authority, Tradition and Time

In *Confessiones* Book 11, Augustine, struggling to define "time" specifically despite being fully aware of it, wrote: *quid est ergo tempus? si nemo ex me quaerat, scio; si quaerenti explicare velim, nescio.*[1] With the rather common term "authority", the same challenge of specificity[2] seems to crop up more so than ever. In this chapter, we shall explore the prevalent presuppositions behind the notion of authority. Taking a cursory look at what the word "authority" often signifies in the twenty-first century, we shall see the etymology of the word in antiquity and look at how the notion of authority had been adapted by Christians in late antiquity. We will see how a specific notion of time within a specific relationship determine the Christian understanding of authority, particularly that of the Scriptures.

1. Authority in Common Parlance Today

The term "authority" is a "concept in motion"[3] that often oscillates between having a positive or a negative connotation[4] — beneficial and indispensable or detrimental and irrelevant — with the context determining what the word actually signifies. Depending on the perceived sources of authority, the term often suggests a "constraining, repressive

---

1 "So what is time? If no one asks me, I know; if I want to explain it to someone who asks me, I do not know". cf 11.14.17 (CCSL 27.202; Williams 210).
2 As Streich observed, "The conceptual history of authority reveals it to be an essentially contested concept because of the many debates about its sources, purposes, and limits, as well as its proximity to the concept of power". Streigh (2005), 181. Interestingly, akin to the notion of time, Bruce Lincoln confessed that the notion of authority can be something that is "hopelessly elusive". Lincoln (1994), 1.
3 See Melvin Richter's "The History of the Concept of *Herrschaft* in the *Geschichtliche Grundbegriffe*" in Ritcher (1995), 58–78 for a comprehensive exposition of the long contribution on *Herrschaft* which was sometimes translated as "authority".
4 As Friedrich remarked, "ever since the eighteenth-century revolt, freedom-loving intellectuals and their following have viewed authority with hostility … [while the] conservatives have … glorified authority beyond all reason … The problem of what makes people accept authority, obey a command or believe a statement, has given rise to a variety of interpretations of authority. In such connections, authority has been contrasted with freedom or with force. It has been praised and condemned in all these juxtapositions. As a result, authority has been made the basis of a pejorative adjective, authoritarian". Friedrich (1972), 45–46.

past"[5] and a "structures of domination"[6] based on some irrational beliefs which find expression in different aspects of life that negate human flourishing. On the other hand, authority will be akin to harmony and right direction in life that many willfully acknowledge as essential to coexistence. Seeing the question of authority as "the first and last issue of life", P. T. Forsyth even remarked that "Our idea of authority lies so near the heart of life that it colours our whole circulation. Men and societies are totally different according as their ruling idea is to serve an authority or to escape it, or according to the authority they do serve".[7] Like "time", therefore, no matter how we "feel" it, we cannot avoid some forms of "authority". One way or another, "authority" always affected us even if we often deny, resist and want to do away with it.

This inevitability is because authority seems to be a natural consequence of relationship, the state of association and interaction between human beings and even with nature and the divine. From a sociological perspective, relationship is defined as "the full gamut of human associations in which behaviour is influenced by the real or imagined presence of another person with whom one has interacted in the past and expects to interact in the future".[8] This relational aspect is central to Jörg Löschke's definition of authority as "having standing to make a claim on another person's actions".[9] "Authority" is acknowledged "when one individual, prompted by his or her circumstances, does as indicated by another individual what he or she would not do in the absence of such indication".[10] Thus, authority basically denoted a "legitimate" and "acceptable" relationship between a superior and a subordinate whereby the subordinate counts on the superior for specific direction, whether it be in the form of expert advice or operational commands.[11]

---

5 Scanlon noted that the term authority is "frequently used in critical discussions, but is rarely treated as posing any particular problem of definition. More than a dozen recent volumes which use the term in their titles treat it rather vaguely as a constraining, repressive past, which the works with which they are concerned struggle against, but they take this view of authority to be sufficiently obvious as to need no particular defense". See Scanlon (1994), 37.
6 Max Weber's *Herrschaft* was translated as "domination" so that in an English translation of *Economy and Society*, we read "Without exception every sphere of social action is profoundly influenced by structures of domination". Although the accuracy of this translation was questioned as it "tends to overemphasise the coercive aspect of rule", it epitomises a negative view of authority. See Ritcher (1995), 58–78; also "Domination (*Herrschaft*)" in Swedberg (2005), 88–91; also "Appendix A" in Tribe (2019), 471.
7 Forsyth (1912), 1.
8 Reis (2009), xliii. This "sociological perspective" is one of the three modern approaches to the question of authority as identified by Lincoln. Another approach is those of the political philosophers with "neoconservative bent, who took the turbulence of the 1960s as a 'crisis of authority' in the face of which they sought to reestablish the legitimacy of the liberal democratic state." The third approach is those of the social psychologists "whose memories stretch back to events of the 1930s and 1940s, who are more concerned with dangers posed by the state than those posed to it, and who have used a variety of experimental data to point up the widespread tendency of citizens, even in liberal democracies, to follow authoritarian leaders." Lincoln (1994), 1.
9 Löschke (2015), 187.
10 Zambrano (2001), 978.
11 Legitimacy attempts to justify why access to, and exercise of, power is rightful for those who have authority, and why those subject to it have a corresponding duty to obey, thereby making authority *authoritative* in a given situation. See Beetham (2004), 107; Wolf (2001), 975, 978.

In various type of relationships where influence is exerted, distinction can be drawn between "an authority" and "in authority" without "separating" them completely: the former suggests theoretical authority based on expertise, as having an authority in matters of belief while the latter suggests practical authority based on office or title, as having an authority over action.[12] The former category can encompass what Parsons called a "professional authority" which is based more on some superior technical competence and seem to be more stable than other forms of authority based on superior status or superior wisdom or higher moral character.[13] The latter category can be associated with what we see in a modern state where authority often suggests "the right to exercise social control" and "the correlative duty to obey".[14] In organisations, there can be a formal/positional authority coexisting with an informal/personal authority.[15] Since there are different layers of human relationships in different contexts, one can be simultaneously "an authority", "in authority" but "under authority".

Today, the alleged "incompatibility" of authority with reason or autonomy poses a big challenge to legitimate an "authority relation" to keep "the relationship from breaking down".[16] The conflicting impulses to maximize one's own authority at the expenses of others is another obstacle to fixing authority concretely to a particular role, institution or person. As Millers asserts, "The need for authority, and the sense of dependency that results, conflicts with individual freedom, another powerful need, and can generate a strong antipathy toward or fear of authority, often reinforced by the behaviour of those 'in authority'".[17] Where legitimacy is lacking, we see instability of systems of authority.[18] So, there is a real sense of "crisis" in authority as all types of authority are neither respected nor deferred to as much as "in the past".[19]

In the past, "authority" seems more concrete, straightforward and assuring, particularly when it was vested upon rulers and patriarchs, institutions and sacred

---

12 See Wolf (2001), 973; Chapman (2008), 498–99; Green (2005), 75.
13 Parsons (1954), 38.
14 McLaughlin (2007), 1. Under the "latter category", another way of discerning authority is in the normative and the empirical sense, where authority denotes either "a right to have orders obeyed or as the capacity to have orders obeyed." Normatively, authority "describes what should happen and who should be obeyed" while empirically, authority "describes what actually happens and who actually is obeyed." Harrison et al. (2015), 8–9.
15 Wolf (2001), 975.
16 Zambrano (2001), 978. This "incompatibility" is the "paradoxes of authority". See Raz (1979), 3.
17 Miller (2008), 9.
18 The main significance of legitimacy, according to Beetham, "lies in the contribution it makes, alongside the organization of the means of administration and coercion, to the reliability, effectiveness, and durability of a system of power". See Beetham (2004), 108–09.
19 Streigh (2005), 182. Reflecting upon this issue, Pollman noted that "currently authority plays no dominant role in our society, or that, where it exists, it is not properly recognized as such". Pollmann (2014), 157. But Forsyth long ago already mooted upon the implications of this mindset, that human liberty is incompatible with authority: "In this unprecedented social revolution ... the question that naturally becomes imperative is the question of an authority ... Is duty dead ... Is obedience a pure curse, and escape from it a pure boon? ... Is all submission but slavery? Is liberty man's chief end, or has it its condition in a prior and creative control? Is the principle of authority the salvation of society or the bane of the race?" Forsyth (1912), 2–3.

texts. Authority ascribed to them was often divinely grounded, externally given and supported by foundational cosmogony. As long as the link to the "external sources" was secure, bearers of authority were rarely questioned. This contrasted with the modern understanding of authority when strong emphasis is laid on the authority of a person.[20] As the foundations of traditionally accepted cosmogonies came tumbling down, human beings became the highest, and even sole measures of all things. And in the web of relationship which determine the nature of legitimate authority, only the human matters and everything else is out of the equation.

At this point, we may ponder if our awareness of time can be connected with, and even seen as a determining factor in, our understanding of authority. If one can simultaneously be "an authority", "in authority" but "under authority" in the different layers of human relationship, can time as "a specific moment" be the factor which determines one's role and standing under the whole gamut of "authority"? Does an absolute claim to time equate an absolute claim to authority then? Likewise, can there be any link between our attitude to authority and our fragmentary reference to time as "past, present and future", "period, eras and ages" and "pre-modern, modern and post-modern"? Is it proper to speak of secular and religious domains in our notions of time? Are "secular" notions of time compatible with "religious" time[21] and what can the implications be on our concept and acceptance of authority? What if a time of crisis concurs with crisis in authority?[22] Ultimately, can there be a valid notion of authority without a specific notion of time and does a certain way of perceiving time suggest and encourage a particular notion of authority, whether in a tentative or absolute sense?

Moving along with these questions which we will attempt to tackle later, we shall explore how "authority" evolved as a dynamic concept and gained momentum in the

---

20 See Streigh (2005), 182; Zambrano (2001), 979; Pollmann (2014), 160; Chapman (2008), 497–98. Conflict in the understanding of authority can be represented either by the notions of "divine right" or "natural law and the notion of contract." This ideological confrontation "raised the question of who held political authority and, as a result, had the right to govern and legitimately to exercise power." Strugnell (2013), 127.

21 John Hassard portray the "gap" between a religious and secular notion of time thus: "Whereas in modern theology linear-time has as its conclusion the promise of eternity, in the mundane, secular activities of industrialism temporal units are finite. Time is a resource that has the potential for consumption by a plethora of activities; its scarcity is intensified when the number of potential claimants is increased". Hassard (1990), 12.

22 This random question has been generated by our modern sense of individual autonomy that has to response to unprecedented events like covid-19 pandemic and ecological crisis that significantly limited our lifestyle and choices. Does the ensuing sense of crisis in "troubled, uncertain times" reshapes our attitudes to, and notions of, authority in terms of acceptance and expectations? When time is commodified so that business done "at the speed of thought" equates power, can the fallout of a catastrophic outbreak upset conventional authority by halting progress and even throw our economic and socio-political systems a step back to "the past"? When the present does not make sense and the future no longer looks infinite and exploitable, do we ever turn to the past, even to traditions to find meanings and values and seek solutions? Can there be hope and assurance in an "uncertain times" with the belief that the present is "a part of the whole" so that "modern times" is actually an "end time" or "the last days" in the whole span of time? Conversely, can a false sense of security by some "religious" notion of time which defy state's political authority jeopardise safety and precautionary measures?

next sections. Going back to the etymology of the term and its usage in antiquity, we shall see how time was a factor in shaping the concept of authority in its abstract and concrete expressions.

2. Authority in Antiquity

Etymologically, the word "authority" comes from the Latin word *auctoritas*. *Auctoritas* comes from the root word *auctor* which basically denotes "the principal in a sale, vendor, seller", "a guarantor", "one who attests or vouches for the truth", "one who persuades, teaches or advices", "originator, cause", etc.[23] *Auctor* was endowed with *auctoritas*, the suffix *tat(i)* describing the quality or characteristic of the *auctor* to "increase".[24]

In a legal context where the term was originally used, *auctor* is someone (e.g., a seller in a sales transaction) "who decisively and effectively endorses the action to be performed by another". In the wider context of life, *auctoritas* can denote an advice or opinion with "the ability to exert significant influence on the resolutions of others by virtue of superior insight". Gradually, *auctoritas* loses this sense of "an expression of opinion that affects others", and only retains that of "the effect by the weight of the person", so that one is influenced by the prestige or reputation attached to *auctoritas* so as to approve willingly.[25] Thus, *auctoritas* infers the weight, influence and persuasiveness attached to someone/something due to their prestige and reputation, which enabled the bearer of *auctoritas* to have the approval of others.

Behind the whole notion of *auctoritas*, we can see the significance of time in that the ability to make a durable influence that can stand the test of time long after an action has been completed is as crucial as the specific time when some decisive events occurred. In fact, the attempt to generate such a durable influence long after the definite event motivated the bilingual *Res Gestae Divi Augusti* (RGDA), an autobiography of the first Roman emperor Augustus, which survived as an inscription in the Temple of Roma and Augustus in Ancyra.[26] As the cognate notion of *potestas* and *auctoritas* suggested by the RGDA still impinge on our insight of what authority "originally" meant, we shall briefly look at the relevant portion.

In chapter 34 which summarizes how his reign and deeds was approved by the Romans, Augustus reports that he returned the republic from his control to the Senate and the people after putting an end to civil wars;[27] for this reason he was given the

---

23 Glare (1968), 205–06.
24 *Auctor nun ist* is qui auget. Heinze (1925), 349.
25 *wer die von einem anderen auszufuhrende Handlung mabgeblichund wirkungsvoll gutheibt ... die Eignung, mabgeblichen Einflub auf die Entschliebungen der anderen kraft uberlegener Einsicht auszuuben ... Wirkungdurch das Gewicht der Person.* Heinze (1925), 351–54.
26 For a historical survey of the recovery of the RGDA from the sixteenth to twentieth century, see Ridley (2003), 3–24.
27 *postquam bella civilia exstinxeram, per consensum universorum potitus rerum omnium, rem publicam ex mea potestate in senatus populique Romani arbitrium transtuli* (Brunt and Moore 34). For the background story of Augustus's rise to power, see Eder (2005), 13–32.

title *Augustus* and other unique honors. In 34:3, Augustus states: ἀξιώμ[α]τι πάντων διήνεγκα, ἐξουσίας δὲ οὐδέν τι πλεῖον ἔσχον τῶν συναρξάντων μοι.²⁸ As the Latin of the first clause is missing from the surviving inscription, Theodore Mommsen who combined all fragments and published a scholarly edition in 1883 had suggested reading *post id tempus praestiti omnibus dignitate*.²⁹ In 1924, Premerstein suggested the reading: *post id tempus praestiti omnibus auctoritate*.³⁰ While the former reconstruction will read, "After this time I excelled everyone in *dignitate*", the latter state, "After this time I excelled everyone in *auctoritas*". In 1925, Heinze promoted Premerstein's reading by asserting that "the only logical contrast to *potestas*, the authority legally due to the incumbent, is not *dignitas*, but *auctorita*".³¹ So, the reading which contrasted *potestas* with *auctoritas* became the conventional interpretation of RGDA 34:3.

Going by Heinze's reading, Augustus had reserved *auctoritas* to himself and assigned *potestas* to the Senate and the people so that he "excelled all in authority", but "had no more *potestatis*" than his fellow magistrates at his accession to emperor. The same logic was reaffirmed in his self-ascribed and unofficial title *princeps* which indicated his leading role in the state without bestowing particular powers.³² The term *potestas* basically denotes "power, possession of control or command over persons or things", "a position of power, office, jurisdiction", "a particular natural force or substance", "a spiritual power".³³

The antithetical implication between *potestas* and *auctoritas* is clearly illustrated by Chapman who writes:

> In Roman politics … *potestas* … was something associated with the magistrate and carried with it the possibility of coercion and force. In distinction, *auctoritas* was used in relation to the advice offered by the Senate, thereby functioning as a check on the unfettered power of the magistrates: whatever power such a form of authority could command had to be earned through respect and guaranteed by the wisdom of those who were held to have authority.³⁴

While *auctoritas* entails some form of legitimacy, *potestas* does not depend on any form of consent of the subordinate, as Heinze asserted, "The *auctoritas* of the gods plays no role in the national Roman religion: the deity is not asked for advice, but its will is explored; it rules, and where there is *potestas* or control, *auctoritas* has no status".³⁵ In

---

28 See Cooley (2009), 98.
29 On this basis, Mommsen's text will read: *Post id tempus praestiti omnibus dignitate, potestatis autem nihilo amplius habui quam qui fuerunt mihi quo que in magistratu collegae*. See Heinze (1925), 348. According to Ridley, "Mommsen insisted on *dignitate*, because the Greek used the word *axioma*". Ridley (2003), 22.
30 Premerstein's text will read: *post id tempus praestiti omnibus auctoritate: potestatis autem nihilo amplius habui quam ceteri, qui mihi quo que in magistratu conlegae fuerunt*. See Heinze (1925), 348.
31 *den einzig inoglichen Gegensatz zu* potestas, *der dem Amtsinhaber rechtlich zustehenden Gewalt, bietet an dieser Stelle nicht* dignitas, *sondern* auctoritas. Heinze (1925), 348.
32 Cooley (2009), 160.
33 Glare (1968), 1417–18.
34 Chapman (2008), 499.
35 *In der nationalen romischen Religion spielt die* auctoritas *der Gotte keine Rolle: die Gottheit wird nicht um Rat gefragt, sondern es wird ihr Wille erkundet; sie herrscht, und wo* potestas *oder* imperium *ist, hat die* auctoritas *keine Statte*. Heinze (1925), 359–60.

other words, *auctoritas* suggest an internal quality emanating/oozing out (*ex manare*) that resulted in the recognition of ability while there is a "transcendental aspect" in *potestas* which can signify imposition of ability by mechanical force or external action.

While this distinction can be drawn particularly when considering their "theoretical" sources, the boundaries between *auctoritas* and *potestas* were neither clear cut nor intended to be in concrete situations. We have mentioned that *auctoritas* gradually loses the discreet sense of "advice" and retained that of a "dominant" influence where autonomy was deliberately negated. In fact, in writing his own "achievements", Augustus sketched a political rhetoric so that *potestas* can be wilfully ascribed to, and vested in his *auctoritas*, as Cooley observed:

> The name "Augustus" was chosen for its complex connotations: related to the Latin words *augur, augurium, auctoritas, and augeo*, it evoked the religious sphere of augury and auspices, as well as ideas of authority and increase ... Above all, [*Augustus*] conveyed the idea of superhuman status ... [that contrasts *humanus*] ... [the name] was pregnant with potent polyvalent implications.[36]

So, we see the achievements of the deified Augustus in bringing the world under the rule of the Romans recounted along with a list of "political moderation"[37] that he maintained before he was given the honorific title *pater patriae*. This noble account was engraved on bronze for public display to exert durable influences, and to sanction and justify historical and institutional continuity.[38] Observing its significance, Cooley noted:

> The use of bronze set the RGDA on a par with Roman legal and other important official documents, and evoked ideals of sacrosanctity and durability. By choosing bronze, Augustus was implicitly elevating his account of his achievements, evoking the moral authority usually enjoyed by texts inscribed on bronze, in accordance with his ambition to act as a role model for the rest of society. At the same time, he could allude to ideas of religious sanctity that underlay his authority in Roman society.[39]

The power symbolism inferred in Augustus's account became obvious when it was freely rendered into Greek. Without the chronological background that *post id tempus* suggests, the Greek translation underplay the sense of achievement and approval of the senate that was intended in the Latin. Literally, a deserved *auctoritat* was ascribed

---

36 Cooley (2009), 261–62.
37 Eder interestingly noted that the *Res Gestae* also contains a long list of *res non gestae* that "could serve only to profile the *princeps* as the incorruptible guardian of tradition who took care, even against the will of Senate and People, not to contradict the constitution of the fathers". Eder (2005), 14.
38 Ridley asserts that "Self-advertisement, especially by the head of state, is probably as old as organised political state" and highlight the similarities of the *Res Gestae* with "the annals of Tuthmosis III (*c.* 1500–1450), the founder of the Egyptian empire in Asia". Ridley (2003), 51. See Güven (1998) for an overview of the "strategic location" of the inscription. As Cooley noted, inscriptions could bolster "the hierarchical structure of Roman society". Cooley (2012), 299.
39 Cooley (2009), 3.

and conferred to Augustus "afterward" while there is a sense of "imposition" in the Greek word ἀξιώμ[α]τι which directly opens the sentence. Commenting upon this, Cooley asserted that the change reflects "a willingness to acknowledge the monarchical nature of Augustus's position at Rome, which would perhaps be less openly acceptable at Rome itself … [offering] a less subtle picture of Augustus's supremacy at Rome than the one developed by Augustus himself".[40] In other words, the inference to "power", implicit in the Latin version was made explicit by the time it was rendered into Greek because Augustus's claim of *auctoritas* was actualized[41] in his display of *potestas*.

Hence, from his RGDA, we can assert the significance of time for Augustus who "constructs" his brand of authority that will generate a durable influence. Establishing a specific point in time that marked the transition from the turmoil of civil wars to a "golden age" or *aureum saeculum*[42] is the determining factor which makes his claim to authority authoritative. This decisive event should be recorded, preserved and exhibited so that Augustus's feat can be authoritative for a long time after the event occurred to ratify historical and institutional continuity. And ironically, in spite of his best attempt to depict Rome as *res publica* where he was conferred *auctoritas* without having absolute *potestas*, Cassius Dio and later Roman historians "elevated" Augustus exactly as a monarch.[43] At this juncture, one should notice how remembrance facilitated authority and ask whether authority can exist and last without a valid commemoration, be that in an oral or a written form.[44] But now, we shall turn to the core of "what is worth remembering" in Christianity, that "which is revealed".

3. Tension of "the Time" in *Aureum Saeculum* and *Consummatio Saeculi*

Interestingly, the term ἀξίωμα which we had encountered in the RGDA was completely missing from the New Testament although both were written in *koine Greek*.[45] In the

---

40 Cooley (2009), 29–30. As Eder insightfully noted, "The more evident [Augustus's] power became in the state during the fifty-seven years of his rule, the more resolutely he opposed the appearance of being a monarch". Eder (2005), 13–14. On why Augustus would avoid being a monarchical figure, see Grebe (2004), 39–40.
41 This is in line with Lincoln's observation that both persuasion and coercion "exist as capacities or potentialities implicit within authority, but are actualized only when those who claim authority sense that they have begun to lose the trust of those over whom they seek to exercise it." Lincoln (1994), 6.
42 On how this *aureum saeculum* was connected with the reign of Augustus in the *Aeneid*, see Grebe (2004).
43 Eder (2005), 15.
44 On how surviving "the sieve of time" can forge authority, particularly in literature and how "the great authorities of tradition are the great survivors of the sieve of time", see O'Loughlin (1999), 75–78.
45 Pollman (2014), 161; Commenting upon the features of the Greek translation which was "considered poor" by scholars in the past, Cooley remarked that this attitude "largely resulted from judging it by the standards of classical Attic Greek rather than those of koine Greek used under the Roman empire". Cooley (2009), 26.

Latin Vulgate, the term *auctoritas* occurs only once — in the Old Testament — while it has no direct equivalence in the New Testament.[46] But, by the time of Augustine who used *auctoritas* and its variant forms over a thousand times in his extant writings, it was already a significantly loaded theological concept. So, how did *auctoritas* acquire a distinct theological meaning?

While there is no direct equivalence of *auctoritas* in the Greek language, it does not mean that the phenomenon which *auctoritas* describes was absent in the Greek speaking world and the New Testament. The Greek term ἐξουσία, often translated as "authority" in English, was usually translated as *potestas* in Latin while the Greek word δύναμις was rendered into English as "power".[47] In ordinary Greek usage, ἐξουσία as the "ability to perform an action" was very close to δύναμις: particularly when ἐξουσία denotes any right in the various relationships similar to and guaranteed by national institutions, it was validated by the δύναμις of the state. But δύναμις denotes external power or force while ἐξουσία has a more inward reference, as the power revealed in the fact that a command is obeyed.[48] In other words, if ἀξίωμα is a "blend"[49] of *auctoritas* and *potestas* in the Greek-speaking world, the New Testament's ἐξουσία expresses the sense that the fluid notion of ἀξίωμα is suggesting.

It is crucial to consider the development of the term ἐξουσία since the power of attorney of Christ (ἐξουσία Χριστοῦ), of which the Gospels speak and which the Latin Bible translates as *potestas*, is addressed in Augustine with the term *auctoritas*.[50] In the LXX, the term ἐξουσία denotes right, authority, permission or freedom in the legal or political sense and also as it is given by God, e.g., in the law. In Daniel and Maccabees, it may be the power of the king or of God.[51] Translating the Aramaic שְׁלַט (*šālaṭ*) as ἐξουσία is very significant for the development of the concept. In the Old Testament, the word family of שלט (*shlt*) is used 15 times in the Hebrew and 33 times in Aramaic and 31 occurrences were from the Aramaic section of Daniel. In Daniel, although its usage as a verb can denote "ruling" in the territorial political sense (2:29), the exercise of authority in a personal sense (5:7,16), the power of fire or wild animals (3:27; 6:25), several times it is predicated of God or of the "heavens" as a substitute for God (4:14, 22, 23, 29; 5:21). The noun *soltan*, peculiar to the Aramaic of Daniel generally means "dominion, kingdom" with a strong apocalyptic and eschatological reference. Theologically, the eschatological end becomes visible against the background of the historical collapse of successive kingdoms (2:39):

---

46 Pollmann (2014), 161; Chapman (2008), 500.
47 Chapman (2008), 500. Commenting on how the translator of the Authorized Version rendered ἐξουσία "as authority or power according to their taste", Williams astutely asserted, "Linguistically they were at fault, but theologically they were not far wrong. For in the New Testament, the ideas of power and authority are very closely related". Williams (1950), 75.
48 Foerster (1964), 562–63.
49 On the interface between persuasion and coercion, and the argument that authority is actually a "third entity" that is distinct yet related to these two categories "in some very specific and suggestive ways", see Lincoln (1994), 4–6.
50 Lutcke (1986), 506.
51 Foerster (1964), 564.

God's "dominion" is manifested in God's "kingdom" in the ultimate apocalyptic battle with other "powers".⁵²

By using ἐξουσία for the Aramaic שָׁלְטָן when the reference is to God's power, the LXX introduces a term that conveys the concept of God's unrestricted sovereignty whose very Word is power (cf. Dan 4:14) far more brilliantly than such expressions of indwelling, objective, physical or spiritual power as κράτος, ἰσχύς, δύναμις. This sense is closest with the usage of the New Testament where ἐξουσία basically denotes the invisible power which decides, signifying the absolute possibility of action which is proper to God.⁵³

If the Old Testament formed the theological background to the notion of God's unrestricted sovereignty, then the New Testament marked the fulfilment of time when God's authority finds concrete and decisive expression: a "revelation" that is worth "remembering". At the beginning of his ministry, Jesus proclaimed that "the time is fulfilled, and the kingdom of God has come near" (Mk 1:15).⁵⁴ The power and authority that Jesus then exercised within the limit of his earthly calling and commission is ἐξουσία. Jesus' power and right to forgive sins was his ἐξουσία (Mk 2:10) as was the power to expel demons (Mk 3:15). The impression that Jesus made to his audiences was also ἐξουσία (Mt 7:29; 9:8). Commenting on these phenomena, Foerster stated that ἐξουσία "presupposes a divine commission and authorization which is also power, and the special feature in this ἐξουσία is that it is inseparable from the proclamation that the kingdom of God is near".⁵⁵

Being in a special relationship with YHWH in a covenantal bond, the belief that God will act decisively in the future was in the horizon of expectation of the Jews. While the Jewish people related the power of God with sovereignty over the natural world, the supreme manifestation of the power of God was his action in history, not nature. YHWH delivered them out of Egypt with a mighty hand and in the light of this belief, they had seen their whole history. God's mighty actions on their behalf "was not a demonstration of merely naked power" but "a power at the command of a moral, personal Being".⁵⁶ Thus the expectation of God to act mightily again.

But Jesus' assertion that the prophecy of Isaiah "has been fulfilled today" does not go down well with the religious leaders of the Jews, as also his subsequent actions (Lk 4:16–29; 6:11; Mk 2:1–12). Besides, as Rome totally dominated the political sphere of Galilee and Palestine, Jesus' proclamation of the imminent 'kingdom of God' would have been regarded as a defiance to Roman's authority by contemporaries

---

52 Saebo (2006), 83–88.
53 Occurring around 102 times in the New Testament, ἐξουσία also denotes the power of government (Lk 19:17; Act 9:14: the Sanhedrin; Lk 20:20: Pilate), the power of self-determination (Act 5:4), the power of kings (Apoc [Rev] 17:12), and "the powers that be" (Lk 12:11; Rom 13:1). It may also mean a realm of control, e.g., the state (Lk 23:7), the domain of spirits (Eph 2:2), or the spiritual powers (1 Cor 15:24; Eph 1:21; Col 1:16; 1 Pet 3:22). See Foerster (1964), 565–66.
54 ὅτι Πεπλήρωται ὁ καιρὸς καὶ ἤγγικεν ἡ βασιλεία τοῦ θεοῦ. All scriptural quotations in Greek from SBLGNT.
55 Foerster (1964), 568–69.
56 See Williams (1950), 76–77.

who viewed the Roman emperor "as 'son of God' and the 'beginning', or first cause, of all good for the inhabited earth".[57]

Despite the hostilities of those who were "in authority", the early Christians believed and proclaimed that Jesus inaugurated the "last days" when the kingdom of God has been coming with power (Act 1:8; 4:20). How Jesus envisaged the "last days" or the "eschaton" has been a subject of much interest and disagreement which we will not deal with in detail here.[58] Suffice to say that the eschatological consummation, the belief that the kingdom of God will soon be concluded with the *Parousia*, "was not simply one aspect of a cognitive theological system, but rather was intimately connected with religious experience within the corporate setting of worship".[59]

So, against the backdrop of the notion of *aureum saeculum* constructed by Augustus and the Roman rulers, Jesus and his disciples likewise envisaged the *consummatio saeculi*. And along this expectation, there are conditions which illuminate the nature of ἐξουσία. Claiming all ἐξουσία after his resurrection, Jesus commissioned his disciples with the promise that he will be with them until the end of the ages (ἕως τῆς συντελείας τοῦ αἰῶνος) (Mt 28:18–20). But when the disciples asked Jesus of the time when the kingdom of Israel will be restored, Jesus answered that it is not theirs to know the times or the seasons (χρόνους ἢ καιροὺς) which the Father put in place by his own authority (ἰδίᾳ ἐξουσίᾳ) (Act 1:7).[60]

This assertion that the power which decides is the Father's, is in line with Jesus' prior teaching that only the Father knows the day and the hour (τῆς ἡμέρας ἐκείνης ἢ τῆς ὥρας) when the Son of man will be seen coming in clouds with great power and glory (Mk 13:26–32). To relate this with our observation in the previous section, Jesus Christ as the Son of God is "an authority", "in authority", but "under authority" of God the Father in this temporal sphere. Furthermore, the early Christian communities were exhorted to be vigilant of the sudden inbreaking of the day and the time (τῶν χρόνων καὶ τῶν καιρῶν) (1 Thes 5:1). Just as ἐξουσία denotes the power which decides,

---

57 Evans (2006), 305.
58 Regarding Jesus' eschatological perspective and Jesus' understanding of his own role within the framework of that perspective, Aune distinguishes four scholarly models: 1) the "consistent eschatology model" (J. Weiß, A. Schweitzer, F. C. Burkitt, B. F. Easton, M. Dibelius, R. Bultmann, R. H. Hiers) that see Jesus as an apocalyptist with an eschatological timetable who ultimately failed since the end that he had anticipated did not arrive; 2) the "realised eschatology model" (C. H. Dodd) that see Jesus teaching the essential presence of the kingdom of God; 3) the "proleptic eschatology model" (J. Jeremias, O. Cullmann, W. G. Kümmel, N. Perrin, G. Lundström, G. E. Ladd) that see Jesus holding a paradoxical juxtaposition of the kingdom of God as both a present reality and a future expectation; and 4) "models de-emphasizing eschatology" (T. F. Glasson, M. J. Borg, B. Mack) which criticized the view that the outlook of Jesus was primarily determined by eschatology. Aune (1992), 599–600.
59 Aune (1992), 597. This belief, deeply rooted in the religious experience of the early Christians, can be contrasted with giving mental assent to some "inerrant propositions" which have been developed out of scriptural data in our contemporary context.
60 Augustine makes an incisive comment in relation to this passage: "Now in fact they had not questioned Him concerning the hour or the day or the year, but the time, when they received this answer". *non utique illi de hora uel die uel anno, sed de tempore interrogauerant, quando istud accepere responsum*. ci 18.53 (CCSL 48.652; Dyson 903).

time as καιρῶν is therefore the specific sphere of the ultimate manifestation of God's sovereignty and authority.[61] And though *auctoritas* has no direct equivalence in the Greek language, the notion of ἐξουσία which accompanied God's revelation, an "inbreaking" into the realm of history with a strong eschatological inference lingers in the background of the term *auctoritas*.

4. *Trado* and the Adaptation of *Auctoritas* in the Early Church

In the previous section, we have indicated how remembrance facilitated authority and raised the question whether authority can exist and last without a valid commemoration, be that in an oral or a written form. This was evidently the case in the early church where the awareness of time as the realm for the ultimate expression of God's sovereignty that finds the definitive embodiment in the incarnation of Christ formed the basis of their hope for the *Parousia*. As these "accounts" of hope, along with the valid responses to and exhortation based upon these hopes, were articulated, remembered and passed on, they gradually evolved into a corpus of writings that formed the core of the New Testament. As we shall see in the next chapter, this was a significant development that marked an important transition since the acknowledgement of the Jewish scriptures "may have been a barrier to Christians creating their own scriptures"[62] in the initial stage of the Christian movement, while "the whole experience of living in the Roman empire, of being ruled by Romans, was overdetermined by the existence of texts".[63]

After the passage of time with the delay of the *Parousia*, it also became crucial to "regularize a system" for passing on the faith and to guarantee that "there were functionaries" who had the authority to teach and who could lay claim to legitimacy. Later New Testament writings even revealed "the emergence of institutions … whereby new legal and traditional patterns of authority were established".[64] However, the significant role of the apostles and the evangelists as "primary witnesses, standing at the point where memory of the events combines with faith in the exalted Lord, is not transmissible" and so, their testimonies were "acknowledged as the norm and canonized as Scripture".[65]

While the need to have valid lasting accounts of the "Christ-event" contributed to the earliest development of Christian writings, the actual adoption and usage of the term *auctoritas* was largely determined by the issue of corroborating those accounts. In fact, the adaptation of *auctoritas* as a theological concept was momentous since modes of thinking was governed by modes of language. Hopkins even asserted that Roman

---

61 Commenting on the New Testament usage of καιρῶν, Cullmann asserted that "it is not human deliberations but a divine decision that makes this or that date a *kairos*, a point of time that has a special place in the execution of God's plan of salvation". Cullmann (1962), 39.
62 Ferguson (2002), 295.
63 Hopkins (2018), 374.
64 Chapman (2008), 501.
65 Williams (1965), 17.

subjects "learnt the language of the conquerors in order to borrow the conqueror's power"[66] and this was obvious in the case of the church's usage of *auctoritas*, both in terms of frequency and in adding new domains to which *auctoritas* can refer to. While some of the Christian writers covered only a few aspects of *auctoritas*, the full spectrum of the term's meanings and contexts were covered in their usages taken together.[67]

Tertullian is the first Latin Christian who employed the term *auctoritas* in his writings. Beside the various aspects of inner-worldly authority already common from the pagan past, he also used the word *auctoritas* to denote the authority of God and the authorities of the apostles, of Holy Scripture, of tradition, of the churches and of the bishops, which are all grounded on God's authority. Adopting the legal aspect of authority in his engagement with "heretics", he argued that the church has authority as bearer and keeper of the authentic and valid apostolic tradition.[68] This implies that the authority of God was embodied in the teachings handed on by the apostles while the institutional church validates those traditions. Later, the significance of "validation" and "authorization" by the church has been succinctly highlighted by Augustine in his assertion against the Manicheans: *ego uero euangelio non crederem, nisi me catholicae ecclesiae conmoueret auctoritas*.[69]

Tertullian's insight was elaborated by Cyprian who identifies the authority of bishops as office holders in legal terms which almost resembles the *potestas* of the "pagan"[70] Roman magistrates, with their episcopal power being grounded on their *cathedrae auctoritas*. This notion contrasted with those of Ambrose who rarely used the term with regard to bishops and the church as he held that bishop's *auctoritas* depended on his person and personality.[71]

For Hilarius of Poitiers, ecclesiastical teachers were akin to authority and this "definition" indicates a decisive moment in the Christian view of authority.[72] At this juncture, we may relate this move with the critical insight of Gadamer regarding authority and reason which, as we have seen in the beginning of this chapter, were often considered incompatible in modern period. Gadamer asserted that the authority of persons is ultimately based on an act of acknowledgment and knowledge, and not on the subjection and abdication of reason. This acknowledgment of authority

---

66 Hopkins (2018), 368.
67 Pollmann (2014), 161–62.
68 Here, Tertullian invokes the sense where the *auctor*, in passing on their property, act as guarantor of and witness to its integrity and vouches for "the authenticity and validity of its content and its efficacy". Pollmann (2014), 162.
69 "I would not believe the gospel if the authority of the Catholic Church did not move me". fu 5.6 (CSEL 25.1.197; Teske 236). But on how Augustine may be grossly misrepresented (*perperam et calumniose*) later, see Calvin, *Institutio* 1.7.3 (CR 30.57).
70 On how "paganism" was constructed, see chapter seven, n. 2 below. Here, it simply denotes the pre-Christian Roman society.
71 Chapman (2008), 502.
72 Veltri asserted that Hilarius utilised the legend of the Septuagint as a "theological basis for introducing his concept of authority ... [Hilarius] does not consider the text as sole authority but also the interpreters of the law ... 'Authority' is nothing but a description of the teachers, successors of the apostles". Veltri (2006), 66.

denoted the awareness of "its own limitations" where trusting the better insight of others amounted to "an act of reason itself". Considered this way, authority "has nothing to do with blind obedience to commands. Indeed, authority has to do not with obedience but rather with knowledge ... that what the authority says is not irrational and arbitrary but can, in principle, be discovered to be true".[73]

Indeed, for the development of the notion of scriptural authority, acceptance of ecclesiastical teachers as "authoritative" proved to be crucial since they mostly engaged with the Scriptures. Commenting on the impact of all these developments, Hopkins stated:

> Sacred texts, exegetical commentaries, letters, written prayers, hymns, sermons and decrees of church councils all helped to integrate Christianity into a coherent if subdivided body; it had a recognisable identity, forged and continually reforged by an argumentative network of writers and readers. The existence of Christian books and readers, emerging from a differentiated set of sub-cultures and disseminated all over the Roman empire, deeply affected the nature of Christian religious teaching and experience ... the Roman empire was conquered by the religious coherence of Christians a century before the western empire was conquered by invading barbarians.[74]

Particularly, the influence generated by these writings[75] along with the adoption of Latin as its medium and the institutions that thrive upon it after the once-persecuted Christianity was officially accepted in the Roman empire[76] was characterized by the pervasive approbation of the notion of *tempora christiana*.[77] In this *tempora christiana*, Scriptures as depository of the apostolic teachings and witnesses served as a crucial

---

73 Gadamer (2004), 281.
74 Hopkins (2018), 379.
75 O'Donnell pointed out the "influence" of Augustine's writings thus: "had he not written, had he not written so much, and had his works not survived so consistently [Augustine] would never have become the authority figure that he did become. He was the right man in the right place at the right time". O'Donnell (2006), 312.
76 As Gaddis remarked, "The end of persecution had been accompanied by an even more dramatic development: for the first time in history, an emperor had openly embraced Christianity ... The bishop combined moral and spiritual authority with canonical powers to impose repentance and forgive sins. Constantine, whose grants of judicial powers and privileges would considerably increase the bishops' effective power, may have envisioned for himself a role that similarly combined didactic and disciplinary obligations. Far from withering away, then, a Christian imperial state would need to take on more responsibilities than ever". Gaddis (2005), 45, 47.
77 *Tempora christiana* will be dealt with more specifically later in chapter seven. Now, we must note that the prevalence of this notion can be seen from Augustine's explicit usage of the word *tempora christiana* in Ev 1.51; ci 12.21; ep 118.21; s 81.7; s Den 24.11.13; s Dol 6.12.13. Markus observed that *tempora christiana* was an elastic concept in Augustine's usage that bore a variety of meanings and must be interpreted according to the context. "He certainly used it to refer to the very recent times — beginning in the early 390s — during which the imperial initiatives for establishing Christianity gathered momentum; but the phrase could also refer to the longer stretch of the empire's history since the conversion of Constantine, or even to the whole period since the incarnation". Markus (2000), 200. The pervasive optimism inherent around this time was reflected in Jerome's ep 107.2

link which maintained and represented the authority of God, although discernment of the signs of times from these Scriptures had been diverged.[78] In later chapters, we will look at how an optimistic "version" of *tempora christiana* that had endorsed triumphalist attitudes was held in tension with a more "apocalyptic" Christian world view and see how Augustine negotiated his own position by invoking the decisiveness of the incarnation of Christ above contemporary historical events.

5. After *Tempora Christiana*: Devolution of Traditions and Authority

So far, we are looking at the conceptual components of authority. We have asserted that at the basic level, authority is a natural corollary of relationship. Exploring the notions of authority in antiquity, we see how different aspects of time has been an indispensable factor which forged the concept of authority in its abstract and concrete expressions. Taking the case of emperor Augustus's quest for power and control, we have asserted that *auctoritas* basically denotes the internal quality of human being, and the ability emanating and increasing until the self-ascribing *princeps* was elevated to superhuman status of *diui Augusti*. The commemoration of the "golden age" that Augustus ushered in through his feats was intended to be a durable, foundational and influential statement which would uphold the hierarchical structure of the Roman society.[79]

Against this background, we see the evolution of the concept of *auctoritas* in the early church that is being grounded in the absolute possibility of action which is proper to God. In "the fullness of time" (Gal 4:4), God's *auctoritas* was revealed in the temporal realm through the "enfleshment" of the Eternal Word (Jn 1:14). If the earthly ministry of Jesus Christ was the foretaste of the kingdom of God, the "last day" was inaugurated through his resurrection and outpouring of the Holy Spirit that endowed power upon the believers (Act 1:17). This "theologically-loaded" concept of the "last day", which has been rooted in concrete historical reality of the Jewish people, determined the Christian notion of *auctoritas*. This concept gradually evolved to take a distinct shape as an eschatological hope maintained by persecuted minorities as prophesied in the book of Daniel, and which Augustine quoted approvingly: "they shall take away his dominion [of God's enemy] …the kingdom and dominion, …shall

---

that he wrote in 403: *solitudinem patitur et in urbe gentilitas, dii quondam nationum cum bubonibus et noctuis in solis culminibus remanserunt; uexilla militum crucis insignia sunt, regum purpuras et ardentes diadematum gemmas patibuli salutaris pictura condecorat* (CSEL 55.292).

78 For example, Bonner asserted that although the way in which the Catholic church adjusted herself to the political change of the Roman empire is "[o]ne of the most remarkable developments in European history" and one which largely altered the prevaling "millenial" expectation of the church, this millennial hope survived "among the masses, for whom the change had been less obviously beneficial". See Bonner (1989), 247–48.

79 We will see more of this in chapter seven where Augustine deconstructed the ideology of the Roman empire.

be given to the people of the saints of the Most High, Whose kingdom is everlasting kingdom, and all dominions shall serve and obey Him".[80]

Therefore, unlike Augustus's account of his grandeur which was endorsed by the external forces that the Roman empire wielded in antiquity, Christians acknowledged and adopted a distinct notion of authority that was based upon their specific vision of history even at the cost of their physical survival. It was their conviction that the incarnation of Christ ushered in the "last age" and it was their expectation of its consummation in the *Parousia* which they commemorated in their Scriptures. At the same time, these Scriptures were subversive texts and the authority ascribed to Scriptures was not coercive but depended on the faith and conviction of Christians who read, passed on, interpreted and preserved them.

Although the meanings drawn from the Scriptures greatly vary in Christendom, the authority ascribed to the Scriptures was never seriously challenged until the "Age of Reason" or "the Enlightenment"[81] which covered the period of the mid-seventeenth century to the early nineteenth century. This period marked the emergence of "forces of intellectual and political opposition" that had challenged not only the essence of "Christian doctrine and the authority of the church" but also "the authenticity of the Christian religion itself". Partially a reaction to the devastating religious warfare and politics of intolerance and confessional divisions prevalent in the day, many questioned the efficacy of scriptural revelation and embraced a natural religion because they considered reason as a sufficient guide to truth. In its more radical expressions, the later "Enlightenment" could be regarded as essentially opposed to Christianity and as a forerunner of "a purely secular world-order".[82]

Besides, greater emphasis upon human freedom and autonomy,[83] coupled with "advance" in researches and criticisms in the field of biblical scholarship in the last two centuries, marked the negation of authority ascribed to church's traditions and the Scriptures even among Christians[84] and the gradual devolution of the Christian concept of time and history. According to Momigliano, "The modern

---

80 *et principatum remouebunt … et regnum et potestas et magnitude regum, qui sub omni caelo sunt, data est santis Altissimi. Et regnum eius regnum sempiternum; et onmes principatus ipsi seruient et obaudient.* ci 20.23 (CCSL 48.742; Dyson 1022).
81 But on how the stress on reason itself was not new and the idea of "the Enlightenment" as a distinctly defined historical object is a modern invention, see Withers (2007), 2–3. The preceding "Middle Ages" marked the ascendancy of the Renaissance humanists "who saw that period as a time of decline and decadence standing between them and a defining more or less 'golden', age in the past" and stressed "the revival of antiquity". Pelikan (2005), 143–44.
82 See Brown and Tackett (2006), 1–6.
83 The "incompatibility" of the Enlightenment mindset with Christian understanding of authority was implied in Ziegler's statement that "heteronomous authority and credulity were set against personal rational autonomy and criticism as the enemies of the pursuit of moral, religious, and political responsibility and maturity." Ziegler (2004), 227.
84 Endorsement of "inward piety" at the expense of traditional-scriptural authority was epitomized in the words of Schleiermacher who wrote: "Every holy writing is merely a mausoleum of religion, a monument that a great spirit was there that no longer exists; for if it still lived and were active, why would it attach such great importance to the dead letter that can only be a weak reproduction of it?" Schleiermacher (1988), 50.

notion of historical periods selected according to the intrinsic importance of the facts and according to the reliability of the evidence is quite clearly part of our pagan inheritance".[85] This can be contrasted with what he called "the essential elements of ecclesiastical historiography: the continuous interrelation of dogma and facts; the transcendental significance attributed to the period of the origins; the emphasis on factual evidence; the ever present problem of relating events of local churches to the mystical body of the Universal Church".[86]

On a more fundamental level, H. E. W. Turner asserted that the challenge of the so-called "Humanist frame is too widely removed from that of previous classical answers *to creation, under which 'time' comes as part of God's creation* [Italics mine] to permit them to be immediately relevant".[87] In other words, in the "aftermath" of the *tempora christiana* — a secular period that vigorously endorses a rational worldview and hails the triumph of scientific method, the "irrelevancy" of a contrasting worldview based on an "outdated" and "expired" religious epistemology represented the undermining of the Christian notion of authorities. As we are living in "a post-religious age that had lost the sense of absolute truth derived from a supernatural source",[88] we seem to witness a real sense of "crisis"[89] in authority, be it an intellectual, political, professional, religious or social authority.

Concluding Remarks

In this chapter, we have been exploring the conceptual components of authority and see how significant events that occur within the realm of time is at the core of this concept. And we have asserted that in Christianity, that "which is revealed" forms the kernel of "what is worth remembering". We also see the role that traditions play for the valid commemoration of these events. In the next chapter, we will see how the Christian Scripture is the medium of this commemoration. Looking at how the Scriptures developed physically, we shall argue that the physical nature of the scriptural texts can largely determine the meaning of, and the theological status ascribed to, the texts.

---

85   Momigliano (1977), 196.
86   Momigliano (1990), 138.
87   Williams (1965), 29. According to Augustine, *nullo ergo tempore non feceras aliquid, quia ipsum tempus tu feceras. et nulla tempora tibi co aeterna sunt, quia tu permanes.* "[T]here was no time at which you had not made anything, because you made time itself. And no times are coeternal with you, since you persist". cf 11.14.17 (CCSL 27.202; Williams 210). Augustine's notion of time radically differed from the nineteenth century naturalists' temporal framework. "Nature was no longer perceived as manifesting a divinely preestablished design; the alleged fixed order of our planet was now replaced by pervasive and ongoing change. Earth time was now recorded in the millions of years, and the origin of this universe had occurred in a remote past lost in the immensity of cosmic time." Birx (2009), xxx.
88   Hoeveler (1974), 658.
89   For an interesting exploration of "the phenomenon of decline rhetoric" which resembles the claim that there is a real sense of crisis in authority today, see Murphy (2005), 586–606. On the revision of the "crisis thesis" and "a crisis of epistemic authority" in early modern period, see Rabb (1975); Shagan (2018).

CHAPTER 2

"Si quam dubitationem attulerit latinorum interpretum infinita uarietas"

Physical Evolution of the Scriptures and its Theological Implications

In the *De doctrina Christiana*, Augustine gives a list of the "complete canon of Scripture" and named "forty-four books" that forms the "authoritative Old Testament" while the New Testament consists of twenty-seven books.[1] Although this statement looks similar and straightforward,[2] what Augustine's accounts suggests for today's reader will probably differ "physically" and "theologically" from what he actually implied.

For readers in the twenty-first century who were accustomed to a printed, identical and complete set of books called "the Bible", it will be difficult to comprehend the "individual characteristics" that Augustine's Scripture then possessed. Unlike a "mass-produced" printed book today, the uniqueness that each manuscript then would possess when copied gives the texts their "individual characteristics".[3] Besides, the physical nature of the texts can largely determine the meaning of, and the theological status ascribed to, the texts.[4] A definitive, uniform set of texts called "the Holy Bible" usually suggests not only a certain degree of dignified authority but also a notion of inerrancy and infallibility ascribed to it. But it has been asserted that Augustine "never laid eyes on a Bible" since his Scriptures was not a complete set but "physical subsets: a volume of Paul, a Psalter, a book of Gospels, and so forth".[5] Therefore, equating our modern notions of "the Holy Bible" with Augustine's *divina*

---

1 *Totus autem canon scripturarum ... quadraginta quattuor libris testamenti ueteris terminatur auctoritas.* do 2.13.26 (CSEL 80.40; Green 69).
2 In fact, Augustine's list became the standard canon among Latin Christians as we see in Cassiodorus (485/90-c. 580). The structure and sequence of the theological curriculum that we see in Cassiodorus' *Institutiones* 1.1–9 came from Augustine's *De doctrina Christiana*. See O'Loughlin (2014), 48–64 for a full treatment of the influence of Augustine on Cassiodorus. Augustine's list is also identical with the canon endorsed by the Council of Trent. See Lienhard (1999), 121.
3 See Parker (1997), 189–92. Augustine displayed this awareness when he acknowledged that there can be error in copying manuscripts. See ep 82.3; ci 15.13; re 1.7.2–3.
4 Houghton noted that the "physical nature of the manuscripts ... has a bearing on the analysis of their text, as does the way in which they were used". Houghton (2008), 22. According to Parker, the existence of scriptural texts "as a manuscript tradition" and how it "grew freely" from the beginning is an essential starting point in "all questions of interpretation and all theological formulations" while failing "to take account of these two key facts are based on *a priori* theorising or prejudice, and not on the actual character of the writings". Parker (1997), 203.
5 O'Donnell (2006), 127,35; for the probability that Latin manuscripts containing the Old and New Testament in a single volume were assembled from multiple manuscripts in the fifth century, see Houghton (2016), 13–14.

scriptura/ scripturas sanctas (do 1.34.73; 2.8.15; 2.28.71; 2.35.88; 2.59.142; 3.51.120) will be grossly anachronistic.

Then again, biblical exegesis today attempts "to reach a purely historical understanding of its texts" that risks estrangement of the Old Testament from the New Testament.[6] So, how can Augustine's presupposition on the harmonious continuity between the Old and the New Testament, thereby forming a "complete canon of Scripture" albeit "physically fragmented", be understood? In order to answer this question, this chapter will look at the early development of Scripture. Starting with the *Vetus Latina* and its precursor, the *Septuagint*, we shall also see how the physical nature of scriptural texts, along with the traditions it was embedded in, can determine the meaning of, and the theological status ascribed to Scripture.

1. *Vetus Latina* — A Brief Sketch of Augustine's "Common Edition" of the Scriptures

For most Christians in Augustine's time, *scripturae* — widely referred to as "the Bible" today — denoted manuscripts of separate books and set of books, comprising of the *libri testamenti ueteris* — translated from Hebrew into Greek and the *libri testamenti noui* — written in Greek.[7] With the expansion of Christianity in the Latin-speaking West, it became necessary to translate the Scriptures for those who do not know Greek, the common language of the primitive Church. So, this scriptural *corpus*, called the *vulgata editio* or the "common edition" by the Latin Fathers,[8] was translated into Latin[9] from the later part of the second century, probably in North Africa.[10] The Greek translation of the Old Testament, which became an important source of the *vulgata editio*, was referred to by Augustine as *Septuaginta* (LXX) and for which he had a high regard.[11] This high opinion was not down to his conviction that it was an

---

6 Muller (1996), 19. For a general survey of Biblical Criticism and the suggestion that "the Enlightenment model of historical criticism has become increasingly problematic", see Baird (1992), 725–36; for a critique of the "Historical Critical" method, see Childs (1979), 39–41.
7 O'Donnell (1999), 100; see do 2.13.29 for Augustine's own account.
8 Cimosa (2014), 516; Houghton (2008), 10; Augustine had *secundum uulgatam editionem* in ci 16.10 (CCSL 48.512).
9 The use of Latin in a Christian context was probably prompted by liturgy. From an oral paraphrase of the Greek, early Latin translation may initially be "an interlinear version written between the lines of a Greek text". See Houghton (2016), 7–8; Burton also noted that "Loose references to 'the Latin Bible' appear to presuppose a single monolithic translation; no such homogeneity has been demonstrated, and the term is therefore misleading". Burton (2000), 3–4.
10 Heine (2004), 131; Bogaert (2013), 505–06.
11 See ep 28.2; do 2.22.53; ci 18.42–43 for Augustine's own account. Modern scholars argued that there is "no one Septuagint", since what Septuagint denoted and included — as well as the texts and editions — widely differed for different faith traditions from the beginning. See Aitken (2015), 1–12; also, Hayward (1995), 29 for Jerome's assertion that "only the five Books of Moses were translated by them". While noting that "the label does not characterize the content but represents a reference to the story of its origins" [Hengel (2002), 25], we will loosely apply the label "Septuagint" to what was considered by Augustine as such for the sake of convenience.

accurate translation but because he was intensely conscious of the weight of authority and tradition that was vested upon this inspired translation.[12]

But the Latin translations, as Jerome was aware, displayed inconsistencies and contained many textual difficulties.[13] This prompted Jerome to make an initial revision based on Origen's version of the LXX (*Hexapla*) and finally a new translation based on the Hebrew texts.[14] After Jerome's translation[15] was designated "the Vulgate" in the sixteenth century,[16] any non-Vulgate form became known as the *Vetus Latina* (VL), the "Old Latin", although this classification is not accurate[17] since a number of manuscripts was actually a fusion of VL and Vulgate form.[18]

It is obvious that Augustine had a large collection of Greek and Latin codices and so was aware of a variety of versions and readings.[19] Augustine explicitly expressed his preference for the *Itala* but without rejecting other versions. The actual meaning of *Itala* is unclear except that it is a pre-Vulgate text.[20] His account in *De doctrina Christiana* suggested that he preferred the *Itala* for its "literal rendering" (*nam est uerborum tenacior*) which tended to follow the words rather than the images. In modern terms, he preferred it because its translation philosophy was that of formal rather than dynamic equivalence.[21] He also referred — apparently in approval — to how some Hebrew words like *amen* and *alleluia* were preserved in the original form for the sake of its more solemn authority (*sanctiorem auctoritatem*).[22]

Here, we can see a common trait evolving — perhaps an awareness of some kind of sacred vernacular — that also corresponds with what we know about the growth of the pre-Vulgate Latin text. In tracing the progressive "Europeanization" of the African texts to be a more accurate rendering of the LXX, Fischer noted: "What in the second century was still a vulgarism or an inelegance of the translator, could have

---

12 Harrison (2013), 677.
13 Everson (2012), 520.
14 Bogaert (2013), 514–18. For a discussion on whether Origen's *Hexapla* constitute an end in itself or a means to an end, a "pure" LXX or a "corrected LXX", see Kamesar (1993), 8–21.
15 Again, we must note that "Jerome himself did not provide a collected edition of his translations" but "were in circulation in the form of separate codices". Bogaert (2013), 518.
16 According to Sutcliffe, the word "Vulgate" gradually assumed its modern sense after the Council of Trent. Sutcliffe (1948), 349. Bogaert observed that referring to Jerome's translation as the *Vulgate* was not exactly accurate since the term is anachronistic and misleading, and its previous usage ambiguous. Bogaert (2012), 69.
17 Burton (2000), 6. For the problems of the "traditional characterization" of the Latin Bible into "Old Latin" and "Vulgate", see Houghton (2016), vii–viii.
18 Houghton (2008), 5, 10; O'Donnell (1999), 101; Bogaert (2013), 511.
19 See Houghton (2008), 24–27, 42; re 1.7.2–3; 1.10.1–3; 1.19.4 for Augustine's own admission.
20 According to Burton, "It is impossible to tie the term *Itala* to a single known tradition; Augustine's many biblical citations and allusions have not been identified with any one extant manuscript type". Burton (2000), 6. For a survey of the possible meaning of the *Itala*, see Metzger (1977), 291–93; Houghton (2008), 7–8.
21 In do 2.19.43, Augustine said, *qui non tam uerba quam sententias interpretando sequi maluerunt* (CSEL 80.46). Dynamic equivalence tries "to make sense of the text" so as to make "sense to its audience". O'Loughlin (2012), 347.
22 do 2.16.34.

already become hieratic-solemn expression by the fourth century because of its use in the Scriptures".²³ So, a certain degree of authority was ascribed to the traditional rendering of the Scriptures by Augustine's time.

Jerome was probably revising this Latin translation of the Scriptures "collectively named the *Itala*" before "relying directly to the Hebrew text".²⁴ When Augustine learnt of this venture, he sent letters to Jerome expressing his desire of seeing a better translation from Jerome to avoid the "terrible defects" of unqualified Latin translators and urging him to make the translation based on the LXX text in Origen's *Hexapla* edition.²⁵ But Jerome persisted and maintained that he wanted "to publish the evidence which had been overlooked or corrupted by the Jews, so that Latin-speakers might know what was really in the Hebrew texts".²⁶ Jerome's freer translation, with its philological underpinning,²⁷ implies a deviation from the crude word-for-word style of the *Vetus Latina*²⁸ and ultimately, the LXX. In the next section, we shall see the basis for Jerome's radical shift from the LXX to the Hebrew text.

2. The Septuagint, *Vetus Latina* and *Hebraica Veritas*

Augustine's preferred text, the Septuagint is the most ancient translation of the Hebrew Scripture into the Greek language. Although how the translation came into being cannot be ascertained, it probably dated back to the third century BCE and was meant for Jews in Egypt who no longer understood Hebrew. While it initially became an authoritative reference within the Greek speaking Jewish community, they later abandoned the LXX when the earliest Christian community who also shared "the belief that the revelation and will of God had been preserved in written documents" had adopted it as their own translation. Conversely, new Greek versions of the Hebrew Scripture — like "the very literal" translation by Aquila and a "more idiomatic" rendering of Theodotian — were produced for Jewish use.²⁹

Prior to the adoption of the LXX by Christians, its legendary origin was narrated in the *Letter of Aristeas* which is initially "an exercise in hellenistic Jewish apologetics

---

23 [W]as im 2. Jh noch Vulgarismus oder grobe Unbeholfenheit des Übersetzers war, konnte etwa im 4. Jh eben durch den Gebrauch in der Hl. Schrift schon hieratisch-feierlich geworden sein. Fischer (1951), 15–16. My translation.
24 Muller (1996), 84.
25 See epp 28.2; 71.4; 82.35. Jerome started translation from the Hebrew in 390. Bogaert (2013), 515. Augustine's attitude represents "ecclesiastical traditionalism". Muller (1996), 89.
26 HI ep 112.20 (White 135).
27 Jerome wanted to promote Scriptures "to a public of cultured Roman readers and conscious that the scriptural text, in its Old Latin versions, was an affront to their sensibilities". Vessey (2004), 320.
28 Bogaert (2013), 516. For an overview of the *Vetus Latina* and Jerome's *Vulgate*, see Kedar (1990), 299–338.
29 McDonald (2002), 10; Bruce (1988), 50; Wasserstein (2006), ix; Metzger (2001), 20; Aitken (2015), 1–12.

joined to Ptolemaic dynastic propaganda". Though this *Letter* does not recount the history of the Greek translation or the methods adopted by the translators, it shows that "the Greek translation of the Jewish Scripture was thought to be important at an early stage in its existence".[30] Soon, Christians adopted the legend, incorporating the miraculous nature of the translation to lend authority to the Greek text, and stressing the credibility of the Seventy translators and their prophetic role.[31] Early Christian writers almost always quoted from the LXX and "many of the terms used and partly created by the Septuagint translators became part and parcel of the language of the New Testament".[32] Augustine, too, accepted the tradition of the miraculous translation that is found in the *Letter of Aristeas* and appealed to the credibility of the Seventy translators in his correspondence with Jerome.[33]

Jerome's insistence on the *Hebraica veritas* was partly an outcome of rabbinic Judaism's attempt to estrange their Scripture from the earliest Christian community after the fall of the Temple in Jerusalem.[34] This was marked by a transition from "books that have a high status" toward "an official list of sacred books to which nothing can be added".[35] Although the exact criteria for this delimitation, viz., the time of writing, the language or origin of the document, theological conformity to Torah, usefulness in the liturgy, cannot be determined, books that formerly have a high status to be included in the LXX were no longer in the list[36] of Hebrew Scriptures from the late first century.[37] This was probably prompted by a prevalent

---

30 Wasserstein (2006), ix, 25.
31 Though the legend mainly consists in that the seventy-two translators bring the text into agreement in seventy-two days, the wondrous process was magnified by the legend of the completely isolated work of the translators to produce the identical text. The miraculous nature of the translation was emphasizes only by Philo among Jewish authors. See Hengel (2002), 26, 78.
32 Metzger (2001), 18. Paget call this process "the creative transmission of the LXX with Christians feeling". Paget (2013), 552.
33 See epp 28.2; 71.4; 82.35; cf. ci 18.43; see also Wasserstein (2006), 95–131.
34 On how Judaism take refuge in the Hebrew language, see O'Loughlin (2012), 344. According to Ulrich, "The texts, later so important for a geographically dispersed faith group, did not exercise such a primary function while the Second Temple stood in Jerusalem and while its sacrificial rituals provided the primary focus of the religion". He also noted that "the phenomenon of a unified Hebrew text appears to be the result of the double threat of the Romans to political identity and the threat of the Christians to religious identity". Ulrich (2015), 10, 282, also 57. Hengel also see the move as "anti-Christian". Hengel (2002), 44–45.
35 See Barton (2013), 152.
36 We must be careful not to equate this with a notion of a fixed canon. As Mc Donald asserts, "only a minority of Jews were interested in a fixed biblical canon in the first century CE … that notion emerges at the end of the first century for some Jews, [but] it was not a popular notion until several decades later among rabbinic Jews and even later for those in the western diaspora. Imposing such notions on the various expressions of Judaism at that time is anachronistic". McDonald (2016), 82–83. Ulrich noted that "no similar term is attested in Jewish writings, including the Septuagint, or in the Hebrew language until comparatively late … If canon as such had been an important concept or reality in Judaism or nascent Christianity, one would expect that authors would discuss or at least mention it". Ulrich (2015), 267. See also McDonald (2002), 5.
37 McDonald (2016), 80. All the additional books which the LXX contains by comparison with the Hebrew Bible are all of Jewish origin. See Barton (2013), 146.

notion in some Jewish circles[38] that the Scriptures inspired by God's spirit came to an end with the last prophetically inspired writers, thereby refuting some books in the LXX along with the Christian literatures currently in circulations.[39] Even within the limit of those books they had retained, for example Is 7:14, Christians openly argue against the wording of the Hebrew text on the basis of the wording of the Greek translation.[40] This urged a greater attention on the details of the text so that from the second century onward, the proto-MT tradition was probably the only one transmitted within Judaism with only minor variants. Jerome principally based his translation of the *Vulgate* upon this pre-MT tradition which will be "one of the forms of the ancient text in the original language".[41]

Jerome became aware of the textual problem of the "Old Testament" and how the LXX "deviates" from the Hebrew text after revising Origen's *Hexapla*. Assuming that the Hebrew Scripture was the pristine original text, Jerome's insistence on the *Hebraica veritas* had certain immediate and long-term implications. In his preface to the *Quaestiones Hebraicae in Genesim* where he first refers to the "Hebrew truth",[42] Jerome suggests that the translators of the LXX deliberately hide mysteries and prophecies about Christ and that they only translated "the five Books of Moses". He also asserted that the Evangelists, the Apostle Paul and Jesus "quote many things as if from the Old Testament, which are not contained in our codices".[43] His version, which supposedly "corrected" these errors, was meant to clarify many passages and refute the Jews.[44] And he holds only twenty-two books[45] which the Jews regarded as Scripture as canonical since the Hebrew text is the norm for Jerome. Ultimately, Jerome's venture largely determines the Christian conceptions of textual authority, canonicity and interpretation.

---

38 Those most concerned with the priestly functions in Judaism hold this notion, particularly in the Hasmonean era. See McDonald (2016), 80.
39 Hengel (2002), 45. This is more an attempt "to fence out, rather than to fence in". See Metzger (1987), 110. Goshen-Gottstein asserted that there never was an official act of introducing certain writings into the canon for Judaism. "The issue was rather which of the various writings which groups had regarded as 'inspired' should be left inside the canon". Goshen-Gottstein (1992), 1018.
40 Muller (1996), 40.
41 Ulrich (2015), 10–11. For the meaning and origin of *Masoretic Text* (MT), see Mulder (1990), 87–135.
42 In ep 112.20 Jerome writes: *ut scirent nostri, quid Hebraea ueritas contineret* (CSEL 55.390). Although he first used the expression *Hebraica Veritas* in his preface to the *Quaestiones Hebraicae in Genesim*, "the concept is already present in the Roman letters". Kamesar (1993), 42.
43 Hayward (1995), 29–30. *Hebraica Veritas* occurs around 85 times in his extant writings. Kamesar remarked that many quotations in the New Testament follow neither the Hebrew nor the LXX and "Jerome has simply exploited the complex nature of the situation in a manner favourable to his own position". Kamesar (1993), 64.
44 White (1990), 37. See his letter to Augustine ep 112.20 where Jerome repeated this assertion.
45 In his *Prologus in libro Regum*, Jerome writes: *Atque ita fiunt pariter ueteris legis libri uiginti duo … quicquid extra hos est, inter apocrifa seponendum … non sunt in canone*. "And so there are also twenty-two books of the Old Testament … what is not found in our list must be placed amongst the Apocryphal writings … [they] are not in the canon". *Vulgata*, 365 (Fremantle 490). But, for Jerome's free use of the LXX, particularly in his commentaries of Pauline letters, see Scheck (2010), 11. See also n. 88 below regarding Jerome's notion of a definitive canon.

3. The *Vetus Latina* and Traditions of the Church Regarding the Septuagint

According to Bogaert "the history of the Latin Bible would have remained that of an infinitely revised version of the Greek Bible" without Jerome's insistence on the *Hebraica veritas*.[46] This is probably right, given that Augustine urged Jerome to make his translation based on the LXX text in Origen's *Hexapla* edition. But if Augustine conceded the efficacy of referring to the *exemplaria praecedentia*,[47] viz., Hebrew and Greek when uncertainty arise in the Latin version, why did he still insist upon the LXX as the textual basis for translation? We shall consider three points in relation to this question.

Firstly, Augustine considered what has been achieved in previous translations, as can be seen from Origen's *Hexapla* edition, which is a six-column synopsis of the Old Testament.[48] Augustine doubts whether anything missed by "those translators", i.e., "the Seventy", could be found in the Hebrew texts or if newer translations could really shed light on obscure things. Implicitly suggesting the "miraculous" unanimity in their translation, he contrasted this with the disagreement among later Greek translators Aquila, Theodotion and Symmachus, who "left out many things which had to be explained and elucidated much later".[49] Augustine therefore lobbied for the credibility of the many translators who were traditionally considered "inspired" against the weight of a single translator, including Jerome.[50]

Secondly, Augustine considered what using a new translation from the Hebrew could entail. He was concerned with how discrepancy would be settled between someone who based their arguments on the Greek and Latin versions of Scriptures once Jerome's version was read regularly in many churches. If the new translation based on the Hebrew came up with "some unusual expression" which was objectionable to the audiences as it was "already ingrained in their memories",[51] "it would be almost impossible to get hold of the Hebrew texts" to refute their objection. In that case, Jerome will be "indispensable" to settle the argument and he can still "be mistaken". Augustine's recurring plea to the "many" was summarized by his question: *tot latinas*

---

46   Bogaert (2013), 514.
47   do 2.16.34.
48   From left to right the parallel columns presented the Hebrew text, followed by a Greek transcription and four translations in Greek including the LXX. For an introduction to Origen's background and his *Hexapla*, see Dorival (2013), 608–11.
49   ep 28.2 (White 66). He reiterated this point in ep 71.6: "The Greek text contains so many divergent readings in different manuscripts that it is almost intolerable [*ut tolerari uix possit*]" (CSEL 34.2.254; White 93–94). But "this may have been the point with the enterprise, because it made the Hebrew text indispensable". Muller (1996), 40; cf. Kamesar (1993), 66.
50   See ci 18.43 where Augustine explicitly refers to Jerome's translation.
51   ep 71.5 (White 92). The issue of "memorization" was substantial as many congregants will be illiterate and few of them will afford to buy books since they are expensive. This implies that they will be "less attached to the written form of the word and encountered it more through the formal oral presentation of liturgical readings and preaching". O'Donnell (1999), 100.

et graecas auctoritates damnari quis ferat?[52] As Kato insightfully remarked, it was likely that "Augustine wanted the source language of the Bible to be Greek to prevent a monopoly by the ones who could read Hebrew, like Jerome, in the realm of biblical translation, and to keep the principle of comparison open to the public".[53]

Thirdly, Augustine further addressed the related question of textual authenticity and authority from the standpoint of the church traditions. He asked why Jerome considered the authority of the Hebrew manuscripts differs from the Greek text since the Septuagint was widely diffused and used by the apostles.[54] In another letter to Jerome on a different issue involving the Manicheans, he expressed a similar stance. The Manicheans refuted a large number of passages in the Scriptures as false although "they were unable to prove their claim either by producing more texts or older ones, or by the authority of an older language from which the Latin books were translated".[55] Although the whole point was that the apostles would not deliberately write a lie, Augustine consistently holds the view that claim of access to older texts or language[56] does not always amount to authenticity and authority while the LXX already carries the weight of traditional claim that it was an inspired translation.

Augustine built upon the same logic in his *De doctrina Christiana*: "If we find in the Hebrew versions something that differs from what [the Seventy] wrote … [i]t may indeed be the case that they translated in a way that the Holy Spirit, who was leading them and creating unanimity, judged appropriate to the Gentiles".[57] Augustine endorsed working "forwards" towards the sense while Jerome was working "backwards" towards the text. So, Augustine sees the divergence of the LXX from the Hebrew text as "a positive move with a spiritual motive" that will benefit the readers while Jerome perceived this as "a negative move that justify a return to the *Hebrew veritas*".[58]

And this same principle applies not only to the texts but also to the books of Scripture: "to prefer those accepted by all catholic churches to those which do not accept". On those books "not universally accepted", preference should be given to "those accepted by a majority of churches, and by the more authoritative ones, to those supported by fewer churches".[59] Augustine's assertion crucially negates the prevailing rabbinic Jewish notion determining Jerome's Old Testament canon that

---

52 "Who would allow so many Latin and Greek authorities to be condemned?" ep 71.4. (CSEL 34.2.252; White 92–93). On how "every word translated in a new way clearly represented a potentially problematic theological option" for Jerome who used a text that was not shared across the Western Church, see Raspanti (2009), 166.
53 Kato (2017), 17.
54 ep 71.6 (White 93).
55 ep 82.5 (White 148).
56 *antiquioribus exemplaribus nec praecedentis linguae*. ep 82.6 (CSEL 34.2.356).
57 do 2.22.55 (Green 81–83).
58 Gallagher (2016), 113–14. For the contradictions in Jerome's translation philosophy which "exhibit adherence to the linguistic structure of the source language" as well as "free rendering", see Kedar (1990), 323–29.
59 do 2.12.25 (Green 67); see also ci 18.43. According to McDonald and Porter, "churches in the larger areas, such as Antioch, Alexandria, Rome, and Ephesus, were more likely to have a greater influence on which books were included than were the smaller churches in rural areas". McDonald (2000), 618.

the Scriptures ended with the last prophetically inspired writers, as prophecy had ceased after the time of the return from the Babylonian exile.⁶⁰

When we consider the stances which Jerome and Augustine had taken toward scriptural translation, we can detect how disparate Jewish and Christian "traditions" lie beneath their notions of textual authority and canonicity.⁶¹ Basing upon these traditions, the LXX had progressively developed a distinct Christian identity that influenced other churches beyond the Latin-speaking one. Therefore, in spite of knowing the significance of the Hebrew text, Augustine insisted upon the LXX as the basis for a new Latin translation of the "Old Testament" because of these traditions. And though referring to the Jewish Scripture as the "Old Testament" which complements the corpus later characterized as the "New Testament" did not go uncontested within Christianity in the formative stage, they nevertheless became an integral part of the Christian Scripture by the time of Augustine. In the next section, we shall see those factors which determine the transformation of these fluid, interacting texts⁶² into a "complete canon of Scripture".

4. Emergence of the "New Testament" and the Notion of a "Complete Canon"

In his writings, Augustine had affirmed that the implications of the Old Testament became explicitly manifested in the New Testament.⁶³ Although one Scripture having two Testaments has since become a "conventional" concept, Pelikan remarked that the development of this novel concept "has been correctly called the most momentous event in the history of early Christianity".⁶⁴ The "concept" simultaneously signified the continuity and diversion of Christianity from the Jewish faith. Mark Edwards even asserted that "the church would have no Old Testament" without a certain reading of the Septuagint while the shapes of its own Testament "if it had one at all, would not be as we now find them".⁶⁵

---

60 On how "rabbis restrict legitimate prophecy to a classical period which coincides with the composition of the canon", see Meyer (1985), 958. Regarding the reception of Jesus' prophetic ministry, see Foerster (1964), 569.
61 Regarding Jerome's use of Jewish tradition to support the case for *Hebrew veritas*, Hayward noted that "Jerome uses the words 'tradition' (*traditio*) and 'hand on as tradition' (*trado*) frequently in QHG of the Jewish material which he transmits". Hayward (1995), 5; see also Kedar (1990), 331–34.
62 Allison noted thus: "The Hebrew Bible itself is a compilation of interacting texts, and the Dead Sea scrolls, the Apocrypha, the Pseudepigrapha and the rabbinic sources in turn regularly cite, echo and imitate those texts". Allison (2013), 479. We will see that this is also the case with all the books in the Christian Scripture.
63 *et in uetere nouum lateat et in nouo uetus pateat* (Gn q 2.73; CCSL 33.106); *quae in testamento uetere uelata in nouo reuelatur* (sp 18; CSEL 60.171).
64 Pelikan (2005), 101.
65 Edwards (2013), 714; On how "the Jewish scriptures may have been a barrier" that "may just as well have served as a pattern" for the development of the Christians scriptures, see also Ferguson (2002), 295.

Indeed, Jesus, the apostles and Paul frequently appealed to, and quoted from, the "Jewish" Scriptures. These Scriptures which bear witness to Jesus Christ (Jn 5:39; Lk 24:25–27) were considered indispensable and were reinterpreted in the light of this conviction. In the apostolic κήρυγμα of Act 2:14–36, we see an instance where "contemporary history is interpreted" in terms of prophecy in the "Jewish" Scriptures, "which itself is interpreted in the light of present fact".[66] And soon, early Christians referred to these Scriptures as "the Old Testament" while the words and deeds of Jesus Christ and the apostles formed the basis of "the New Testament". The Old Testament therefore determined and complemented the development and meaning of the New Testament.

The New Testament consists of a mixture of early Christian literature in several relatively diverse genres. An important factor that determine its development "was the sheer passage of time, as the church needed to discover whatever resources it could to bind it to its past and to guarantee its continuance in the tradition of the faith".[67] Beside the testimony of the apostles and other eyewitnesses to Jesus and the stories about the early activities of his disciples, books of instruction for moral life, prayers and confessional materials particularly relevant for liturgy were circulated in Christian circles. By the end of the second century, books that were associated in one way or another with the name of an apostle[68] and their close associate came to be regarded as "canonical"[69] and the four Gospels, the Epistles of Paul, and some other Epistles "were being used as Scripture".[70]

While the internal need of Christian communities to remember the "Christ-event" determined the emergence of literatures that recorded the traditions about Jesus, the "inverted" need to draw distinct lines from those who are in the periphery of these traditions soon ensued. "Syncretistic" Gnostics who created "rival gospels, acts, and apocalypses" on their dualistic philosophy compelled the church to define the valid Christian stances in relation to Judaism and of the cogent merit of the Old Testament which many Gnostics rejected. The Church also had to be wary to receive nothing which did not carry "the stamp of apostolic guarantee" to avoid the Gnostics' "secret

---

66 Williams (1950), 26. O'Loughlin succinctly noted thus: "The Christians may have seen themselves as the followers of Jesus, but they did so as a community which already possessed a library of distinct sacrality". O'Loughlin (2015), xi.
67 Pelikan (2005), 114.
68 An important criterion for authoritative books was being "handed down" or "received". Irenaeus mentions Valentinus's "*Gospel of Truth*, which he contrasts with the gospels 'handed down from the apostles' that he classifies as 'scriptures'". Ferguson (2002), 295, 312.
69 As Metzger interestingly remarked, "'canonical' means authoritative books, but 'the canon' means the only authoritative books. Use does not equal canonicity; though a certain kind of use does, namely, use that excludes any other". Metzger (1987), 24. See also O'Loughlin (2015), xi.
70 Pelikan (2005), 102, 115, 116; Ferguson (2002), 295–98. It was asserted that there were no generally accepted terms beside "Scripture" to identify this collection of Christian writings as the term Old Testament and New Testament had not gained sufficient recognition in the second century. McDonald (2000), 615. But "we can see the outline of what may be described as the nucleus of the New Testament". Metzger (1987), 75.

traditions" which were highly disruptive. Indirectly, this resulted in "a devaluation of oral tradition, which ... Papias towards 130 still preferred to books".[71]

Within the Christian community, Marcion of Sinope led a movement to reject the Old Testament which he considered "superseded by the gospel" and thus "having no relevance or authority for Christians". Deeming Paul as the only apostle who preserved the teaching of Jesus in its purity, he asserted that the original apostles had perverted this with a mixture of Jewish legalism. Marcion also discerned the God of the New Testament from the God of the Old.[72] The term "Old Covenant" and "New Covenant", which stressed that the two covenants came from the same God, was adopted in "a thrust against Marcion and some Gnostics".[73] Thus, in his *Stromateis*, Clement of Alexandria (*c*. 150–215) referred to Prov 19:17 and 3:27 as the law from "the Old Testament"[74] and also asserted that "If prophecy promises the same homes for us and the patriarchs, one single God is revealed in both the Testaments".[75]

The Montanist movement and the persecution of Christians under emperor Diocletian further contributed to the formation of a Christian canon of Scripture.[76] In short, what eventually became the "Christian Scripture" has been simultaneously forged and shaped by two disparate and almost exclusivist "theological" views: one that disregarded the other as "prophetically" void (the "New Testament" by Rabbinic Jews) or as superseded by the "New" (the Old Testament by Marcion and other "Christian" groups who had Gnostics tendencies, for example the Manicheans of whom we will later see more about). And as the Christian Scripture treads between these two extreme views to assume a distinct identity, the enigma of "time" as the "already" and "not yet" which various "groups" of the early Christians grappled with was thereby documented in the formative history of the Scriptures.

Apart from these fundamental theological issues, another important factor that contributed to the emergence of "a Christian Scripture" and its canon was the

---

71 Metzger (1987), 77–78; Ferguson also asserted: "The gnostic controversy made imperative a clarification of what writings accurately expressed apostolic teaching and apostolic authority". Ferguson (2002), 314. For Gnostic and Manichaean interpretation of the Scriptures, see also Lohr (2013), 584–604.
72 See Bruce (1988), 134–36; Harnack asserted that Marcion was "the first to construct a formal canon of Christian Scripture and that the Church followed his lead". Metzger (1987), 98.
73 Ferguson (2002), 307. See n. 70 above on how this notion had not yet gained sufficient recognition in the second century.
74 Παλαιὰ Διαθήκη νομοθετεῖ/ *leges in Ueteri Testamento. Stromateis* 3.6.54 (PG 8.1159-60).
75 Εἰ δὲ αἱ αὐταὶ μόναι ὑπὸ τῆς προφητείας ἡμῖν τε αὖ καὶ τοῖς Πατριάρχαις καταγγέλλονται, εἰς ἀμφοῖν ταῖν διαθήκαιν δείκνυται ὁ θεός/ *Si autem eaedem mansiones a prophetia et nobis rursus et patriachis annuntiantur: ostenditur unum esse Deum utriusque testamenti. Stromateis* 2.6.28 (PG 8.963–64; Ferguson 177–78). Ferguson remarked that "This is directed against Marcion (second century A.D.) and some of the Gnostics who set the God of the Old Testament in contrast with the God of the New Testament". See Ferguson (1991), 177–78. Clement also asserted that "the Testament and the commandments (τὴν διαθήκην καὶ τὰς ἐντολάς/ secundum testamentum et praeceptum) ... chronologically two, granted in the divine economy with an eye to the stage of progress, are one in power, Old and New (δυνάμει μιᾷ οὖσαι, ἡ μὲν παλαιά, ἡ δὲ καινή/ *cum potestate quidem unum sint, illud quidem novum, hoc vero vetus*), being presented by the one and only God through his Son". See *Stromateis* 2.6.29 (PG 8.963–64; Ferguson 178).
76 For a detailed study, see Metzger (1987), 75–112; Ferguson (2002), 309–17.

physical evolution of manuscripts during the formative stage of Christianity. This physical change may even influence the textual deviation of the LXX from the Hebrew Scripture. It has been noted that the Christian LXX was characterized by the use of the codex[77] rather than the Jewish scroll even before there was a "New Testament". Christian codices were also discernible as the Tetragrammaton — God's mysterious name YHWH/יהוה — was replaced by κύριος, χριστός and other *nomina sacra*. This distinction clearly implies to a new beginning meant to differentiate between the use of Scriptures in "church" and "synagogue".[78]

Moreover, the table of contents of the Scriptures, which was a mental notion with scrolls which usually contains one or two books, became a physical object when a codex contained many books included in that table of contents and no others.[79] In the Hebrew Scripture, the books were arranged into three sections, Torah, Prophets and Writing which provides the basis for the acronym Tanakh.[80] In the LXX, it was arranged in such a way that the prophetic books were placed at the end. This arrangement "may be connected with the transmission of the Greek Bible in Christian circles, since when the Bible is written on a codex the prophetic books then lead into the New Testament where their predictions are seen as fulfilled".[81] Thus, the physical development of manuscripts actually paved the way for what Augustine referred as a "complete canon of Scripture" comprising of the Old and the New Testament.

---

77 On what a codex is and how it may serve to distinguish Christians "from the wider book-copying culture of the time", see Hurtado (2013), 63–80. According to Bar-Ilan, "it seems that in Christianity, as a new religion without a scribal tradition, there was no objection to the change in form". Bar-Ilan (1990), 24. Gamble stated thus: "Almost without exception, the earliest Christian books known have the form not of the papyrus roll but of the papyrus codex, or leaf book ... It is possible ... that the codex was first employed in primitive Christianity for collections of texts (*testimonia*) from Jewish Scripture. Judging from the predominantly atomistic citation of Jewish Scripture ... this would not have been a matter of producing continuous transcriptions of Jewish scriptural books, but rather of compiling excerpta, that is, selective proof-texts". Gamble (1995), 49, 65. But Skarsaune cautioned: "Very likely one should rather think of the 'testimony tradition' as part and parcel of the growing theological heritage within early Christianity, which was transmitted within the 'mainstream' of early Christian literature, in varying literary formats". Skarsaune (1996), 420.

78 Hengel (2002), 41. In his *Prologus in libro Regum*, Jerome specifically wrote: *Et nomen Domini tetragrammaton in quibusdam graecis uoluminibus usque hodie antiquis expressum litteris inuenimus*. "And we find the four-lettered name of the Lord in certain Greek books written to this day in the ancient characters". *Vulgata*, 364 (Fremantle 489).

79 Ulrich (2002), 25. But regarding an actual pandects, Houghton asserts that manuscripts containing the Old and New Testament in a single volume in Latin are not attested until much later than the time of Augustine although the earliest single-volume copies of Scripture in Greek date from around his time. "Instead, books were bound in smaller collections, such as the Epistles or the Gospels, or circulated individually". Houghton (2008), 22. To have an idea of how a codex and codices can hold together books, or how books can become too many to combine in a single volume, see Augustine's own suggestion to Firmus regarding his *De civitate Dei*, as quoted in Dyson (1998), xiii.

80 According to Barton, "It is traditional Jewish teaching that there is said to be a diminution of inspiration as one moves from the centre to the periphery. The Torah is direct divine revelation; the Prophets are divine revelation mediated through prophetic figures; the Writings are human reflection on revelation". Barton (2013), 162.

81 Barton (2013), 146, 162.

Regarding the "theological" issue of canonicity, unlike Jerome whose stance on the "Old Testament canon" was clear cut, Augustine seems to think of Scripture as a library and it has a fluid, fuzzy edge.[82] In the *De doctrina Christiana*, Augustine listed an "unusual" forty-four books, instead of the traditional twenty-two books, as forming the authoritative Old Testament.[83] And probably due to his gradual acquaintance with Jerome's translation and his arguments in favour of following the Hebrew canon, Augustine modified the order of his canon that he originally presented in the *De doctrina Christiana* without changing the structure[84] in the *De civitate Dei*. In this significant work, Augustine asserted some of his arguments basing on its presence in "the canonical Scriptures, Hebrew and Christian".[85]

However, Augustine sees the Scriptures not as a closed system that can contain the fullness of truth, whether as a closed canon or as Jerome's *Hebraica veritas*, but a temporal set of signs that actually points towards the Eternal Truth.[86] The divine messages of the Scriptures will never be exhaustible nor fully comprehensible only through the text itself but must be studied along with creation in a process of mutual illumination.[87] Augustine also regarded church traditions as the works, and continuing guidance of the Spirit that stood in a mutual relationship with the Scriptures.

Beside the "absence" of a definitive canon in Augustine,[88] the distinctive characteristics that each of Augustine's manuscripts of Scriptures have can negate our

---

82 Augustine, unlike Jerome, "experienced no difficulty in allowing into canon the Greek portions of Daniel and Esther" and he "does not counsel abstinence from non-canonical literature, but rather a critical reading by those well grounded in the truth of the canonical Scriptures". La Bonnardière (1999), 35; Gallagher (2017), 226. And Gallagher asserts that Jerome generally "follows the synagogal criterion, which necessarily allows for literature only in Hebrew", although "he is able to be pushed in debate to the point of permitting documents outside the Jewish canon if they are written in Hebrew". Augustine "seems to reject the Hebrew criterion for canonicity, instead relying solely on Christian tradition to establish the content of the Bible. In fact, in his possible rejection of the Hebrew criterion, Augustine's view challenges Christian tradition, which had generally upheld this standard". Gallagher (2012), 104.
83 Noting that this total is unusual, Gallagher state, "Augustine's total increases because he includes the deuterocanonical books within his canon, but also because he counts separately several books that are usually counted jointly … Only in the case of the Minor Prophets does he acknowledge the tradition of counting these books jointly, … But Augustine's total forty-four for the entire Old Testament requires that one count the Minor Prophets individually, despite Augustine's comment to the contrary". Gallagher (2017), 228.
84 See La Bonnardière (1999), 35–39.
85 *Igitur secundum scripturas canonicas Hebraeas atque christianas* ci 15.23 (CCSL 48.491).
86 See do 1.38.81–39.85; cf 10.6.9; 11.6.8. According to Gallagher, Jerome's fundamental belief in the stability and authenticity of the Hebrew text available in his day differs from Augustine's who insisted upon "the importance and originality of the Hebrew but rejected the idea that the Church's Bible should match textually the Hebrew". See Gallagher (2012), 103, 200–01.
87 See O'Loughlin (1999), 58–59; Toom (2013), 80.
88 Cf. SanPietro who recently argued that Augustine was "committed to the idea of a canon" while Jerome wanted "to keep the Christian corpus open-minded and expansive". SanPietro (2017), 236, 257. This is an interesting hypothesis but does not seem to take sufficient account of Jerome's actual statements in the prologues to the books of the Vulgate. For example, in the prologue to the four books of the Kings he gives a complete canon list which he imagines as being closed with a specific

modern obsession of going to the original languages on a "stabilized" original texts to "extract" scriptural messages.[89] Most crucially, "the perfection of Scripture" is the most fundamental aspect of "Scripture's authority"[90] for many Christians today. But, considering that Augustine's texts and "canon" were not as rigid and definitive as our "Bible" today, it will be safe to surmise that his notion of inspiration[91] and scriptural authority will be different from what many of us "fundamentally"[92] hold today.

Finally, Augustine's affirmation that the meaning of the Old Testament became explicitly manifested in the New Testament can be seen as another way of describing the inner harmonious continuity between the two "Testaments", which is rooted in God's redemptive work in history. As we shall see later, this affirmation also suggested the intimate relationship between Christ and the church, as that of a head and body,[93]

---

number of books equal to the number of elders in Apoc [Rev] 4:4–10 (see *Prologus in libro Regum, Vulgata*, 364–66), while in the prologue to "the books of Solomon" he makes his, now famous, distinction between fully canonical books and those which are read *ad aedificationem plebis, non ad auctoritatem ecclesiasticorum dogmatum confirmandam* (see *Prologus in libris Salomonis, Vulgata*, 957). See also n. 45 above. In fact, these *Prologus* are indispensable, as O'Loughlin remarked, "If one wants to appreciate how a Latin Christian viewed either 'Scripture', 'the Scriptures', an individual book, or somewhat later, 'the Bible' at any time during the medieval period, then it is with these short texts that one should begin". O'Loughlin (2015), xiii.

89 This obsession is largely the consequence of the medieval scholastic-humanist debate on literary, academic, and doctrinal issues. Those scholastics who were unwilling to correct or revised "Jerome's *Vulgate*" regarded the philologists as unqualified to engage in scriptural studies while the humanists argued that lack of language training hampered proper scriptural exegesis. The impact of the humanists, whose pioneer Erasmus draw great inspiration from Jerome too, was ultimately assisted by the new medium of the printing press. See Rummel (2008), 1–13. For the effect of the printing press on "stabilizing the text" of Scripture, see Pelikan (2005), 145–48.

90 McKim (1992), 1035. John Goldingay asserts that the New Testament does not explicitly link authority with Scripture (the Old Testament) while the Church Fathers simply assumed that the scriptures should determine the nature of Christian faith and life. "Such linkage came about in the context of modernity and of the existence of rival understandings of the nature of Christian faith [when] thinkers asked what was the authority for forms of belief and behavior. They wanted to be sure that the theological and ethical edifice was built on secure foundations. One way of attempting to do that was to see the scriptures as the foundation of all else. If the scriptures have authority, then beliefs and behavior built on them are secure". Goldingay (2007), 30.

91 Regarding the notion of inspiration in the early church, MacDonald and Porter makes an interesting observation: "Inspiration, though often assumed to be a criterion for acceptance, was in fact more of a corollary to a writing's canonicity than a criterion. In other words, if a writing was accepted as Scripture and a part of the biblical canon, it was also assumed that the writing was inspired by God. Inspiration, however, was never limited by the early church to sacred writings but was extended to what was considered true, whether it was written or taught/preached orally". McDonald and Porter (2000), 618.

92 For an introduction to the "fundamentalist impulse" where "the authority of the Bible is defended primarily by reference to its factual reliability", see Harris (1998).

93 In Ev 1.54, Augustine stated, *Hoc magnum et inenarrabile sacramentum, hoc regnum et sacerdotium antiquis per prophetiam reuelabatur, posteris eorum per euangelium praedicatur ... quandoquidem membra eius id operata sunt, quod dictante capite cognouerunt.* "This great and unutterable mystery, this kingdom and priesthood, was revealed by prophecy to the men of ancient time, and is now preached by the gospel to their descendants ... He stands to all His disciples in the relation of the head to the members of His body". (CSEL 43.60; Salmond 101).

in this temporal realm. Therefore, what is seemingly a physical fragmented text is a complete canon for Augustine because the Scriptures recounts the work of a single *auctor* toward a definite goal.

Concluding Remarks

In this chapter, we are looking at the underlying theological assumptions in the process of the development of the Christian Scripture. We have seen how the awareness of time as having a new and definitive orientation in the ministry and teachings of Jesus contributed to the formation of the Scriptures as constituting the Old and the New Testament. And we have asserted that the physical nature of the Scriptures can have significant theological implications subsequently. Looking at the various factors at play in the developmental process, we can affirm that the main issues with Scripture were clearly defined by the time of Augustine, although they were far from being settled.[94]

The issue more pressing for Augustine was the poor Latin translations of the Scriptures and the textual basis for the task of a much-needed revision. Nonetheless, this issue still proves to be a stumbling block for Augustine. In fact, the lack of eloquence in the Latin Scripture and his misgiving regarding the teaching of the Old Testament (cf 3.5.9; 3.7.12–13) deterred Augustine when he read the Scriptures as a young man. Even later in his *De doctrina Christiana*, Augustine referred to the infinite variety of Latin translations (*latinorum interpretum infinita uarietas*) produced by those who could not read Hebrew and were thus ignorant of the particularities of the language (*signa propria*).[95] In Augustine's eyes, their eagerness to translate Greek texts into Latin outran their linguistic ability. Augustine believed that the Latin manuscripts of the Old Testament should be corrected from the LXX and the New Testament from the Greek, particularly from "those found in the more learned and diligent churches".[96]

---

94   In 367, Athanasius wrote to the churches of Alexandria concerning the canon of Scripture. The list contained twenty books of the Old Testament, twenty-seven books of the New Testament and the list of books "not canonized, but prescribed by the fathers to be read to those who have recently joined … They, themselves, are able to refute heresies: the Manicheans, the Marcionites, the Montanists, Arians, and their parasites, the Melitians". Gallagher and Meade (2017), 118, 120; Gribomont asserts that Athanasius "was thinking less of the universal church but more for his own flock, [especially] the monks, who continually drew edification from pious apocryphal texts. This list, however, automatically became widely read". Gribomont (2014), 512. Metzger also noted that "not all in the Church were ready to accept precisely the canon as identified by Athanasius, and throughout the following centuries there were minor fluctuations in the East as well as in the West". Metzger (1987), 7. Nevertheless, Athanasius' list, particularly of the New Testament books, may provide the basis which was later adopted and affirmed by various Councils. The Council in Trullo, convened in 692, "may be taken to have formally closed the process of the formation of the New Testament canon for East and West" while the status of the Old Testament canon was never really settled and there never really has been a vote on the biblical canon which all Christians would feel bound to accept up to the present day. See Pelikan (2005), 117; Gallagher and Meade (2017), 2.
95   See do 2.16.36.
96   *et maxime qui apud ecclesias doctiores et diligentiores reperiuntur*. do 2.22.56 (CSEL 80.49; Green 83).

In the next two chapters, we shall explore the background behind the emergence of these convictions in Augustine's thought. Starting with his initial negation of the Scriptures in his *Confessiones*, we shall see how Augustine evolved into an ardent expositor of the Scriptures in the *De doctrina Christiana*. As we see the changing socio-political and religious-theological background behind these two works, we shall argue that much of the problems and the solutions recounted therein lies with Augustine's own engagement with the enigma of time. We will also assert that the incarnation of Christ is the pivotal event determining Augustine's understanding of the authority of Scripture.

CHAPTER 3

"Our Hearts are Restless until they Rest in You"

The Longing for the Fullness of Time in the Confessiones

In the last chapter, we have seen the physical evolution of the Christian Scripture that has been forged and shaped between two disparate and almost exclusivist theological views: one that disregards the other either as "prophetically" void or superseded. We have asserted that the physical nature of the Scriptures can have theological implications subsequently. In this chapter, we will see how Augustine resolved his scriptural conundrum by aligning these theological and physical factors with the decisiveness of Christ's incarnation. Starting with the ambivalence of authorities behind his quest for the Truth, we will see how Augustine embraced the Scriptures and expressed his understanding of scriptural authority in the *Confessiones*.[1]

1. The Ambivalence of Authorities in Augustine

Augustine believes in authority. This can be deduced from his experience of being a seeker initially, and subsequently being a figure of authority himself. In his extant writings, the term "authority" occurs 1281 times.[2] As Augustine was not systematic in his usage of the term, the general sense can be determined from the context although it will not be possible to reduce them to have a single consistent sense. Following the traditional usage of the term especially in his early writings, "authority" can denote the reputation and persuasiveness of human, non-Christian authorities like Plato, Pericles and Varro. Above all, the authority of Christ, the Scriptures, the church and its ministers were connoted, particularly later in his arguments with opponents in the church.[3] These different aspects of authority which operated in and influenced Augustine's life, can be seen in his *Confessiones* where he went beyond the abstract, theoretical treatment of the subject that he had made in his earlier writings.[4]

---

1   Augustine wrote his *Confessiones*, after he succeeded Valerius as the Bishop of Hippo in 395/6, as a recollection of his spiritual odyssey. Written between 397–400 when he produced a spurt of literary activities, the *Confessiones* can be seen as an interacting text with other works which we will explore in subsequent chapters.
2   These numbers were collected using the cag-online.net database. According to Pollmann, the word occurs 1256 times "from his earliest extant work, the *contra Academicos*, onwards" while Lütcke noted that Augustine used the term 1235 times. See Pollmann (2014), 161; Lutcke (1986), 499.
3   See Lutcke (1986), 498; Chapman (2008), 503.
4   The theoretical explanations of the meaning and function of authority are more likely to be found in the writings up to *c.* 395 and the *Confessiones* was written *c.* 397. See Brown (2000), 154; Lutcke (1986), 499.

In the *Confessiones*, Augustine's whole narrative was interpolated[5] between various scriptural quotations. While this reflects a shift in emphasis from his earlier works,[6] it also highlights his acknowledgment of the authority of Scripture with which he initially struggled against. This struggle, epitomized by a "restless heart" (*cor inquietum*), was compounded by misguided preoccupations in a series of *quaerens*[7] for Truth, the source of the *beata uita*.[8] And in retrospect, this whole process of seeking, searching and learning presupposed some forms of authority. Augustine recounted his infancy and boyhood when he learnt to speak and was subject to the authority of his parents (cf 1.8.13). His mother, his teachers at school and even friends were "figures of authority" who influenced his behaviour and development till his youth (cf 1.10.16; 1.11.18; 2.3.5; 2.8.16). In his youth, Augustine came across the "authoritative" Cicero "whose tongue practically everyone admires"[9] and whose writing, *Hortensius*, changed the direction of his mind and gave him a new purpose and ambition.

With high expectation of finding values, Augustine initially turned to the Scriptures. But, resonating "a strong aesthetic assumption" prevalent in his culture that "truth and beauty (style) had an important reciprocal relationship",[10] he deemed the Scriptures unworthy when compared to the impressiveness of Cicero's work.[11] This lack of eloquence was compounded by his concern with the origin of evil (cf 3.7.12), his misgiving with an anthropomorphic depiction of God, the "immorality" of some Old Testament's characters, the nature of Christ's incarnate body, and the assumption that the New Testament had been corrupted by the Jews (cf 3.7.12–13; 5.11.21). Hence, Augustine could not bring

---

5   Cameron noted that the "conversion narrative does not merely quote texts; in many ways Scripture itself tells his story" while Martin asserted that the "intersection of Augustine's voice and the biblical voice progresses in such a way that it is not always evident where one ends and the other begins". Cameron (2012a), 200; Martin (2003), 185.

6   According to Wills, "Though Augustine wrote three dialogues in his retreat at Cassiciacum — a breakthrough after the long silence after his first (lost) book — none of them has any deep reflection on Scripture, typological or otherwise. They are pious, but in a philosophical way". Wills (2011), 56. La Bonnardière notes that "until 384 Augustine's biblical knowledge had been acquired more by listening to either the Manicheans or Ambrose that reading the Scripture". La Bonnardière (1999), 17. For Chadwick, the *Confessiones* is "a profound modification of the very Neoplatonic *Soliloquies* where Augustine was in dialogue with Reason". Chadwick (1986), 68.

7   See cf 2.6.13: *et ambitio quid nisi honores quaerit et gloriam*; 3.1.1: *quaerebam quid amarem*; 3.2.4: *et quaerebam, ut esset quod dolerem*; 3.6.11: *sed secundum sensum carnis quaererem*; 4.12.18: *non est requies, ubi quaeritis eam, quaerite quod quaeritis, sed ibi non est, ubi quaeritis. beatam uitam quaeritis in regione mortis* (CCSL 27.36; 27.27; 27.28; 27.33; 27.50); also cf 5.3.4; 6.3.3; 6.6.9.

8   "The happy life is joy in truth, and Truth is God: not truths, multiple, fragmented, partial, but Truth, one, whole, and complete". Williams (2019), xv. Augustine was *desperabam de inuentione ueri*. cf 6.1.1 (CCSL 27.73); see cf 6.10.17 for the relations between truth and happy life; also Harrison (1999), 852.

9   *cuius linguam fere omnes mirantur*. cf 3.4.7 (CCSL 27.30).

10 Martin (2003), 188. According to Cameron, "Augustine's original problem with the Bible was not intellectual but rhetorical: not that it was unphilosophical but that it was un-Ciceronian". Cameron (2012b), 27; see also Brown (2000), 155. In cf 3.6.10, we read: *pulchritudo pulchrorum omnium. o ueritas, ueritas* (CCSL 27.31). Cf. cf 5.3.3 and 5.13.23 regarding his concern with "eloquence". On the proposal to reread the *Confessiones* "in terms of aesthetics", see Steinhauser (1992), 20.

11 *sed uisa est mihi indigna quam tullianae dignitati compararem*. cf 3.5.9 (CCSL 27.31).

himself (literally *inclinare ceruicem*, "bend" his "neck") under the "authority" of Scripture (cf 3.5.9).

Augustine was then caught between contrasting and conflicting voices of authority[12] as he keeps on seeking and searching for understanding. He was enticed by the Manicheans who "kept calling out 'truth, truth'".[13] Drawing from his accounts beyond the *Confessiones*, TeSelle asserted that "the type of Christianity ... which stressed reverence for divine authority at the expense of rational enquiry" deterred Augustine while the Manicheans' claim "to lead men to God through reason alone"[14] appealed to him. But, ten years after he negated and abhorred the Holy Scriptures, he was still disappointed by those whom he had taken to be an authority, particularly Faustus the Manichean and the Academics.[15] While in this state of mind, he listened to the preaching of Bishop Ambrose in Milan "rightly handling the word of truth"[16] that gradually dispelled his misgiving upon the Scriptures. If previous authorities that influenced his *quaerens* were often futile and misplaced, we can see Augustine introducing, and alluding to other aspects of authority in, Bishop Ambrose — an unexpected "teacher of the truth"[17] — at this juncture. But why Bishop Ambrose? And why now?

2. Augustine's Tryst with the Authority of Scripture

After the publication of Pierre Courcelle's *Recherches sur les Confessions de Saint Augustin* in 1950 that produced "a Copernican revolution in Augustine scholarship", the extensive research done on the *Confessiones* actually yields little consensus.[18] There is no consent on whether the work is an autobiography or a philosophical and theological treatise, or if an event like the "Milan garden scene" (cf 8.12.26) is to be taken literally or symbolically. While some focused on "Augustine 'behind' the text", others stressed on "the readers 'in front of' the text".[19] As the "quest for biographical fact and its appropriate assessment"[20] still raved on, the "authority"

---

12 *ipsorum auctorum mouebat auctoritas; auctoritate plenaria*. cf 4.3.6; 5.5.8 (CCSL 27.43; 27.60).
13 *Et dicebant, Ueritas et ueritas, et multum eam dicebant mihi*. cf 3.6.10 (CCSL 27.31; Williams 34).
14 TeSelle (1970), 27. For the irony in the Manichean's insistence on *credere*, see cf 5.3.6. For a summary of his problem with the Scriptures that led him to the Manicheans, see also Teske (2009), 111–26; Burns (1990), 376.
15 cf 5.7.13; 6.11.18. In retrospect, he said, *ceterum cor inane ueri*. cf 3.6.10 (CCSL 27.31). Of the Academicians, he said, *de omnibus dubitandum esse censuerant nec aliquid ueri ab homine comprehendi posse decreuerant*. cf 5.10.19 (CCSL 27.68).
16 *uerbum ueritatis recte tractantem* ... cf 6.3.4 (CCSL 27.76; Williams 81).
17 *doctorem ueri* ... cf 5.13.23 (CCSL 27.70; Williams 76).
18 O'Donnell (1992a), xxi; Drobner (2000), 19. For a survey on these researches, see Starnes (1990), 277–89; O'Donnell (1992a), xx–xxxii; Kotze (2004), 7–43.
19 Kotze (2004), 3.
20 O'Donnell (1992a), xx. On how truth and fiction were not always "mutually exclusive" and how "fictional elements are used as a vehicle in the narrative", see O'Meara (1992), 77–96; regarding its performative aspect as drama script, see Ferrari (1992), 102–03.

that Augustine ascribed to Bishop Ambrose of Milan and what authority Ambrose actually "commanded" can also be seen and analysed from different perspectives.

Bishop Ambrose came from an aristocratic family and was educated in philosophy and rhetoric at Rome.[21] While serving as a provincial governor of Aemilia and Liguria in northern Italy, Ambrose was appointed "against his will"[22] as Bishop of Milan to succeed Auxentius, a deceased "Arian"[23] bishop. Ambrose's tenure at Milan coincided with the time when "it was effectively the western capital" and functionaries, aristocrats, and intellectuals from that province came to the city to meet the emperors.[24] And according to Chadwick, "Congregations normally expected their bishop not only to get them to heaven by his teaching but also to care for their worldly interests by squaring the secular authorities at government house or the tax office or the lawcourts".[25] In regard to this, we can say that the learned Ambrose, who dared to defy three Roman emperors — Gratian, Valentinian II, and Theodosius, exceeded expectations.[26] Ambrose was seen as playing a crucial role in replacing pagan influences with Christian practices in the public sphere,[27] and portrayed as the champion of Nicene orthodoxy.[28] Besides, as bishop of an imperial capital, he "operated for much of his career at close quarters to the court, an environment where the clerical leadership was often discomfited by the expansive piety of a wealthy

---

21 On how social status determined good education, see Rapp (2005), 181–82.
22 According to Ramsey, "The accent in antiquity was clearly more on the discernment and the will of the local church, clergy and laity, than on the desires and wishes of the person under consideration for ecclesiastical promotion. In Ambrose's case the people had determined, for whatever reason, that he was capable of the episcopate". See Ramsey (1997), 19.
23 "Homoian" is considered a better "label" since "what writers in the patristic era collectively called 'Arianism' represents several distinctly different theological viewpoints" which was "rhetorically conceived in a polemical context". So, "Arianism" is historically and theologically inaccurate term. Williams (1995), 1. According to Rist, "Arianism was a theological syndrome rather than a single necessarily fixed set of doctrines". Rist (1996), 395.
24 Berardino (1999), 561. The significance of "various churches in the empire was often seen as being related to the political importance of the places where they were located". Moorhead (2013), 2. Thus, "the Milanese cathedral had a much higher social profile than the churches of Rome and Carthage". McLynn (1999a), 17.
25 See Chadwick (2009), 65–66.
26 According to Brown, the "courage of the philosopher, not the peremptory authority of a Catholic bishop, was what he wielded most effectively" in his early tenure. Brown (1992), 111. See Wills (2011), 48–50 for Ambrose struggle with the rulers; Ambrose's epp 40.6; 41.28 for his understanding of the authority of bishop.
27 See Ambrose, ep 11.17–18; Ramsey (1997), 4–5. O'Donnell also asserts that Ambrose "would live to see the emperor he supported and chastised ban all non-Christian public religious practice in the empire and thus force a huge population into the churches of Ambrose and his fellow bishops". O'Donnell (2006), 75. Later, we will see more of this in chapter seven.
28 See Lossl (2017), 98. Liebeschuetz remarked that "Ambrose succeeded in winning Milan for Nicene Christianity". Liebeschuetz (2011), 73; cf. Ramsey (1997), 6, 14–15. But according to McLynn, Ambrose "impose his own interpretation upon events, conjuring elaborate ideologies and strategies from his slogans". McLynn (1994), xxii. It was also asserted that the "Arian" opposition in Milan was largely conjured up by Ambrose himself, lumping together critics and outsiders in order to secure and justify his own authority. See Williams (2017) regarding the "politics" of heresy in Ambrose of Milan.

Christian elite".²⁹ Such "an authority" as epitomized by Bishop Ambrose³⁰ can still be felt in Milan even to this day.³¹

Augustine first introduced such a figure of authority in Book 5 of the *Confessiones* where he compared the "preaching Ambrose" with Faustus. Initially, he was more impressed by the kindness of Ambrose than the content of his speech (cf 5.12.23), while Monica was immediately swayed by his authority so that she willingly abandoned her cherished African custom (cf 6.2.2; cf. epp 36.32; 54.3). Ambrose gradually dispelled Augustine's dilemmas regarding the Scriptures although the moral challenge was still hefty for Augustine. The *Confessiones* vividly recounted Ambrose's consolation of Monica (cf 8.2.2), his persistent defiance of heresy (cf 9.7.15) and his strategic appropriation of sacred relics (cf 9.7.16). Most decisively for Augustine, he was baptized by Ambrose in April 24, 387 (cf 9.6.14)

In recounting these events, Augustine played a crucial role, perhaps not intended initially,³² in promoting Ambrose directly and indirectly. It was remarked that Augustine would "never correspond with Ambrose, never dedicate a work to him, or request a book from him after leaving Milan" but "only begins to use Ambrose in later life when he needs him".³³ But the period in Milan which revolved around Ambrose amounted to "thirty-eight percent of the first nine books"³⁴ of the *Confessiones*. Considering the "cultivated detachment from particulars"³⁵ Augustine maintained in the *Confessiones* that he wrote ten years later, and in which he "has imposed a drastic, fully conscious choice of what is significant",³⁶ this is remarkable. We can say that the period in Milan where Bishop Ambrose made his authoritative presence was the kernel of the *Confessiones*.

A number of "readings" were proposed regarding the motifs of Augustine's *Confessiones* that also touch upon why Ambrose's authority matters.³⁷ There are

---

29 McLynn (1994), xxi–xxii.
30 Ambrose "pulled every string he could at court and played the crowds with great skill to support his aims". O'Donnell (2006), 69.
31 Regarding how Milan still "bears the mark of Ambrose, even sixteen centuries after his death", see Wills (2012), 19. According to Ramsey, "The western world to this day experiences, whether consciously or not, the force of Ambrose's views regarding the relationship between Church and state, articulated over the course of numerous clashes between the Bishop of Milan and the imperial authorities". Ramsey (1997), 48.
32 Although Augustine, in retrospect, acknowledges that he was led to Ambrose by God (cf 5.13.23), he finds Ambrose busy and detach (cf 6.11.18) when he first approaches him, though his eagerness to engage in dialogue with Ambrose may be a "Manichean reflex". O'Donnell (1992b), 343. For the "resentment" that Augustine may felt during those days, see Wills (2011), 46–47, 50–51.
33 Wills (2011), 47, 51. O'Donnell noted: "For such an inveterate letter-writer, Augustine surprisingly appears never to have corresponded with Ambrose during or after the time he spent in Milan, though the older man lived until 397". Interest in his work was revived in the anti-Pelagian period "when quoting Ambrose for his side was a guarantee" of Augustine's own orthodoxy. See O'Donnell (2006), 74; O'Donnell (1992b), 321–22.
34 O'Meara (1992), 84.
35 O'Meara (1992), 93. On how "Things that we expect, or even demand, from autobiography are missing" from the *Confessiones*, see Wills (2011), 51; also O'Donnell (1992b), 419.
36 Brown (2000), 163.
37 For "the Interpretive Conundrum" of the *Confessiones*, see Fredriksen (2012), 87–98; Kotze (2004), 7–43.

"competing narratives" about Augustine in Africa from the Manicheans and the Donatists whose "accusations had both a public and personal dimension": Augustine was fighting for his own reputation as well as the community where he served as a bishop and this compelled Augustine to write the *Confessions*.[38] Augustine alluded to Ambrose whose "authority" can give weight to his account.[39] O'Donnell even asserts that Augustine downplays his childhood familiarity with Christianity in order to make the impression that he truly confronted authentic Christianity for the first time from Ambrose. Augustine also makes a "theological point" in relating his "detachment" from Ambrose. In the late antique society where the "private study-circle of master and disciples" was typical, what Ambrose had to say was indeed his plain public message and not some secret inner doctrine.[40] Augustine's crucial encounters with the preaching Ambrose therefore explicate and substantiate his own orthodoxy.

Another "reading" which saw Augustine's motif beyond "apology" stressed that after a series of his encounters with "disappointing" authorities that he previously recounted, Augustine saw Ambrose, and wanted to invoke him, as the ideal Bishop. Stock asserted that there is a narrative design behind Augustine's lack of opportunity for exchanging ideas with the Bishop in depth. Augustine wanted to portray "to posterity" a picture of Ambrose "who enjoyed his periods of leisure by himself".[41] "Ambrose of the Confessions" embodied the kind of teacher that he wants to grow into, "who combines faith, philosophy, and biblical erudition".[42] According to Williams, Augustine replicated Ambrose in his awareness of his own limitations and his reluctance to pose as an expert. The authority Augustine accorded to Ambrose depended on his example as a reader as much as a writer.[43]

Therefore, in the layer of meanings embedded within the *Confessiones*, we can "read" a blend of the apologetic, polemical and even didactic aspects behind invoking the credence of Bishop Ambrose. Augustine was influenced by the "authoritative statement" of Ambrose and his subsequent intellectual and moral conversions were sealed by a full admission into the Catholic community through baptism. Besides, the contemplative intellectual Ambrose who submitted himself before the Scriptures was contrasted with the shallow verbose "others" who ultimately disappointed and frustrated Augustine in his *quaerens*.[44] In fact, Ambrose effectively embodied the

---

38 Martin (2003), 192, 197.
39 According to Mark Edward, because of his early death in 397, Ambrose was already a classic author by the time Augustine wrote *Confessiones*. "If one purpose in writing the Confessions was to outflank any accusation that the Donatists might bring against Augustine, the patronage of this irreproachable figure would be a shield against calumny, both for the neophyte and for the church that had made him a bishop". Edward (2012), 221.
40 O'Donnell (2006), 52–53, 74; O'Donnell (1992b), 322, 339–42.
41 Stock (1996), 62; see also cf 11.2.2.
42 Stock (2010), 29; see also O'Donnell (1992b), 341–42.
43 See Williams (2012), 238–39.
44 He expressed his frustration thus: *iam tricenariam aetatem ... dum dico, "eras inueniam; ecce manifestum apparebit, et tenebo; ecce Faustus ueniet et exponet omnia, o magni uiri Academici! nihil ad agendam uitam certi conprehendi potest? immo quaeramus diligentius et non desperemus*. cf 6.11.18 (CCSL 27.86).

fusion of "eminent authority" and "holy humility"[45] in the Scriptures that is so central to the whole Milan episode.

3. Discerning the Principle behind the Authority of Scripture

If we assert that "the preaching Ambrose" took the centre stage tentatively to point toward the authority of Scripture which is the overarching theme in this entire episode, how did "Ambrose's preaching"[46] actually facilitates Augustine's understanding of the scriptures? The *Confessiones* recounted two instances on which Ambrose's preaching had markedly influenced Augustine's understanding of the Scriptures and gradually lifted the "mystical veil" (*remoto mystico uelamento*) from scriptural texts to uncover the spiritual meaning of things which did not make sense to him when taken literally (cf 5.14.24; 6.4.6). Though we cannot determine these sermons with certainty now,[47] Ambrose's sermons and writings that will reflect his "doctrine" like *De Iacob et uita beata, De interpellatione Iob et David* were dated to the time of Augustine's stay in Milan while Augustine was acquainted with *de Isaac uel anima* and the *de bono mortis*.[48]

Going back to the question, Augustine tells us the "principle" he heard from Ambrose "that would lay open all Christian teaching"[49] to him. Ambrose diligently recommended 2 Cor 3:6 as a rule to his audience: "the letter kills, but the spirit gives life".[50] This rule involves a non-literal reading of texts that describe one thing while representing something else as well. Harmless asserts that a more accurate rendering for Ambrose's "spiritual" reading that was often denoted as an "allegory" would be "figurative" reading.[51] *Figura* basically denotes "a form of speech departing from the straightforward and obvious" while *allegoria* comes from the Greek word that takes its roots from ἄλλα and ἀγορεύω, "to speak other things".[52] But in using the term *allegoria* and *figura*, Augustine was neither consistent nor did he precisely define

---

45 *auctoritatis emineret ... sanctae humilitatis ...* cf 6.5.8 (CCSL 27.79).
46 This differentiate the Bishop's personality from the content of his preaching. See Burns (1990), 378. On how Ambrose considered preaching an important duty and make the Scriptures his "principal source for his sermons" and "relies upon allegorical exegesis for the entire Old Testament", see McHugh (1972), 2.
47 On Courcelle's attempt to date Ambrose's sermon, Moorhead remarked that "not only does the dating of these works remain open, but what Augustine later remembered as having learned from Ambrose was a general principle of biblical interpretation ... rather than any doctrine which can be traced to Neoplatonic sources". Moorhead (2013), 172. See also O'Donnell (1992b), 418; McHugh (1972), 4.
48 See O'Donnell (1992b), 325. According to McHugh, a portion of a passage from *de bono mortis* is cited (*c.* 420) in Augustine's Pel 4.11.31. See McHugh (1972), 9, 76. Noting the significance of Ambrose particularly for Augustine's later works, Markus asserts, "Here we strike, as so often in Augustine's writings and sermons, once more, the old Ambrosian, bedrock of his faith". Markus (1991), 924.
49 O'Donnell (1992b), 349.
50 *Et tamquam regulam diligentissime commendaret ...* "*littera occidit, spiritus autem uiuificat*". cf 6.4.6 (CCSL 27.77; Williams 82).
51 Harmless (2010), 157–58; Harrison used the term together in Harrison (2013), 680. On the scope and justification of "figurative readings", see also Edwards (2013).
52 Glare (1968), 700; Hoek (2007), 9. For some technical terms of Greek Exegesis, see Bate (1922), 59–66.

their meanings in relation to one another so that trying to resolve them in line with "a set of systematically organised categories" may be pointless and even misleading.[53]

As for Ambrose, being a student of Philo and Origen, he used the hermeneutical tools of the Alexandrians and the Neoplatonists[54] "to defend the Old Testament Scriptures from charges of self-contradiction" and not solely "to read philosophical doctrines into the passages he considers".[55] This "spiritual" reading universalized the meaning of Scripture, thereby "widening its impact from telling a single historical event in the past, present or future, to having concrete and contemporary relevance to a potentially universal readership".[56] Although Ambrose's discourse, despite all his learning (*eruditioris*), lacked the "sparkle and lightness" of Faustus (cf 5.13.23), it nonetheless opened Augustine's eye to the "theological significance of humility"[57] that he lacked when he first studied the Scriptures (cf 3.5.9). In other words, seeing "beyond" the physical and literal aspects of the Scriptures enabled Augustine to hear God addressing him though the Scriptures.

To what extent this rule initially "converted" Augustine is still a matter of debate.[58] But through Ambrose's preaching, Augustine realized that the Catholic faith could be defended against the attacks of the Manicheans regarding immaterial reality, the origin of evil and the humanity of Christ, and that the Scriptures is a tool used by God to guide both the educated and the ignorant.[59] Cameron asserts that Augustine suddenly discerned a strategy at work that he had known from his rhetorical training. In interpreting difficult written texts, Cicero made a distinction between a law's written form (*scriptum*) and the will or intention (*uoluntas*) of its author. A deeply spiritual message from God was actually hidden at what seems like a jumbled collection of stories written in an undignified style, about some people with contentious morals and an unspiritual love for worldly things. "The insight not only untied certain knotty passages for Augustine; it opened

---

53 Dawson (1999), 365.
54 Gerson and Dillon suggest that the term "paleo"- Platonists will be more accurate than "neo" for these "non-innovating expositors and defenders of Platonic philosophy" since there is "a fine line between saying what one thinks the master meant and saying something, in fact, new". Gerson (2004), xiii–xiv.
55 Vaught (2003), 136. Chadwick asserts that "Ambrose's debt to Plotinus was combined with caution about pagan philosophy as a guide to truth". Chadwick (1986), 17. For Augustine's own "high praise" and "unyielding criticism" of the Platonists, see O'Donnell (1992b), 414.
56 Pollmann (2009), 321.
57 Burton (2007), 113. See cf 7.18.24 for Augustine's own account of Christ's humility.
58 For example, Vaught asserts that there are three pivotal encounters between God and the Soul in Books VII–IX of Augustine's *Confessiones*: his philosophical conversion, his conversion to Christianity, and his mystical experience at Ostia. Vaught (2004), 1. But Cary points out that "intellectual conversion" is not Augustine's phrase but a scholarly invention which "reflects a deeply ingrained modern tendency to read the [*Confessiones*] … as a story whose high point must be a conversion experience". Cary (2000), 33. Cary also asserts that Augustine "is already a Catholic believer" when he comes upon the books of the Platonists as he describes in book seven of the *Confessiones*. "Contrary to centuries of misreading that assimilates Book Eight to Protestant narrative of conversion to Christ, Augustine want us to know that he already had faith in Christ in Book Seven". Cary (2003), 120–21. For the "history of conversion" in antiquity, see Nock (1988).
59 See cf 5.14.24; 6.3.4–5.8. Augustine later hold that "Evil is not to be found in creation but in the way a certain object is deficient in its measure, form and order". Lieu (1994), 189.

him to perceiving Scripture, in its entirety, as a work of divine eloquence".[60] Augustine was convinced that the wisdom which he had desired since he read Cicero's *Hortensius* at age nineteen can be attained through "the Scriptures and the church's way of life".[61]

4. Implications of Ambrose's Principle in Augustine's Reading of the Scriptures

While Book 6 of the *Confessiones* relates how Ambrose's preaching offers a working principle for reading the Scriptures as "divine eloquence", Book 7 introduces the aspiration of this principle — Truth.[62] Dawson asserted that this principle transforms human beings from creatures who oppose the divine will expressed in the Scriptures "into those who live in joyful obedience to it". This process of spiritual transformation entails "tensions between preservation and novelty, and eternity and temporality" in that it "preserves something from the past while bringing about something new" when reading scriptural texts.[63] And momentously for Augustine, this principle rectifies his misapprehension of Truth, the incarnated Christ.[64]

Although Augustine revered Christ throughout his entire life,[65] he always struggled with how to grasp the "nature" of Christ's incarnate body. After he renounced the Manicheans' docetic view which denies Christ's "enfleshment",[66] he read certain books of the Platonists[67] where he learnt of the eternal pre-existent Word of God (cf 7.9.13) and heeded their admonition to seek incorporeal truth.[68] Although the Platonists' method of "philosophical ascent" of the mind elevates Augustine from

---

60 Cameron (2012a), 203; On how "Augustine's reorientation to Scripture ... was rhetorical before it was philosophical", see also Cameron (2012b), 29–30.
61 Burns (1990), 378.
62 According to O'Donnell, the focus of Book 7, which also "stands in the middle" of the *Confessiones* is Christological. O'Donnell (1992b), 409, 413. In the *Confessiones*, the noun *ueritas* and its derivatives occurs 136 times while the noun *uerum*, the adjective *uerus* and its derivatives occurs 309 times (these numbers were collected using the cag-online.net database).
63 Dawson (1999), 365–66.
64 *et dixi: numquid nihil est ueritas ...? et clamasti de longinquo: immo uero "ego sum qui sum". Et audiui, sicut auditur in corde, et non erat prorsus* "I said, 'Then is truth nothing ...?' And you called from afar, 'No indeed; truly, I am who I am'. And I heard, as one hears in the heart; and I no longer had any room to doubt". cf 7.10.16 (CCSL 27.104; Williams 110).
65 *Stabiliter ... haerebat in corde meo ...* cf 7.5.7 (CCSL 27.97).
66 *Metuebam itaque credere in carne natum, ne credere cogerer ex carne inquinatum.* cf 5.10.20 (CCSL 27.69); see also cf 7.18.24: *non enim tenebam deum meum Iesum humilis* (CCSL 27.108). Interestingly, Lieu remarked that Augustine's counter-arguments against Manicheanism "rested on the teaching of the Church on the consubstantiality of the Persons of the Trinity ... which might have meant little to Mani ... Mani did not see himself as an apostle of the historical Jesus but as the Apostle of 'Jesus of Light'". Lieu (1994), 163.
67 cf 8.2.3; see also vit 1.4. On why Augustine stumbled upon these books, see Brown (2000), 85. There is a consensus that they included works of Plotinus (see Cary [2000], 31–44) and Porphyry, though Augustine's decision "to leave the texts unidentified ... is in itself a form of commentary on them". See O'Donnell (1992b), 421–24.
68 *incorpoream ueritatem ...* cf 7.20.26 (CCSL 27.109).

bodily thing (*corporibus*) to God's invisible attributes (*inuisibilia tua*), it was entirely insufficient.[69] As Augustine listed to what had been missing from the books of the Platonists, his account amounted to saying that "the Platonists taught of the existence of the Logos, but not that the Logos took flesh and died for us".[70] In other words, the Platonists were so near and yet so far as they could see the end without sufficient means to reach that end (cf 7.21.27). In retrospect, Augustine identified this position as a "Photinian" view of Christ that denied the divinity and the pre-existence of Jesus. Without knowing of the mystery of the Word made flesh, Augustine had considered Christ as a person of outstanding wisdom whom no one could equal and who had earned great authority as an ethical teacher.[71]

Perhaps, the most crucial corollary of this new insight into the "incarnation" is that Christ is the "Person of Truth"[72] and not merely someone who had "a more perfect participation in wisdom".[73] For the Platonists, God is remote and not gracious while their "truth" is a quality contemplated through the intellect.[74] But on reflecting upon the Christian notion of God in the light of the incarnation, Augustine began to realize the absolute centrality of the concept of *creatio ex nihilo*[75] where nothing created can be co-eternal with the creator.[76]

---

69 O'Donnell asserts that "this is a clear statement of the plenitude of the experience" although it was not the beatific vision and a "relapse into the material world is inevitable". See O'Donnell (1992b), 414–15, 442, 457–59. On a similar note, Ortiz asserts, "Augustine learned from the Platonists that God is utterly transcendent to the world and therefore totally present to it without competition. The Catholic understanding of the incarnation deepens this understanding of God's transcendence, but also clarifies and reveals more about how God and the world are related". Ortiz (2016), 105–06.

70 See O'Donnell (1992b), 426, 436, 459. For the *non ibi legi … non habent illi libri … non est ibi*, see cf 7.9.13–14 (CCSL 27.101–02).

71 *Quid autem sacramenti haberet uerbum caro factum, ne suspicari quidem poteram.* cf 7.19.25 (CCSL 27.108).

72 *persona ueritatis* cf 7.19.25 (CCSL 27.109). As O'Donnell remarked, the "truth" of which Augustine spoke "was not merely a quality of a verbal formula, but veracity itself, a quality of a living human person". He also noted that "Augustine's Christianity represents a mighty effort at bringing the two [fundamental fault-line in Western thought, between being and discourse, reality and truth] into harmony" while "the rejection of that Christianity leaves moderns to face again the unbridged chasm". O'Donnell (1992a), xvii.

73 *perfectiore participatione sapientiae …* cf 7.19.25 (CCSL 27.109). For Augustine, "Christ is the very incarnation of eternal wisdom, and true philosophy meant the love of Christ … [for] true wisdom cannot merely be knowledge of earthly, temporal things but actually must be the desire for eternal things … the philosopher seeks to transcend the world … otherwise his knowledge is vain and empty, mere *vana curiositas*". Moran (2014), 514.

74 According to Gerson, "the locus of eternal truth is Platonic Forms". Gerson (1994), 56. Plotinus "adheres to the principles underlying any theory of Forms … Among these principles are that eternal truth exists; that eternal truths are truths about eternal entities; and that eternal truth is complex". Gerson (1999), 6.

75 In cf 8.1.2, he succinctly stated thus: *uniuersa creatura inueneram te creatorem nostrum et uerbum tuum … per quod creasti omnia.* "[B]y asking my questions of the whole of creation I had discovered you, our Creator, and your Word … through whom you created all things". (CCSL 27.114; Williams 120). As Soskice remarks, "*creatio ex nihilo* is not a teaching about the cosmos but about God … The teaching centrally concerns the power, goodness, and freedom of God, and the dependence of 'all that is' … on God's free choice to create and to sustain". Soskice (2018), 38.

76 He implicitly suggested creation *ex nihilo* in cf 12.17.25 and 12.22.31: *uerum tamen quia non de ipsa substantia dei, sed ex nihilo cuncta facta sunt.* "[A]ll things were made, not from the substance of God, but from nothing"; *cur non informem quoque illam materiam … ex deo factam esse de nihilo ideoque illi*

For the Manicheans and the Platonists, creation is *ex materia* and *ex deus*,[77] which entails an "eternal" principle or pre-existing matter. While evil was a self-originating principle for the Manicheans, the Platonists stressed that there is no separate principle opposed to the One so that there is no reality to evil.[78] Creation emanates from itself in eternity, according to the Neoplatonists, "as an out-of-time act of descent from the higher to the lower levels of existence, which is best illustrated by the ontological series of remaining (*monē*), procession (*proodos*) and return (*epistrophē*)".[79] The natural divinity of the human soul therefore nullifies the necessity of the incarnation for salvation and the resurrection of the body.[80]

In contrast, Christians consider creation as a free, unique act of God,[81] with temporal origin and not out of some pre-existing material.[82] Evil was the result of

---

non esse coaeternam. "[T]he formless matter … was made from nothing by God and is therefore not coeternal with God" (CCSL 27.228; 27.233; Williams 235, 239–40). For an indirect reference to the notion, see cf 7.11.17; 11.5.7; 11.7.9.

77 According to Jason BeDuhn, "The Manichaeans were thoroughgoing materialists". BeDuhn (2001), 5. A Manichaean myth asserts: "Then the Living Spirit commanded three of his sons, telling one to kill and another to flay the archons, sons of darkness, in order that they be brought to the Mother of Life. And the Mother of Life [gave her orders, and the Living Spirit] spread out the sky with their skins and made eleven heavens. Then the three sons of the Living Spirit threw their corpses onto the land of darkness and made eight earths [layers of the world]". See Tardieu (2008), 78. Likewise, in Neoplatonism, there are a number of texts that "contain references to a principle named 'the creator god' (*opifex deus*), 'the god who is artificer and creator of the world's substance' (deus mundanae molis artifex conditorque), or 'the god making all things' (*deus omnium fabricator*)". See Gersh (1986), 548. Both views can be seen as a varying form of *ex nihilo nihil fit*, "nothing comes from nothing", in that the universe is formed from eternal formless matter.

78 According to Rist, "Plotinus's account of divine production was … an unhistorical one. All depends on the One in that it could not exist without the One's productive power, but there is no beginning of the physical universe: hence matter has always existed, though it has always been dependent for its existence on the One itself". Rist (1996), 391.

79 Dimitrov (2014), 532. For Moran, "The aim of all things and the explicit aim of Neoplatonic meditation or contemplation (*theōria*) is becoming one (*henōsis*) [by returning] to the One". Moran (2014), 513.

80 The soteriological implication was highlighted by O'Donnell who remarks that *creatio ex nihilo* negated "Gnostic/Priscillianist emanation" and "Platonic procession. Hence the possibility of sin". O'Donnell (1992c), 308. For the assertion that *creatio ex nihilo* "is formulated as an antithesis to the Greek model of world-formation", see also May (1994). According to King, "Augustine's complaint about neoplatonism's lack of the Incarnation/Redemption was thus more than a mere test for dogmatic orthodoxy: it rests on a solid philosophical basis". King (2005), 224.

81 As Moran noted, "Christian Neoplatonists never think of this outgoing as a necessary emanation … rather it is because of the boundless freedom, generosity and grace of the One that it seeks to mirror itself in all the levels that follow from it … the kind of necessary relation which holds between creation and Creator is one-sided: necessary from the point of view of the dependent created being; neither necessary for, nor even known by, the Creator whose Oneness transcends all relation to anything outside itself. Other things come into being by participating in the One. The divine will is a kind of open invitation for things to come into being in order to emulate it". Moran (2014), 513.

82 Copleston asserts that the doctrine of free creation *ex nihilo* "is not to be found in neo-Platonism". But Augustine "is not so concerned with developing a philosophical doctrine for its own sake as with emphasising the essential dependence of all creatures on God". Copleston also asserts that the related concept of *rationes seminales*, "the germs of those things which were to develop in the course

human frailty and without adequate resources within ourselves to return to God, we need divine help in the form of grace.[83] Against the Platonists' insistence that "there are many ways to so great a mystery", Augustine thus asserts that there is only one Way and this Way has been revealed when God has descended in Christ to bring us where on our own we could not ascend.[84] If Cicero's *Hortentius* lead Augustine away from the truth and into Manichaeism, the books of the Platonists lead him towards, and even afford him a temporary glance at, God. But knowledge alone is not salvation and the Platonists served as an example of how pride impedes a true response to the knowledge of God (cf 7.9.13; 7.21.27; 10.42.67). It was only when he "has an encounter with the Word made flesh, with Christ Incarnate", that Augustine started "to acquire the requisite humility to recognize the truth about Christ, a truth which is made possible by the insights of the Platonists, but which, in turn, will profoundly deepen them".[85]

After recounting how Ambrose's "principle" opened his eyes to the "Truth" of the Scriptures in Book 7, Augustine depicted his encounter with the *persona ueritas* in the "conversion" scene of Book 8.[86] He now realized the futility of his philosophical endeavour alone and the necessity of humbling himself for the truth of the Scriptures

---

of time", was to be found in the philosophy of Plotinus, which is rooted in the Stoics' notion of λόγοι σπερματικοί, "but it is an idea of rather vague content" for them. Augustine's own "assertion was the result of an exegetic, not a scientific problem ... so that it is really beside the point to adduce him either as a protagonist or as an opponent of evolution in the Lamarckian or Darwinian sense". See Copleston (1993), 74–80. Cavadini also asserts that Augustine's "use of this idea is to evoke 'creation' as a mystery that must remain, essentially, a mystery, one that ... refuses to resolve itself into a clear and distinct philosophical idea, though it certainly has philosophical implications". Cavadini (2018), 151. For a summary of the doctrine of *creatio ex nihilo* as held by the Byzantine Fathers, see Ierodiakonou and Zografidis (2010), 865.

83 On the "frailty" of the will, see cf 7.21.27. Commenting on the difference between Augustine's position and the Manicheans, Fredriksen stated: "Exactly in the place where the Manichees had read proof of external coercion, of the good soul's struggle against the incursions of the forces of evil, Augustine saw the thrashing around of the will divided against itself. Human will is indeed 'free', but only in the sense that nothing outside of itself forces its self to sin. Wounded by sin, the will fights against itself". Fredriksen (2010), 207.

84 Rist (1996), 407–08. See cf 7.18.24 for Augustine's own acknowledgment.

85 Ortiz (2016), 104. On how Augustine see Christianity as the fulfilment of philosophy, see O'Daly (1999a), 392.

86 On "conversion", see n. 58 above. Noting the "redemptive, salvific, and decisive" significance of the "event", O'Donnell said, "For Augustine, after all, it is the incarnation pre-eminently that redeems, and to come to understand that incarnation accurately and to acquire in his life a pattern of conduct that he thought required by an understanding of that incarnation — that, for Augustine, is a very Christian, and Christ-centered, conversation". O'Donnell (1992a), xxxvii. Ortiz also asserts, "In the Confessions, [Augustine] says of his new understanding, 'I acknowledged the whole man in Christ, not just the body of a man, or a soul with a body but without a mind, but an actual man [cf 7.19.25]'. This is obvious, he says, from the fact that Christ moved, acted, and experienced emotions in places and times, as the Gospels amply attest. Christ is also true God, 'equal to God and God with God and simultaneously one God' [cf 10.43.68]". Ortiz (2016), 104.

to address him.[87] Commenting upon Augustine's turn from "philosophizing" toward the Scriptures, O'Donnell remarked that "the specific texts put in front of him brought him new light and new frustration, and thus had the effect of driving him towards scriptural authority, where, in [Book] 8, the real resolution of his difficulties would be worked out".[88] In other words, we can say that when Augustine read the Scriptures anew, he was faced with the reality and implications of the tension of time that the "Christ-event" set in motion in the course of "salvation" history.

Accordingly, the anguish of a tormented soul[89] that cried "Let it be now; let it be now"[90] was calm (*tranquillo*) when the reading of Rom 13:13 promptly produced the desired effect.[91] If Augustine's relationship with the Scriptures had been severed ten years ago after reading the *Hortentius*, it has now been restored as God addressed him through the incarnate Word in the Scriptures. In retrospect, Augustine used the words *exciperet* and *traiceret* to describe the change in relationship brought by this new insight.[92] *Exciperet* can denote "to accept, receive, greet" and "to take under one's care or protection, take in, give shelter to"[93] which reflected the "welcome" extended by the Scriptures. *Traiceret* can denote the "transference", "to move from one position to another" and reflected the outcome that brings one closer to God.[94] Commenting on this passage, O'Donnell remarked that for Augustine, "authority is in its origin empirical rather than innate; the respect shown to scriptural texts is itself the proof

---

87 Augustine summed up the process thus: *et placuit in conspectu tuo reformare deformia mea. et stimulis internis agitabas me, ut impatiens essem, donec mihi per interiorem aspectum certus esses*. "And it was pleasing in your sight to take my deformity and give it form again, and by your inward goads you spurred me on so that I would be impatient until my inward gaze beheld you with certainty". cf 7.8.12 (CCSL 27.101; Williams 107).
88 O'Donnell (1992b), 415. Interestingly, O'Daly remarked that although certain philosophical themes preoccupy Augustine, he does not construct a philosophical system. "At times he understands by 'philosophy' the Graeco-Roman tradition of rational inquiry, as opposed to Christianity ... At other times, however, he does not distinguish between the philosophical and theological aspects of his thought". O'Daly (1999a), 392.
89 *Sic aegrotabam et excruciabar* ... cf 8.11.25 (CCSL 27.129). It is interesting to note that the Bishop Augustine did not pour out his tale of misdeeds and transgressions "out of him and onto the page in a torrent of tormented introspection during some dark night of the soul. Augustine performed the *Confessions*, declaiming its beautiful phrasing always in the presence of at least one or two other people, the skilled *notarii* taking shorthand dictation. What moderns take to be intimate self-portraiture is often the product of their own presentism, overstimulated by Augustine's rhetorical artistry". Fredriksen (2010), 201.
90 *Ecce modo fiat, modo fiat*. cf 8.11.25 (CCSL 27.129; Williams 135).
91 *Nec ultra uolui legere nec opus erat. Statim quippe cum fine huiusce sententiae quasi luce securitatis infusa cordi meo omnes dubitationis tenebrae diffugerunt*. "I had no desire to read further; there was no need. As soon as I reached the end of this sentence the light of assurance was poured into my heart and all the clouds of doubt melted away". cf 8.11.29 (CCSL 27.131; Williams 138).
92 *ut exciperet omnes populari sinu et per angusta foramina paucos ad te traiceret* ... "[Scripture] welcomes all people into its very center, and through the narrow passage of the needle's eye it brings a few to you". cf 6.5.8 (CCSL 27.79; Williams 84).
93 Glare (1968), 635.
94 Glare (1968), 1959–60. Scripture thus served as "the divinely constructed bridge between eternity and time". Fredriksen (2010), 206.

of authority".[95] And in humbling himself,[96] Augustine could therefore enter into a new relationship with God,[97] the "author" of the Scriptures.

As Augustine gets more acquainted with the Scriptures, he moved beyond the "spiritual principle" of Ambrose to a more literal reading, as we see in the last three books of the *Confessiones*. According to O'Daly, Augustine contends that even if Christian beliefs are initially valid "only because the believer subjectively accepts divine authority, these beliefs are in principle accessible to, and explicable by, rational inquiry". Augustine seeks "to broaden the basis of authority, stressing, for example, the role of historical evidence and wide acceptability in the tradition of Christ's life and teaching".[98] We will see more of the development and implications of these insights in subsequent chapters.

But ultimately for Augustine, adopting any principle and rule in reading the Scriptures, "far from bringing full knowledge, requires belief".[99] Augustine, who formerly sought to understand to have intellectual certainty[100] rather than to believe, now realized that he needed humility to believe prior to understanding the meaning of Scripture.[101] Instead of seeking an understanding in order to believe, faith and trust in authority will lead him to understanding. Thus, Augustine asserted, "What I wanted was not to be more certain about you, but to be more firmly grounded in you".[102]

Like Ambrose, Augustine therefore learns to subordinate his own personality to the Scriptures. Augustine can make no claim to authority as this rule opens "the continual possibility of displacing the literal constraint of any particular historical limit" where there is a "text which continually transcends its own textuality, a signifier grounded on the endless possibilities of signification".[103] At the same time, the historicity of the incarnation and of creation validate the search for the meaning of time.[104] While Neoplatonism downplayed the significance of the temporal order,

---

95 O'Donnell (1992b), 354.
96 According to Conybeare, this is the "humility to accept the prose of the bible for what it is, humility to believe in the truth of its meanings and to accept that they cannot all be immediately unlocked. From some of his earliest writings onward, Augustine attached great importance to a sentence from the Vulgate version of Isaiah: 'Unless you believe, you will not understand' (Is 7:9)". Conybeare (2016), 53.
97 Commenting on cf 6.5.8, Williams insightfully noted thus: "The words here translated 'very center' and 'embrace' are *sinu* and *gremio*, respectively. Both mean 'bosom' or 'lap': Lazarus in the parable in Luke 16 is carried in *sinum Abrahae*, 'to Abraham's bosom', and the Prologue to John says that the only Son is in *sinu Patris*, 'in the bosom of the Father'". Williams (2019), 84.
98 O'Daly (1999a), 393.
99 Flores (1984), 58.
100 *certum, certus* ... cf 6.4.6 (CCSL 27.77).
101 cf 6.5.8. Thus he asked, *sed unde scirem, an uerum diceret?* cf 11.3.5 (CCSL 27.196).
102 *ablata mihi erat, nec certior de te, sed stabilior in te esse cupiebam*. cf 8.1.1 (CCSL 27.113). And in *De doctrina Christiana*, Augustine stated that seeking God's will firstly involves "to know these books; not necessarily to understand them but to read them so as to commit them to memory" after which "the matters which are clearly stated in them ... should be examined carefully and intelligently". do 2.14.30 (Green 71).
103 Scanlon (1994), 46–47. For this surplus of meaning see Cameron (2012a), 208; also cf 12.31.42.
104 As Fredriksen remarked, the Scriptures for Augustine was not just "a peculiar physical incarnation of the Word of God" nor "solely an infinite treasury of Jewish types and figures whose deepest meanings lay off in the Christian future". The Scriptures "contained meanings about events and ideas whose

Augustine realized that the notion of history as "a progress toward the divine" was an important message of Christianity. Augustine was aware that a valid Christian philosophy "must see time and history as real and indeed as playing a crucial role in the divine plan for the salvation of humans".[105] Although Augustine develops this notion and expounds it more exhaustively in his *De civitate Dei*, the later part of the *Confessiones* form the philosophical groundwork of this perspective. Augustine therefore locates the Scriptures in the realm of time where the accounts of God's eternal plan find the fullness of expression in the incarnated Word.[106] In other words, as "Words forged in time reveal the One who is beyond time",[107] Augustine acknowledges the authority of Scripture accordingly.

Concluding Remarks

In the *Confessiones*, we have seen the different aspects of "authority" and its concrete expressions. Unlike the commemorative RGDA that emperor Augustus constructed to ratify his authority, the *Confessiones* narrates Bishop Augustine's vulnerability and his total reliance upon God's mercy. It describes how Augustine initially failed to appreciate the value of the Scriptures, until Bishop Ambrose's preaching gradually helps him see the authority of Scripture in a new light. If Ambrose who advocated the "spiritual" reading embodied the Scriptures which is a fusion of "eminent authority" and "holy humility" that addresses human being courtesy of the eternal Word, Augustine certainly appropriated this principle as he admitted his own frailty.[108] Contrary to emperor Augustus's project, Augustine's personal narrative in the *Confessiones* was therefore eclipsed by the acknowledgement of God's authority whose eternal Word speaks through the Scriptures. Augustine's plight was epitomised by the prayer much denounced by Pelagius, "Grant what you command and command what you will".[109]

For Augustine, acknowledgement of scriptural authority was not simply a resolve between faith and reason but a new perception and awareness of time which makes faith and trust in authority for a specific end reasonable. Once he realized his temporality and the tentativeness of his experience in time, Augustine

---

interpretive point of reference lay within the time frame of its own narrative, thus at a point in the past". Fredriksen (2010), 242.
105 Moran (2014), 514–15.
106 According to O'Daly, Augustine "believes that the links between the temporal and the eternal are only realized in the incarnate Christ, who is both *sapientia* and *scientia*, and in the doctrines which emerge in Christianity (Gn li 1.21.41)". O'Daly (1999a), 393.
107 Bright (2006), 44.
108 "Now a bishop himself", asserts Brown, "he will tell his readers exactly how he still had to struggle with his own temptations; and in the last three books of the *Confessions*, as he meditates on the opening lines of the book of Genesis, he will carry his readers with him into his thoughts as he, also, sat in his study, as he had once seen Ambrose sit, wrapt in the silent contemplation of an open page". Brown (2000), 155.
109 *Da quod iubes et iube quod uis.* cf 10.29.40 (CCSL 27.176; Williams 184). See pers 53 where Augustine highlighted Pelagius's reaction.

sees the Scriptures not as fragmented texts but as a coherent whole narrative of the eternal God and he fits his life into this bigger narrative.[110] Moreover, he draws upon various scriptural passages to construct his narratives in the *Confessiones*, and specifically reflected on the contradistinction between a created being in time that stands in relationship with God the creator, an eternal Being beyond time. Beyond the recognition of an absolute dependence upon God in this present life, the chasm between the creator and the creature, and the deep tension which the recognition of this temporality engendered, was profoundly depicted in the longing for a fulfilment which Augustine expressed thus: "you have made us for yourself, and our heart is restless until it comes to rest in you".[111]

This chasm between the creator and the creature, as Augustine realized, was bridged in the incarnation which is an event in time and recorded in the Scriptures. As Fredriksen succinctly remarked, "God's grace, incarnate in history — through the Bible, through the church, and most especially through the Son — works to close this gap between his creature and himself, until time would be dissolved in eternity".[112] Augustine's "restless heart" that started his account in the *Confessiones* therefore represents the tension and anticipation of the "now and not yet" which is characteristic of the whole New Testament's hope for the *consummatio saeculi*. For Augustine who closed the last three books of the *Confessiones* with an exposition of the creation account of Genesis, his "restless heart" will find "the peace of rest" on "the peace of the sabbath" because God makes "the rest that comes when time shall be no more".[113]

In the next chapter, we will look at the *De doctrina Christiana* where the focus of Augustine's scriptural odyssey shifts from Bishop Ambrose of Milan to Tyconius the Donatist. As Augustine attempts to reveal "the rules to be observed in the process of understanding" the Scriptures,[114] we will see how the practical implications of the enigma of time determined the rules of his scriptural expositions.

---

110 Wills succinctly remarked thus: "Augustine is trying to acknowledge the graces that make his life part of sacred history — whence the constant use of Scripture". Wills (2011), 22.
111 *quia fecisti nos ad te et inquietum est cor nostrum donec requiescat in te.* cf 1.1.1 (CCSL 27.1; Williams 1).
112 Fredriksen (2010), 239.
113 cf 13.35.50; 13.37.52 (Williams 277).
114 do *prol* 8.17 (Green 9).

CHAPTER 4

"Exercet autem hoc tempore et purgat"

Discerning the Signs of the Time in the De doctrina Christiana

In the last chapter, we had mentioned that thirty-eight percent of the first nine books of the *Confessiones* centres around Bishop Ambrose and the time that Augustine spent in Milan. Augustine's baptism by Bishop Ambrose in Milan in 387 was followed by a short period of retirement at Cassiciacum, after which he gradually returned to Carthage in Africa in the late 388. But his hope of living a secluded life with his mother Monica and his son Adeodatus along with like-minded friends was shattered by their death[1] as well as the practical need of the Catholic church when he arrived at Hippo in 391.[2] And soon, he came across the work of Tyconius (died *c.* 390), a lay theologian who immensely influenced Augustine for the rest of his life.[3] If the political power that Milan represented and the ensuing struggle for authority between Bishop Ambrose and his opponents initially determined Augustine's understanding of, and his approach to, the authority of Scripture, a shift in geographical location and character, viz., North Africa and Tyconius the Donatist, brings out another dimension of his understanding of the authority of Scripture in the *De doctrina Christiana*.

According to Kannengiesser, there are three important reasons why Augustine wrote the *De doctrina Christiana*. Firstly, as Augustine realized the centrality of Scripture after he assumed the role of a Pastor, he also needed to establish himself as a reputable expositor of Scripture. So, Augustine's personal and long-term commitment to the reading of Scripture developed into the *De doctrina Christiana*. Secondly, his professional background as a teacher of rhetoric motivated him to reassess and transfer

---

[1] Augustine lost Monica in Ostia, and Adeodatus and Nebridius in Thagaste. As Brown remarked, "It may well be that grief and a sense of emptiness now pressed Augustine into a more active life. ... It is not the first time in Augustine's life that grief, and some inner discontent, drove him from the small, tight society of his home town down into a wider and more busy world". Brown (2000), 128, 130. For O'Donnell, "a prime reason for continuing stewardship of the family property evaporated" with the death of Adeodatus. O'Donnell (2006), 24.

[2] Kannengiesser asserts that the two and a half years in Africa before Augustine's involvement in church affairs, when he was chosen as a priest in Hippo, was a period of a "holy leisure" which was "a form of private elitism". Kannengiesser (1999), 149. According to Brown, "The Catholics in Hippo were a harassed minority. The rival church, that of the 'party of Donatus', was predominant both in the town and the surrounding countryside. It was supported by prominent local landowners and enjoyed the tacit recognition of local officials". Brown (2000), 132. Regarding Augustine's aloofness "from churchmen and churchgoing when he returned to Africa" and then the recovery of his "childhood loyalty" to the church, see O'Donnell (2006), 213–14.

[3] Commenting on the significance of his influence, Frend remarks that Tyconius may perhaps have shared with Ambrose "the honour of finally winning Augustine from Mani to Christ" while Bonner suggest that in the long run, the influence of Tyconius upon Augustine's theory of scriptural exegesis may even be stronger than that of Ambrose. Frend (1951), 205; Bonner (1970), 555.

his skills into his new role as a church leader. Thirdly, the local context of Hippo and its ecclesiastical surrounding motivated him.⁴ This chapter will primarily focus on how Augustine's pastoral context in Africa and his appropriation of Tyconius's works determined his readings of the Scriptures and structured the shape of the *De doctrina Christiana*.

If the Christian Scripture is a subversive text that challenged and defied secular authority in the hands of the cultured Ambrose in Milan, how does Tyconius's reading of Scripture differ, especially as a Donatist? Do the specific contexts or a pervasive notion of time determine these readings? Where did Augustine stand in relation to Ambrose and Tyconius regarding the authority of Scripture? In order to answer these questions, we shall first look at the background of Tyconius. We will see how the church in Milan differs from the church in Africa, and how these differences prompted Augustine to negotiate and chart his own understanding of the authority of Scripture.

1. Tyconius and the Socio-Political and Religious Context of the "Donatist" Controversy

Tyconius produced at least four books, of which only the *Liber regularum* regarding the principles of scriptural exegesis that he wrote *c.* 382 survived intact.⁵ His works, and Augustine's appropriation of them, were largely determined by Tyconius being a "Donatist". In his polemic against the "Donatist" Bishop Parmenius, Augustine refers to Tyconius's notion of the universality of the church⁶ and seeks to defend it. Augustine was, however, conscious and cautious of Tyconius's "Donatist inclination" whenever he refers to Tyconius's works.⁷ So, what is the context which determined Tyconius's "Donatist" label⁸ and what does *Donatista haereticus*⁹ mean for Augustine?

---

4   Kannengiesser (1995), 4–5.
5   His books were the "polemical" *De bello intestino, Expositiones diuersarum causarum*, and the more "exegetical" *Liber regularum*, and *In Apocalypsin*. Bright (1988), 163. For Tyconius's brief biography, see Anderson (1974), 1–8; Fredriksen (1999a), 853–55.
6   *ecclesiam praedicaret toto orbe diffusam.* Par 1.1.1 (CSEL 51.20).
7   Some examples are: *Tychonium, hominem quidem et acri ingenio praeditum et uberi eloquio, sed tamen Donatistam* (Par 1.1.1; CSEL 51.19); *Tychonius quidam, qui contra Donatistas invictissime scripsit, cum fuerit Donatista; Caute sane legendus est non solum propter quaedam, in quibus ut homo errauit, sed maxime propter illa quae sicut Donatista haereticus loquitur* (do 3.42.92; 3.43.97; CSEL 80.101, 106).
8   We need to be wary of this "label", since Augustine "never engaged the Donatists as people with a perspective that might have merit or explanation. Labelling them as 'schismatic' made it unnecessary for him to deal with them as people". O'Donnell (2006), 217. Consequently, "scholars portrayed the Donatists as an intransigent, monolithic, and millennialist sect of Christianity which never adjusted to the end of the Roman persecutions, for that is the portrait their opponents in the fourth and fifth centuries painted of them". Tilley (1996), viii. On how these labels sometimes "cohered with an accepted reality, but in others they did not", see Shaw (2011), 5.
9   Alexander Ever assumes that Augustine would have been familiar with the "Donatists" since they dominated large parts of the province where he grew up although Augustine formally dealt with them "after his own ordination to the priesthood in the year 391 [when] he found himself in an area where

The Donatist controversy and the schism within the church of North Africa was the consequence of the Diocletian persecution in 303–305 and it lasted till the Vandals' invasions of Africa in the early fifth century. This persecution was preceded by a vigorous propaganda war against the Christians epitomized by Porphyry's fifteen books where he used historical and literary criticism to undermine claims of the divine origin and prophetic value of their Scriptures and defend traditional Roman religion against the irrationality of Christianity.[10] On 23 February 303, the emperor Diocletian issued an edict — soon followed by three others — that demanded the confiscation and burning of Scriptures and the demolition of Christian churches.[11] This prompted fanatical resistance along with prudent, conciliatory compromisers in many churches. While many members of the clergy forfeited their properties to imperial authority, the handing over (*tradere*) of copies of the scriptures was particularly considered a serious apostasy by those who adamantly resisted the edicts. Although this resulted in conflict in the church, it was kept under control by Mensurius, the Bishop of Carthage whose loyalty during the persecution was also questioned as being one who "hands over" (*traditor*).[12]

In 311–312, Mensurius died and Caecilian, one of his deacons, was elected as the new Bishop of Carthage. But Caecilian, who was consecrated in great haste in the absence of the bishops from Numidia, was accused of being consecrated by bishops who were guilty as *traditores* and unworthy of the clerical state, among other charges. In a council of 70 bishops convened by Secundus of Tigisis, the primate of Numidia,

---

they constituted a clear majority". Ever (2012), 379. And J. S. Alexander asserted that the Donatists were not heterodox in the strictest sense. "Wishing to put an end to the schism by bringing the Donatist within the ambit of anti-heresy legislation, Augustine was content to have them officially labelled heretics through their practice of rebaptism ... [and] he insisted on the principle that persistent schism amounted to heresy". Alexander (1986–1994), 622.

10 On Porphyry's main arguments and how these "fragmented" works were not known as a single writing with the title *Against the Christians* until several centuries after Porphyry's death, see Berchman (2005), 1–16. On Porphyry's three-fold purpose and the four main charges brought against Christianity by these "pagan" intellectuals, see Simmons (1995), 23, 28–31. Regarding the constrasting views of whether the persecutions were based on religion to maintain divine favour of the traditional gods or on the Christians' refusal to obey the reasonable requests of magistrates to pay homage to *di nostri*, see Streeter (2006), 3–34. However, these views may not be mutually exclusive, as Gaddis observed, "Pious fear of the gods and sense of public duty blended with anger, frustration, and sometimes outright prejudice against the obstinate disobedience of the Christians". Gaddis (2005), 34.

11 On how the confiscation and burning of the Scriptures will be "no small loss in an age before the printing-press, when books were scarce and the labour of producing them immense", see Edwards (1997), xi. On the probable contents of the First Edict, see de Ste. Croix (2006), 35–36. On the significance of the date of the First Edict of Persecution, see Leadbetter (2009), 132. For an overview of imperial persecutions of the early Christians, see Frend (2006), 503–23.

12 Bright (1999a), 281; Markus (1999), 284–85. Pose (2014), 1:735. Regarding the meaning of *traditores* that "was applied not only to the persons who literally engaged in these acts, but also to their ecclesial descendants, generation after generation" and how *The Acts of the Abitinian Martyrs* preserved the story that "North African Christians conspired with the state to harass other Christians", see Tilley (1996), ix, xi.

Caecilian was declared "deposed" and Majorinus was "elected" in his place. This double election of Bishop of Carthage was at the root of the controversy when the questions of imperial recognition between two rival churches was raised after the advent of emperor Constantine.[13]

After Majorinus was dead around 313, he was succeeded by Donatus who held the see until he was exiled from Africa in 347. Donatus' expulsion and the subsequent repression of his supporters by the imperial agents Paul and Macarius[14] sealed their reputation for being the church of the martyrs.[15] Donatus' successor Parmenian provided strong leadership and ensured the stability of the "Donatist" church. The name of Donatus was adopted by opponents to label the party of Majorinus although the "Donatists" rejected the designation and referred to themselves simply as Christians while they also discredited the "Catholics" as "Macariani".[16] Parmenian's death in 391/92 resulted in a major schism between his successor Primian, who represented the Numidians and the more radical elements of the church, and his opponent Maximian, who reflected the more moderate opinions of the Donatists of Proconsular Africa and Byzacena.[17]

Tyconius wrote his first two books when the "Donatists", who were estranged from their reviled "Catholic" because of their "collusion" with secular authorities, were the dominant party in North Africa. In *De bello intestino*, written around 370, Tyconius asserts the universality of the church while *Expositiones diuersarum causarum* was subsequently written around 375 in defence of his position. Tyconius was condemned by a Donatist council c. 380 since his assertion that the church must be universal and her membership mixed, undermined the ecclesiological principles of his own

---

13 Bright (1999a), 282–83; Markus (1999), 284–85. On Optatus' account that Caecilian "incurred the animosity of a rich woman named Lucilla, because he had objected to her extravagant veneration of a martyr", and how this version "is manifestly incomplete", see Edwards (1997), xviii–xx.
14 On how Paul and Macarius was sent by emperor Constans which resulted in "the creation of a new crop of martyrs, and the composition of new martyr stories", see Tilley (1996), xvi–xvii.
15 Markus (1999), 285. According to Gaddis, "their self-conception as the 'Church of the Martyrs' was central to their identity and ideology". Gaddis (2005), 41. Tilley stated that "the military actions … merely succeeded in creating heroic Donatist martyrs instead of subservient new Catholics". Tilley (1996), xvi. But, as Dillistone observed, "The blood of the martyrs may be the seed of the Church: the zeal of martyrs can easily prove to be the disruption of the Church". Dillistone (1979), 176. On how "the enterprise of seeking a universal definition of martyrdom … is misguided" since martyrs "are not defined [but] are made", see Middleton (2006), 11.
16 This is a reference to the imperial officer Macarius. See Frend (1951), 196. According to O'Donnell, the "Macarian persecution" became a rallying cry for the rest of their history. O'Donnell (2006), 211. Tilley noted that "the name 'Donatist' perdures as a term of opprobrium until the era of Gregory the Great (c. 540–604)" but "the issues of the schism do not seem to have been vital for North Africans after 450". Tilley (1996), xvii. Interestingly, Dearn observed: "Catholics and Donatist polemicists used the martyrs of the past to demarcate their own idealised group from that of their opponents, creating and strengthening the antithesis between 'us' and 'them'; between the pars Donati and the Macariani. For Donatists, this meant denying that persecution belonged only to the pre-Constantinian world and legitimising the victims of Catholic violence as martyrs". Dearn (2016), 72.
17 Bright (1999a), 281; Markus (1999), 284–85; Pose (2014), 1:736–37.

party who see themselves as "the visible faithful remnant waiting the return of the Lord".[18] Nonetheless, Tyconius produced the *Liber regularum* where he explains the logic of the scriptural texts with reference to the mystery of the union of Christ and the church as Head and body. Discerning the proper reference of texts between Christ and the church will help in determining its Christological and ecclesiological signification.[19] The church as the body of Christ is *corpus permixtum* and not pure, as the Donatists insist.[20]

For Tyconius, temporal designations and duration of time is symbolic and qualitative rather than quantitative. As numbers do not quantify but symbolize aspects of spiritual truths, they cannot serve as the basis for calculating when that eschatological perfection of the Lord's body will come. The coming of the Son of Man referred to the presence of Christ in the church and not to the *Parousia*.[21] By reversing the eschatological categories of Scripture, many traditionally apocalyptic verses became symbolic descriptions of the church's present situation.[22] In other words, Tyconius "de-eschatologized" the traditional *consummatio saeculi* and "eschatologized" the *tempora christiana* in his ecclesiology.

Augustine, who returned to Africa when the "Donatist schism" further charged the passion within the Christian community, was greatly impressed by Tyconius's interpretative method. But as Augustine's conception of the "Donatist" label was partisan, he considered Tyconius "absurd"[23] since Tyconius's theology obviously transcended this narrow "Donatist" identity.

---

18 Fredriksen (1999a), 854; Bright (1988), 11. See ep 93.43–44 for Augustine's own account.
19 For Tyconius, "not the head, which is the same from the beginning, but the body grows from the head". Anderson asserts that "Tyconius subsumes his ecclesiology under his Christology" since the Church is "Christ's continuing presence in the world". See Anderson (1974), 18, 29. And according to Bright, Cyprian's typology is Christological whereas Tyconius uses typology ecclesiologically. Bright (1988), 70.
20 Commenting on Rule 2 of Tyconius's *Liber regularum*, Bright asserts that Tyconius was concerned with the "Bipartite Body of Christ" and not the "true church" or the "counterfeit church" which will not be visibly separated until the Judgment. "It was this repudiation of the necessity of a withdrawl from a 'tainted' church that made Tyconius's ecclesiology such an anomaly in Donatist circles". Bright (1999b), 114–15.
21 Tyconius held a double interpretation of the Second advent: the second advent is occurring even now on an individual basis while the Second coming will be a world-encompassing event in the *eschaton*. "The growth of the Church is a kind of Second Advent, but it is not the final return of Christ". See Anderson (1974), 28, 33.
22 See Fredriksen (1999a), 854. According to Anderson, Tyconius was mainly interested in relating the Scriptures to "the contemporary Church existence and history in North Africa" in each of the Rules. Anderson (1974), 18. So, in Tyconius's exposition, "the apocalyptic visions of John's Revelation were given immediate relevance for the present situation of the church". Robinson (2017), 4; see also Bright (1988), 8.
23 *illic inuenitur absurdissimi cordis.* do 3.42.92 (CSEL 80.104). In his letter, Augustine repeated this sentiment thus: *de ecclesia toto orbe diffusa et quod neminem in eius unitate macularent aliena peccata, ab Afrorum se tamen quasi traditorum contagione remouebat et erat in parte Donati.* ep 93.44 (CSEL 34.2.487).

2. Discerning the Underlying Theological Issue in the "Complex" Donatist Controversy

Today, there is an awareness that "a much more complex web of multiple, often competing narratives" existed behind the Donatist controversy which was often reduced to "a binary sectarian narrative" involving the "Catholic" and the "Donatist" parties.[24] And it is critical to see Augustine against his socio-political context and identify the assumptions he brings into his engagement with the Donatists.[25] Then again, our "modern" sensibilities with their scholarly tendency to "detach" often reduce the schism to nothing more than "church politics".[26] Ployd remarks that the non-theological aspects of the religious disputes was the sole focus of many studies at the expense of the underlying theological issues which became "merely instruments of political power struggles" while Mark Edwards warned against drawing such a line "between theology and what we now call the politics of the church".[27] Bourke also asserts that Augustine "was forced by circumstances to act and write about political matters, at times" and that "the political order was not the focal point" of his thinking.[28] So, although the Donatist controversy was rooted in, and produced by, the socio-political reality of the day, one should avoid the tendency to overstress only these aspects at the expense of the underlying theological issues.

Regarding the theological issues of the Donatist controversy, Bonner grouped them under three main headings: (i) The nature of the Church; (ii) the Sacraments and their validity; and (iii) the relationship between Church and state with regard to the employment of state coercion of schismatic and heretical Christians.[29] Pose asserts that "Donatism began as a revolt against what many Christians in N. Africa considered a betrayal of the faith by their own leaders, and continued as a protest

---

24 Miles (2016), 1. See also Pose (2014), 1:735; Edwards (2016), xxi. Here, I put "Catholic" and "Donatist" inside quotation marks to highlight the fact that they often are a complex labels and ideological construct.
25 Eno pointed out that there were "some nuances" on the Donatists' attitudes on certain issues and were not so "monolithic" as Augustine had asserted. As the Donatists were confined to Africa, Augustine seems to make a valid point when he insisted that his party, who is in communion with the rest of the Christian world is the true universal church. But Bishop Emeritus of Caesarea retorted that "the fact that Augustine's party is in communion with the rest of the Catholic Church prove nothing except that the rest of the Catholic Church is in communion with the wrong group". Regarding Augustine's assertion that "the Donatists claimed to be a Church uncontaminated by the presence of sinners, known and unknown", "some responsible Donatist opinion" asserted that they acknowledged sinners present among them but "claimed that they, unlike the Catholics, made a real effort to purge their ranks of known sinners. Secrets sinners ... would be dealt with at the Last Judgment". Eno (1976), 418–20.
26 For an overview of the trend in interpreting the Donatist movement, see Markus (1999), 285–86. But on the "partiality" of scholar like de Ste. Croix's, whose "hostility to Christianity" guided his inquiry "to understand the form that Christianity developed in the Roman Empire and its historical consequences", see Streeter (2006), 4.
27 Ployd (2015), 14; Edwards (2016), 102.
28 Bourke (1973), 209.
29 Bonner (1986), 278.

against the effects of the *christiana tempora* initiated by Constantine".[30] According to O'Donnell, the quarrel finds concrete expression as a "liturgical issue". While the Donatists "took the sin so seriously that they insisted the seriously lapsed be baptized again", the Catholics "took the sacrament so seriously that they insisted baptism could be administered only once".[31] Tilley sees "Donatism" as a religious movement "in response to a crisis of ecclesiology. The specific point at issue was the relationship of the Christian community to the larger society. All the disputes between Catholics and Donatists were rooted in their different approaches to the matter".[32]

While these specific points formulated by modern scholars can be regarded as only a partial contention, given the complex nature of the controversy, we can identify a mutual concern being addressed and reflected upon among the Christian writers in Africa. This "affinity" was recapped in the words of Edwards, who summed up the response that Tyconius, Optatus and Augustine more or less maintained against the Donatists, thus:

> The tendency to sin being universal and its effects being often secret, no Christian has the right to judge another, and to act as the Donatists do is to pre-empt the work of Christ on the final day. The Church is a field that bears both wheat and tares, a net containing every kind of fish.[33]

Without going into detail and giving an assessment of the arguments in the controversy,[34] we will assert that a specific notion of time is the key which underlies the whole argument. In chapter one, we had argued that Jesus and his disciples envisaged the *consummatio saeculi* against the background of a notion of the *aereum saeculum* that emperor Augustus and other Roman rulers constructed. Now, in the light of these scriptural teachings, Christians try to make sense of the different convictions that church members display in the changing socio-political context. As they try to assert their identity and discern a working relationship between the church and the larger society,[35] what is the valid implication of the impending *aduentus* of Christ and the final judgment or of belonging to the body of Christ in the interim period before the *Parousia*? What does *consummatio*

---

30 See Pose (2014), 1: 736, 740.
31 See O'Donnell (2006), 210.
32 Tilley (1996), xii.
33 Edwards (1997), xxii. For the significances of Optatus, see Bogan (1968), 155. Regarding Augustine's specific stance, Portalie summed up his writing against the Donatists as developing "the fundamental theories of the visibility of the Church, which harbors even sinners in her boson, the efficacy of the sacraments independently of the disposition of the minister, and the impossibility of validly repeating baptism, even if originally conferred outside the Church". Portalié (1975), 5. But see n. 25 above for some nuances in the Donatists' ecclesiology.
34 On the general assessment of the controversy, Bourke noted that "even after the lapse of fifteen centuries, the Donatist movement is still viewed with some favor by representatives of various national reforms in Christianity and with some disfavor by Catholics who stress the continuity and unity of their religious traditions. Perhaps, it is not possible for a scholar with definite religious convictions to be wholly impartial in interpreting the meaning of schism". Bourke (1973), 207.
35 On how the "Catholic" and the "Donatists" were "faced by the fundamental problem of the relationship of any group to the society in which it lives", see Brown (2000), 209–10.

saeculi imply in the light of the *tempora christiana* that emperor Constantine initiated and how can they meaningfully relate it with their existential realities?

These concerns are essentially different from the issues raised by the Manicheans, more of which we will see in subsequent chapters. While Augustine needs to assert the harmony, and the "unique" authority, of the Christian Scripture against the "syncretizing" Manicheans,[36] his main concern in engaging with the Donatists was to discern the correct signification of that Scripture in the *tempora christiana*.[37] The theological implication of this exegetical concern,[38] which ultimately shows the centrality of theological issues in the Donatist controversy, was substantiated by Ayres's remark that "early Christians did not distinguish 'exegesis' and 'theology' in the way that modern scholars tend to do".[39] And if Augustine had ever pondered upon the meaning of the *tempora christiana* in Milan under the highly influential Bishop Ambrose, he will be compelled to reconsider it as a marginal cleric and as a reader of Tyconius's intriguing works in the North African context: How can a Donatist's exposition of the Scriptures affirm that the church is a mixed body, called to repentance by the Holy Spirit, thereby negating their fundamental belief of the apostasy of the non-Donatist Christian church? As a Catholic bishop, how will Augustine assess Tyconius's appropriation of the *tempora christiana*?

3. Engaging Tyconius's *Liber Regularum* in the *De doctrina Christiana*

Although Ambrose's spiritual reading inspired Augustine to approach the Scriptures anew at Milan, he finds Ambrose's advice to meditate upon the book of Isaiah

---

36 Regarding Mani's own syncretistic background, see Henrichs (1979). But on the problem of the concept of "syncretism" which "falsely suggests that there are religions that are, somehow, pure", although "Mani *deliberately* and *explicitly* welded elements from the religions he knew", see de Jong (2015), 131.

37 Harrison asserts that Augustine's argument with the Manicheans was rooted in scriptural exegesis where his allegorical interpretation of Genesis clashed with their literal interpretation. See Harrison (2013), 682. But the affinity between the "Catholic" and the "Donatists" in North Africa were much closer. Alexander Evers states that they "were two Christian communities divided by a single language of communion" and by Augustine's time, the main issue "was the source of the spiritual authority of the clergy". Ever (2012), 375, 383. According to Bright, both sides invoked the Scriptures "in the claim to be heir to hallowed tradition and look on the vindication of their claims when Christ was to reappear in the glory of his Second Coming — soon!" Bright (1988), 19. Frend maintain that the questions that divided the "Donatists" from the "Catholics" were "not of doctrine" but "those of discipline and politics". See Frend (1953), 14. On how Augustine was caught unprepared by the Donatist controversy, see Brown (2000), 269.

38 According to Pollmann, "a stronger interest in hermeneutical questions arises when there is a fixed and canonical text to consider … the obscurity of a text and the difficulty of understanding it are the results of its age and the circumstances of its transmission. This factor acquires additional importance when a text is granted religious or quasi-religious authority, with the implication that its message needs to be understood". Pollmann (2005), 208.

39 Ayres (2006), 18. On how "the hermeneutical circle of biblical text, tradition and interpretation" determines Christian theology in the early church, see Froehlich (1984), 1; see also Bright (1988), 13.

initially daunting.[40] Although his "scriptural knowledge as of 388 was solid and well grounded",[41] and in spite of his previous secular learning, Augustine feels that he still lacked so much[42] to minister to others. Therefore, he asked Bishop Valerius a time off to study the Scriptures when he was ordained as a priest in Hippo in 391. Brown asserts that Augustine wished to replicate the atmosphere of Milan among his friends in the African churches by drawing on "the Greek East, the traditional source of a high Christian culture" but then fall back "on its own resources" — the *regularum* of Tyconius.[43] This new development, where Augustine grappled with "an idiosyncratic hermeneutical method" of Tyconius, is also seen as "Augustine's gradual 'inculturation' into his own African milieu".[44]

According to Anderson, Tyconius wanted to develop an interpretative method "more rational, thorough and objective than the subjective, haphazard and (often wildly) allegorical methods of his day".[45] Tyconius regarded the Scriptures as "a seamless, living oracle of God, made incomprehensible only by the human failure to grasp its logic".[46] This "logic" basically works from the future backward and it involves the reversal of the usual terms of scriptural interpretation. According to Fredricksen, Tyconius's scriptural interpretation, which "sought to understand the Bible ... historically", flouts the usual philosophical and typological allegory which often established a relative inferiority of the prototypes in the Old Testament with what is completed and perfected in the New Testament. He stressed the theological harmony of the two testaments, bound together by a single divine plan of salvation where "the difference between these two historically distinct dispensations was only one of measure (*modo*), not of kind (*genere*)". This implies that the "righteous within Israel" not only prefigured the future church but were actually "a continuous community of the redeemed".[47] Instead of the shape of future eschatological events, the present spiritual realities were revealed and illumined by the Spirit, the Author of Scripture. Therefore, Tyconius rejected a literal thousand year reign of Christ but perceived Christ's earthly reign as "the exercise of spiritual authority over the

---

40 cf 9.5.13; cf. ci 18.29. In fact, La Bonnardière remarked that Augustine had paid little or no attention to the book of Isaiah during his entire Manichean period and Ambrose's preaching had failed to arouse his interest in it. Augustine's works "from 387 to 388 include only two citations of Isaiah ... [His] knowledge of Isaiah, which would remain limited to certain texts, would result from his pastoral work as priest and bishop, and mainly from his discussions with the heterodox". La Bonnardière (1999), 21.
41 La Bonnardière (1999), 23. In Augustine's own admission, *auderem enim dicere scire me et plena fide retinere, quid pertineat ad salutem nostram.* ep 21.4 (CSEL 34.1.52).
42 *Tam multa autem sunt, ut facilius possim enumerare, quae habeam, quam quae habere desidero.* ep 21.4 (CSEL 34.1.52).
43 Brown (2000), 268–69. We can see this "circle" in his correspondence with Jerome, where Augustine stated that "all the learned members of the African churches" (*nobiscum petit omnis Africanarum ecclesiarum studiosa societas*) joined him in his query to Jerome. See ep 28.2 (CSEL 34.1.105; White 66).
44 Bright (1999c), xiv.
45 Anderson (1974), v, 10–12.
46 Kugler (1999), 129; see also Anderson (1974), 19.
47 Fredriksen (1999a), 855; Fredriksen (2010), 158–60.

members of the Church in this world until the Eschaton".[48] This notion of time that stressed the decisiveness of the present as the point where the past and the future collate,[49] is one of the most significant insights that Augustine draws from Tyconius.

Augustine explicitly mentioned Tyconius 31 times in his writings. His *Contra epistulam Parmeniani* was written around 400 as a refutation of Bishop Parmenian's letter to Tyconius. Here, Augustine criticized what he considered as an inconsistency in Donatist ecclesiology, drawing many of his arguments from Tyconius and mentioning his name ten times.[50] But it was in the *De doctrina Christiana* where he most clearly depicted the influence of Tyconius's thought. In this work, Augustine makes the most of his professional background as teacher of rhetoric and his personal commitment to the reading of Scripture to gracefully express the principles of scriptural exposition.[51] Initially, he asserts that all scriptural interpretation depends on two things: discovery (*inueniendi*) of what we need to learn and presentation (*proferendi*) of what we have learned. The first three of the four books is a guide to "discovery", with Book 1 focussing on the theological questions regarding the purpose of Scripture for salvation, Book 2 focussing on significations of words and Book 3 focussing on "the task of analysing and resolving the ambiguities of the scriptures".[52] Notably though, we can see from his *Retractationes* that Augustine completed the book only partially and much later, he added more materials to Book 3 and finished the *De doctrina Christiana* with Book 4.[53]

On why it was "interrupted" as such, Kannengiesser assumed that Augustine was no longer satisfied with his own distinctions of "figurative expression" in his *capitulam* 25 of Book 3.[54] And while Book 3 of the *De doctrina Christiana* finally endorsed the *Liber regularum* (LR), Augustine's explicit espousal of Tyconius's ideas was not

---

48 See Bright (1988), 9–11; Anderson (1974), 5.
49 Regarding the "complex backwards and forwards view of the prophetic text" and its implication for the present in Tyconius's exposition of the Scripture, see also Bright (1988), 73.
50 Tilley (1999), 312. In re 2.17.43, Augustine highlighted the two points in his argument: *utrum in unitate et eorundem communione sacramentorum mali contaminent bonos, et quemadmodum non contaminent* (CCSL 57.103). According to Eric Plumer, Augustine's personal engagement in the Donatist controversy should not be regarded as starting only with his first major work against the Donatists written in 400, "but much earlier, with his ordination to the priesthood in 391 and his acceptance of the pastoral responsibilities that went with it". Plumer (2003), 251. M. I. Bogan remarked that "Augustine's treatment of the Church and the Sacraments ... is considered a development of the doctrine of Optatus". Bogan (1968), 155. Bright remarked that Tyconius's position was a middle path between Optatus and Parmenian. While Tyconius defended the Donatists as the victims of persecution, he also insisted that the Church was beyond the confines of Africa. Bright (1988), 20.
51 As Bright asserted, "Augustine found the rhetorical skills acquired in his classical education indispensable to his new task as biblical commentator, and he sought to combine them with the Church's traditional rules of exegetical practice". Bright (2006), 42. And according to Pollmann, "Augustine's hermeneutics teaches a discipline ... that enables people to decipher ... what they already know". Pollmann (2005), 211.
52 do 1.1.1; 1.39.85; 3.1.1 (Green 13, 49, 133).
53 In his own word, *libros de doctrina christiana, cum inperfectos conperissem, perficere malui quam eis sic relictis ad alia retractanda transire*. re 2.4.1 (CCSL 57.92).
54 Kannengiesser (1995), 8. Van Fleteren opined that Augustine "well may have stopped writing because he did not know what to say about the hermeneutic of Tyconius". Van Fleteren (2013), 285.

instantaneous.⁵⁵ His letter to Aurelius, written around 397, suggests that Augustine probably came across Tyconius's writings around 394.⁵⁶ While we can still detect a tinge of suspicion in this letter, and though he did not mention it yet, Tyconius's LR was considered to inspire Augustine to write the *De doctrina Christiana*.⁵⁷ If the LR was Tyconius's response to the censure of his fellow Donatists and thereby his account of "the rationale for his ecclesiology",⁵⁸ Tyconius's reputation was probably "what initially commended his work to Augustine's attention".⁵⁹

Even though Augustine did not mention Tyconius in the first instalment of the *De doctrina Christiana* that he wrote in 396, he was comfortable to invoke Tyconius's insights against the Donatist by 400, which indicated his familiarity with Tyconius's works. And after thirty years of ministry when he became a reputable bishop, Augustine finally made a bold move of incorporating, endorsing and critiquing the LR in the sequel to his *De doctrina Christiana*.⁶⁰ Nonetheless, this is an exceptionally unusual move "in the Christian literature of the patristic era" since Augustine, as "a strict guardian of ecclesiastical orthodoxy", endorsed the work of a "heretical" writer, "and more so specifically for the study of the Holy Scripture".⁶¹ So, what makes the LR so appealing and worthy of recommending for Augustine after all?

In his preface to the *De doctrina Christiana*, Augustine stated his intention to communicate the rules that can illuminate "the obscurities of divine literature/scriptures".⁶² And we can see from the LR that Tyconius also considers that "the

---

55 Kannengiesser asserts that Augustine was not yet ready to incorporate Tyconius's *Liber regularum* that was initially "a stumbling block for Augustine, still infused with his allegiance to the Platonizing high culture which he had enjoyed so much in Milan". Kannengiesser (1995), 7. On why "Augustine suppresses the influence of Tyconius", see also TeSelle (1970), 181–82.

56 Augustine stated: *nam et ego, quod iussisti, non neglego et de Tychonii septem regulis uel clauibus, sicut saepe iam scripsi, cognoscere, quid tibi uideatur, expecto*. ep 41.2 (CSEL 34.2.83).

57 According to Kannengiesser, *De doctrina Christiana* is Augustine's "needed response of a sound biblical hermeneutic in a Catholic framing". Kannengiesser (1995), 8. Green suggested that Tyconius's work "showed him the possibilities of a hermeneutical treatise and encouraged him to provide something better". Green (1995), xi.

58 Bright dubbed his "exegetical basis of ecclesiology" that we see in the LR as "contrariness of signification" or "duality of reference" where a single referent can be either blameworthy or praiseworthy depending on a particular context. Bright (1995), 25. Anderson asserts that their indigenous quality partly makes Tyconius's work appealing, though his LR also contains traces of his attempt "to justify the Donatist ecclesiology, revised somewhat according to the biblical image and even slightly critical of the party line". Anderson (1974), 4, 6.

59 See Fredriksen (2010), 158.

60 Bright (1988), 21–22.

61 Kannengiesser (1995), 12; see also Kannengiesser (1999), 153. M. S. Williams remarked that Augustine rarely make direct citations "outside of specific controversies … The unexpected exception of Tyconius is perhaps to be explained by his doubtful status in the church as an ex-Donatist — so that here Augustine expressly acknowledges the source of his exegetical ideas partly in defence of Tyconius, and partly in order explicitly to delimit the extent of his indebtedness to this dubious source". Williams (2012), 228.

62 *diuinarum litteratum operta; diuinis scripturis obscura.* do prol 1.1; 3.6 (CSEL 80.3–4). Interestingly, in the *De doctrina Christiana*, the words *obscura* occurs 8 times, (out of which 3 occurrences were in connection with Tyconius's LR), and *obscurum* and *obscure* occurs 2 times each. In his extant works,

immediate task of Christian hermeneutics is to address the obscurities of the biblical text".[63] Eventually invoking the LR, Augustine introduced it with Tyconius's own "preface" that the correct application of the principle therein will bring light to obscure things. Although he instantly qualifies Tyconius's "preface" with some words of caution, Augustine still acknowledges its helpfulness to understand Scriptures.[64] And in summarizing his own "summary" of the LR, Augustine asserted that other than the third rule titled *De promissis et lege*, these rules basically "state that one thing is to be understood by another".[65]

Regarding Tyconius's explication of his third rule *De promissis et lege*, which Augustine deemed effective but not exhaustive discussion,[66] it is interesting to note that Tyconius drew heavily upon Pauline thought. Augustine adjudged Tyconius as "less attentive and less on his guard" to the core Pauline insight that "even faith itself is a gift of God, who distributes to each individual his or her measure".[67] Although Tyconius extensively supported his notion of the "bipartite body of Christ" with various imageries,[68] Augustine, who disagreed with Tyconius's notion of a "bipartite body",[69] rather abridged his "deliberation" of the third rule by pointing out that he had "dealt with them [that faith and understanding is God's gift] often in various places".[70] It will be very interesting if we can see Augustine's initial impression of this rule, as his summary of the LR thirty years later had been determined by his engagement with the Pelagians. Nonetheless, as Cameron pointed out, the LR offers Augustine "a prophetic, christological and indeed christo-ecclesiological hermeneutic".[71]

In studying Augustine's summary, Bright actually asserts that Augustine misrepresented Tyconius's exegetical theory and that "they had diametrically opposed views

---

Augustine used the word *obscura* 146 times. Apart from his *Enarrationes in Psalmos* where the word *obscura* occurs 41 times (15 times in Psalm 10), *De doctrina Christiana* is the work where Augustine most frequently used this particular word (these numbers were collected using the cag-online.net database).

63 Bright (1988), 60.
64 See do 3.42.93. According to Stock, "In the early draft, written in 396, Aurelius may have discouraged Augustine from borrowing heavily from the interpretative principles of the Donatist Tyconius … However, by 426–427, when the revision took place, the Donatist controversy was behind him". Stock (1996), 384. Kannengiesser asserts that in 426, Augustine introduced a much more adequate and theological distinction than he did in 396 in his treatment of ambiguities. See Kannengiesser (1995), 12.
65 *Hae autem omnes regulae … aliud ex alio faciunt intellegi.* do 3.56.133 (CSEL 80.117; Green 193).
66 *bene, sed non plene.* do 3.46.103 (CSEL 80.108; Green 179).
67 *minus attentum minusque sine … sollicitum … fidem donum esse illius qui eius mensuram unicuique partitur* do 3.46.104 (CSEL 80.108; Green 179).
68 Tyconius made references to "the bipartite nature of Jacob", "the two-fold seeds of Abraham, that is, of peoples [Jacob and Esau] struggling in the one womb of mother Church", "from Abraham the bipartite seed was shown", i.e., Hagar and Sarah, Ismael and Isaac. See Anderson (1974), 52–96.
69 *Secunda est de domini corpore bipertito, quod quidem non ita debuit appellare; non enim re uera domini corpus est quod cum illo non erit in aeternum, … quia non solum in aeternum, uerum etiam nunc hypocritae non cum illo esse dicendi sunt, quamuis in eius esse uideantur ecclesia.* do 3.45.100 (CSEL 80.106).
70 *Plura sunt et alia testimonia, quibus id ostenditur, … Alibi autem atque alibi saepissime ista egimus.* do 3.46.105 (CSEL 80.108; Green 181).
71 Cameron (1999), 93.

on key issues in hermeneutics".[72] For Kannengiesser, "Augustine's main concern was obviously to relativize Tyconius's authority from the start" and that "the Tyconian rules are emptied of most of their proper signification".[73] He asserts that Augustine misread Tyconius by "conflating the two interpretative categories, the *regulae* and the *claues*". Hence, Augustine "thought Tyconius was boasting about his personal achievement as an interpreter" by claiming that "whatever is closed will be opened and whatever is dark will be illumined" by his seven *regulae*.[74] Regardless of these flaws in his summary, it has been acknowledged that Tyconius's legacy was preserved and appropriated later in the church because Augustine endorsed them in the *De doctrina Christiana* which is one of his most significant works.[75]

Moreover, this "misrepresentation" is explicable since Augustine incorporated the LR into his ongoing project of scriptural exposition. Augustine may need to "bend" the LR to fit into his overall purpose and adapt them for his specific audiences.[76] In fact, Augustine exhibited certain differences in his view and approach to the Scriptures as a whole. According to Kugler, Tyconius understands Scripture as speaking for itself without the need for explanation while Augustine regards Scripture to need interpretation. While grasping the logic is the key for Tyconius, Augustine believes that one needs to decipher the signs obscured by language to get to the meaning of the word.[77] Augustine stressed the temporality of the text in that it was an accommodation of the eternal Word (do 1.12.25; 1.42.92–43.93) and pointed out the tentativeness of any exegetical method (do 3.35.78; 3.42.93) which cannot be used in a fixed and rigid way.[78] In Tyconius's hermeneutical theory, "the scriptures bear the impress of the Spirit rather than the dual nature of the Incarnate Word"[79] while Augustine juxtaposed "the Incarnate Word of God with the words of Scripture"[80] in his theology of Scripture. And most importantly, Tyconius's notion of the "bipartite" church, which largely determined his exegesis, was not really shared by Augustine.[81]

---

72 For a detail assessment, see Bright (1988), 22–23.
73 Kannengiesser (1999), 152, 174.
74 Kannengiesser (1995), 8–9; see also Kannengiesser (1999), 155–57.
75 As Jean-Marc Vercruysse remarked: "Qu'on se rappelle à ce sujet le décret du pseudo-Gélase, au début du VIe siècle, qui cite Tyconius parmi les auteurs que 'l'Église romaine, catholique et apostolique' ne peut admettre en aucune façon et que 'les catholiques doivent éviter'. La stature et l'autorité morale d'Augustin furent telles que sa version abrégée du *Livre des Règles* évita à son auteur de tomber dans l'oubli mais dispensa pour longtemps de recourir à l'original". (Remember on this subject the decree of pseudo-Gelasius, at the beginning of the sixth century, which cites Tyconius among the authors that the "Roman, Catholic and Apostolic Church" cannot in any way admit and that "Catholics must avoid". Augustine's stature and moral authority were such that his abridged version of the *Book of Rules* saved its author from being forgotten, but for a long time dispensed with the need for the original). Vercruysse (2004), 94. My translation.
76 On whether Augustine misunderstood Tyconius or intentionally reshape his insights, see Kugler (1999), 143.
77 Kugler (1999), 140, 148.
78 See O'Loughlin (1999), 252.
79 Bright (1988), 175.
80 Bright (2006), 44.
81 For an overview of their difference in ecclesiology, see Bright (1988), 28–29.

4. Fitting Tyconius's *Liber Regularum* into Augustine's Wider Exegetical Concerns

Even though Augustine suppressed the influence of Tyconius in 396, yet we can see a change in his scriptural exposition that can be ascribed to Tyconius's. Though it will be difficult to determine those insights exhaustively,[82] one remarkable feature will be Augustine's new reading of Paul. According to Brown, the last decade of the fourth century saw a renewed interest in the Latin church toward the writings of Paul and this interest[83] had even brought Tyconius, who drew his ecclesiological principles particularly from the writings of Paul, "closer to Augustine than to his own bishops".[84] During 394–396, Augustine was preoccupied with the chapters 7–9 of Paul's epistle to the Romans. Babcock asserts that his study of and writing on the Pauline epistles resulted in a fundamental shift in Augustine's views on "the interaction between God's grace and man's freedom". While Augustine previously depicted human's moral life as a linear progression toward God from the perception of God as the eternal good, now he has envisaged "a human state in which a person must struggle against a self which is not merely resistant to the will, but is actually beyond his own control".[85]

Without seeing in detail how the notion of grace developed in Augustine, we should point out that there is a close parallel between Augustine's emerging views and Tyconius's notion of "Promises and Law" which he outlined in the LR. Anderson remarked that Tyconius's attempt to reveal "the continuity between the Old and New Testaments and of demonstrating that every part of Scripture is capable of Christological interpretation". Going beyond the distinction between law and promise that he established in Rule 1 and 2 of the LR, Tyconius now maintains the "continuity of purpose and relationship that law and promise have in the two Testaments and how to interpret their function within God's plan of salvation".[86] Babcock argued that Tyconius's assertion that the spiritual children of Abraham are not justified because they fulfil the law but observe the law because they are justified was very

---

82 Anderson asserts that Tyconius's three hermeneutical approaches which profoundly influenced Augustine were his "spiritual interpretation of the millennial reign of Christ, his image of the church as the earthly body of Christ and the portrayal of the conflict between the kingdom of God and the kingdom of the Devil". Anderson (1974), vi. According to Bonner, Augustine drew upon Tyconius's second rule "to resolve the problem of how the church militant, which contains both the elect and the reprobate, can be the kingdom of Christ" while Tyconius's fourth rule helped him "understand the rule of the martyrs with Christ as including the pious dead, who are commemorated at the offering of the Eucharist". See Bonner (1989), 245–46.
83 On why Paul's theology, particularly his ecclesiology, may be avoided before this period of "renewed interest", and how two contrasting traditions of Pauline exegesis — antignostic and gnostic — have emerged from the late first century through the second, and how the gnostics of the second century could claim Paul as their "great pneumatic teacher" if he was so "unequivocally antignostic", see Pagels (1975), 5, 10, 161.
84 Brown (2000), 144, 269; Anderson (1974), 4.
85 Babcock (1979), 56–61.
86 Anderson (1974), 72. In another place, Anderson pointed out that Tyconius established three significant points in terms of hermeneutical principle: that the New Covenant is not a new entity unto itself but a fuller revelation of the Old Covenant; that the law and promise have always had the

close to Augustine's characterization of the law as *minister mortis*.[87] Fredricksen even asserts that Tyconius inspired Augustine to reimagine his "reading of the double canon of Scriptures" that enabled him "to understand Paul's letters in a new way". He encountered Tyconius "when the first flush of the liberation worked through Plotinus and Porphyry was fading", resulting in "a new historical understanding of Paul and of Scripture that led ultimately to the mature masterworks of the *Confessions*, the great commentary *ad litteram* on Genesis, and the *City of God*".[88] Although it will be difficult to determine the precise degree of how Augustine appropriated the third rule of Tyconius, it will be reasonable to assent to TeSelle's remarks that "what Augustine learned with Tyconius's aid had such an impact that it constitutes the major turning-point in his thought", although "the end product was Augustine's own".[89]

This new way of reading Paul also encouraged Augustine to initiate a correspondence with Jerome, who emphasized the necessity of knowing the "original languages" and its context to qualify as an expositor of the Scriptures. Augustine also acknowledged the efficacy of knowing the "original languages" and even referred later to Jerome's translation affirmatively as the work of "an expert in both languages" in the *De doctrina Christiana*.[90] However, he essentially differs with Jerome regarding the veracity of the *Septuagint*, the indispensability of Hebrew and its exegetical implications. Basing upon the hermeneutical key of "double love" that was profoundly drawn from Paul's letters (1 Cor 13:13; 1 Tim 1:5), Augustine suggested "certain rules for interpreting the scriptures" by which those willing to study will be "finding illumination for themselves".[91] This assertion is in line with Babcock's observation that Augustine's awareness of the helplessness of the flesh without grace is "an antidote to the inevitably elitist character of a Christian sensibility set apart from the Christian population at large".[92] Ironically, if the "rules" in *De doctrina Christiana* were Augustine's implicit response to Jerome's insistence on the need for another form of "elite" — learned, professional interpreters of Scripture,[93] Augustine will be obliquely inspired and convinced by Tyconius the Donatist in this respect.

---

same mutual relation and have performed their respective functions throughout both covenants, and that justification of the person of faith was the result of the work of the Holy Spirit. See Anderson (1974), 74.
87 See Babcock (1979), 69, 73–74.
88 Fredriksen (2010), 158; Fredriksen (1999a), 855; Brown also asserts that Augustine "would carefully sift Paul for his true meaning" and he would turn to "Tyconius for the 'better treatments' that would enable him to make up his mind". Tyconius "deflected Augustine's thought into some of its most distinctive channels: for Tyconius also was a drastic interpreter of S. Paul, a man whose thought was dominated by the idea of the Church, who already saw history in terms of the destinies of the 'City of God'". Brown (2000), 146, 268–69.
89 TeSelle (1970), 180–82.
90 do 2.16.34; 4.15.48.
91 do *prol* 1.1 (Green 3); see also do 1.40.86–44.95.
92 Babcock (1982), 1211.
93 See Vessey (1993), 178–79, 190–95; Vessey (1999), 58. Highlighting Vessey's arguments, Williams remarked that "Augustine's encounter with Jerome has been proposed as the source of much of the theory subsequently articulated in *On Christian Teaching* and in the *Confessions*". Williams (2012), 229.

Concluding Remarks

In this chapter, we are mainly focusing upon one important factor that determined the shape of Augustine's *De doctrina Christiana*: the existential reality of the church in North Africa. Christians in Africa still adapted to living in the *tempora christiana*. As they grappled with questions regarding the valid implications of the impending *aduentus* of Christ, the final judgment and of belonging to the body of Christ in the interim period before the imminent *Parousia*, Tyconius's LR gave answers to these concerns from the Scriptures. In his Christo-ecclesiological hermeneutic, Tyconius embraced both the Old and New Testament harmoniously as a continuum under a single divine scheme. Tyconius also interweaved *tempora christiana* and *consummatio saeculi* by applying many apocalyptic scriptural passages immediately to the church's present situation. In other words, if the urgency felt at an impending *Parousia* has been decelerated by the *tempora christiana*, Tyconius's affirmation of Christ's existing presence and reign in the church makes the present situation momentous.

This notion of time that stressed the decisiveness of the present as the point where the past and the future collate is a very crucial insight that Augustine draws from Tyconius. Bright asserts that the primary basis of Augustine's theology of Scripture, which juxtaposed "the Incarnate Word of God with the words of Scripture", is introduced comprehensively in the *De doctrina Christiana* and the *Confessiones*.[94] In the *Confessiones*, the "eminent authority" and "holy humility"[95] of the Scriptures signify the Word made flesh who "has built for himself a humble home from our very dust".[96] Now in the *De doctrina Christiana*, the "theology" of the indwelling (*habitaret*) or "enfleshment" of God to save or heal humanity was conveyed with the exegetical "principle of contrariety" and "similarity". At the present time, the church, as Christ's body and "his bride", has been trained and purged "by means of various disagreeable medicines so that when it has been saved from the world [Christ] may take as his wife for eternity 'the church, which has no spot or wrinkle or any such thing'".[97] Considering the rigorous ecclesiology of the North African Christians, the intrinsic theology that Augustine resorts to in this vital passage with its Pauline imagery resonates the ecclesiological principles that Tyconius developed in his LR.[98]

Although Augustine only incorporated the LR into the *De doctrina Christiana* late in his career, the crucial insights that he had initially drawn from Tyconius still makes it worth acknowledging and recapping the LR for the Bishop Augustine. The LR has therefore left a permanent impression upon Augustine's theology. It has even

---

94 See Bright (2006), 41–44.
95 *auctoritatis emineret ... sanctae humilitatis ...* cf 6.5.8 (CCSL 27.79).
96 *in inferioribus autem aedificauit sibi humilem domum de limo nostro.* cf 7.18.24 (CCSL 27.108; Williams 114).
97 *Exercet autem hoc tempore et purgat medicinalibus quibusdam molestiis, ut erutam de hoc saeculo in aeternum.* do 1.15.33 (CSEL 80.16; Green 27). Cf. do 1.11.23: *Cum ergo ipsa sit patria, uiam se quoque nobis fecit ad patriam* (CSEL 80.14).
98 On how Tyconius's exegetical principle of "the contrariness of signification", which Augustine probably emulates in the "principle" here, challenged the rigorous ecclesiology of the Donatists, see Bright (1995), 25–31.

been asserted that while Augustine helped to define the Donatist controversy, the Donatist controversy also moulded Augustine.[99] Following this line of argument, Tyconius can also be considered as the most constructive of the Donatists that shaped Augustine's thought. Tyconius's influences upon Augustine stretched beyond his arguments with Parmenius and his explicit endorsement of the LR in the *De doctrina Christiana*. Indeed, Tyconius endowed Augustine to read and understand the apostle Paul in a way that opened a whole new vista in his understanding of the nature and authority of Scripture. In Augustine's reading of Paul, the dialectic of the "already" and the "not yet" that traditionally suggested an eschatological connotation was interiorized in the perpetual struggle of the self that is helpless without the grace of God. In the next chapter, we will see how a new understanding of Paul's letters emerged in Augustine which contributed to a long and passionate correspondence with Jerome who claimed to herald a new dawn in Latin Scriptural interpretation.

---

99 Miles (2016), 10. In almost an identical way, Wilken observed: "Christianity became the kind of religion it did, at least in part, because of critics like Celsus, Porphyry, and Julian … They helped Christians clarify what they believed, and without them Christianity would have been intellectually poorer". Wilken (2003), xi.

CHAPTER 5

"Instead of doing what I had asked you, you thought up a new argument"

The Emergence of Paul in the Correspondence between Augustine and Jerome

Augustine (354–430) and Jerome (347–419), the two most eminently remembered Fathers of Latin Christianity, engaged in a correspondence over a period of twenty-five years, sending over 17 letters.[1] In his earliest letter, i.e., ep 28, Augustine implored Jerome to translate the Old Testament from the Septuagint and not directly from the Hebrew. And disagreeing with Jerome's interpretation of Gal 2:11–14, he requested Jerome to explain his position on the points he disputed. Reiterating these points in his second letter, i.e., ep 40, Augustine who did not receive a reply to his first queries from Jerome, also questioned the criteria in compiling the work that Jerome titled *De viris illustribus*. The question of *efficacy* in translating the Old Testament from the Hebrew, the *validity* of the interpretation of Gal 2:11–14 and the *criteria* for determining heresy and orthodoxy formed the core of the ensuing correspondence for the next 10 years[2] before they moved on to other subjects.

This correspondence between Augustine and Jerome reflects how authority was constructed in late antiquity by evoking orthodoxy and rebuking heresy, a "technique" Augustine was aware of and which he employed in some of his arguments.[3] From his responses to the issues that Augustine raised in the correspondence, we can also see the scholarly views and peculiar characteristics of Jerome to a certain extent. Jerome was a great scholar whom Alypius[4] — who met him personally — highly recommended to Augustine for his scholarship. Augustine was hoping for "many benefits and provi-

---

[1] According to White, these extant letters were written between 394–419 and "there are apparently some letters missing to which Jerome and Augustine refer". White (1990), 1, 10, 17. More precisely, Fuhrer asserts, "Twenty-six letters are attested and 18 preserved, half from each of the correspondents". Fuhrer (2012), 281. Altogether, Augustine's extant letters includes 249 letters that he wrote, and 49 letters written to him. There are 9 letters which were relevant to him although they were neither written by nor for him. Eno (1999), 306.

[2] Augustine again brings up the issue of the "authority of the Septuagint" in ep 71 and ep 82, written in 403 and 404/5 respectively while Gal 2:11–14 was discussed in ep 40, written in 397 and ep 82. For the dating of the letters, compare White (1990), 1, 17–18 with Eno (1999), 299–305 who also remarked that one should be cautious since the dating of Augustine's letter is often inaccurate.

[3] On how Augustine increasingly make extensive citations of Greek and Latin fathers in order to prove that his doctrine had ecclesiastical authority and to avoid the charge of innovation in his debates with the Pelagians, see TeSelle (1970), 181. On how avoiding innovation gradually became "the characteristic of good theology" and "opinions whose orthodoxy was recognised" was repeated to "shelter under their authority", see O'Loughlin (1999), 69.

[4] For a brief introduction to Alypius, see Fitzgerald (1999a),16. For his significance in the introduction to the letter, see Ebbeler (2012), 76–78.

sions"⁵ from such an able scholar and even sent his writings to Jerome for an honest assessment of the works.⁶ We can ascertain from ep 28 and ep 40 that Augustine was acquainted with Jerome's translation of the book of Job.⁷ He was also familiar with Jerome's commentary on Galatians and his work titled *De viris illustribus*. As we shall see, the interest that Jerome's works had aroused, and the cautious and diplomatic approach that Augustine exercised in the correspondence, shows how influential and resourceful Jerome was considered to be by Augustine and his colleagues.

The issues that Augustine raised in the first two epistles did not happen in a vacuum. Augustine started writing to Jerome in c. 394, roughly three years after his ordination and three years prior to writing the *Confessiones* and the *De doctrina Christiana*. This was the crucial period when "one literary project after another fell to pieces"⁸ in Augustine's hands except his *Epistolae ad Galatas expositio* (394/5). Although ep 28 was largely prompted by his pastoral concern, Augustine found his voice as a writer by the time he wrote ep 40.⁹ And interestingly, Augustine became more assured in his "reading" of Paul within this ten-year period (394–404) and his replies to Jerome became more and more exhaustive.

Considering the remarkable development of Augustine, what are the new insights that he gained? How much did the new insights that Augustine gained upon the "logic" of Paul's letters determine his stance? How were these new insights revealed in the question regarding "a feigned dispute/white lie" of Gal 2:11-14 in his correspondence with Jerome? In order to see this, we shall firstly look at how Jerome's "preface" of his commentary on Galatians and *De viris illustribus* set the tone for Augustine's arguments and explore the stances Augustine and Jerome had taken in their respective commentary on Paul's epistle to the Galatians. We shall see the development of their arguments in the course of their correspondence. We shall then specifically look for traces of a "new" reading of Paul's letters in Augustine and ask if that insight can throw more light on Augustine's notion of the nature and authority of Scripture.

1. The "Great Prefaces" to the Correspondence

Jerome wrote the commentary on Galatians in 386/7 under the patronage of Marcella and dedicated it to Paula and Eustochium.¹⁰ Even before the actual exegesis, his

---

5   ep 28.1 (White 66).
6   *Sane idem frater aliqua scripta nostra fert secum.* ep 28.6 (CSEL 34.1.113).
7   Augustine probably obtained Jerome's work based upon the Hexaplaric Greek in 494 and greatly admiring it, he wanted to have the rest of the book which Jerome translated from the Septuagint and not the Hebrew.
8   O'Donnell (1992a), xlii.
9   According to O'Donnell, "What freed his pen for the prolific career and the masterworks we know was the writing of the *Confessions* themselves. He discovered at length how to make 'confession' in his special sense come to life through his writing". O'Donnell (1992a), xliv.
10 Cain (2010), 16–18, 55–57. For their significance to Jerome, see Kelly (1975), 91–103; Scheck (2010), 48–49. On how Jerome later attempt to show to a Roman Christian audience that "his controversial Hebrew scholarship was in demand among the spiritual elite", see Cain (2009), 169–96.

"Prefaces" are loaded with meanings. An inquisitive Marcella, whom Jerome met in Rome, is presented as an "un-Pythagoreans" student because she did not "consider correct whatever [Jerome] had said in response" and Jerome's authority "did not prevail with her if it was not supported by reason".[11] Depicting the mourning Marcella who sought Jerome's comfort as a very committed Christian was an "indirect compliment to himself" that highlighted his own "spiritual and exegetical authority in a subtle but powerfully symbolic way".[12]

In writing this commentary, Jerome also claimed to "undertake a work that no Latin writer"[13] before him had attempted and stressed that he cautiously followed the commentaries of Origen and consulted the works of Didymus, the Laodicean [Apollinaris], the ancient heretic Alexander, Eusebius of Emesa and Theodore of Heraclea.[14] He contrasted his approach to the eloquent but incompetent Marius Victorinus who was the first Latin writer to produce a commentary on Galatians while Jerome deliberately failed to acknowledge the work of Ambrosiaster on Galatians. By branding Victorinus as "completely ignorant of the Scriptures" and overlooking Ambrosiaster's work, who were both his predecessors, Jerome claimed to be "the real inaugurator of the Pauline commentary in Latin".[15]

Summarizing the argument of the epistle, Jerome mostly focused on the incident where Paul rebuked Peter. This particular point addressed the request of Paula and Eustochium to clarify the incident and Jerome's explanation was aimed at Porphyry who wrote that the leaders of the churches disagreed among themselves so that the whole Christian teaching was "fabricated".[16] And eager to present himself as a "watchdog of theological orthodoxy", Jerome also alluded to a dozen more heretical sects and teachers in his main exposition.[17]

Interestingly, the commentary, divided in three books, had separate prefaces. In the preface to Book 3, Jerome who "adorned" his work with classical literature, now bemoaned the popularity of eloquent speech and Greek rhetoric among the Christians

---

11 *Commentarii in epistulam ad Galatas prol* 1 (Cain 56).
12 Cain (2010), 17.
13 *Commentarii in epistulam ad Galatas prol* 1 (Cain 56).
14 See Cain (2010), 21–30, 56–57. Cain noted that due to the sheer amount of materials he used in preparing the work, Galatians is the most research-intensive one among Jerome's four Pauline commentary while "the preface to Book 1 could plausibly serve as the general prolegomenon to his entire Pauline corpus". Cain (2011), 92, 101. According to Scheck, "Jerome's is the lengthiest and most learned of the ancient patristic commentaries on Galatians". Scheck (2010), 23. Plumer remarked that Jerome's *Commentarii in epistulam ad Galatas* "extends over some 130 columns in Migne" while it occupies 43 columns in Augustine's, 51 in Victorinus's, 36 in Ambrosiaster's and 19 in Pelagius's. See Plumer (2003), 33.
15 Cain (2010), 33. Jerome depicted his effort as "putting Pauline studies in Latin back on track after Marius Victorinus ... had completely derailed them". Cain (2011), 92. See n. 120 below.
16 *Commentarii in epistulam ad Galatas prol* 1 (Scheck 52). Determined by his "reading public", Jerome's rebuttal of Porphyry was highly significant. Simmons listed thirty-one "names of ancient Christian writers who either wrote works against Porphyry or whose works contain anti-Porphyrian material, beginning with the early fourth century and ending in the sixteenth century", including Augustine. See Simmons (2015), 52–53.
17 See Cain (2010), 42, 59–60.

at the expense of the harsh sounding Hebrew. Jerome alluded that his elegant and charming Latin was ruined by his "tireless study of Hebrew". This "deterioration", prompted by his "extremely advanced knowledge of Hebrew", is essentially "a subtle but potent affirmation of his authority as a Biblical scholar".[18] Still playing upon "the foolishness of the Gospel message", Jerome then suggested that "the Christian church had triumphed over the pagan intellectual past" since Plato and Aristotle were studied by "only a few idle old men" in "a corner".[19]

Regarding the *De viris illustribus* that he wrote in c. 393,[20] Jerome claimed in his preface that this book was a "brief treatment of all those who have published anything memorable on the Holy Scriptures from the time of Christ's passion" down to the present.[21] This work is seen as "Jerome's attempt to fix a canon of Christian literature" and "to write himself into that canon" by which he stood at the zenith of the Christian literary tradition.[22] Jerome ascribed the preparation of *De viris illustribus* to Dexter, the son of a recently deceased bishop of Barcelona, Pacianus.[23] That Dexter urged Jerome to follow the example of Tranquillus[24] can be seen as an acknowledgment of Jerome's ability as well as Jerome's own assertion than he can emulate Cicero "who stood at the pinnacle of Roman eloquence".[25]

Jerome admitted that there may be some writings that were known to others which remained unknown to him "in this corner of the earth".[26] Then specifically naming Celsus, Porphyry and Julian and others who think that "the church has had no philosophers, no orators, no men of learning", Jerome asserted that there are "men who founded, built, and adorned the church". Jerome urged those "ignorant" people to "stop accusing our faith of such rustic simplicity",[27] prior to parading a "bio-bibliographical"[28] catalogue of 135 Christian writers which culminates in him.

---

18 See *Commentarii in epistulam ad Galatas prol* 3 (Scheck 205–07; Cain 203–04).
19 *Uix in angulis otiosi eos senes recolunt. Commentarii in epistulam ad Galatas prol* 3 (PL 26.401; Cain 206–07; Scheck 209); see also Cain (2011), 104.
20 Kelly (1975), 174.
21 *De viris illustribus prol* (Halton 1).
22 Cain (2010), 10.
23 Pacianus and Dexter were both included in Jerome's *De viris illustribus* at chapters 106 and 132 respectively.
24 Suetonius Tranquillus "pursued the anecdotal history of Latin grammarians and rhetoricians from the 'origins' of those professions at Rome down to his own time". Vessey (2015), 30; Jerome would be "the first and only person in antiquity to conceive of the idea of 'following Suetonius' … with or without additional prompting from his friend Dexter". Vessey (2012), 246. In ep 47.3, Jerome states: *scripsi librum de illustribus uiris ab apostolis usque ad nostram aetatem imitatus Tranquillum Graecumque Apollonium* (CSEL 54.346).
25 *De viris illustribus prol* (Halton 1). Cicero, in his *Brutus* "provided more or less chronological lists or 'canons' of authors worthy of imitation, down to [his] own generation or the one before". Vessey (2015), 29.
26 *in hoc terrarum Angulo. De viris illustribus prol* (Ceresa-Gastaldo 56; Halton 2).
27 Halton (1999), 2. Jerome writes: *et desinant fidem nostram rusticae tantum simplicitatis arguere, suamque potius imperitiam agnoscant. De viris illustribus prol* (Ceresa-Gastaldo 58).
28 Vessey (2015), 30.

Right from the prefaces, therefore, we can see how Jerome affirms his intellectual and spiritual authority and validates it with appropriate cases. These can serve to promote his agenda to his influential patrons and readers in Rome, especially since Jerome's new translation project was a "radical" move.[29] Raspanti even asserts that one likely reason that Jerome commented on Galatians was to defend his translation agenda.[30] Indeed, Galatians provided a good opportunity to correct the Old Latin version against the Greek and highlight the advantage of reading the original text. In the commentary itself, he made a number of "a more accurate translation from the Greek"[31] and corrected faulty translation in the Latin texts.[32] Jerome also stressed that every time "the apostles" quote from the Old Testament, he will go back "to the sources of these quotations" and examine them "in their original context", thereby suggesting his expertise over Victorinus who could not read Hebrew.[33]

Jerome's prefaces also set the stage for asserting his orthodoxy, particularly in invoking the name of Porphyry as the nemesis for Christians and refuting his disputation. Ironically, he preferred to consult the "ancient heretic Alexander" for his commentary over Victorinus who is not "able to discuss competently what he does not know".[34] As Cain remarked, this can stress how Jerome's commentary "emerged from a devotional context" against Victorinus's "empty exercise in ivory-tower pedantry that is out of touch with the practical spiritual needs of the common Christian".[35] And it is also notable that in many of his writings, Jerome equates "corner" with those who are in the periphery or whose influence diminishes, thereby making an implicit reference to his relegation after his "fall from grace" in the power struggle within the church.[36]

Hence, Jerome's motives in these prefaces can explain his hostile reaction to Augustine's "criticism" of his works. If Jerome dedicated the commentary on Galatians to his patrons with the hope of gaining their support for his translation project and

---

29 Kamesar (2013), 663. Jerome was not popular among "conservative readers" who branded him "a sacrilegious forger" when they see an unfamiliar taste in his revisions. Kelly (1975), 87. See HI ep 27.1 for his own account. On why a "spiritual advisee" from Rome is very significant for Jerome, see Cain (2011), 102–04.
30 Raspanti (2009), 171.
31 *Commentarii in epistulam ad Galatas* 1.1 (Cain 85).
32 For a list of correction that Jerome made, see Cain (2010), 39.
33 *Commentarii in epistulam ad Galatas* 2.3 (Cain 135); Cain (2011), 98–101, 104.
34 *Commentarii in epistulam ad Galatas prol* 1 (Cain 56–57); on what "heresy" and "orthodoxy" connotes in the early church, see Cain (2010), 41–43. On his "criteria" in *De viris illustribus*, Rebenich noted: "Jerome did not hesitate to canonize his understanding of orthodox staunchness, ascetic championship, and literary brilliance. So, Diodore of Tarsus is criticized for his ignorance of secular literature, … while Lucifer of Cagliari is praised for his theological constancy and his willingness to meet martyrdom … Jerome's personal preferences and his hostility are apparent. He either omitted or chastised contemporaries he disliked". Rebenich (2002), 48.
35 Cain (2011), 104.
36 Cain asserted that "while the Roman church was responsible for prosecuting him, the case against Jerome was actually instigated by members of Paula's immediate family unsympathetic with her ascetic piety and upset over her close association with Jerome, whom they saw as a meddler in their domestic affairs". Cain (2009), 10.

to amend his tarnished public image in Rome where he was marginalized, asking Jerome to correct his stance — to "sing a palinode"[37] — would amount to a challenge of his scholarship and questioning of his credibility and discrediting his venture. In fact, in his reply to Augustine's letters, the same assertions that Jerome made in his prefaces resonated. What is the "criticism" that Augustine levelled against him? What does Jerome's reaction tell us about his disposition?

2. Jerome and the Notions of Authority in the Correspondence

Jerome's portrayal of Marcella's attitude to authority resembled Augustine's own tryst with authority in the *Confessiones* until he finally posits that faith and trust in authority will lead him to understanding. While Augustine saw humility as the requisite to approach Truth in Scripture, Jerome seems to recommend scholarship and reason.[38] This difference in approach seems to underlie Augustine's contention that Jerome's interpretation of Gal 2:11–4, where Paul pretended to rebuke Peter "for committing a dangerous act of deceit",[39] was dubious.

According to Jerome, assuming that Paul truly opposed Peter for withdrawing "himself a little from association with the Gentiles" will be a contradiction and hypocrisy since Paul "is convicted of having done the very same thing". Among the things done by Paul "that very openly derive from the ceremonies of the Jews" were shaving of his head in Cenchrea, making an offering in Jerusalem, having Timothy circumcised and taking part in a bare-footed procession.[40] Jerome suggested that "unless it be the case that Peter was pleased to be convicted like this", Paul would not dare "convict the greatest of the apostles, so impudently and so persistently". Drawing from his own experience of arguing in fictitious lawsuits, he deducted that Paul's rebuke of Peter will be "a feigned dispute" which was meant to "bring peace to the believers and bring the faith of the church into harmony by means of a holy quarrel between them".[41] According to Jerome, if one deems either that Peter had gone astray or that Paul had rudely rebuked him, "they give Porphyry an opportunity to blaspheme".[42]

But Augustine believed that Peter was really rebuked, not simply for observing the Jewish custom but for wanting to "impose" the custom and "force the Gentiles

---

37 ep 40.7 (White 80).
38 In his preface, Jerome wrote: *Neque uero more Pythagorico quidquid responderam, rectum putabat: nec sine ratione praejudicata apud eam ualebat auctoritas. Commentarii in epistulam ad Galatas prol* 1 (PL 26.307). It is interesting to compare this with Augustine's preface to *De doctrina Christiana*: *Immo uero et quod per hominem discendum est, sine superbia discat, et per quem docetur alius, sine superbia et sine inuidia tradat quod accepit. do prol* 5.11 (CSEL 80.5).
39 ep 28.3 (White 67).
40 *Commentarii in epistulam ad Galatas* 1.2 (Scheck 97–98).
41 *Commentarii in epistulam ad Galatas* 1.2 (Scheck 100).
42 *Commentarii in epistulam ad Galatas* 1.2 (Scheck 101).

to live like Jews". Paul's observation of certain Jewish customs that "were regarded as the accepted practices in all circumstances ... does not mean that he had fallen into hypocrisy". Moreover, "[T]his incident serves as a great example of humility, which is the most valuable Christian training, for by humility love is preserved [while] nothing violates love more quickly than pride".[43] Insisting that Paul writes the truth, Augustine therefore considered Jerome's interpretation as a "defence" and "recommendation" of lying that can shake one's "confidence in the authority of the Holy Scriptures" and requested him to consider his interpretation more carefully.[44] Later, we will see more of Augustine's argument on this particular passage which also became more elaborate in the course of the correspondence.

The preface to the *De viris illustribus* seems to be even more crucial when Augustine questioned the criteria that Jerome employed in compiling it: Is it proper, as he was told, to title the book an epitaph? Then, why did Jerome mention the works of many people who were alive? In what ways are the heretics, particularly Origen, unreliable and departing from the true faith? And while Augustine acknowledged that Jerome included those whom he could remember, he still questioned why some people are omitted. This amounted to asking how Jerome could really not know them. With these points, Augustine questioned the principle on which Jerome compiled his *De viris illustribus* and requested him to consider and include these points as that would make the book more helpful for "people whose other duties allow them no spare time or who are unable to read ... a foreign language".[45]

In defending these works, we can see Jerome's peculiar characteristics, and his understanding of, and attitude to, authority. Jerome often received "consulting" letters from "eager" disciples and in replying, he "comes through ... as a magisterial figure perfectly comfortable with dispensing advice about the spiritual life and the Bible". But in the way Augustine initiated the correspondence, he "was asking to be treated as a scholarly equal by one who was far more accomplished".[46] In knowing about, and receiving Augustine's letters, Jerome was offended and referred to them as an attack, a challenge, a provocation, and a criticism.[47] Jerome also accused Augustine of seeking "fame for oneself by attacking illustrious men", desiring "praise and fame and popularity", seeking "to increase your reputation at my expense", and as someone who was "showing off" his learning but whose "statements" Jerome deemed "to be heretical".[48]

Beside Augustine's bold approach in initiating the correspondence, another crucial backdrop to Jerome's initial hostility was that Augustine's letter, which Jerome

---

43 Gal 15 (Plumer 143–45); for a brief summary of the Greek and Latin tradition of interpreting Gal 2:11–14, see Cooper (2005), 203–12.
44 ep 28.3–5 (White 67–69); ep 40.4–7 (White 77–80). See n. 84 and 97 below.
45 ep 40.2; 40.9 (White 75–76, 80–81). For the significance of Jerome's omission of certain writers, see Cain (2010), 33.
46 Cain (2009), 210; Ebbeler (2012), 78–79.
47 HI epp 102.2; 105.3; 112.1 (White 87–88, 96–98, 112).
48 HI epp 102.2; 105.2; 105.5 (White 87, 95, 98). Thus, Cain classified Jerome's epp 102 and 105 as "threatening" letters. See Cain (2009), 207–19 for a classification of Jerome's letters.

labelled as "the honey-coated sword", did not reach Jerome but was in circulation at Rome. Jerome suspected that this letter was directed against him.⁴⁹ Around the same time, Jerome was in a bitter dispute with Rufinus who translated Origen's *Peri Archon*. Rufinus asserts that heretics tampered with Origen's texts and that where Origen seemed to hold incompatible beliefs, only the "orthodox" alternative was to be attributed to him. Rufinus, who was also critical of Jerome's scriptural translation, points out how Jerome's work had suffered the same fate and how Jerome also relies much on Origen and how he follows Jerome's lead. Jerome, who praised Origen so highly before and aspired to be the Latin Origen, reversed his stance and considered Origen an apparent heretic which resulted in a bitter exchange of allegations with Rufinus.⁵⁰ Jerome sent Augustine a copy of his brief and partial reply to Rufinus as a foretaste of what was to come if Augustine rattled him. This dispute seems to determine Jerome's perception of Augustine's letter as a criticism on his works.⁵¹

In response, Jerome highlighted his arduous effort, saying that he "have spent the whole time from my earliest youth until now sweating over my work", reading many relevant books and "mentally absorbed many things".⁵² Although Augustine insisted that they were both striving for the same thing, Jerome vividly stressed their difference in fortune, stature, orthodoxy and knowledge. Jerome portrayed himself as an old man living in rural seclusion of his little monastery in contrast to a young Augustine who was "a son in years but a father in merit", "firmly established at the summit of episcopal dignity".⁵³ In defending his interpretation of Gal 2:11–14, Jerome insisted that he was in the company of Origen and John Chrysostom while Augustine, in his fear of Porphyry's blasphemies, was actually reintroducing the wicked heresies of Cerenthius and of the Ebionites into the Church.⁵⁴ While Augustine, "the most famous bishop in the whole world" tried to convince his fellow-bishops of the view that converts from Judaism still need to keep the law after the coming of Christ, Jerome and his "fellow sinners in this little hut of mine" renounce such a view.⁵⁵

In retaliating to his "perceived" opponents and the "others" — in the correspondence and other works related to it — Jerome often infers that they were not

---

49 See HI epp 102.1; 105.1–4 (White 86, 95–97). For Augustine's explanation, see his epp 71.2 and 82.1.
50 Jerome was eager, and even consider it an honour, to be associated with Origen's name. In his preface to the *Quaestiones Hebraicae in Genesim* that he wrote c. 391, Jerome even stated that "Adamantius, whose name ... is more hateful than my name ... because in his sermons which he delivers to the common folk he follows the common edition ... but in his books ... he is overcome by the Hebrew truth ... I should wish, along with hatred of his name, also to have knowledge of the Scriptures". See Hayward, 29–30. For an introduction to Rufinus and his relationship with Jerome and on how "their friendship became a casualty of theological politics", see Cain (2010), 11–12; Vessey (2004), 322–26; Kelly (1975), 227–58; Clark (1992), 159–93.
51 See HI epp 102.2 (White 86–87). For Augustine's reaction, see ep 73.
52 HI epp 105.4; 112.4 (White 97, 115); Jerome also stressed that he read the writing of his predecessors.
53 *aetate fili, dignitate parens; in pontificali culmine constitutus*. HI epp 105.5; 112.22 (CSEL 55.246; 55.393; White 99, 137). On how Jerome was the victim of episcopal elitism, see Cain (2009), 143–44.
54 HI ep 112.6; 112.13; 112.16 (White 117, 125–26, 130). For a brief introduction to Cerenthius and the Ebionites, see Myllykoski (2005), 213–46 and Häkkinen (2005), 247–78.
55 HI ep 112.5; 112.8 (White 117, 120).

competent for the "task". We have pointed out that Jerome considered Victorinus, who was "engrossed in secular learning" and "completely ignorant of the Scriptures", not competent to discuss the Scriptures.[56] Similarly, Jerome's insistence upon the "consistency" of the act of Peter and Paul was to refute Porphyry who calumniated untold number of scriptural passages "because he did not understand them".[57] And in his reply to Augustine's query why his later translations of the Old Testament omitted asterisks and commas that were used in his earlier translations, Jerome remarked that Augustine did not "appear to understand" what he asked and expressed his "amazement" that Augustine was "not reading the Septuagint in the original form".[58]

Perhaps, this resonated Augustine's statement that "attempting to reach an understanding of the Holy Scripture" demands "a high regard for the sanctity and truth of the sacred writings" and one "should pass over what he does not understand" without attaching "more value to his own ideas than to the truth".[59] As we had already seen in the previous chapters, Augustine seems to suggest that the authority of reason must give way to the authority of tradition and the authority of Scripture. But, in stressing the significance of reading the "original form" even to be "a true admirer of the Septuagint", Jerome "ridiculed" Augustine and his naïve reverence of the LXX. Indirectly, Augustine was counted among those "commentators" who hold "little streams of opinion" while Jerome "rush[es] back to the very source from which the Gospel writers drew" and reached back to "the Hebrew words themselves". A reliable text with which to work was needed before one can properly comment on the Scriptures. So, regardless of their learning and their position in the church, these commentators "were rank amateurs in the field of Biblical exegesis because they were ignorant of Hebrew" while his expertise in Greek and Hebrew established "his credibility as a Biblical scholar".[60] Ultimately, this knowledge is Jerome's credential even against "all those translators" of the Septuagint which Augustine "accorded preeminent authority in this field". After all, Jerome attempted "to publish the evidence which had been overlooked or corrupted by the Jews, so that Latin-speakers might know what was really in the Hebrew text".[61]

Jerome's self-depiction in his initial response, therefore, was of a zealous veteran who ran the course to the best of his ability and deserved "some rest".[62] Since Augustine, his antithesis, did not approach him as an "eager disciple that Jerome had come to expect from an otherwise unknown correspondent",[63] Jerome stressed that he was far

---

56 *Commentarii in epistulam ad Galatas prol* 1 (Cain 56–57).
57 *Commentarii in epistulam ad Galatas* 1.2 (Cain 109).
58 HI ep 112.19 (White 133).
59 ep 28.4 (White 68, 69).
60 See HI ep 20.2; Cain (2010), 36–37, 40.
61 ep 28.2 (White 66); HI ep 112.20 (White 135).
62 HI ep 102.2 (White 87); see also HI epp 105.3; 112.22. On "Jerome's sophisticated use of literary artistry to construct spiritual and intellectual authority for himself through idealized epistolary self-presentation", see Cain (2009).
63 Ebbeler (2012), 79.

more profound and accomplished than the "criticism" that Augustine pointed out.[64] As a grand master in the field of Scripture, Jerome was not interested to engage with a "novice" he suspected to have ulterior motives. In fact, Jerome advised Augustine to teach his people and "fill the Roman storerooms with the fruits of Africa" while he was "satisfied to whisper to one poor listener or reader in some little corner of my monastery".[65]

From Jerome's reply, we can clearly see how authority was constructed in late antiquity through episcopal and ascetic zeal for orthodoxy and in reproaching heresy. In chapter one, we have pointed out that interpreters of scriptural texts also became "an authority". Now, we can sense a tension rising between someone like Jerome whose expertise and innovation was "an authority" against someone like Augustine whose ecclesiastical office amounted to being "in authority".[66] Although Augustine expressed his "great desire to be fully acquainted" with Jerome, this background tension guided Jerome's assumption of Augustine to a great extent. In other words, Jerome was more concerned with what to know, how to know and who should know that he made a completely wrong presumption on why Augustine really wanted to know.

Augustine was dismayed by Jerome's resentment towards him and remarked that he was "injured", "beaten and harassed" by Jerome's scathing and bitter reply. He bemoaned that Jerome "jumped to the conclusion that I was that kind of person" and "had rashly formed an estimate" of him.[67] How much of Jerome's *rash estimation* on Augustine's nature reflected his own character and high ambition — particularly as someone who once aspired to succeed Pope Damasus[68] — we can only assume.

This does not mean that Jerome's innovative approaches, and vigorous effort and exceptional contribution, to Biblical scholarship was not commendable. Cain observed that Jerome made many "otherwise mostly lost antiquarian" Greek exegetic material more accessible to Latin Christians, and adapted their "form and substance" to an entirely new cultural and linguistic environment.[69] Kamesar also remarked that Jerome's "achievements as editor, translator and scholar are perhaps unparalleled in Antiquity".[70] And as we have pointed out in chapter two, "the history of the Latin Bible would have remained that of an infinitely revised version of the Greek Bible" without Jerome's insistence on the *Hebraica veritas*.[71]

---

64 Before putting forward "evidences" from Scripture to support his explanation, Jerome played down Augustine's "criticism" by remarking: "All this on the question of the interpretation of one chapter of the Epistle to the Galatians". HI ep 112.6 (White 117–18).
65 HI ep 112.22 (White 137–38).
66 See chapter one, section 1 above for the difference between "an authority" and "in authority".
67 ep 73.1–2; 73.9 (White 100–01, 107–08).
68 Although Jerome was eager to depict himself as "the primary latter-day bearer of the patristic torch" in his *De viris illustribus*, Cain remarked that "the thorniness of his profile forever impeded his ambitions". Cain (2009), 3. For Jerome's rise and fall in Rome and his "quest" for the Papacy, see Kelly (1975), 80–115.
69 Cain (2011), 108–10.
70 Kamesar (2013), 674.
71 Bogaert (2013), 514.

3. Augustine and the Notion of Scriptural Authority in the Correspondence

Despite Jerome's initial hostility and aloofness, Augustine continued to engage him until the tone of the dialogue became more mellow and open. Jerome's irritable character evident in the correspondence thus only confirms that Jerome was such a sublime biblical scholar and an indispensable authority for his day that even his angry and sarcastic response could not deter Augustine from tactfully approaching him again. This merits the questions, what did Bishop Augustine ultimately hope to achieve through the initially tempestuous dialogue with the scholar Jerome? Why did Augustine want to know what he wants to know? How much does this "motif" set the tone of the issues raised as well as the ensuing dialogue? We will go back to Augustine's commentary of the epistle to the Galatians and follow the development of his arguments and its logical implication in the correspondence to answer these questions.

In the preface to his commentary, Augustine outlines the reason why Paul writes the epistle to the Galatians. Although God's grace freed the Gentile Christians from the law, some people claimed that they have to circumcise and observe some Jewish custom to benefit from the gospel. This claim confounded the Galatians and they had suspected Paul as not holding the teaching of the other apostles, who were persuading Gentiles to live like Jews. Even Peter had yielded to such people to avoid offending them and had been led into hypocrisy, as if he also believed that only fulfilling the burdens of the law will benefit the Gentiles of the gospel. Augustine asserts that Paul calls Peter back from this hypocrisy,[72] thereby resonating Marius Victorinus's position that "the very thing reprimanded in Peter by Paul was what the congregation reprimanded as well. From there it follows that the Galatians too are sinning".[73]

However, in expounding this particular passage in the course of the correspondence, Augustine became more and more exhaustive, which shows the significance he attached to it. In the commentary itself, Augustine had taken for granted that Peter was wrong to force the Gentiles to live like Jews.[74] Then going beyond Marius Victorinus who accepted some form of pretense but not a collusion between Peter and Paul,[75] Augustine stressed Paul's "genuine" rebuke and Peter's humbleness in

---

72 Plumer (2003), 125.
73 Cooper (2005), 278.
74 *Non enim ait: si tu, cum Iudaeus sis, gentiliter et non Iudaice uiuis, quemadmodum rursus ad consuetudinem Iudaeorum reuerteris? sed quemadmodum, inquit, gentes cogis iudaizare?* Gal 15 (CSEL 84.70).
75 Victorinus hold that "because Peter also put on a pretence, he none the less sinned in so doing. ... Paul shows that he also understood Peter to have gone along with the Jews only by way of a pretence, but that he was none the less sinning". Cooper (2005), 278. According to Plumer, "While Victorinus in his exegesis of Gal 2:11–14 speaks repeatedly and emphatically of Peter's 'sin' (*peccatum*), Augustine does not use the word 'sin' but speaks only of Peter's 'error' (*error*). ... [But] unlike Jerome, [Augustine] does not try to avoid the strong term 'hypocrisy' (*simulatio*) that Paul uses for Peter's action (Gal 2:13) but rather highlights it by using it twice in the *Preface* to his Commentary ... So, while Augustine does not judge Peter's action as severely as Victorinus does, he does not trivialize it either". Plumer (2003), 145.

accepting his "error" which was not just "signs of spiritual realities" but "the spiritual realities themselves".⁷⁶ Peter's humility in accepting the rebuke — a "new and unexpected visible" occurrence — can arouse those present around them "to seek a faith in things invisible".⁷⁷ As we shall see later, the movement from *signa* to *res* has sacramental significance in Augustine's scriptural exposition.

Beside this significant insight, one key term which determined Jerome and Augustine's reading of Galatians was the word *simulatio* (Gk. ὑποκρίσει). Although Augustine does not pay exegetical attention to the term *simulatio* in his main commentary, which he already used twice (*simulatione, simulationem*) in the preface, his arguments largely hang on the signification of *simulatio* in the ensuing correspondence.⁷⁸ Augustine used the noun *simulatione* once in ep 28, and twice each in ep 40 and ep 82, while he used the noun *simulationem* five times in ep 82 and the verb *simulate* ten times in ep 82. In his reply to Augustine, Jerome used the words *simulatione* three times and the words *simulationem* four times in ep 112. Crucially, Augustine contrasted "mercy and compassion" with "deceit and pretence" (*compassione misericordi, non simulatione fallaci*) in ep 40.4. Then, in ep 82, he contrasted "pretention" and "hypocrisy" with "sincerity" and "reverence" (*non uere sed simulate ab apostolis obseruatas esse credamus* [82.13], *nec simulate sed religiose* [82.14]), and paired "pretence and deceit" (*simulate ac fallaciter* [82.16]) again. As Plumer observed, Augustine understood *simulatio* "in a very unfavourable sense" while Jerome "interprets Peter's *simulatio* in a favourable sense, noting that 'even our Lord himself ... assumed the likeness (*simulatio*) of sinful flesh'".⁷⁹

Regardless of this basic difference, a common preoccupation determined their arguments. In their exposition of the epistle to the Galatians, Augustine and Jerome attempt to "safeguard the truth"⁸⁰ against those who revile the Scriptures. We had mentioned that Jerome targeted a number of heretics in his *commentary*. Porphyry, who writes against the Christians and their Scriptures, was the immediate target of Jerome in his exposition of Galatians 2:11–14, whereas he was a secondary concern for Augustine. Cole-Turner even asserts that his concern for the validity of his anti-heretical arguments, initially against the Manicheans and later the Pelagians, give Augustine a "sense of urgency in discussing Galatians 2 with Jerome".⁸¹ While Augustine engaged with specific teachings that he encountered as a young man and then as a bishop, Jerome approached the issue as a "freelance" scholar at the behest of his patrons.

---

76 *Illa enim signa sunt rerum spiritualium, mitem autem esse et humilem caritatis conseruatorem res ipsae spirituals sunt.* Gal 15 (CSEL 84.71; Plumer 145).

77 *ad quas per illa ducuntur, qui oculis corporis dediti fidem inuisibilium, quia iam de usitatisque non possunt, de nouis et repentinis uisibilibus quaerunt.* Gal 15 (CSEL 84.71; Plumer 145–47).

78 Cooper (2005), 209.

79 Plumer (2003), 125. Scheck translated this passage as "even our Lord himself ... adopted the pretence of sinful flesh" while Cain translated the passage as "our Lord himself ... pretended to take on sinful flesh". See Scheck (2010), 99; cf. Cain (2010), 107. Jerome's interpretation justify pretension out of a sense of duty.

80 See ep 28.4 (White 68).

81 Cole-Turner also observed that "until 399, Augustine's primary concern was with the Manichees" while the Donatists become the main target since 400. See Cole-Turner (1980), 156–57.

This determines the tone and the shape of Augustine's argument. Augustine vowed to "use whatever strength the Lord grants me" to defend his argument and wanted a more definitive statement from Jerome on the issue he raised. But Jerome, who was engaging in a more general discourse, said that he just "expressed the ideas" of the Greek authors he read and "leave[s] it to the reader to decide" for themselves whether to approve these things or not.[82]

Displaying these preoccupations in their exposition beside the Greek and Latin exegetical traditions they inherited, Jerome attempted to refute Porphyry's charge of inconsistency by insisting that Peter and Paul agree to "feign a quarrel ... by means of a holy dispute": they had agreed in advance "to stage a public confrontation for the benefit of the Gentile and Jewish believers".[83] But Augustine argued that Paul really rebuked Peter so that Jerome's reading would amount to Paul deceiving and lying to his audiences: "Once we admit even a useful lie in that supreme authority ... at no point in the sacred books will the authority of pure truth stand firm".[84] In other words, Jerome attempts to uphold the authority of Scripture from abuse by stressing the consistency of the characters while Augustine attempts to uphold the authority of Scripture from abuse by insisting upon the truthfulness of the content.

4. From *Signa* to *Res* in the "New Argument"

In the course of the correspondence, Augustine attempted to corroborate the truthfulness of the content of Scripture by insisting that the accuracy of Paul's account does not contradict the gospel of freedom and that Paul was not hypocritical in observing some Jewish customs himself. As he supported his arguments with a long treatment of its historical background, Jerome asserted that Augustine "thought up a new argument"

---

82 ep 28.5; HI ep 112.4; 112.13 (White 69, 116, 126). Riches remarked that Origen, Chrysostom and Jerome "developed a highly strained apologetic which ... was based principally on the belief that the apostles were all to some greater or lesser extent engaged in a stratagem which was designed to encourage Jewish Christians". Riches (2013), 107. For Jerome's view on the purpose of a commentary and why he "report the views of many exegetes", and the criticism that he provided "erudition but not insight", see also Kamesar (2013), 673.

83 *Commentarii in epistulam ad Galatas* 1.2 (Cain 105, 108). "If one believes either that Peter had gone astray or that Paul had impudently rebuked the chief of the apostles", Jerome argues, "they give Porphyry an opportunity to blaspheme". See Scheck (2010), 101.

84 ep 28.3–4 (White 67–68). In men 3.3 that he wrote in 395, Augustine state, *quapropter ille mentitur, qui aliud habet in animo et aliud uerbis uel quibuslibet significationibus enuntiat*. In men 21.43, he commented on Gal 2:14 and said, *cum enim uolunt Petrum ab errore atque ab illa, in quam inciderat, uiae prauitate defendere, ipsam religionis uiam, in qua salus est omnibus, confracta et comminuta scripturarum auctoritate conantur euertere. in quo non uident non solum mendacii crimen, sed etiam periurii se obicere apostolo in ipsa doctrina pietatis, hoc est in epistula, in qua praedicat euangelium* (CSEL 41.415; 41.465). According to Boniface, "Augustine's theology of lying is typical of his moral theology in general, in that it operates *sub specie aeternitatis* rather than from the perspective of human temporality; this meant, in effect, that the human sufferings which might be entailed in telling the truth had to be weighed against eternal values of immeasurably greater consequence, and that, thus, human suffering would always have to be borne for the sake of truth". Boniface (1999), 557.

beyond the scope that he set in his commentary.⁸⁵ This "new argument" refers to Augustine's assertion that "Paul had abandoned only what was bad". Specifically, Paul abandoned whatever the Jews observed in order to establish their own righteousness, and those they regarded as necessary for salvation, and those which resulted in the persecution of the Christian preacher of grace. Paul observed some of the Jewish law that are kept in the traditional way without counting them essential for salvation. Therefore, Paul was neither disrespectful to Peter nor hypocritical.⁸⁶

But Jerome considers Augustine's "new argument" as contradictory as it supposedly implies that "the Gentiles who had believed in Christ were free from the burden of the law" while "all who have been converted from Judaism have a duty to keep the law". Elaborating why he insisted that Paul did not really rebuke Peter nor fought like children as Porphyry maintained, Jerome asserted that he just followed the exposition of the Greek authors like Origen and John Chrysostom and admitted that he was willing "to err in the company of such men".⁸⁷ Jerome also "put forward some pieces of evidences from Scripture", mainly from the Acts of the Apostles and insisted that the incidence was "a matter of honest diplomacy".⁸⁸ Jerome considered Augustine's position as a relapse into the heresies of Cerenthius and of the Ebionites since he allegedly propounded that the Jewish believers were right to observe the commandments of the law even after the gospel of Christ.⁸⁹ He then contrasted this "grace of the law" with "the grace of the gospel which is everlasting, and instead of the shadows and types of the Old Testament, truth has come through Jesus Christ". For Jerome, observing "the rituals of the law cannot be neither good nor bad — it must be either one or the other".⁹⁰

In reply, Augustine discerned his respect of the Scriptures from the writings of other scholars. While he "firmly believe that none of the authors" on these books in the Scriptures "has erred in writing", and ascribed any fault in them "which appears to conflict with the truth" either as textual error, wrong translation or lack of proper understanding of the meaning, he did not consider other authors to be free from all error "however holy and learned they may be". Augustine did not consider their writings as true unless their arguments persuaded him that it was based upon the Scriptures or that it was "not at odds with the truth".⁹¹ Williams asserts that Augustine's

---

85 In his commentary, Jerome write, "But if this interpretation displeases anyone, whereby neither Peter sinned nor is Paul shown to be impudent in having accused his superior, he should explain what the consequences are of Paul's reproving in another what he himself has done". Scheck (2010), 102. Replying to Augustine and quoting the above statement, Jerome said, "If then you considered anything in my explanation worthy of criticism, it was up to your learning to find out whether what I had written was to be found in the writings of the Greeks, so that if they had not said them, then you could justifiably condemn my opinion … Instead of doing what I had asked, you thought up a new argument". HI ep 112.4–5 (White 116).
86 ep 40.4–6 (White 77–79).
87 HI ep 112.5–6 (White 116–17).
88 HI ep 112.6–11 (White 117–24).
89 HI ep 112.13 (White 125).
90 HI ep 112.14–16 (White 127–30).
91 ep 82.3 (White 146).

actual concern in his reply to Jerome is to challenge the "very principle of argument from (scholarly) authority ... The point is that authorities can always be wrong, with the sole exception of Scripture, and that all Jerome's learned citations are therefore irrelevant to the real debate".[92] And Augustine may even make an implicit "swipe" at Jerome's *De Viris illustribus* when he suggests that Jerome's "pious humility" and "true opinion" of himself would not allow him to claim his "books (*libros*) to be read as if they had been written by prophets and apostles".[93]

Augustine then asserted his case that Paul wrote only the truth and argued that if Paul was lying to "his sons" — the Galatians — by "some kind of prudent dissimulation", he cannot be certain that Paul "is not deceiving me in what he writes or what he says".[94] Drawing examples from other scriptural passages, Augustine elaborated his argument to uphold the truthfulness of the content of Scripture over the consistency of the characters therein: what matters for him was what Paul wrote and not what Paul did.[95] Peter acted deceitfully, he argued, when Peter forced the Gentiles to live like the Jews since "the apostles had already decided in Jerusalem itself that no one should force the Gentiles to live like the Jews".[96]

At this point, Augustine reiterated the stance he had made in ep 28: Accepting that there is a useful lie in the Scriptures even once undermines the whole integrity of the Scriptures,[97] particularly against those "misguided men" like the Manicheans who condemned marriage, which is what Paul foretold about them.[98] Conceding that the apostles themselves wrote lies will amount to negating the prophetic value of the Scriptures. It will ultimately give the Manicheans a great opportunity to claim that there are indeed false passages in the Scriptures. Since the Manicheans rejected the Acts of the Apostles, it is significant that both Augustine and Jerome comprehensively based their arguments on the events recorded therein.[99]

Interestingly, we also see Augustine substantiating his concept of the authority of Scripture in relation to time. For Augustine, God's decisive act of redemption in the realm of time has been recorded in Scripture so that falsification of these accounts would amount to shaking the foundation of scriptural authority. And he believes that grasping the essence of this "redemptive time" is key to overcoming seemingly contradictory passages in Scripture. We have already seen how Jerome, who insists that Paul also acted as a Jew among fellow Jews and "did some things that were contrary to

---

92 Williams (2012), 230.
93 Augustine asserted: *prorsus, inquam, non te arbitror sic legi tuos libros uelle tamquam prophetarum uel apostolorum, de quorum scriptis, quod omni errore careant, dubitare nefarium est. absit hoc a pia humilitate et ueraci de temet ipso cogitatione.* ep 82.3 (CSEL 34.2.354; White 146).
94 ep 82.4 (White 147).
95 *non nunc quaero, quid fecerit; quid scripserit.* ep 82.7 (CSEL 34.2.356; White 148).
96 ep 82.10 (White 151–52).
97 *Admisso enim semel in tantum auctoritatis fastigium officioso aliquo mendacio, nulla illorum librorum particula remanebit, quae non, ut cuique uidebitur uel ad mores difficilis uel ad fidem incredibilis, eadem perniciosissima regula ad mentientis auctoris consilium officiumque referatur.* ep 28.3 (CSEL 34.1.108); see also n. 84 above.
98 epp 28.4; 82.6 (White 67–68, 148).
99 See ep 82.9–11; HI ep 112.7–10.

evangelical freedom in order to avoid scandalizing the Jews", supported his arguments from other scriptural passages.[100] For Jerome, the grace of the law is a tentative, temporary phase.[101] But against Jerome's inference that "the rituals of the law cannot be neither good nor bad", Augustine maintains that these rituals were neither to be imposed on the Gentiles nor to be detested and condemned or to be rejected as detestable and idolatrous.[102] Being "the sacraments" which signified Christian salvation,[103] the law of Moses was the shadow of things to come, while the grace of Christ which justifies the believers was "formerly in the future but now present and at hand".[104]

For Augustine, then, law and gospel are neither alternatives nor opposites but "stand together as two historically specific modes of a single divine initiative of redemption".[105] Paul, who lived at "the time of Christ's physical presence and during the apostolic period", was in that special transition period before "all that activity of shadows would disappear".[106] In this way, he asserted that Paul "really did observe those ancient customs when obliged" while also insistently urging that "it was not by means of them but by the grace of faith revealed that the faithful will be saved".[107] Here, we can see how the dialectic of the "already" and the "not yet" which preoccupied the early church was still very much an interpretative conundrum during the time of

---

100 *Commentarii in epistulam ad Galatas* 1.2 (Cain 106–07); On how Jerome supported his arguments from other scriptural passages, see HI ep 112.7–14.
101 Basing upon Lk 16:16, Jn 5:18 and Jn 1:16–17, Jerome argued: *pro legis gratia, quae praeteriit, gratiam euangelii accepimus permanentem et pro umbris et imaginibus ueteris instrumenti ueritas per Iesum Christum facta est.* HI ep 112.14 (CSEL 55.383).
102 *Sed quamuis gentibus inponenda non essent, non tamen sic debuisse auferri a consuetudine Iudaeorum tamquam detestanda atque damnanda … non tamquam detestanda et similis idolatriae uitaretur …* ep 82.15 (CSEL 34.2.365; White 155–56). In ep 82.13, Augustine says: *ego uero apostolis non tam exemplum philosophorum timeo, quando et illi in sua disputatione ueri aliquid dicunt, quam forensium aduocatorum, quando in alienarum causarum actione mentiuntur* (CSEL 34.2.363). See n. 90 above.
103 ep 82.8 (White 149). In ep 40.4, Augustine asserted: *nam utique Iudaeus erat, christianus autem factus non Iudaeorum sacramenta reliquerat, quae conuenienter ille populus et legitime tempore, quo oportebat, acceperat* (CSEL 34.2.73–74).
104 *non illis umbris rerum ante futurarum tunc iam uenientium atque praesentium.* ep 82.15 (CSEL 34.2.365; White 155). Noting that Augustine altered his allegorical readings of the Old Testament, Cohen stressed how Augustine also "insists that its words mean exactly what they seem to mean … a blood sacrifice really is a blood sacrifice, and circumcision really is circumcision." In observing these rituals, the ancient Hebrews "before the time of Christ are obeying God's will. This innovation introduces a historical and subjectively relativistic perspective into Christianity." Further reflecting upon this innovation, Cohen asserts that "Augustine's temporal thinking results in a literalist rehabilitation of the Hebrew Bible integral to an allegorical approach in which the Old Testament prefigures the New, in which the history of the Jewish people is a figure that finds fulfillment in the life of Christ. This outlook inheres in rejection of pure antimaterialism, of radical antiworldliness." Cohen (2017), 74–75.
105 Fredriksen (2010), 242. In ep 82.8, Augustine says: *utique nefas est, ut credentes in Christum discindantur a propheta Christi tamquam eius doctrinam detestantes atque damnantes, de quo ipse Christus dicit: si crederetis Moysi, crederetis et mihi; de me enim ille scripsit* (CSEL 34.2.358).
106 *quos praesentia carnis domini et apostolica tempora sic inuenerant, omnis illa actio consumeretur umbrarum.* ep 82.15 (CSEL 34.2.365; White 155–56).
107 *Quod Paulus utique non cogebat ob hoc illa uetera ueraciter, ubi opus esset, obseruans, ut damnanda non esse monstraret, praedicans tamen instanter non eis sed reuelata gratia fidei saluos fieri fideles, ne ad ea quemquam uelut necessaria suscipienda compelleret.* ep 82.15 (CSEL 34.2.366; White 156).

Augustine. And as we shall see in the next chapter, the notion of time that Augustine expressed in his correspondence with Jerome is also something he developed alongside his argument against the Manicheans and had implications for his whole interpretative framework of the Scriptures and his approach to scriptural authority.

5. Humility, *Caritas* and Authority

In defending his argument that writing the truth will not make Paul a hypocrite, Augustine also asserts that the truthfulness of the scriptural content is the principle which must be accepted before one tries to reach an understanding of, and expound, the Scriptures. Augustine categorically restated the principle he asserted in ep 28[108] when he expounded the implication of the action of Peter and Paul. In defending the character of Peter, Jerome stressed the respect shown by Paul to his superior Peter.[109] But Augustine emphasized not only the truthfulness of Paul's writing but also his "frankness of love" in rebuking Peter, and the sincere penitence of the chastised Peter, which serves as "a model for the behaviour of the Christian who is corrected".[110] Paul was a model in showing "how those lower in authority may dare to stand firm in defending the truth of the gospel, as long as they do with brotherly love". He also insisted that praising Paul's fairness and outspokenness and Peter's humility in receiving the rebuke "would have provided a better defence against Porphyry's criticisms".[111]

For Augustine, these virtues of humility and brotherly love take ethical precedence over the quest for "what to know" and "how to know": "For it is possible that you do not see things as they really are", Augustine insists, "but the important thing is that all your actions should be inspired by love".[112] This stance can be related with Augustine's request regarding the *De viris illustribus* to Jerome. With "brotherly love together with my humility", Augustine asked Jerome to include "some indication of the points on which the authority of the Catholic church has condemned" all the heretics that Jerome named. This addition would help those people who are too busy in other duties or "who are unable to read and learn so many things because they are written in foreign language".[113] Augustine thereby proposed a "radical shift" in audiences and "reading public"[114] that goes beyond the "exclusive" addressee in

---

108 *Agendum est igitur, ut ad cognitionem diuinarum scripturarum talis homo accedat, qui de sanctis libris tam sancte et ueraciter existimet, ut nolit aliqua eorum parte delectari per officiosa mendacia, potiusque id, quod non intellegit, transeat, quam cor suum praeferat illi ueritati. profecto enim cum hoc dicit, credi sibi expetit et id agit, ut diuinarum scripturarum auctoritatibus non credamus.* ep 28.4 (CSEL 34.1.110).
109 On the things that Paul "says in summation in praise" of Peter (*et caetera qua in ejus laudes perorat*), see *Commentarii in epistulam ad Galatas* 1.2 (PL 26.340; Scheck 100).
110 Cole-Turner (1980), 155.
111 ep 82.22 (White 164); see also do 1.43.93: *indiget scripturis nisi ad alios instruendos* (CSEL 80.32).
112 ep 73.3 (White 102); see also ep 73.9; TeSelle (2002a), 32–33.
113 ep 40.9 (White 81).
114 See n. 16 above. In chapter three, we have mentioned that there was also a shift in emphasis from a more philosophical theme in Augustine's earlier works towards a deeper reflection on the Scripture. The *De doctrina Christiana* was written so that "the person who knows how to read, on finding a book,

Jerome's preface like the prominent Dexter, Paula and her daughter Eustochium and Jerome's ideal pupil Marcella.

This "shift" in audiences that Augustine proposed was part of the answer to our preliminary question, "why did Augustine persistently want to know?" Beside the initial "Manichean-inspired" request he made to Jerome to reconsider his exposition of Galatians 2, Augustine wanted to break the "exclusive mould" that Jerome constructed through his literary activity: what to know, how to know and who should know. According to Vessey, the traditions of the ancient Greco-Roman world were enshrined in their texts and freeborn high-aspiring male should model their development on those exemplary persons. In that context, Jerome established a textual tradition where the role model would publicly renounce one set of morally and culturally normative texts for another after choosing to follow Christ. Instead of the exemplars offered by the classical *paideia*, Jerome introduced a new model of "Christian professional identity — monastic, semi-martyrial, Scripture-centered (and Jerome-centered)". Striving for a different outcome while engaging with the Scriptures like Jerome, Augustine attempted to show that "One could be a good and faithful student of Christian Scripture without becoming an accredited *scriptor ecclesiasticus* in Jerome's exalted and exclusive sense".[115]

Ultimately, the attempt to break Jerome's "exclusive mould" could be related to Augustine's notion of God's redemptive scheme and the way salvation finds expression in history while the correspondence should be seen as "interacting texts" that falls within the larger context of Augustine's attempt to make Paul's account foundational to his theological stances. Jerome's attempt to imitate Suetonius Tranquillus[116] in his *De viris illustribus*, whereby he stood at the pinnacle of Christian literary tradition, resonated with the "triumphalist Rome-Eusebius theology"[117] that Jerome endorsed. But, in Augustine's evolving scriptural understanding, we see the centrality of God's redemptive act through the incarnation and a privileging of scriptural canon that bears witness to this event.[118] Unlike Jerome, he denied this privileged status "to any other interpretations of historical events",[119] while the significance Augustine ascribed to any works on the Scriptures has also been largely determined by the salvific value they offer to the readers. In fact, we can say that preoccupation with God's redemptive act and its appropriation largely determined the issues Augustine raised, and directed the focus of the arguments and the stances he propounded in his lengthy correspondence with Jerome.

---

does not require another reader to explain what is written in it" (do *prol* 9.18). And in his later works on the book of Genesis (Gn Ma 1.1.1–2), we will see how Augustine shifted his style of exposition as he was aware of the mental capacity of his audiences.

115 Vessey (2012), 244–53.
116 Regarding Tranquillus, see n. 24 above.
117 See n. 22 above. We will see more of the "triumphalist Rome-Eusebius theology" later in chapter seven.
118 Thus, Bright asserts that the focus of Book 1 of *De doctrina Christiana* "is on theological questions concerning the role of scripture for salvation, rather than on the praxis of biblical exegesis". Bright (2006), 42. On how Augustine was influenced by Tyconius in making Paul's account foundational to his theology, see chapter four, n. 88 above.
119 Markus (1970), 43. See do 2.58.139 for Augustine's assessment of "any branches of [secular] learning" (Green 121).

Concluding Remarks

From the correspondence between Augustine and Jerome, we can see how authority was constructed in late antiquity. Jerome's attempt to achieve literary "monumentalization" through his *De viris illustribus* and his claim to be "the real inaugurator of the Pauline commentary in Latin"[120] can be juxtaposed with Augustus's RGDA as well as Augustine's *Confessions*.[121] And we can also see the fine line between heresy and orthodoxy, and the frictions between those "in authority" and those who are "an authority", as well as the chasm between the Greek and Latin expository traditions in the early churches. We see the interplay between diverse and conflicting notions of, and claim for, authorities which can ultimately have a bearing on the evolving concepts of the authority of Scripture.

When we look at Augustine's arguments in the correspondence, we can see that he was not just reacting spontaneously upon, and picking random issues from, Jerome's works. Augustine makes a sincere, persistent and elaborate effort to maintain and express what he believes is the truth regarding the Scriptures and his stance was largely shaped by his pastoral concern. This concern is at the background of Augustine's questions to Jerome, and it also explain the sense of urgency he attached to these questions. At the same time, Augustine's Latin tradition as well as the new insight he gained from reading Tyconius's works determines his approach to scriptural exegesis.

In this regard, one significant development we can see from the correspondence is how Augustine asserted that grasping the essence of time is key to overcoming seemingly contradictory passages in the Scriptures when Jerome alluded to the question of the imposition of Jewish rituals upon the Gentiles. Based upon this understanding, Augustine maintained that the whole Scripture has salvific significance and that all scriptural exposition should attempt to draw out this salvific meaning.[122] Therefore, as Augustine fine-tunes his arguments with Jerome, we can also see the blueprint of his scriptural theology: that fallible human being has been rebuked by Truth, that Scripture is the reliable witness of the incarnated Word and that readers need humility to appropriate the deeper meaning of the Scriptures.

From the issues raised and the ensuing correspondence, we see an exchange of scholarly views and insights into their character. And as Augustine and Jerome exchanged views and allegations they gradually gained and displayed more mutual

---

120 Cain (2010), 33. For Jerome, "*aggrediar opus intentatum ante me linguae nostrae scriptoribus, et a Graecis quoque ipsis uix paucis, ut rei poscebat dignitas, usurpatum*". *Commentarii in epistulam ad Galatas prol* 1 (PL 26.308). See also n.13 and 15 above.
121 In fact, Vessey believe that Augustine read *De viris illustribus* in 397 although he may "come across an earlier edition of the same work of Jerome's between 393 and 397". Among the various factor contributing to the genesis of the *Confessiones*, according to Vessey, was Augustine's "recent reading or rereading of Jerome's [*De viris illustribus*]. The *Confessions* talks back to Jerome's [*De viris illustribus*]. It is Augustine's attempt to assert a personal ideal of Christian profession as a way of living among texts, against Jerome's monumentalization of himself in an imaginary postclassical Forum of Trajan". Vessey (2012), 241–42, 253. See do 2.59.141 for Augustine's indirect reference to Jerome's work.
122 On how this insight is in line with Tyconius's hermeneutical principle, see n.86 of chapter 4.

respect, and by the end of their correspondence they seemed to appreciate each other greatly.¹²³ Augustine not only honed and developed his arguments but draws upon Jerome's scholarship and utilizes it particularly in his epic *De civitate Dei*.

Before we turn to this epic work, we will look at the immediate outcome of the correspondence in the next chapter when Augustine engaged with the Manicheans. We have seen that Augustine and Jerome had an awareness of Luke's interpretative framework of history¹²⁴ in writing the Acts of the Apostles and they both engaged with this writing to support their specific stances regarding the authority of Scripture in their correspondence. Against the Manicheans who rejected the Acts of the Apostles in favour of other Gnostic's *Acta*,¹²⁵ the correspondence with Jerome substantially enabled Augustine to think through and develop his understanding of the Scriptures, particularly as he interpreted the letters of Paul. Therefore, in the next chapter, we shall see how the concerns and arguments that Augustine articulated and defended in his correspondence with Jerome was related to his engagement with the Manicheans. And we shall see how his understanding of the authority of Scripture was reflected in his readings of the Pauline epistles and his exposition of the book of Genesis.

---

123 In ep 167.6.21, written around 415, Augustine stated that "the literature of the Church in the Latin language has advanced more than was possible ever before" through Jerome. And in his short ep 141, written around 418, Jerome stated that Augustine was famous throughout the world and had been revered and honoured by the Catholics as "the second founder of their ancient faith". See White (1990), 225, 230.
124 It is interesting to see that Jerome was aware of this "historical interpretive framework". In refuting the explanation that Cephas and Peter are two different people, Jerome interestingly asserted that "the historian Luke was silent about this quarrel" that Paul recounted in his epistle, which implies that Luke was "making use of his freedom as an historian. And it is not immediately a contradiction if what one person thought was worthy to relate for some reason, someone else leaves out". Scheck (2010), 101. This argument will justify the stances he takes in many of his writings, particularly *De viris illustribus*. And Augustine's engagement with *De viris illustribus* also display his awareness of this "historical interpretive framework".
125 According to Teske, "the Manichees rejected from the New Testament the Acts of the Apostles. In fact, they were reluctant even to mention it, because this book reported the coming of the Paraclete, whom the Manichaens held to be Mani himself". See Teske (2009), 116.

CHAPTER 6

"Ea ipsa est simplex fides, qua credimus"

Retrieving Paul Through the Book of Genesis

In the previous three chapters, we have seen how Augustine drew, developed and defended his understanding of the Scriptures and his exegetical principles from Ambrose, Tyconius and Jerome. And we have seen the centrality of Paul, whose account had been read and reread as Augustine engaged with these men. Drawing upon Paul's insight that "the letter kills, but the spirit gives life", Ambrose lays down the principle which removes the veil that makes Augustine see the Scriptures, particularly the Old Testament, in a whole new perspective. Augustine's appropriation of Tyconius's works, particularly the *Liber Regularum* resulted in a new historical understanding of Paul that greatly determined Augustine's theology. Augustine takes great interest in Jerome's works, particularly his exegesis of Paul's letter to the Galatians, to initiate a correspondence where Augustine honed and developed his arguments and make Paul's accounts foundational to his theological postures.

Augustine's acquaintance of Paul can be seen as a three-stage process: as a Manichean,[1] as a new "convert"[2] in a devotional context in Milan,[3] and as a priest and bishop in Africa. These three stages can correspond with what Michael Cameron called the three paradigms of Augustine's interpretative structures: "materialist" paradigm, "spiritualist" paradigm and "incarnational" paradigm.[4] And in retrospect, Augustine's subsequent endeavours can be seen as a long process of unravelling

---

1 In Gn Ma 1.2.3, he states: *certe et ipsi Manichaei legunt apostolum Paulum et laudant et honorant et eius epistulas male interpretando multos decipiunt.* "Now the Manichees themselves certainly also read the apostle Paul, and praise him and hold him in honour; and by misinterpreting his letters they lead many people astray" (CSEL 91.69–70; Hill 41). In cf 7.21.17, he admitted that he once considered Paul to "contradicted himself and that the drift of his writing was at odds with the witness of the law and the prophets". (Williams 116). BeDuhn stressed Augustine's ineptness to the Manicheans and asserted that Augustine "had already been committed to Christ as a Manichaean". See J. D. BeDuhn (2013), 1–18. Frend also asserted that Augustine had no thought of renouncing Christianity by becoming a Manichee. Frend (1953), 24.
2 Regarding his "conversion", see n. 58 in chapter three above. van Oort asserted that "whether characterized as a *secta* or typified as a *haeresis*", Manichaeism was always a form of Christianity for Augustine. van Oort (2013), x.
3 See cf 7.21.17; 8.6.14. According to Bammel, Augustine was "replacing his earlier Manichaean reading of Paul with a new 'Platonising' understanding". Bammel (1993), 1. But Harrison asserts that "Augustine evidently read Paul not just as a confirmation and corrective of the Platonists but also in the context of ascetic renunciation and conversion" so that in Augustine's early works, we see "Pauline inspired understanding of conversion and the Christian life". Harrison (2006), 118.
4 Cameron (1999), 74–75.

from his initial enticement to the Manicheans and their "materialist" reading of the Scriptures.[5]

In this chapter, we will see how Augustine retrieved and rehabilitated Paul through his intertextual reading of the scriptures. Looking at how the Manicheans interpreted Paul to substantiate their teachings, we will see how Augustine's rereading of Paul initially recast his notion of the book of Genesis, and how Augustine interpreted Paul and forged his theology based on Genesis in a circular, mutually illuminating process.

1. "Paul" of the Manicheans

In chapter two, we have seen how the Christian Scriptures, comprised of the Old and New Testaments, evolved and developed in the midst of rival gospels, acts and apocalypses produced by the syncretistic Gnostics[6] on the one hand, and the rejection of the Old Testament mainly by Marcion and some Gnostics on the other hand. In chapter four and five, we have also seen how Porphyry spearheaded a vigorous propaganda war against the Christians by undermining the divine origin and prophetic value of their Scriptures. The Manicheans that Augustine encountered in Africa can be considered both as the remnant of the Gnostics,[7] who also attempted to justify Christianity to the pagan critics.

In fact, Frend asserts that these Manicheans, just like the Gnostics two hundred years before them, were troubled with exactly the same problems, and they responded in precisely the same manner. They both share the tendencies to be hostile toward "the Old Testament and Jehovah", while heavily relying on the words of Paul to endorse their teaching. "Rejection of the Old Testament led in Africa to an almost exaggerated respect for the Epistles of St Paul, and also for the various Gnostic *Acta* of

---

5 Commenting on how anti-Manicheism is a dominant concern in Augustine's exegetical writings, O'Donnell asserts that "Everything exegetical in [Augustine] down to 400 at least must be taken as having an anti-Manichean sub-text". O'Donnell (1992a), xlix. Van den Berg remarks that Augustine "dedicated no less than one-third of his literary output to the refutation of the teachings of his former co-religionists". van den Berg (2010), 1. According to Torchia, "Augustine's anti Manichaean polemic was not merely directed against a single sect, but against an entire outlook that permeated late antiquity". Torchia (1999), 67. Interestingly, John Kevin Coyle claim that "one understands Augustine more the better one understands Manichaeism". Coyle (2009), 307.
6 According to Metzger, the three main features of the various "Gnostic systems" includes "a philosophical dualism that rejected the visible world as being alien to the supreme God; belief in a subordinate deity (the Demiurge) who was responsible for the creation of the world; and, in some systems, a radical distinction between Jesus and Christ, with the corollary that Christ the Redeemer only seemed to be a real human being". Metzger (1987), 77. Spat remarks that the Church Fathers made Simon, who first appears in the Acts of the Apostle, "not just the first Gnostic, but the father of all heretics, the ultimate source of all heresies professing dualist ideas, the first link in the chain of demonic succession". See Spat (2004), 5–11; also Rm in 15–16 where Augustine brings up the case of Simon Magus who was rebuked by Peter.
7 Bonner regarded Manichaeism as the last and the greatest manifestation of Gnosticism. Bonner (1986), 161.

the Apostles".[8] Likewise, Bammel affirms that Faustus's *capitula* that are set forth as a reply to Catholic questions aimed at the Manicheans, also propounded "a religious system which meets and disarms many of the pagan criticisms of Christianity".[9] As Brown rightly remarked, the Manicheans can be considered as "the most radical and self-confident of Paul's expositors" that Augustine encountered and most of the specific questions which he had to settle for his audience at Carthage were due to them.[10]

There are two main sources of knowledge relevant for our study regarding the Manicheans' exposition of Paul: firstly, the anti-Manichean writings of Augustine — particularly the *Contra Faustum*, in which he fully quotes Faustus's book against the Catholic Christians,[11] the *Contra Adimantum*,[12] where he summarises all the points of Adimantus's attack on the law and the prophets, and the accounts of his debates with Fortunatus[13] and Felix at Hippo; and secondly, in other Manichean writings, particularly the *Cologne Mani Codex* (CMC). Since they are foundational to the Manichean teachings that Augustine encountered in Africa,[14] we shall first look briefly at the CMC to see how Mani and his followers, who "adopted New Testament phraseology, especially from St Paul",[15] interpret Paul's letters in their writings.

Discovered in Egypt and deciphered in 1969, the CMC[16] asserts to be an autobiography[17] of Mani and related his early life among a Jewish Christian baptist sect in

---

8   Frend (1953), 15, 17, 21.
9   According to Bammel, "An obvious point for attack on the Christians was their reliance on their own and the Jewish scriptures, and it was here that Porphyry went much further than Celsus. In this respect Faustus simply accepts and takes over the pagan criticisms ... The particularity of the Christian view of salvation history, which Celsus found offensive, is largely done away with by the rejection of any special role for Judaism ... The Catholic attachment to the body, shown in the doctrines of incarnation and resurrection, is found particularly disgusting by Celsus. This however is abandoned by the Manichees, since they view the fleshly nature as evil, and adopt a docetic Christology". See Bammel (1993), 8–9.
10 Brown (2000), 144.
11 For a study of the scriptural quotations that Faustus made in the *capitula*, see van den Berg (2013), 19–36.
12 For a thorough examination of Adimantus's views on the Scriptures, see van den Berg (2010).
13 For an assessment of Augustine's debate with Fortunatus, see BeDuhn (2011).
14 According to Henrichs, "The Syriac works of Mani and his disciples passed through Greek channels before St Augustine could read them in Latin". Henrichs (1979), 353.
15 Henrichs (1979), 356. According to J. R. Harrison, Paul's letters were regularly cited alongside the Gospels and the Old Testament as "Scripture" from 200 CE onwards and "differing ecclesiastical traditions appropriated Paul for their own theological and social agendas instead of allowing the apostle to the Gentiles to speak to his first-century context". Harrison (2004), 24.
16 According to Henrichs, "No other Manichean document of comparable importance is written in a language so widely accessible as Greek, or covers such varied aspects of Manichean tradition within the limited space" as the CMC. Henrichs (1981), 724. On how the CMC "makes it easier to understand the complex development of Manichaeism from a Christianized Judaism which was subject to the growing influence of gnosticism", see Koenen (1978), 154–95. For an account of the earliest stages of decipherment of the CMC, see Henrichs (1979), 339–67; for a recent overview of the CMC, see Aitken (2000), 161–76; van Oort (2004), 139–57.
17 Identifying the CMC as "a specimen of devotional literature", Henrichs remarked that the CMC "was actually the earliest part of a continuous biography which has thrown unexpected light on the darkest period of Mani's life, his first twenty-four", and that it had been written by his disciples

southern Babylonia. It also recounts Mani's separation from that sect,[18] the revelations he received from his heavenly twin, the σύζυγος — which is "the personification of a typically Gnostic concept",[19] and his missionary activities. Translated from Syriac into Greek,[20] the CMC is titled Περὶ τῆς γέννης τοῦ σώματος αὐτοῦ and can be rendered as "On the Birth/ Genesis of His Body". Koenen asserts that this title is a good example of how "the theological language of the new codex is partly influenced by Paul", since it was rooted in "the language of the Pauline formulation of the church as the body of Christ".[21] If the Manichaean Church (the ἐκκλησία, which Mani used explicitly in CMC 35,13; 36,14; 111,15 and 116,14)[22] was labelled as the body of Mani, it would emulate Paul's description of the Church as the body of Christ in his letters.[23]

Likewise, the opening words of the *Living Gospel*[24] from the CMC-fragment read: *I, Mani, Apostle of Jesus Christ, through the will of God, the Father of Truth*. This expression is very similar to the opening passages of the Pauline epistles like 1 Cor 1:1; 2 Cor 1:1; Col 1:1; Eph 1:1, and Henrichs even expressed his amazement that "The author who introduced himself in the manner of St Paul was no less a man than Mani himself".[25] Koenen asserted that for the Manichaeans, the title "Apostle of Jesus Christ" suggested that Mani was the Apostle of the heavenly "Jesus the Splendour" and not the historical Jesus. And Mani's apostleship made sense because Paul's

---

who "apparently reproduced what Mani himself had told them". See Henrichs (2019), 570; Henrichs (1979), 340, 352; also Henrichs (1981) for a literary criticism of the CMC.
18 Koenen, who assumed this sect to be the Elchasaite, opined that Mani regarded himself as a reformer who wanted to restore the true Christian beliefs by freeing the Elchasaite teachings from Jewish influences. Mani's point of view was not, of course, historically correct. "The Elchasaites had Jewish roots, and the Christianity Mani experienced was gnosticized. Similarly, Manichaeans later thought that they were adhering to the true teachings of Christ when they eliminated the Old Testament". Koenen (1978), 187.
19 Henrichs (1979), 340. For Koenen, this gnostic term may be evocative of Phil 4:3. "The *Nous* of Mani and his Twin are the two complementary aspects of Mani's identity … one complete Mani". Koenen (1978), 170, 173.
20 Mani's "theological vocabulary was originally Syriac", written in "his own variant of the Palmyrene script" while the Greek translation "imitates the Greek of the Septuagint and of the New Testament". See Henrichs (1973), 33; van Oort (2004), 147; Henrichs (1979), 353.
21 Koenen (1978), 164–65.
22 See van Oort (2013), xi.
23 Koenen stated that "His Body" could either denoted "the mystical body (1) of Mani, (2) of the 'Apostle of Light', (3) of the 'Light — Nous' and (4) of Jesus. Theologically all these were interchangeable". Koenen (1978), 166. For Heinrichs, "In the literal sense, Mani's body was the vehicle of his earthly life, and it was appropriate to refer to it in the title of Mani's biography. In the pneumatic sense, which was influence by Pauline christology, Mani's body was Mani's church so that the story of Mani's life became the first chapter in the history of his church". Henrichs (1979), 340; v. Oort noted how "His Body" could either mean the physical body of Mani or the Manichean Church, though "it could well be that both are quite correct". van Oort (2004), 142.
24 According to van Oort, Mani composed a sevenfold canon of authoritative writings in order to securely establish the doctrine of his Church: 1) The Living (or Great) Gospel; 2) The Treasure of Life; 3) The *Pragmateia* (or Treatise or Essay); 4) The Book of Mysteries (Secrets); 5) The Book of the Giants; 6) The Letters; 7) The Psalms and Prayers. See van Oort (2004), 147.
25 Henrichs (1979), 349.

apostleship was also founded upon the call he received from Jesus in the vision at Damascus after the lifetime of Jesus. "Mani could understand this as a call by Jesus, the heavenly Father. Hence Mani could feel entitled to call himself an apostle of Jesus in the *exordia* of his letters as Paul did".[26]

Betz thoroughly examined how Paul's apostleship served as a paradigm for Mani's awareness of his own vocation and mission in the CMC.[27] According to Betz, the influence of Paul on the CMC can be distinguished into: 1) A general image of Paul; 2) Stylistic and literary imitation of Paul's letters; 3) Pauline conceptuality and theology derived from Paul's authentic letters and the deutero-Pauline letters, especially Colossians and Ephesians; 4) Quotations from Galatians and 2 Corinthians; 5) Material drawn from post-New Testament Paulinist traditions.[28] Observing that the quotations from the letters of Paul show a strong preference of the letters to the Galatians and the Corinthians, Betz suggests that Mani did not simply read the letters of Paul but saw and interpreted Paul "through the medium of later Paulinism which was close to Ephesians".[29]

Beside the CMC, the writings of the Manicheans that Augustine refuted tell us how the Manicheans used Paul's writings and considered Paul central to their teaching. Although there are instances where he seems to have misunderstood the Manicheans in his refutations, Augustine's attempt to persuade them by identifying the flaw in their teachings will prevent him from intentionally misrepresenting their beliefs[30] as well as their reading of Paul.

Augustine mentioned how the Manicheans read and praised the Apostle Paul so that they had convinced him that Paul's writings disagree with the teaching of the Old Testament.[31] And we can see how the Manicheans built their argument for the "discrepancies of scriptures" based on Pauline teachings in *Contra Adimantum*.[32]

---

26   Koenen (1978), 168; see also van Oort (2004), 147, 149, 157; Betz (1979), 75.
27   The CMC "presents Mani not only as an imitator of the apostle Paul, but as a congenial interpreter of Paul's [Galatians]; Mani uses [Galatians, particularly in CMC 64.1–15, 71.1–72.7] and its theology to justify his break with the Elchasaite sect, … just as Paul justifies his break with Judaism". Betz (1979), 6, 63, 65.
28   Betz (1994), 164.
29   Betz (1994), 164, 181–82.
30   See Coyle (1999a), 40. For Koenen, "Augustine tried hard to understand the Manichaean concept, but he interpreted their terms as used in the dogma of his church". Directed against the beliefs of the Manichaeans of his time, his theological interpretation is marked by his misunderstanding of Manichaean theological terms. Koenen (1978), 176. On how competently Augustine knew their cosmogony and how accurately he reproduced them in his works in the light of the Manichean *Kephalaia*, and on the "plausibility" of the allegations by Beausobre, Alfaric and other scholars that Augustine's testimony will be "unreliable", see Maher (1979).
31   See n. 1 above. This is in line with Harrison's remark that by the mid second century, the gnostic circles had so effectively "kidnapped" Paul that "the early fathers found it difficult to appeal to Paul as an authority. This explains the scarcity of reference to Paul's letters in the early patristic literature". See Harrison (2004), 25.
32   *Quod autem etiam testimonium apostoli adiungunt, quod ait de domino nostro Iesu Christo: "ipse est primogenitus totius creaturae; et omnia per" "ipsum facta sunt in caelis et in terris, uisibilia et" "inuisibilia" et hoc capitulum aduersum esse dicunt Genesi.* Ad 1 (CSEL 25.1.116); see also Ad 12.1–5; 14.1–3; 16.1–3; 25.

In Augustine's debate with Fortunatus regarding the source of evil, i.e., due to human's free choice of the will or a principle co-eternal with God, Fortunatus tried to invoke Paul by quoting Phil 2:5–8; Eph 2:1–18; 1 Cor 15:50; Rom 7:23–25; 8:7; 9:20; Gal 5:17; 6:14.[33] In his debate with Felix, Augustine asserted that Paul, through the Holy Spirit, foretold of the coming "deceiving spirits" like Mani who claimed to be an apostle of Christ. In reply, Felix argues that the promised Holy Spirit only came in the person of Mani, who preached and taught as the Paraclete, and which was not yet present in Paul who claims only to know in part (1 Cor 13:9).[34]

The popularity of Paul among the Manicheans in Africa was also evident from the *capitula* of Faustus, who refers to the *Acts of Paul and Thelca*[35] in his argument. Commenting upon the *capitula*, van Gaans asserts that they were written as a Manichaean polemical manual and not just a literary adaption of actual debates held between Faustus and his Catholic opponents. Faustus's Christian language was clearly inspired by his "reading of the Pauline epistles".[36] Basing upon the letter of Secundinus[37] who invoked Paul and Mani to build his arguments,[38] van Oort also asserts that Secundinus had "a certain knowledge of the *Corpus Paulinum* (Ephesians, Romans, 1 Timothy, Philippians) and of the Gospel in one form or another".[39]

Looking at these evidences, we can therefore affirm that Mani and his disciples, and the successive Manicheans that Augustine encountered in Africa, largely drew their inspirations from the letters of Paul, with certain adaptation and selectiveness.[40] From their reading of Paul, the Manicheans considered the Jewish scriptures as an obsolete antitheses to the New Testament,[41] and the "true" Christian belief as "needing correction" from Jewish influences.[42] They would also invoke Paul to endorse their

---

According to van den Berg, "Adimantus' acquaintance with the New Testament documents triggered off an associative and creative process in his mind for the application of this knowledge in order to reject the Hebrew Scriptures". van den Berg (2010), 137.

33 See Fo 7; 16; 19; 21; 26.
34 See Fel 1.8; 1.9; 1.13.
35 See Fau 30.4.
36 van Gaans (2013), 225.
37 For an introduction to Secundinus and his letter, see Coyle (1999b), 759–60.
38 In his *ep. Sec.* 894.9, Secundinus writes: *Hoc Paulus, hoc ipse testatur Manichaeus* (This is what Paul testifies, and this is what Manichaeus himself testifies). See van Oort (2001), 163.
39 van Oort (2001), 167, 173.
40 On the selective usage of the Old Testament's "antediluvian" prophets, see Frankfurter (1997), 60–73. As Ayres remarks, "Paul's corpus does not seem to have been treated by Manichees as 'scriptural' in the way it was by Catholic Christians; Paul was rather an authoritative source to be approached via commitments to the fundamental Manichean myths and texts. But Paul's contrasts — law versus gospel, flesh versus spirit — were easily taken up and read within a highly dualistic system which wanted to present itself as the true Christianity". Ayres (2011), 345.
41 Betz believe that "Mani relied on the canon of Marcion". Betz (1994), 181.
42 Interestingly, Koenen remarks that "the early Manichaeans thought of themselves in much the same way that they did in the time of Augustine. They claimed that after the Christian church turned away from the genuine teaching of Christ, the Manichaean church was sent into this world. Consequently,

radical dualism, their moral determinism and their docetic Christology. As we shall see in the next sections, these are exactly the focal points that Augustine contended with in his response to the Manichean.

2. Augustine's Early Responses to the Manicheans

In the *Confessiones*, Augustine recounted how his "materialist" reading of passages from the Old Testament, apparently contradictory with the New Testament according to the Manicheans, had been demystified by Ambrose's spiritualist interpretation.[43] Ambrose's reading motivated Augustine to ponder if he could produce certain proof of the errors of the Manichaeans and unmasked their deception from his mind. Though Augustine was not able to conceive of a spiritual substance then, he decided to leave the Manicheans since even the "Academics" philosophers, who were without the saving name of Christ, hold the more probable views about the structure of the world.[44]

If Augustine's reading of Cicero's *Hortentius* preceded his disillusionment with the Christian Scriptures and led him to the Manicheans, "certain books of the Platonists" informed him of the eternal pre-existent Word of God and inspired him to seek incorporeal truth after a period of scepticism. Soon, Augustine eagerly seized (*auidissime arripui*) upon "the noble writing of [God's] Spirit", and especially finds Paul aligning with, and surpassing, what he read in the books of philosophers.[45]

In his early responses to the Manicheans after his baptism, Augustine's preoccupation and outlook seems to have been largely determined by the neo-Platonic philosophy.[46] In the three dialogues that he wrote in his retreat at Cassiciasum (cf 9.4.7), as well as

---

Faustus thought of his church as the fulfillment of the Christian church just as the Christian church understood itself as the fulfillment of the synagogue". Koenen (1978), 166.

43 In cf 5.14.24, he writes: *maxime audito uno atque altero et saepius aenigmate soluto de scriptis ueteribus, ubi, cum ad litteram acciperem, occidebar. spiritaliter itaque plerisque illorum librorum locis expositis iam reprehendebam desperationem meam illam dumtaxat, qua credideram legem et prophetas detestantibus atque inridentibus resisti omnino non posse* (CCSL 27.71).

44 In his own words: *tum uero fortiter intendi animum, si quo modo possem certis aliquibus documentis Manichaeos conuincere falsitatis. quod si possem spiritalem substantiam cogitare, statim machinamenta illa omnia soluerentur et abicerentur ex animo meo: sed non poteram ... non arbitrans eo ipso tempore dubitationis meae in illa secta mihi permanendum esse, cui iam nonnullos philosophos praeponebam: quibus tamen philosophis, quod sine salutari nomine Christi essent.* cf 5.14.25 (CCSL 27.71–72).

45 See cf 7.9.13; 7.10.16; 7.21.27. As O'Donnell remarks, "Augustine reads philosophy and turns [cf 3.5.9] to scripture, ending in frustration. The same sequence of readings occurs at [cf 7.9.13], in changed circumstances, with a different result". O'Donnell (1992a), 162.

46 On the debate whether Augustine in 386 converted to neo-Platonism but not to Christianity, or he converted to Christianity and rejected neo-Platonism, or he converted to Christianity and was also a neo-Platonist or he committed to Christianity without utterly rejecting neo-Platonism but aimed to develop a Christian faith that was informed by neo-Platonic insight, see Boone (2015). According to O'Donnell, Augustine's "reading of the *Hortensius* lingered in his mind for half a century". O'Donnell (1992a), 165.

the first book of *De libero arbitrio*[47] and the *De duabus animabus*,[48] Augustine used standard philosophical arguments for free will instead of engaging in a deep reflection on Scriptures to counter Manichean moral determinism.[49]

In the *De moribus ecclesiae Catholicae et de moribus Manicheorum* (387–389), Augustine identified the "two snares of the Manicheans by which the unwary are led astray so that they want to have them as their teachers": criticising the Scriptures through false interpretations and pretending to lead a high moral life.[50] In order to validate the "Catholic teaching concerning life and morality" and to "heal" the Manicheans of their errors, he "investigate[s] by reason how a human being ought to live".[51] Augustine frequently quoted from the New Testament to support this "philosophical" arguments,[52] particularly from Paul's writings[53] as they were the testimonies from the scriptures that the Manicheans have to believe, thereby allegedly avoiding the testimonies which the Manicheans considered to be an interpolation.[54]

Disputing the Manichean claim that the scriptures were corrupted with Jewish interpolation, Augustine asserted that the good life that Christians were commanded to live by "the Lord" in the gospel and by Paul in his letters, is to love God, and that "the authority of the Old Testament is also in accord with these statements".[55] Arguing that the Manichean "interpret in a bad sense an idea and a statement" that

---

47 In the *De libero arbitrio* Book 1 (387–88), the only Scripture he quoted were Is 7:9, *nisi credideritis, non intellegetis* and 1 Cor 1:24, *dei uirtutem et dei sapientiam nominamus* (CSEL 74.6); In lib Book 3 (391–95), Paul figured more prominently and there are 11 direct quotations from different verses of Pauline letters: Rom 1:21 (3.24.72); 1:22 (3.24.72); 7:18 (3.18.51); 7:19 (3.18.51); 11:36 (3.11.33); 1 Cor 3:17 (3.14.40), 6:3 (3.9.28); Gal 5:17 (3.18.51); Eph 2:3 (3.19.54); 1 Tim 1:13 (3.18.51); 6:10 (3.17.48).

48 In *de duabus animabus* (391–95), Augustine explicitly quoted the Scriptures 21 times. Interestingly, not only were these quotations taken from only 12 verses of the New Testament, six verses were from the Gospel of John, which was quoted 14 times, while John 8:47 alone was quoted 7 times. Except for 5 times, all of the 21 quotations occurred in 2 an 7.9, which was a refutation of the Manicheans exposition of Jn 8:47, "You do not come from God". He countered this with Paul's words, "All things come from God" (1 Cor 11:12). (Teske 123).

49 See Plumer (2003), 62; Fredriksen (1988), 89.

50 *Sed quoniam duae maxime illecebrae sunt Manichaeorum, quibus decipiuntur incauti, ut eos uelint habere doctores.* mor 1.1.2 (CSEL 90.4; Teske 31).

51 mor 1.2.4 (Teske 32). He used the word *quaeramus* 5 times in mor (1.2.4; 1.3.6; 1.4.6; 2.3.5; 2.9.15).

52 For example, *secutio igitur dei beatitatis appetitus est, assecutio autem ipsa beatitas.* mor 1.11.18 (CSEL 90.22). Coyle asserted that although he "has begun in a philosophical vein", and though there is no exegesis in the strict sense, *De moribus* is "Augustine's first serious use of Scripture [where] his method is to present passages from the Old Testament with strong semantic echoes in the New Testament … though he goes further in insisting on a basic harmony (*concordia*) between them". Coyle (1999c), 571.

53 Of the 76 quotations he made explicitly from the New Testament, 49 were from the Pauline letters.

54 mor 1.1.2. He actually makes around 31 direct quotations from the Old Testament, where more than half of them (18 times) were from the books of Psalms and Wisdom.

55 *Uideamus, quemadmodum ipse dominus in euangelio nobis praeceperit esse uiuendum, quomodo etiam Paulus apostolus … "diliges", inquit, "dominum deum tuum" … age nunc inuestigemus uel potius attendamus, praesto enim est et facillime uidetur, utrum his sententiis ex euangelio atque apostolo prolatis etiam testamenti ueteris auctoritas congruat. quid dicam de superiore sententia, cum manifestum sit omnibus, eam de lege quae "per Moysen data est" esse depromptam? … ibi enim scriptum est: "diliges dominum" "deum tuum, ex toto corde tuo et ex tota anima tua, et ex tota" "mente tua".* mor 1.8.13; 1.9.14 (CSEL 90.15–16; Teske 36–37); see also 1.16.26; 1.21.39; 1.28.57; 1.30.62.

which they did not really understand, he stressed that the Catholic church interprets "the law and the prophets far, far differently than you suppose", and benefit from what "we accept in good sense".[56] The rest of his arguments can be summed up as an assertion that "these two commandments [love of God and neighbours, upon which] human life is ordered in the most salutary and the best way" can be found in "the two testaments",[57] and that love is the real defining factor of Christian morality, and not merely chastity and abstinence which the Manicheans boasted to observe.[58]

In the *de moribus Manicheorum*, he engaged in a more philosophical question, "What is evil?" to argue that knowing the essence of evil is a more important issue to investigate than asking where evil comes from.[59] Contending that the Manicheans taught blatant errors regarding the nature of good and evil, he thereby "debunked" the "three seals" upon which the Manicheans' morality was established.[60] To support these arguments, Augustine used only one passage from the Old Testament (in contrast to *De moribus ecclesiae Catholicae* where he made 31 quotations) but a variety of passages from the New Testament, particularly from the Pauline letters.[61]

When he returned to North Africa, Augustine wrote the *De Genesis contra Manicheos* (389) to tackle the Manichean criticism head-on since they are in "the habit of finding fault" with the book of Genesis where the creation account (Gen 1–3) was utterly contrasting to their basic doctrine of the two eternal principles.[62] As the Manichean's criticism was intended "to undermine the credibility of a Church that took this questionable text as a document of revelation", he had to supplement his refutation of the Manichean cosmogony with a positive exposition of the church's teaching.[63] Therefore, after stating his key "target audiences", namely the "unlearned"[64]

---

56 mor 1.10.16 (Teske 38); also 1.17.30.
57 mor 1.28.57 (Teske 57); also 1.32.69.
58 *Manichaei, perfectorum christianorum, quibus summa castitas non laudanda tantum sed etiam capessenda uisa est, mores et continentiam singularem, ne uos impudenter iactare apud animos imperitorum quasi difficillima rerum abstinentia, si quid in uobis pudoris est, audeatis ... caritas praecipue custoditur ... sciunt hanc commendatam esse a Christo et apostolis, ut si haec una desit, inania, si haec adsit, plena sint omnia.* mor 1.31.65; 1.33.73 (CSEL 90.69; 90.79).
59 *Percunctamini me unde sit malum; at ego uicissim percunctor uos quid sit malum. cuius est iustior inquisitio?* mor 2.2.2 (CSEL 90.89; Teske 69–70).
60 *Sed quoniam ostendi, ut arbitror, de bonis et malis generalibus in quantis tenebris et in quanta falsitate uersemini, nunc uideamus tria illa signacula, quae in uestris moribus magna laude ac praedicatione iactatis. quae sunt tandem ista signacula?* mor 2.10.19 (CSEL 90.104).
61 In the *de moribus Manicheorum*, his sole quotation from the Old Testament in support of the nature of evil is Is 45:7: *ego facio bona et creo mala* (2.7.9) while he also quoted at length Rom 14:1–15:3 (2.14.32), 1 Cor 8:4–13 (2.14.33), 1 Cor 10:19–25, 28–11:1 (2.14.34) to negate the Manichean notion of "unclean foods". He also quoted Mt 10:31 (2.13.28); 15:11 (2.14.31), Lk 2:14 (2.7.10); Jn 8:36, Gal 5:13 (2.11.22); Rom 13:14, 14:21 (2.14.31).
62 *qui inscribitur Genesis, sic solent Manichaei reprehendere.* Gn Ma 1.2.3 (CSEL 91.68; Hill 40). Even before his return to Africa, "St Augustine had frequented the Bible (St Paul and the Psalms in particular), and the requirements of the Manichaean controversy had very quickly obliged him to study Genesis carefully, especially the accounts relative to the origin of the world". Mosher (1982), 17.
63 Hill (2002), 25, 27.
64 *imperitioribus ... imperitorum ... indocti ... infirmos et paruulos.* Gn Ma 1.1.1–2 (CSEL 91.67).

who would struggle to understand his "other books", and others who could benefit from seeking to know the true meaning of Scripture, Augustine appealed to the writing of Paul to suggest that the Manicheans were just one of the many heretics to come along with various errors to awaken many people "from their slumbers".[65]

Expounding the meaning of Gen 1:1, *in principio fecit deus caelum et terram*, which the Manicheans ridiculed in the light of their dualistic cosmogony, Augustine appealed again to the writing of Paul in Tit 1:1–2 to assert that the Manichean "thoughtlessly try to find fault with something about which they should instead have been making earnest inquiries".[66] On the question why God decided to create heaven and earth, he asserted that God, who is "the cause of everything there is" (*uoluntas dei omnium causa*), wills that everything be so. For Augustine, becoming friends with God should precede knowing the will of God, and this could only be attained by the "total integrity of life and conduct and by means of that end of the commandment of which the apostle says: Now the end of the commandment is love coming from a pure heart and a good conscience and a faith unfeigned (1 Tim 1:5)".[67] Augustine therefore turns the Manicheans' taunt on its head by suggesting that "they thoughtlessly try to find fault with something about which they should instead have been making earnest inquiries".[68]

Interestingly, we can find a great resemblance between Augustine's arguments here with that of his own experience which he described in the *Confessiones*. In the *Confessiones*, Augustine described how the Manicheans unsettled (*perturbabar*) him with such questions as where evil comes from, whether God is bounded by bodily form or if the patriarchs of the Old Testament were righteous. And recounting how he had already perplexed many unlearned people with certain questions (cf 3.12.21), Augustine acknowledged that he sought God according to the sense of the flesh and not according to the understanding of the mind, and that he was ignorant of the true meaning of the Scriptures (cf 3.7.12). We can therefore say that straight from his own experiences, Augustine basically described in the *De Genesis contra Manicheos* what he would later refine in the *Confessiones*.

In the ensuing expositions in the *De Genesis contra Manicheos*, Augustine reiterated his point that the Manicheans were ignorant of the truth by firmly basing his arguments

---

65 *Sed ideo diuina prouidentia multos diuersi erroris haereticos esse permittit, ut, cum insultant nobis et interrogant nos ea quae nescimus … propterea et apostolus dicit: oportet multas haereses esse, ut probati manifesti fiant inter uos. hi enim deo probati sunt qui bene possunt docere.* Gn Ma 1.1.2 (CSEL 91.68).

66 *Certe et ipsi Manichaei legunt apostolum Paulum et laudant et honorant et eius epistulas male interpretando multos decipiunt; dicant ergo nobis, quid dixerit apostolus Paulus: agnitionem ueritatis quae est secundum pietatem dei in spem uitae aeternae, quam promisit non mendax deus ante tempora aeterna. aeterna enim tempora quid ante se habere potuerunt? hoc ergo cogantur exponere, ut intellegant se non intellegere, cum temere uolunt reprehendere quod diligenter quaerere debuerunt.* Gn Ma 1.2.3 (CSEL 91.69–70; Hill 41).

67 *Non autem quisque efficitur amicus dei nisi purgatissimis moribus et illo fine praecepti, de quo apostolus dicit: finis autem praecepti est caritas de corde puro et conscientia bona et fide non ficta.* Gn Ma 1.2.4 (CSEL 91.71); cf. cf 3.8.15: *numquid aliquando aut alicubi iniustum est diligere deum ex toto corde ex tota anima ex tota mente* [Mt 22:37] *et diligere proximum tamquam te ipsum* [Mt 22:39]? (CCSL 27.35; Hill 42).

68 Gn Ma 1.2.3 (Hill 41).

from Paul's letters and asserting that there can be a spiritual interpretation beyond "a purely literal, material sense".[69] Thus, the seed-bearing grasses and fruit trees and green plants signifies the emotions of the spirit which need to be restrained and crucified until "death is swallowed up in victory".[70] On the Manichean mockery of the notion of God resting on the seventh day (Gen 2:2–3), and their appeal to Jn 5:17 (*My Father is working up until now*) to argue that "the New Testament contradicts the Old", he asserts the "sacramental significance of the sabbath" against a carnal notion of the Sabbath basing upon 2 Cor 3:12 and Rom 8:26.[71] Augustine also supported his notion that the six days of creation represent the six ages of the world from various Pauline writings. The sixth day when God created human beings (Gen 1:26–27; 2:7) corresponded with "the age of the old man" (Eph 4:22; Col 3:9) when the new man is also born (Eph 4:24; Col 3:10) as well as the six days of our personal lives.[72]

In these two particular responses he initially made to the Manicheans, we can thus see certain common themes emerging in Augustine's arguments. The two commandments to love God and to love our neighbours is central to Christian beliefs and conducts.[73] These two commandments can be found in the "two testaments" so that the authority of the Old Testament is in accord with the message of the New Testament.[74] The abuses that the Manichean hurled at the Old Testament was due to their ignorance[75] and because their arguments were built on false premises.[76] While Augustine refuted the Manichean allegations that the Jewish Scripture is obsolete and true Christian belief needed correction from Jewish influences, his significant insight that love is the goal of, and the hermeneutical key to, the Scriptures has been emerging. Augustine also laid the exegetical foundation to his argument that Genesis is a legitimate part of God's revelation in the history of salvation through his allegorical readings which he largely validated from the Pauline epistles. And

---

69 *non carnaliter haec esse intellegenda.* Gn Ma 1.20.31 (Hill 59).
70 He quotes Gen 1:28; 1 Cor 15:24 and Gal 5:24 to support his argument. See Gn Ma 1.20.31 (Hill 59).
71 *quibus persuadere conantur nouum testamentum ueteri testamento aduersari ... non intellegunt sabbati sacramentum.* Gn Ma 1.22.33 (CSEL 91.101–02; Hill 60–61).
72 See Gn Ma 1.23.40; 1.25.43. He also quotes 1 Cor 3:1, Rom 7:25 to support his spiritual readings here. In the Second book of Gn Ma, he quoted from Rom 13:10; 1 Cor 1:24; 2:11; 11:7–12; 11:19; 13:2; 13: 8, 12; 15:46, 2 Cor 2:11; 3:3; 11:2–3; 11:3; 12:17; Eph 2:2; 5:31–32; 1 Tim 1:20; 5:6; 2 Tim 2:25; 4:4; Phil 2:7.
73 See mor 1.8.13; 1.11.18; 1.25.46; 1.28.57; 1.32.69; Gn Ma 2.23.36; cf. Gn Ma 2.27.41; rel 12.24; 46.86; do 1.21.41; 1.27.57; 2.10.18; 2.25.64; cf 3.8.15; 10.37.61; 12.25.35; 13.24.36. TeSelle noted that prior to Augustine, the love commandment had not been used very much as a summary of the Christian life. "Now he was drawn toward it because of its comprehensive applicability to all possible situations and its reliability as a guide to all acts of willing". TeSelle (2002a), 32–33.
74 See mor 1.9.14; 1.28.57; cf. mor 1.16.29; 1.17.31; Gn Ma 1.17.27. In mor 1.21.39, he stated: *huic ergo auctoritati, si de ueteri testamento quaeram quid comparem, plura quidem inuenio* (CSEL 90.44).
75 In mor 1.25.46, he stated: *haec est hominis una perfectio, qua sola impetrat ut ueritatis sinceritate perfruatur, haec nobis testamento utroque concinitur; haec nobis hinc atque inde suadetur. quid adhuc scripturis, quas ignoratis, calumnias innectitis? quanta imperitia lacessitis libros, quos et soli reprehendunt qui non intellegunt et soli intellegere nequeunt qui reprehendunt* (CSEL 90.51).
76 For instance, they usually asked about the origins of evil. Augustine highlighted the significance of this question for them: *saepe atque adeo paene semper, Manichaei, ab his quibus haeresim uestram persuadere molimini, requiritis unde sit malum.* mor 2.2.2 (CSEL 90.89).

though we see Augustine developing his theology and exegetical skills considerably in subsequent works, they were "already set forth, in a nutshell"[77] on this early commentary of Genesis.

Significantly though, Augustine later commented on his *Retractationes* that he "was not yet familiar" with the Scriptures[78] when he wrote the *De moribus ecclesiae Catholicae*, and that in the *De Genesi contra Manichaeos*, he misread Paul in the way the apostle himself meant it in quoting the text of Gen 2:7 to support 1 Cor 15:45.[79] In fact, Augustine already realized that he "still lacked so much"[80] that he asked Bishop Valerius for a leave to study the Scriptures once he was ordained in 391. It maybe the recognition from his own experience that the less educated were particularly vulnerable to the Manicheans' "corruption"[81] which compelled Augustine to study the scriptures, particularly the works of Paul, so that he can base his arguments more on the scriptures at the expense of the method of philosophical argumentation he earlier adopted.[82] So, when he intensified his refutations of the Manicheans later, we can see some changes in his approach. But what are these changes?

3. Retrieving Paul through the Book of *Genesis*

In many of his polemics against the Manicheans, Augustine largely resembled, and probably followed, the approaches of other earlier polemists. The *Acta Archelai* of Hegemonius is the account of two public debates between the heresiarch Mani and the Bishop of Carchar, Archelau. Composed between 330 and 348 in Syria, it was the first Christian work written against Manichaeans. Eszter Spat asserts that all the key elements of anti-heretical polemics are seen in "the *vita*: the motifs of false Christianity, taking the name of Christ, plagiarism, compiling their system from all sources after the fashion of patchwork, hunger for power and attempts to trick and corrupt the mind of simple men".[83] But it was the specific context of Africa,

---

77 Hill (2002), 31.
78 *in quibus nondum assuetus eram*. re 1.7.2 (CCSL 57.18; Ramsey 38).
79 *Nec illud apostoli ubi adhibet testimonium de Genesi dicens: factus est primus homo Adam in animam uiuentem, sicut ille uoluit intellexi, cum exponerem quod scriptum est: insufflauit deus in faciem eius flatum uitae, et factus est homo in animam uiuam uel in animam uiuentem*. re 1.10.3 (CCSL 57.32).
80 *Tam multa autem sunt, ut facilius possim enumerare, quae habeam, quam quae habere desidero*. ep 21.4 (CSEL 34.1.52).
81 In mor 1.34.75, he asserted: *nolite mihi colligere professores nominis christiani neque professionis suae uim aut scientes aut exhibentes. nolite consectari turbas imperitorum, qui uel in ipsa uera religione superstitiosi sunt uel ita libidinibus dediti ut obliti sint quid promiserint deo* (CSEL 90.80). See also mor 2.12.26–13.27; 2.17.60; Gn Ma 1.1.1; cf 3.12.21.
82 Plumer asserts that after becoming a priest, Augustine "realized that this method of argumentation would be of little benefit to ordinary parishioners. African Manicheism was in a sense a 'Pauline' heresy, and so Augustine had to 'reclaim' Paul from the Manichees". Plumer (2003), 62. According to Babcock, "Augustine's ordination compelled him to depart the Christianity of the philosophic elite and to enter the Christianity of the North African crowd". Babcock (1979), 55.
83 Spat (2004), 1–3.

where the scriptures were highly esteemed by his interlocutors,[84] which ultimately defined and determined the polemical approach of Augustine. When he confronted the Manichean "version" of Paul again, Augustine therefore added a "new angle" to retrieve Paul through his allusion to the book of Genesis.

In *Contra Fortunatum Manichaeum disputatio* (392), Augustine refuted the Manichean notion of the vulnerability of God,[85] and the nature and origin of the soul and evil.[86] Remarkably, in the course of the debate, Augustine asserted that his interlocutor, Fortunatus, had taken refuge in the scriptures again, even though their "listeners have imposed upon us the task of discussing in rational arguments the belief in two natures", which compelled Augustine to "descend" to the scriptures. There was even an outburst among the listeners who wanted the two debaters to use rational arguments instead, since Fortunatus "did not want to accept everything that was written in the book of the apostle".[87]

Fortunatus then asked whether God "establish[es] evils or not" and if God "establish[es] an end of evils". And boldly asserting that he can "in no way show that my faith is correct unless I confirm the same faith by the authorities of the scriptures",[88] Fortunatus quoted from Rom 7:23–25; 8:7; Gal 5:17; 6:14 as well as Jn 15:22 to support his argument. In reply, Augustine quoted the Pauline letters six times (Rom 5:19; 8:2; 1 Cor 15:21; Gal 5:13; Eph 5:6; 1 Tim 4:4) but referred explicitly to Genesis (3:19) only once. At the same time, Augustine implicitly based his argument on the creation account of Genesis to support his argument on the source of evil, sin and the free choice of the will.[89]

In his other works like the *De Genesi ad litteram imperfectus* (393) and *Contra Adimantum* (c. 394), Augustine asserted that Paul endorsed the book of Genesis and the Old Testament, and the Old Testament corroborated Paul. In *De Genesi ad litteram imperfectus*, for example, Augustine pointed out that Gen 1:2 did not mention

---

84 In chapter four, we have seen how the "Donatists" were willing to sacrifice their lives to prevent their scriptures from confiscation by the Roman officials while in the previous section, we have seen how the Manicheans make use of the writings of Paul to support their fundamental beliefs.
85 See Fo 1; 23.
86 See Fo 12; 13.
87 *Rationibus ut discuteremus duarum naturarum fidem, interpositum est ab his, qui nos audiunt. sed quoniam ad scripturas iterum confugisti, ad eas ego descend ... hic strepitus factus est a consedentibus, qui rationibus potius agi uolebant, quia uidebant eum non omnia, quae in apostoli codice scripta sunt, uelle accipere.* Fo 19 (CSEL 25.1.96–97; Teske 153).
88 *Hoc ergo propositum est a me, et quod interrogo nunc, utrum deus mala instituerit necne, et utrum ipse finem malorum instituerit ... et quia nullo genere recte me credere ostendere possum, nisi eandem fidem scripturarum auctoritate firmauerim, id ergo est, quod insinuaui, quod dixi.* Fo 20 (CSEL 25.1.99; Teske 154).
89 *Nam omnia deus et bona fecit, et bene ordinauit; peccatum autem non fecit et hoc est solum, quod dicitur malum, uoluntarium nostrum peccatum ... etenim ut bonus est deus, quia omnia constituit, sic iustus est, ut uindicet in peccatum. cum ergo omnia optime sint ordinata, quae uidentur nobis nunc aduersa esse, merito contigit hominis lapsi, qui legem dei seruare noluit ... ille sic factus est, ut nihil omnino uoluntati eius resisteret, si uellet dei praecepta seruare. postquam autem libera ipse uoluntate peccauit, nos in necessitatem praecipitati sumus, qui ab eius stirpe descendimus.* Fo 15; 22 (CSEL 25.1.91–92; 25.1.104). He concluded his argument with 1 Cor 15:21 (Fo 25).

that "God made the water" although "the Spirit of God was being borne over the water". He then deduced that "God made the water" since the apostle Paul says God is the one "from whom are all things, through whom are all things, in whom are all things" (Rom 11:36).[90] And in his exposition of Gen 1:4, "And God divided between the light and the darkness", he implicitly refuted the Manichean cosmogony that light and darkness mingled by insisting that darkness is the absence of light. Augustine supported his argument with Paul's word, "For what fellowship does light have with darkness" (2 Cor 6:14).[91]

Against Adimantus's allegation that the Old Testament contrasted the New Testament, Augustine asserted that God inspired both the two Testaments.[92] For instance, refuting the Manichean argument that the creation story of Gen 1:1–5, which did not mention the Son, opposed Jn 1:10 and Col 1:15–16, where the Son is the agent of the creation, Augustine asserted that in Rom 11:36, Paul did not mention the Son either: "But just as the Son is not mentioned here but is nonetheless understood, so he is in Genesis".[93] Against the Manichean insistence that Gen 2:18–20, regarding the union of man and woman, contradicted the gospel passage that exhorted a man to leave his wife (Mt 19:29; Mk 10:29–30; Lk 18:29–30), Augustine quoted Mt 19:3–9; 1 Cor 7:12, 15; Eph 5:22, 25, 32, 33 to assert that "there are forceful commandments in the New Testament about loving one's wife".[94] On these particular pieces, we can therefore see how Augustine uses Paul to support Genesis and by implication, asserted that Genesis is in line with Paul.

But it was in his treatises on the Pauline epistles where Augustine altered his approach[95] and prolifically drew upon Genesis to retrieve and rehabilitate Paul from the Manichean expositions. In the years 394–395, Augustine was believed to engage in a systematic study of the Pauline letters, which resulted in his treatises on Romans and Galatians.[96] As we have seen in his correspondence with Jerome around this time, one of the concerns he could not suppress and discard was the Manichean's exposition of the scriptures.[97] Not only did Augustine read the Pauline letters

---

90 See Gn im 4.13 (Hill 120).
91 See Gn im 5.23 (Hill 125–26). Another instance is Gen 1:27 and 1 Cor 11:17, regarding the image of God in human (see Gn im 16.61).
92 *sed omnia tam in uetere quam in nouo testamento uno sancto spiritu conscripta et commendata esse sentirent.* Ad 3.3 (CSEL 25.1.121).
93 *Quomodo autem hic filius nominatus non est, intellegitur tamen, ita et in Genesi.* Ad 1 (CSEL 25.1.116; Teske 176).
94 Ad 3.1–3.3 (Teske 177–78).
95 Fredriksen asserts that his debate with Fortunatus "apparently touched a nerve" and thereafter, "Augustine proceeds against the Manichaean Paul by arguing exegetically". Fredriksen (1988), 89.
96 See Mosher (1982), 19.
97 In ep 28.4, Augustine asked Jerome, *quid respondebimus, cum ex surrexerint peruersi homines prohibentes nuptias*, if Paul was considered to have been lying in his letters to the Galatians. Then, in ep 82.6, he argued, *Manichaei plurima diuinarum scripturarum, quibus eorum nefarius error clarissima sententiarum perspicuitate conuincitur, quia in alium sensum detorquere non possunt, falsa esse contendunt, ita tamen … itane non intellegit sancta prudentia tua, quanta malitiae illorum patescat occasio, si non ab aliis apostolicas litteras esse falsatas, sed ipsos apostolos falsa scripsisse dicamus?* (CSEL 34.1.109; 34.2.356).

exegetically but he also attempted to build a coherent "theology" upon them through a deeper reflection on Scriptures. And the notion of grace and the anthropology congruent with it, which Augustine developed henceforth in his treatises on the epistle to the Romans[98] and the Galatians, depended heavily on an implicit and explicit reading of Genesis.

In his *Epistolae ad Galatas expositionis* (394/5), the Manichean's favourite Pauline epistle,[99] Augustine expounded Paul's key argument against the "Judaizers", who insisted upon the observance of the Mosaic law by the Gentile Christians, that "a person is justified not by works of the law but through faith in Jesus Christ" (Gal 2:16). According to Augustine, this implies that "a person fulfils the works of the law when his weakness is aided not by his own merits but by the grace of God".[100] Paul substantiated his argument that a person can avail the fulfilment of God's promise by faith in Christ with imageries drawn from the book of Genesis.[101] While the morality of the patriarchs, following the explications of the Manicheans, was once a "stumbling block" for Augustine, he now argued that Abraham did not use women to satisfy his lust but to have descendants. Both Abraham and Sara had indeed acted consistently with the rule of righteousness which Paul also commended in 1 Cor 7: 4: the wife does not have authority over her own body but the husband does, and similarly, the wife has authority over her husband's body too.[102] But, while Augustine also alluded to Gen 2:22, *formauit eam in mulierem* to clarify Gal 4:4, *misit deus ... filium suum factum ex muliere*, rather than targeting the Manichean "Docetism" in this particular passage,[103] he was more concerned with refuting the denial of Mary's virginity and the Arian's assertion that the Son is a created being and not of one being with the Father.

In his expositions of the epistle to the Romans, *Epistulae ad Romanos inchoata expositio* (394/5) in an important piece which delineated Augustine's notion, and the focus of his reading, of the Scriptures from the Manicheans. We have seen how Fortunatus asserted to confirm his faith by "the authorities of the scriptures" while

---

98 These are *Epistula ad Romanos inchoate expositio, Expositio quarandum propositionus ex epistula apostoli ad Romanos*, questions 66–74 of the *De Diversis questionibus* and the first book of *ad Simplicianus*. Here, we should remember Babcock's insightful remark that Augustine was more interested and effective in producing "a kind of *quaestio*-format [literature] which allowed him to deal with individual passages of particular significance rather than forcing him to discuss each text in the scriptural book under consideration", as we have seen in the case of his unfinished *De Genesi ad litteram imperfectus* and *Epistulae ad Romanos inchoata*. See Babcock (1979), 56.
99 Betz (1994), 181–82.
100 *impleat opera legis adiuuante infirmitatem suam non merito suo sed gratia dei*. Gal 15 (CSEL 84.71; Plumer 147).
101 They are Gen 12: 3; 16: 1–3; 21: 9–10.
102 *Non enim tales homines, qualis erat Abraham, ad explendam libidinem utebantur feminis, sed ad successionem prolis ... Antiqua enim iustitiae regula est, quam commendat ad Corinthios idem apostolus: Mulier sui corporis potestatem non habet sed uir, similiter autem et uir sui corporis potestatem non habet sed mulier*. Gal 40 (CSEL 84.110–11).
103 On the anti-Manichean element in his *Commentary on Galatians* and how Augustine does not use Gal 4:4 "to affirm the reality of Christ's birth in the face of the Manichees' denial of it", see Plumer (2003), 63–68.

Adimantus taught that Gen 1:1–5 was not compatible with Jn 1:10.[104] Augustine's explication of *Epistulae ad Romanos inchoata expositio* chapters 4 and 5 started with an evaluation of the validity of prophecies about Christ beyond the Jewish Scriptures. But it was only those writings that bear witness to the dual identity of Christ — who was the descendent of David "according to the flesh" and the son of God with power "according to the Spirit of Sanctification"[105] — which qualify as Holy Scripture.[106] While he already pointed out in his debate with Fortunatus that the Manichean always denied that Christ really take "the flesh"[107] because of the corruptibility of the human body,[108] Augustine now highlights the opposite sense where Paul used "according to" to distinguish Christ's divine dignity (*diuinitati dignitatem*) from his humanity. Jesus Christ is not only the "seed" of David[109] but the very Word of God through whom all things were created.[110] Therefore, in his exposition of this passage, Augustine linked creation with the incarnation of the Word of God by explicitly referring to Jn 1:1,14 while he implicitly alluded to the creation account of Genesis 1.

In his other work *Expositio quarandum propositionus ex epistula apostoli ad Romanos* (394/95),[111] Augustine propounded the concept of the four stages (*quattuor istos gradus*) of the appropriation of grace by sinners in relation to the Law and the freedom of the human will to obey the Law of God. Commenting on Rom 3:20, "Nobody can be justified before him by observing the Law, because by the Law comes the conscience of sin", he argued that the Law is good since it informed us of the precepts of God. But apart from the grace of God, it cannot be fulfilled and is futile to resist the stronger

---

104 See n. 88 and n. 93 above.
105 *qui secundum carnem factus est ex semine Dauid* [Rom 1:3] ... *filius autem dei in uirtute secundum spiritum sanctificationis* [Rom 1:4]. Rm in 5 (CSEL 84.151).
106 *Et ne quisquam etiam prophetas aliquos remotos atque alienos a gente Iudaeorum forte praeferret* ... *ne quis tamen aliqua huiusmodi praeferens, quia ibi Christi nomen ostendat, eas potius sanctas scripturas esse asserat non eas, quae populo Hebraeorum sunt diuinitus creditae satis opportune mihi uidetur adiungere cum dixisset: in scripturis sanctis* [Rom 1:2]. Rm in 4 (CSEL 84.148).
107 *Uidemus apostolum de domino nostro nos docere, ut et uirtute dei ante carnem praedestinatus fuerit et secundum carnem factus sit ei de semine Dauid. hoc uos cum semper negaueritis et negetis, quomodo scripturas flagitatis, ut secundum eas potius disseramus?* Fo 19 (CSEL 25.1.96).
108 Koenen asserts that there was no room for a sinless body of Christ in Mani's system. "[A]ll bodies were the work of the powers of Darkness. Since Mani ... knew that such a body was not fitting for Christ, he simply adopted the docetism of Marcion and of Christian gnostics". Koenen (1978), 192.
109 It is interesting to see that in his previous explanation of the passage "according to the flesh", Augustine interpret it allegorically: *item reliquit et matrem, id est synagogue ueterem atque carnalem obseruationem, quae illi mater erat exsemine Dauid secundum carnem* [Rom 1:3], *et adhaesit uxori suae, id est ecclesiae, ut sint duo in carne una* [Gen 2:24]. Gn Ma 2.24.37 (CSEL 91.161).
110 *Occurrendum autem erat etiam illorum impietati, qui dominum nostrum Iesum Christum secundum hominem tantummodo, quem suscepit, accipiunt, diuinitatem autem in eo non intellegunt ab uniuersae creaturae ... quae non solum semini Dauid ... quandoquidem ipsum est uerbum dei, per quod facta sunt omnia*. Rm in 4 (CSEL 84.148–49). These passages seem to be a longer, more detail treatment of Rm 1 and 59.
111 See re 1.23.1 for the context and re 1.25.1 for the time of these expositions.

desire to sin.[112] Augustine saw the origin of such desires as an inheritance from "the sin of the first man, of whom we are corporally descended".[113] Explicating Rom 7:11, "For sin, taking the stand of the commandment, deceived me" he alluded to Gen 3:6 to support his argument: "The desire for the forbidden fruit makes it sweeter".[114]

The "anti-Manichean" tendency in Augustine's notion of the "human will"[115] became explicit when he reached Rom 8. The "enemy of God" in Rom 8:7 is "the one who does not abide by his law" and not "some being from an adverse principle, not created by God, and who is dedicated to making war against God",[116] as the Manicheans had contended. Further commenting on Rom 8:19–23, "So the creature awaits with a strong expectation the manifestation of the children of God", he asserted that the Manicheans erred in believing that trees or vegetables or rocks or any other similar creatures are capable of feeling pain or complaining.[117] Insisting that all of them are contained in "humankind", which consists of spirit, soul and body,[118] he substantiated his distinction between human — including believers and non-believers — and other creations with Gen 2:17, "You will die without remedy".[119] In other words, due to the

---

112 *Bona ergo lex quia ea uetat, quae uetanda sunt, et ea iubet, quae iubenda sunt. sed cum quisque illam uiribus suis se putat implere, non per gratiam liberatoris sui, nihil ei prodest ista praesumptio, immo etiam tantum nocet, ut et uehementiore peccati desiderio rapiatur et in peccatis etiam praeuaricator inueniatur.* Rm 13–18 (CSEL 84.7; all English translations of Rm from https://sites.google.com/site/aquinasstudybible/home/ romans/augustine-of-hippo-two-question-about-the-epistle-to-the-romans). Cf. Gn Ma 1.23.35–40. As Fredriksen noted, "The four historical stages, which stretch from humanity before Israel to the second coming of Christ, are recapitulated in the spiritual development of the individual believer … But where, in the earlier scheme, the six ages corresponded to successive stages in God's dealings with humankind, five relating to Old Testament history and the six to New Testament times, the four-age scheme united history into one development. … As such, it was a radical defense of the Old Testament against the criticisms of the Manichees". Fredriksen (1988), 90.

113 *Sed quoniam ista desideria de carnis mortalitate nascuntur, quae trahimus ex primo peccato primi hominis, unde carnaliter nascimur.* Rm 13–18 (CSEL 84.8). Later, this is a point of contention with the Pelagians.

114 *Ideo dictum est, quia desiderii prohibiti fructus dulcior est.* Rm 39 (CSEL 84.17).

115 According to Canty, "locating the source of evil in the human will transformed Augustine's understanding of God, the universe, and humanity, and Augustine came to find Paul's letter to the Romans to be the interpretive key for understanding the drama of human salvation. Paul affirms the goodness of God and creation while simultaneously removing the possibility of blaming anything for being the source of evil except oneself". Canty (2013), 126.

116 *ne quis putaret tamquam ex aduerso principio aliquam naturam, quam non condidit deus, inimicitias aduersus deum exercere. Inimicus ergo dei dicitur, qui legi ipsius non obtemperat.* Rm 49 (CSEL 84.22).

117 *sic intellegendum est, ut neque sensum dolendi et gemendi opinemur esse in arboribus et oleribus et lapidibus et ceteris huiuscemodi creaturis — hic enim error Manichaeorum est …* Rm 53 (CSEL 84.26). In studying the CMC, Koenen commented, "What seemed to be Augustinian irony turns out to have been told by the Manichaeans as educational stories which expressed their beliefs. A palm tree defends its branches and calls its pruner a murderer. Vegetables literally weep and cry with human voices, and they bleed when they are cut with a sickle". Koenen (1978), 180.

118 *cum interituri utique non sint, sed omnem creaturam in ipso homine sine ulla calumnia cogitemus … omnis autem est etiam in homine, quia homo constat spiritu et anima et corpore.* Rm 53 (CSEL 84.26).

119 *Peccatori enim dictum est: morte morieris* [Gen 2:17] *… sed ne quis putaret de ipsorum tantum labore dictum esse, subiungit etiam de his, qui iam crediderant.* Rm 53 (CSEL 84.27–28). Augustine made a similar point in q 67.3 where he quoted Gen 3:19. "For creation, it says, has been subjected to vanity …

punishment for their sin, it was humankind — who are qualitatively different from other creatures — who groan and moan and struggle in their will against sin, and not the other creation as the Manichean insisted.

Augustine later repeated this stance with more clarity in Book 1 of his *ad Simplicianum* (396–398). In explicating Rom 7:7–25, he asserted that "the law was given not that sin might be instilled nor that it might be extirpated but only that it might be made manifest",[120] and referred to Gen 2:16–17.[121] Further commenting upon Rom 7:21 on the subject of the law and free will, Augustine asserted that the law of sin which opposed the law of the mind "was assigned as punishment by divine judgment and imposed by him who warned the man when he said, *On the day you eat, you shall die* (Gen 2:17)".[122] Asserting that Paul considered the law which prohibited sin as good, Augustine countered the Manichean allegation that the "good" law is the Gospel and not the law that was given to the Jews.[123]

In his defence of human free will and the justice of God, an interesting word which we find in Augustine's explication of Rom 9:20, 21 in *Expositio quarandum propositionus ex epistula ad Romanos* is *massam luti*. How Augustine contoured this *massam luti* into different "shapes of sin" between his reading of Gen 2:7, 16–17; 3:6 in various works related to the epistle to the Romans is very interesting. According to his manuscripts of Gen 2:7, God formed humankind from the dust of the earth.[124] However, he seems to "theologically" equate "the dust of the earth" with "clay" in Romans, as can be seen from his response to Simplician: "All human beings come from the ground, and from the earth Adam was created ... Like clay in a potter's hand, for shaping and forming, all its way according to his plan, so is man in the hands of the one who made him".[125] More remarkably, based on his reading of Genesis, this *massam luti* became *massa peccati*, *massa peccatorum*, simply *massa*, and then in

---

[To human] it is said, *In toil, you shall eat your bread*. Creation, then, has been subjected to vanity not of its own will". (Ramsey 112).

120 *Quare intellegendum est legem ad hoc datam esse, non ut peccatum insereretur neque ut extirparetur, sed tantum ut demonstraretur.* q Si 1.1.2 (CCSL 44.9; Ramsey 175).

121 *in praeuaricatione primi hominis, quia et ipse mandatum acceperat.* q Si 1.1.4 (CCSL 44.10).

122 *quia iure supplicii diuino iudicio tributa et inposita est ab eo qui praemonuit hominem dicens: qua die manducaueritis morte moriemini* [Gen 2:17]. q Si 1.1.13 (CCSL 44.17; Ramsey 181).

123 *Hoc, rursus dicunt, non de illa lege quae Iudaeis data est sed de euangelio dictum est. Manichaeorum est enim tam ineffabiliter caeca ista peruersitas.* q Si 1.1.16 (CCSL 44.20).

124 Augustine's manuscripts were very consistent in his explicit and implicit quotations of Gen 2:7, which can be seen as follows: *de limo terrae* in Gn Ma 2.1; 2.8; 2.9; 2.37; Gn li 3.22.34; 6.3.4; 6.5.8; 6.6.11; 6.12.21; 6.13.23; 7.5.8; ci 13.24; Ps 89.3; *limo uel puluere* in Gn li 7.6.9; *puluere uel limo terrae* in Gn li 6.11.19; *de terrae puluere* in Gn li 6.9.16; pec 1.4; ci 13.24; 14.11; *puluerem de terra* in Gn li 6.1.1; ci 13.24; Ps 118.18.2; *puluerem terrae* in Gn li 6.11.19; Jul im 2.178.

125 *et homines omnes de solo, et ex terra Adam creatus est ... quasi lutum figuli in manu ipsius, plasmare illud et disponere, omnes uiae eius secundum dispositionem eius, sic homo in manu illius qui se fecit, reddet illi secundum iudicium suum.* q Si 1.2.20 (CCSL 44.51; Ramsey 203). Augustine makes a similar point in q 68.2 by quoting Gen 3:19: "and because he did not want to obey [God] by whom he was created, [he] fell back into that out of which he was created, and after his sin he deserved to hear: *You are earth, and to the earth you shall go*. To persons such as these the Apostle says, *o man, who are you that you talk back to God?*" (Ramsey 117).

his later works, it became *massa damnata*, which all reflected his pessimistic view of the human condition due to the transgression against, and as a punishment for disobeying, the law of God (Gen 2:16–17; 3:6).[126] So, it was obvious that without being based upon the book of Genesis, his reading of the Pauline epistle will neither be sensible nor his theology credible.

From his treatises on the epistle to the Romans and Galatians, we have seen how Augustine retrieved and rehabilitated Paul from the Manicheans by alluding to the book of Genesis and established that Genesis is in line with Paul. There are considerable passages where he cited a piece of Genesis[127] and the Pauline epistles to substantiate his theology, and he continued to draw imagery from Genesis in his later works. In *De libero arbitrio*, where he used standard philosophical arguments for human free will in Book 1, Augustine related Paul with Genesis in Book 3 to argue that a good human being can be led astray and that sin entered the world through free will.[128] Even the famous garden scene in the *Confessiones* could be reimagined now that we see such a link between Genesis and Paul. When the voice tells Augustine to "pick up and read" and he picks up Paul, the fact that Augustine does it in a garden in Milan is itself reminiscent of being in the garden of Eden.[129]

Augustine reiterated the argument that Genesis is in line with Paul in *Contra Faustum Manicheum* (c. 408–410) where he refuted the *Capitula* of Faustus systematically. Fautus's *Capitula* asserted that the Manicheans rejected the Old Testament since it was opposed to the New Testament, and it repudiated the genealogies of Jesus as God was not defiled by human flesh. Faustus also stressed that the Hebrew patriarchs led lives of scandalous immorality to support his negation of the Old Testament.[130] Without seeing in detail what Augustine referred to as a "large work against Faustus",[131] we shall highlight Book 12 where he frequently cited the book of

---

126 We had seen *massa peccati* in q 68.3; q Si 1.2.16; *massa peccatorum* in q Si 1.2.19, and *massa* 9 times in his treaties on the Roman epistles. *massa damnata* emerged in ci 21.12; Jul 6.2; ench 27; Jul im 1.141; epp 190.9; 194.14. For the development and significance of *massa* in Augustine's though, see Fredriksen (1999b), 345–47.

127 In Augustine's extant works, there are around 3194 explicit references to the book of Genesis, with around 1100 references to chapter one and 142 references was made to the first verse of chapter one (these numbers were collected using the cag-online.net database).

128 In lib 3.24.72, Augustine stated: *ex quo intellegitur etiamsi sapiens primus homo factus est potuisse tamen seduci, quod peccatum cum esset in libero arbitrio, iustam diuina lege poenam consecutam. ita dicit etiam apostolus Paulus: "dicentes se esse sapientes stulti facti sunt* [Rom 1:22]*". superbia enim auertit a sapientia, auersionem autem stultitia consequitur. stultitia quippe caecitas quaedam est, sicut idem dicit: "et obscuratum est insipiens cor eorum* [Rom 1:21]*". unde autem haec obscuratio nisi ex auersione a lumine sapientiae? unde autem haec auersio nisi dum ille cui bonum est deus, sibi ipse uult esse bonum suum, sicuti sibi est deus? itaque "ad me ipsum", inquit, "conturbata est anima" "mea"; et: "gustate et eritis sicut dii* [Gen 3:5]*"* (CSEL 74.150).

129 See cf 8.12.29. For an examination of how Augustine's conversion in cf 8.12.28–29 integrated the exhortation of Paul with imageries of the Garden of Eden, see Vaught (2004), 90–99.

130 See Teske (2007), 9–10 for a summary of Faustus's arguments.

131 *scripsi grande opus ...* re 2.7.1.

Genesis and Pauline epistles in a three-part argument to refute Faustus's allegation that he had found no testimonies about Christ in the prophets.[132]

Quoting a number of passages from the Pauline letters as a proof, Augustine argued that the word of God was exclusively entrusted to the Jews and "the New Testament was symbolized in the Old".[133] Since the Manicheans refused to "listen to Moses and the prophets" (Lk16:29, 31), Augustine asserted that they "not only do not believe Christ who rose from the dead but do not at all believe that Christ rose from the dead".[134] Arguing that Paul correctly summed up in Rom 3:21; 10:4 and 2 Cor 1:20 how Christ was foretold in the Old Testament prophecy, Augustine alleged that Mani "tells a long and foolish myth" that opposed Paul's testimony.[135] Regarding the place in the Old Testament "where Christ was foretold by the prophets of Israel", Augustine argued that God's promise to Abraham to bless all the nations of the earth through his descendants (Gen 26:4) has been fulfilled in Christ whom all the nations come to believe, as Paul himself wrote in Rom 9:6–8 and Gal 3:16.[136]

For Augustine, the six days of creation in Genesis signified the six ages of the human race through the passages of time: the first age is from Adam to Noah; the second from Noah to Abraham; the third from Abraham to David; the fourth from David to the Babylonian exile; the fifth from the exilic period to the incarnation of Christ; and the sixth, which is now passing and will conclude with the coming of Christ for judgement. The sixth day when Adam "is formed into the image of God" corresponded with the sixth age of the world when human beings were renewed in God's image. Basing upon this scheme, Augustine asserted that "everything that we read" regarding the creation of Adam and Eve in God's image foretells Christ and the church "when it is considered clearly and piece by piece". Adam foreshadowed "the one to come" (Rom 5:15) while his union with Eve prefigured Christ and the church (Eph 5:31–32). The "New Adam" who "emptied himself, taking the form of the servant (Phil 2:6–7) … became a partaker of our nature so that we might be the body of that head".[137] The sacrifice of Cain, who refused to suppress his anger even after God's counsel when his offering was rejected (Gen 4:7 LXX) prefigured the Jews who were "filled with pride over the works of the law" while Abel prefigured Christ, "the head of the younger people" who "is killed by the older people of the Jews". Thus, Augustine used Genesis to support Paul's writing that "not knowing the righteousness of God and wanting to establish their own" (Rom 10:3), the Jews "tripped on the stumbling block" (Rom 9:32).[138]

Asserting again that the pages of the Old Testament are brimming with prediction of Christ,[139] Augustine alleged that Faustus "does not knock with pious faith [at

---

132 *Faustus dixit … dic potius, si quid habes, cur debeamus prophetas accipere … propter testimonia, inquit, quae de Christo praefati sunt. ego quidem nulla inueni.* Fau 12.1 (CSEL 25.1.329).
133 Fau 12.3 (Teske 127).
134 Fau 12.4 (Teske 128).
135 Fau 12.5 (Teske 128).
136 Fau 12.6 (Teske 128).
137 Fau 12.8 (Teske 130).
138 Fau 12.9 (Teske 131).
139 *cui praedicendo omnes illae paginae uigilant.* Fau 12.25 (CSEL 25.1.325; Teske 141).

the closed door of divine mystery], but mocks with proud impiety [so that he] has eyes for reading but does not have heart for understanding".[140] Continuing to explore the prefiguration of Christ in the Old Testament while refuting the possible objection that he cleverly used "those things, which occurred at their own time in the course of history ... to signify Christ", Augustine invoked the authority of Paul to support his interpretation: *All these things happened to them in figure* (1 Cor 10:10) and *These were all symbols of us* (1 Cor 10:6).[141] For Augustine, failing to understand the meaning does not mean, and is no reason to doubt, that "all those events that are found in the old canon of the holy scriptures ... signify something".[142] He then insisted that believing precedes understanding (Is 7:9) so that, in simple faith "we believe that the providential plan of his humility ... was for good reason foretold so long ago by prophets, by means of a prophetic nation, a prophetic people, and a prophetic kingdom".[143] Finally, Augustine defended the conduct of the patriarchs and prophets who, according to Faustus, did not live in a way worthy of their prophecies, by quoting Paul's writings that "Abraham believed God, and it was credited to him for righteousness" (Gal 3:6; also Rom 1:17; 4:11–12; Gal 3:8).[144] By deducing that Faustus actually "blames those men [whom] Paul the apostle praises",[145] Augustine also inferred that the Manicheans in fact contradicted and misread Paul whom they used to substantiate their teachings, particularly against the Catholic Christians.

Although many of his arguments in *Contra Faustum Manicheum* were a reiteration of what he already spelt out against the Manicheans, Augustine was more aware of the significance of the incarnation in understanding the relation of the two testaments of the Scriptures. Pointing out the implication of this deeper insight, Cameron remarked that if Christ as the *res significans* of God was not just witnessed by history but had acted in history, then every historical sign can convey something of its *res*, either before or after the incarnation. This new insight made the Old Testament into a bearer of New Testament grace, and opened prophecy to be understood as sacramental. "Where Augustine had once thought the prophetic sign acted as the diaphanous and obsolescent pointer to the future reality, Christ was now understood to have present within the sign both to denote and communicate his power".[146] In other words, Christ was not only prefigured and predicted in the Old Testament in a one way process or direction but already "enjoyed" by people of the Old Testament.

---

140 *Et clamat Faustus oculis clausis nihil se in illis litteris inuenisse, quod ad praenuntiationem Christi pertineat! quid autem mirum, si oculos habet ad legendum et cor ad intellegendum non habet, qui positus ante ostium clausum diuini secreti non fide pietatis pulsat, sed elatione inpietatis insultat?* Fau 12.30 (CSEL 25.1.359; Teske 145).
141 Fau 12.37 (Teske 149).
142 *Ita prius illa omnia, quae sunt in uetere instrumento scripturarum sanctarum, quisquis non peruerso animo legerit, sic oportet moueatur, ut aliquid ea significare non ambigat.* Fau 12.37 (CSEL 25.1.364; Teske 149).
143 Fau 12.46 (Teske 156).
144 Fau 12.47 (Teske 156).
145 *Nunc uero illos homines Faustus Manichaeus uituperat, Paulus autem apostolus laudat.* Fau 12.48 (CSEL 25.1.377; Teske 157).
146 See Cameron (1999), 96–97.

Perhaps, Augustine's most significant treatment of the book of Genesis was *De Genesi ad litteram* (*c.* 400–415), which was considered to be one of the great works of his religious and philosophical maturation alongside *De Trinitate* and *De civitate Dei*. No longer written to refute just the Manichean errors but concerned with all the false views of the text of Genesis, this book is "an impressive testimony to the way in which Augustine lovingly immersed himself in the scriptures".[147] Asserting that the two categories of Scripture — namely the two testaments — contain four types of information, viz., about eternal realities, about the facts of history, about future events and about moral precepts, Augustine saw Genesis as an account of actual events and book of facts.[148]

Remarkably, from his reading of Paul, Augustine also insisted that the actual bipartite quality of the scriptures "is not its obvious division into two testaments, but its all having a figurative and a literal meaning".[149] In Augustine's evolving interpretative structures, this two-fold meaning of the scriptures corresponded more with the incarnational paradigm than the spiritualist paradigm: he was conscious of the Christ-ian meaning of Genesis where "the creation came through the Word and the Word entered the creation in Christ".[150] Therefore, Augustine attempted to draw out the two-fold meaning of Genesis alongside each other so that "each gives a true and real" but distinct meaning. In this "twin-track" approach, Augustine's "exegesis moves backwards and forwards between the questions of metaphysics and cosmology, between the Son as Logos and incarnate Saviour, and between questions of human truth and salvation history".[151]

Without going into his detailed exegesis, we shall take Augustine's explication of "Paradise" to show how he drew out the two-fold meaning of Genesis and blended it with Pauline accounts. Against those who understood Paradise only figuratively while accepting "the authority of these writings", he insisted that Paradise should be understood according to the proper literal sense.[152] He reconciled what was said about Paradise with what was written about the third and the sixth days of creation so that

---

147 Hill (2002), 155, 166; Teske (1999), 376. In *De Genesi ad litteram*, he still referred implicitly to the Manicheans in 7.11.17; 8.2.5; 10.13.22 and 11.36.49 while 7.2.3 and 11.13.17 were an explicit reference to the Manicheans.
148 *Omnis diuina scriptura bipertita ... quae duo etiam testamenta dicuntur. ... quae ibi aeterna intimentur, quae facta narrentur, quae futura praenuntientur, quae agenda praecipiantur uel admoneantur. in narratione ergo rerum factarum quaeritur, utrum omnia secundum figurarum tantummodo intellectum accipiantur, an etiam secundum fidem rerum gestarum ad serenda et defendenda sint.* Gn li 1.1.1 (CSEL 28.1.3). See O'Loughlin (1999), 168.
149 Hill (2002), 168. According to Augustine: *nam non esse accipienda figuraliter nullus christianus dicere audebit, adtendens apostolum dicentem: omnia autem haec in figura contingebant in illis* [1 Cor 10:11], *et illud, quod in Genesi scriptum est: et erunt duo in carne una* [Gen 2:24], *magnum sacramentum commendantem in Christo et in ecclesia.* Gn li 1.1.1 (CSEL 28.1.3–4).
150 See O'Loughlin (1999), 204. See also n. 110 above for Augustine's own treatment of this passage.
151 O'Loughlin (1999), 171.
152 *qui auctoritatem harum litterarum sequuuntur.* Gn li 8.1.4 (CSEL 28.1.231; Hill 347). Cf. Gn li 8.2.5 with Gn Ma 2.2.3; 2.9.12 for his previous figurative interpretation. Hill remarked that for Augustine, "to relativize the historical character of the paradise story was ... to relativize also the truths of faith that were closely bound up with the account". Hill (2002), 161.

the trees laid out in Paradise are of the same varieties which the earth still went on producing in their proper time while the seed-bearing fodder contains "the things that were going to spring up over the earth from that generative power which the earth had already received".[153] Although the tree of life in the middle of Paradise and the tree of knowledge of discerning good and evil (Gen 2:9) "were themselves bodily realities", in its "forward reference that was figurative … the tree of life also was Christ".[154]

If Augustine read the "factual events" in Genesis alongside the figurative meaning that Paul hinted, he also attempted to read Paul in the light of Genesis. As we see in Book 12 of the *De Genesi ad litteram*, Augustine attempted to answer some questions regarding "the problem raised by the apostle's apparently locating Paradise in the third heaven" in 2 Cor 12:2–4. Starting with the question, "how did Paul see Paradise?", Augustine considered three kinds of visions: bodily, spiritual and intellectual vision.[155] These three visions corresponded with the three strata of heaven. The first heaven can be taken as the "bodily sky" and whatever is above the waters and the earths that can be seen with bodily vision, as described in Gen 1:6–8. The second consists in the "bodily likeness which is perceived in spirit", as seen in Act 10:10–12. The third is that one that is observed by the mind, which has been snatched away from the senses of the flesh, where one "see and hear the things that are in that heaven, and the very substance of God" through the power of the Holy Spirit.[156]

Basing on the ecstatic experience of Paul, Augustine inferred that Paul was "snatched away" to the "paradise of paradises": "If the good soul, after all, finds joy in the good things in the whole of creation, what could outdo the joy which is to be found in the Word of God, through whom all things were made?"[157] Then, he neatly connected the "actual historical events" in Genesis and the rapturous experience of Paul with the future by moving to the question of the resurrection of the body: until the resurrection of the body, it had been necessary to be "snatched away from the senses of this flesh" to gaze upon God as this flesh "mars and weighs down the soul, deriving as it does from the handing on of the first transgression".[158]

---

153 *Sed cum ex his generibus sint ista ligna instituta in paradiso, quae iam terra tertio die produxerat, adhuc ea produxit in tempore suo … quae super terram exorta erant ex illa uirtute generandi, quam terra iam acceperat.* Gn li 8.3.7 (CSEL 28.1.234; Hill 350).
154 *Aliud quam erant illa omnia significauerunt, sed tamen etiam ipsa corporaliter fuerunt. et quando a narrante commemorata sunt, non erat illa figurata locutio, sed earum expressa narratio, quarum erat figurata praecessio. erat ergo et lignum uitae quemadmodum petra Christus.* Gn li 8.4.8 (CSEL 28.1.235–36; Hill 351); see also Gn li 8.5.9.
155 Gn li 12.2.5; 12.24.51 (Hill 466, 492).
156 Gn li 12.34.67 (Hill 504).
157 *Non incongruenter arbitramur et illuc esse apostolum raptum et ibi fortassis esse paradisum omnibus meliorem et, si dici oportet, paradisum paradisorum. si enim animae bonae laetitia in rebus bonis est in omni creatura, quid ea laetitia praestantius, quae in uerbo dei est, per quod facta sunt omnia?* Gn li 12.34.67 (CSEL 28.1.432; Hill 504).
158 *Porro autem, si tale sit corpus, cuius sit difficilis et grauis administratio, sicut haec caro, quae corrumpitur et adgrauat animam, de propagine transgressionis existens, multo magis auertitur mens ab illa uisione summi caeli: unde necessario abripienda erat ab eiusdem carnis sensibus, ut ei quomodo capere posset illud ostenderetur.* Gn li 12.35.68 (CSEL 28.1.433; Hill 505).

We can therefore see Augustine's hermeneutical ingenuity in relating Paul with Genesis. While Paul determined Augustine's reading of Genesis, Genesis in turn shed light even on the ambiguous words of Paul. While Paul's account of his "rapture" seems incompatible with the scheme of *De Genesi ad litteram* particularly as a conclusion to an exposition of the book of Genesis,[159] Augustine understands Genesis and the Pauline epistles as mutually illuminating and complementary accounts of factual events within time. Both accounts occurred within the realm of time where the Word entered creation in Christ so that Christ determined and opened the deeper meaning to these passages.

Concluding Remarks

In this chapter, we have seen how Augustine retrieved and rehabilitated Paul from the Manicheans, particularly through the book of Genesis and argued that without the book of Genesis, Augustine's reading of the Pauline epistles will neither be sensible nor his theology credible. Against the Manicheans, Augustine credibly asserted that the two testaments of the Scriptures are in perfect harmony. Largely drawing from the book of Genesis, Augustine negated the Manichean dualism by affirming that all the creations were created by and through the Word of God. The transgression of God's commandment without external coercion but solely through their own free will severed the relationship of human with God. The incarnation of the Word of God in creation to save and restore this broken relationship negated the Manichean docetic Christology. Against the Manichean's assertion that God was not defiled by human flesh, Paul's analogy of the church as the body of Christ based upon the book of Genesis became a significant insight for Augustine.

Drawing from both Genesis and the Pauline letters, Augustine asserted that bearing witness to the dual identity of Christ became an important criterion which qualifies "writings" as the "Holy Scripture". The eternal Word of God addressing the "infirm" human being through the lowly scriptural passages determines the authoritative status of Scripture within the realm of time. Without intensely drawing upon Genesis to substantiate his reading of Paul, he will not be able to establish these points against the Manicheans. Conversely, without Augustine's reading of Paul that greatly shaped and determined subsequent readers even till today, the messages that we draw from the Pauline epistles in particular and the whole Scripture in general will be quite different. Therefore, the intellectual conversion[160] of Augustine that we had seen in this chapter has been relevant for subsequent readers of the Scriptures.

---

159 Thus, Hill observed that Book 12 "offer autonomous theological treatises on subjects that are only distantly connected with the texts of Genesis but were of special interest to Augustine or his readers". Hill (2002), 162.
160 But see chapter three, n. 58 above regarding the argument that the phrase "intellectual conversion" is just a "scholarly invention".

This does not imply that Augustine offers a "definitively" correct reading of Paul, but that he offers a systematic reading of Paul which is in line with the teaching of the Catholic church that also negated the Manichean and other "gnostic" readings.[161] And while his reading of Genesis against the Manicheans was neither completed nor rigidly set, the cases Augustine built against them prepared the ground for his argument with the Donatist so that "the conclusions harvested in the former controversy germinated seeds of argument for the latter".[162]

Ultimately for Augustine, the inbreaking of the eternal Word of God within the realm of time in specific historical settings affirms that history has a definite meaning and moves in a particular direction. In the next chapter, we shall see how Augustine perceives this salvation history as witnessed and recorded in the Scriptures, which he expounded in the *De civitate Dei*.

---

161 On the accuracy of Augustine's reading of Paul which determined later interpretations, and whether he overlooked those facets of Paul which embraced some kind of apocalyptic eschatology and cosmic dualism and replaced it with a "juridical" concern for justification or a more introspective approach of the human situation, see Patte and TeSelle (2002).
162 Cameron (1999), 98.

CHAPTER 7

"There we shall rest and see"

Beyond "Time" and "the Authority of Scripture" in the De Civitate Dei

De civitate Dei can be considered as one of the most epic writings of Augustine. In his other works that we have seen in the previous chapters, Augustine mostly dealt with issues of Christian orthodoxy in the light of, and in relation to the Scriptures. Unlike his interlocutors in those works, *De civitate Dei* was prompted by the criticisms levelled at *tempora christiana*[1] particularly by "pagan"[2] intellects who held views antagonistic to the Christian religion (*opiniones christianae religioni aduersariae*), and Augustine touched upon a wide-ranging theme in this "monumental undertaking" (*grande opus*).[3] Painstakingly drawing upon the written historical traditions of Rome apart from the Scriptures, Augustine developed his argument that the heavenly "City of God" (*ciuitatem dei*) whose security is eternal (*illa stabilitate sedis aeternae*) and where perfect peace (*pace perfecta*) will be established, stand in contrast with the earthly "city" "which aims at dominion", and though served by all nations, "is itself dominated by that very lust of domination".[4]

In this chapter, we will see the general background to the "formation" of the *De civitate Dei*. Specifying how the main arguments in the *De civitate Dei* had in fact already taken shape in, and interrelated to, Augustine's works[5] that we had seen in the preceding chapters, we will see if they align with the more recent developments

---

1   On how this is an "elastic concept" in his usage, see chapter one, n. 77 above. *Tempora christiana* will denote in this context the "present time" when Christianity supplanted traditional religious beliefs of the Romans.
2   On how the term "paganism" as a generalization, "creates a standard of imprecision that easily leads to theologically-based judgments about religion 'apart from' Christianity", and how these "intellectual pagans [often] had more in common with the Christian fathers they opposed than with the villagers and pilgrims who crowded shrines in an effort to resolve quotidian crises", see Frankfurter (2006), 544–45. According to Cecilia Ames, "Tertullian institutes this form of discursive construction in Latin". Ames (2007), 459.
3   See re 2.43.1.
4   *de terrena ciuitate, quae cum dominari adpetit, etsi populi seruiant, ipsa ei dominandi libido dominator ...* ci *prol* 1 (CCSL 47.1; Bettenson 5).
5   The interrelation of the *De civitate Dei* with his other works has long been acknowledged. For example, Markus remarked that *De genesi ad litteram* "contains the first germs of many of the ideas which we meet later in the *De civitate Dei*" while Edmund Hill asserted that "The thoughts that Augustine will develop on a large scale later on" in his *De civitate Dei* are "already set forth, in a nutshell" here. Dyson traced the emergence of "two cities" in *De catechizandis rudibus* and surmised that "a *City of God* in some form or other would have been written even had the sack of Rome not occurred, and even without the correspondence with Marcellinus". See Markus (1965), 75; Hill (2002), 31; Dyson (1998), xiii.

in his thought. Focusing on his exposition of some passages from Genesis, we will see if previous stances that Augustine now abandoned or retained, and new insights that he incorporated into a more coherent structure of the *De civitate Dei*, can give us a better idea of his understanding of the nature and authority of Scripture.

1. "Rome" as an Ideological Construct

In 410, the invading Goths under Alaric sacked Rome.[6] In the *Retractationes*, Augustine recalled how the "pagans" were attempting "to impute the devastation to the Christian religion" so that he decided to write the books "in answer to their blasphemies and errors".[7] Who are these "pagans" and why did they blame the Christian religion for the downfall of Rome and how did Augustine respond to their allegations?

In chapter one, we have seen how emperor Augustus commemorated his achievements in the RGDA. Recounting his feats in battles, the expansion of the Roman empire, subjugation of the neighbouring peoples,[8] and establishment of colonies,[9] Augustus asserted that he inaugurated a period of stability and peace.[10] In chapter 12 of the RGDA, Augustus stated that the senate decreed that an altar of Augustan Peace should be consecrated on the field of Mars to commemorate his return. And in chapter 13, Augustus declared that the gates of Janus, which were closed in times when Rome was at peace, were closed three times under his leadership while in the whole period before him, they had been closed only twice since the foundation of the city.[11]

Augustus also proclaimed that he restored and built temples, introduced new laws, and revived many ancient customs that were already becoming obsolete, and personally "handed down to later generations exemplary practices for them to imitate".[12] Commenting on the "impressive number of repairs, restorations, and constructions of cult places" listed in the RGDA, Scheid remarked that Augustus's pious actions "were

---

6   On the origins and identity of Alaric's Goths who were "[h]alfway between a besieging army and a band of refugees", and why they sacked Rome after besieging the city for two years, see Kulikowski (2007).

7   re 2.43 (Ramsey 147); see also ci 4.2.

8   *Omnium provinciarum populi Romani quibus finitimae fuerunt gentes quae non parerent imperio nostro fines auxi*. RGDA 26 (Brunt and Moore 30).

9   See RGDA 28.

10 *Plurimaeque aliae gentes expertae sunt [populi Romani] fidem me principe quibus antea cum populo Romano nullum extiterat legationum et amicitiae commercium.* RGDA 32 (Brunt and Moore 34).

11 See ci 3.9 for Augustine's own comment on the closing of the gates of Janus.

12 *Legibus novis me auctore latis multa exempla maiorum exolescentia iam ex nostro saeculo reduxi et ipse multarum rerum exempla imitanda posteris tradidi.* RGDA 8 (Brunt and Moore 22); see RGDA 19–20 for the list of temples that Augustus built and restored. On the significance of these feats, Galinsky noted: "The rebuilding, first and foremost, was a matter of signifying the return to stability. Roman religion was not a religion of salvation, but it was intimately connected with the civil order of the state ... The gods were there to protect the community, to safeguard its values, and to help instill proper civic behavior. When their shrines fell apart it was a sign of the fraying of this fabric. Their restoration signified the return of divinely ordered civic stability". Galinsky (2007), 74.

firmly rooted in the ideological sphere of traditionalism" that helped to construct the emperor's image[13] and rise of the "umbrella phenomenon" known as the "imperial cult".[14] Augustus sums up his achievements in chapters 34–35 by claiming that he ended tumultuous civil wars[15] and restored the *res publica* at Rome that earned him the "deserved" title *Augustus* and *patrem patriae*. All of Augustus's victories and military honours "goes hand in hand with his claim to have brought peace to Rome. He intended his rule to go down in history as the *pax Augusta*".[16]

Another significant renovation/innovation that was also cloaked with Augustus's ideology was the implementation of the Julian calendar. Stating that calendars are "a fundamental aspect of social life, an organizing principle of human experience, a constitutive component of culture and world views" and not just "a technical curiosity", Sacha Stern emphasised that "their development was closely related to the political changes that transformed the ancient world from the mid-first millennium BCE to late Antiquity".[17] And remarking that calendar involved more than a mere reckoning of time, Galinsky stated that calendar reform of Caesar marks the arrival of expert professionals who "bring their knowledge to regularizing a haphazard system, and they are employed and appropriated by the new leader of the state", at the expense of the nobility. Augustus continued this process of "opening up of formerly restricted opportunities to a much larger segment of the populace (with the obvious exception of governance at the top)".[18] Seeing calendar as a significant aspect of the imperial propaganda, Jörg Rüpke also asserted that the dates of the Julian calendar not only "model the history of the Imperial Age: they paint a cosmic picture that transcends Empire. In the context of time at least, and its measurement, Rome and the cosmos become one entity".[19]

The introduction of the Julian calendar therefore coincided with, and seems to enhance, the notion of *Pax Romana* that Augustus ushered in, and which he prudently commemorated in the RGDA.[20] This period lasted for almost two hundred years

---

13 Scheid (2009), 275–77. According to Alaric Watson, "Augustus understood, and fully exploited, the ideological nexus linking political authority to the divine sanction implicit in military victory that has come to be known as the 'theology of victory'". Watson (1999), 3.
14 On how the so-called imperial cult "was not a centrally steered phenomenon", see Galinsky (2011), 1–21; on how this cult did not negated traditional Roman religion in late antiquity, see Salzman (2013), 371–97.
15 On Augustine's own comment on the role of Augustus in the *crudelia bella ciuilia*, see ci 3.30 (CCSL 47.96).
16 Eck (2007), 123. Cooley also asserted that underestimating the innovation involved in introducing the cult of *Pax Augusta* to Rome is easy but misleading. "Such deities did become commonplace under later emperors, but this was the first known instance of an 'august(an)' deity: not only did the new deity's title encapsulate the idea that Rome could now enjoy a special relationship with the gods specifically through the mediation of Augustus, but it also facilitated the dissemination of such cult beyond Rome, contributing to cultural unification of the empire". Cooley (2009), 156.
17 Stern (2012), v.
18 Galinsky (2007), 72.
19 Rüpke (2014), 146–48.
20 Rüpke remarked thus: "Despite their great number, the Augustan temples did not simply represent elements of a major architectural programme. As in the Republican Period, many of the cult structures, and these the most important ones, resulted from specific historical events, often military

during which the Roman Empire attained its largest territorial extent. This notion of *Pax Romana* converged with the prevalent idea that Rome is the "Eternal City".[21] According to Kenneth J. Pratt, *Urbs aeterna* appeared prior to *Roma aeterna* which was used from the time of the emperor Hadrian (117–138), while the first explicit reference to the city as "eternal" was made by Tibullus (c. 19 BCE). When they spoke of Rome as eternal, the Romans initially mean the "possibility of the state's perpetual security" while the notion "was to undergo new expressions and credence with increased theological meaning".[22] If Augustus's imperial ideology ascribed the peace, stability and enduring safety which the "Eternal City" of Rome enjoyed to the restoration of ancient customs and rituals that had been neglected due to civil wars, falling away again would therefore disrupt peace and safety and mark the gradual demise of Rome.

Thus, long after the heyday of Augustus, when the "relegated" Rome — yet "the symbolic heart of empire"[23] — was sacked by Alaric in 410, pagan aristocrats and intellectuals who flew to North Africa attributed the event to the Christian religion.[24] Initially as a response to these allegations, Augustine wrote the *De civitate Dei* where he "deconstructs the ideology of Rome as the eternal city, whose peace and justice are the peace and justice of the world".[25]

Using "the cultural expectations and literary training he shares with the classically educated members of his audience" to deconstruct their ideology, Augustine presented "a Christian interpretation of events"[26] in the light of his reading of the Scriptures. Rhetorically referring to his interlocutors as "the unlearnt" and "the inexperienced",[27] Augustine invoked the written historical tradition of Rome

---

successes, to which they referred in their decor. Thus, in recording these events, the calendar again acquired a historical dimension, even though in a largely contemporary context". Rüpke (2011), 126.

[21] We can see how Augustus "etched" his achievements with the "identity" of the city of Rome from Denis Feeney observation: "Augustus over the years created a profound reconfiguration of the systems of representing the past time of the city. This reconfiguration centered on his own person and that of his heir, in the process forging links with Rome's divine origins and creating a new imperial dating era. The Republican time systems appear to be still in place, but by the end of Augustus's reign their symbolic power, iconography, and resonance have been compromised and redrawn". Feeney (2007), 181–82.

[22] See Pratt (1965), 25–27.

[23] Kulikowski (2007), 4. In the words of Markus, "Rome had long since ceased to be a first-class city", economically, administratively and culturally. See Markus (1963), 341.

[24] See ci 3.12. Previously, the emperor Theodosius I, by his edict *Cuntos populos* of 384, established Christianity as the official religion of the empire. Abolition of the worship of Rome's ancient gods was followed by numerous anti-pagan edicts. Particularly in the Roman aristocratic world, the events of 410 were attributed to this change of allegiance: "Rome is now suffering … because she has forsaken the gods of her fathers in favour of a God Who counsels meekness and submission". Dyson (1998), xi–xii. On the issue whether Rome ever "fell" or just underwent transition and even accomodated the barbarians, see Ward-Perkins (2005).

[25] Dyson (1998), xxix.

[26] Conybeare (1999), 63.

[27] On *indoctum … inperitis*, see ci 4.1. Evans pointed out that the references were "a rhetorical ploy rather than a statement of facts" while Conybeare asserted that Augustine created "a fictional audience … for the rhetorical purpose of toying with them". See Evans (2003), xl–xli; Conybeare (1999), 62.

from which he listed "the many and diverse calamities" which have befallen the city before the incarnation of Christ and the Christian religion grew up.[28] From the books in which Roman authors "have recorded and published the history of times gone by", Augustine claimed to demonstrate that "matters are far other than the ignorant suppose" while there will be endless historical examples to prove his contention.[29]

2. "Eternal Rome" in the "Collective" and "Personal" Memories: Reading *Confessiones* as a Subversive Literary Device

Since Augustine utilized Latin classics to build up his arguments in his responses to the "pagans" allegations, it will be apt to ask: Even if there was anything to deconstruct about the history of the Roman empire, the myth of Rome or the many gods who protected the City, can Augustine and his method[30] be considered credible for the task? In tackling this question, many modern researchers focussed upon Augustine's "external" sources: how, why and in what way did he use these historical and philosophical sources, explicit and implicit, in the *De civitate Dei*? Did he use "primary" and "secondary" sources and how exact are his quotations? Did he recollect them from memory or did he reread them?[31]

Although they are important aspects of scholarship, we shall not dwell upon the crucial questions posed about Augustine's "external" sources since they defy definite answers and they may not really bother his interlocutors.[32] Instead, we shall look at a more immediate question they would probably asked: what did

---

28 *quibus calamitatibus res Romanae multipliciter uarieque contritae sint* ... ci 2.3 (CCSL 47.37). According to O'Donnell, "after the early works (*c.* 386–391, before Augustine's ordination) there is a long dry spell for classical allusions in his theological works, until the early 410s, when Augustine began a fresh program of classical readings to fortify himself for the writing of the *De civitate Dei*". O'Donnell (1980), 147.
29 *De libris, quos auctores eorum ad cognoscendam praeteritorum temporum historiam memoriae mandauerunt, longe aliter esse quam putant demonstrandum fuit ... si haec atque huius modi, quae habet historia, unde possem, colligere uoluissem, quando finissem*? ci 4.1 (CCSL 47.98–100; Dyson 143).
30 According to Markus, "Augustine's reflections on history owed much both to the development of Christian historiography during the fourth century, and to the challenge of his own troubled times". Markus (1970), 2. For a good analysis of Augustine's method, see also O'Daly (1999b) and the articles in Vessey (1999).
31 For a general survey of the extent and limitation of his reading, his methods of citation, and whether he quoted "the classics from memory" or "read them again, enlarge his book knowledge, look up the passages when writing", see Hagendahl (1967), 15, 690–729. O'Donnell advocated a "cynical" or "minimalist" approach to Augustine's reading that stressed "the act of reading rather than the practice of citation". See O'Donnell (1980), 145. For a recent treatment of this question, see O'Daly (1999b), 234–64 and Shanzer (2012), 161–74.
32 On what may preoccupy Augustine's educated contemporaries which determined his approach, see Fortin (1980), 253. On the methodological "fallacy" of abstracting Augustine's texts from their rhetorical and pedagogical contexts, see Lamb (2018), 591–624.

the man from North Africa, a provincial bishop, know about the inner dynamic and powerplay of Rome to make his critique of Roman cultural memory and collective consciousness authoritative? Since Augustine wrote little about his time in Rome, we shall try to cull evidences from his *Confessiones*,[33] without assuming that his interlocutors will necessarily read this work, to see the making of the "Roman" Augustine. We shall see the expectations he would bring to Rome as a "provincial man", as the Greek historian Ammianus did in his *Res Gestae*, and see how significant Augustine's personal experience[34] could be in his reading of these "external" sources.

In Book 1 of the *Confessiones*, Augustine recounted his early education[35] where he learned Greek[36] and Latin literatures[37] including the marvellous tales (*suauitates graecas fabulosarum*) of Homer and Virgil's *Aeneid*.[38] In the early pages of the *Confessiones*, not only did Augustine cite "all four standard school authors" of his time, namely Cicero (cf 1.16.25), Virgil (cf 1.13.21–2), Terence (cf 1.16.26) and Sallust (cf 2.5.11), he quoted all but Sallust when he gave a "moralizing reading"[39] of the story of Jupiter, a "character" who recurred frequently in *De civitate Dei*.[40] Remarking that his enjoyment of Jupiter's exploits gave him a reputation as a gifted young man,[41] Augustine therefore made a big statement that even at that age, he was immersed in, and was well aware of the "fictitious" nature of, the Roman mythology.[42]

---

33 *Confessiones* is "the groundwork for the constructive project of the City of God". Vessey (1999), 9.
34 As McLynn argued, Augustine's earthly city was first of all a product of his own experience while his political horizons as Bishop of Hippo will determines his presentation of imperial authority. McLynn (1999b), 29, 33.
35 *in scholam datus sum, ut discerem litteras ... ubi legere et scribere et numerare discitur.* cf 1.9.14; 1.13.20 (CCSL 27.8; 27.11). On the three stages of schooling that probably originated in "Hellenistic Greece, whence it was adopted by the Romans in the last century of the Republic, to endure thereafter throughout the history of the Empire", see Kaster (1983).
36 On his hatred for Greek (*graecas litteras oderam*), see cf 1.13.20; 1.14.23. Greek is "a language spoken by a substantial minority of the North African population with links to Sicily and South Italy where Greek was widespread". See Chadwick (2009), 6. Augustine had "limited but usable knowledge" of Greek that he later enhanced "to expand his knowledge of Greek patristic literature". O'Donnell (1992a), 75.
37 Chadwick remarked that Augustine's "culture and training were initially more literary than philosophical, and merely as a literary figure he must rank as one of the most remarkable writers of his age". He also asserted that "education at the Thagaste school was principally in Latin language and literature, a subject which ancient men called 'grammar', taught by the Grammaticus". Chadwick (2009), 1, 6.
38 See cf 1.13.20–1.14.23. Homer was mentioned in cf 1.14.23; 1.16.25; ci 3.2; 4.26; 21.8. Beyond this two works, Homer "is named only at *haer.* 7". O'Donnell (1992a), 82. Pointing out that Augustine's quotation of Virgil, whom he quoted "about seventy times" in the *De civitate Dei*, was "more than the total of his quotations from all the other poets", S. Angus remarked that "Augustine knew his Virgil intimately". Angus (1906), 12.
39 See O'Donnell (1992a), 89; cf 1.18.28.
40 In fact, Jupiter was mentioned around 175 times in the *De civitate Dei* alone (these numbers were collected using the cag-online.net database).
41 *libenter haec didici et eis delectabar miser et ob hoc bonae spei puer appellabar.* cf 1.16.26 (CCSL 27.15).
42 On the *figmentorum poeticorum* and its dramatization in the stages, see cf 1.17.27.

Augustine recounted how his studies took him from Thagaste to Madaura and then to Carthage where he advanced his career by teaching the art of rhetoric.[43] Around 380–381, Augustine wrote a book called *De Pulchro et Apto* that was dedicated to Hierius, an Orator in Rome.[44] Attracted by the "hearsay" that students in Rome, unlike Carthage where "students enjoy a disgusting, unrestricted freedom", were better behaved and more disciplined,[45] Augustine left for Rome around 383.[46] But his short stay in Rome was "marred" by the nature of how he left his mother Monica behind in Africa, his sickness upon arrival and his association with the Manicheans' "elect" in Rome, and finally his realization that students in Rome presented another set of problem.[47] Thus, when there was an opportunity to be a professor of Rhetoric in Milan, Augustine applied for the post and was sent by the prefect Symmachus who approved of a public speech that he delivered for the occasion.[48]

In spite of Augustine's brief stint at Rome, the timing was highly significant in that he was commissioned by Symmachus — who had written his famed *Relatio* 3 recently, and that the Greek historian Ammianus Marcellinus was in Rome around the same time. In his *Res Gestae* which is "Roma-centric Latin historiography",[49] Ammianus, who had been expelled as a foreigner from Rome in 384 during a food shortage (14.6.19), had presented a realistic[50] and idyllic side of the city.[51] Probably completed soon after 390, Ammianus saw "a link between the fortunes of emperor

---

43 See cf 2.3.5; 3.1.1; 4.2.2. On how Carthage was the largest city in western Africa and the regional center of power where many of the sons of the elite went for the highest levels of education, see Sears (2017), 37–43. "Carthage had a substantial concentration of sophisticated people of high Latin culture" where "a poet or an orator or a civilized bishop" were welcomed by high officials of the Roman administration. Chadwick (2009), 9.
44 cf 4.13.20–14.23. On the significance of *De Pulchro et Apto* for an understanding of Augustine's intellectual and spiritual evolution, see Burchill-Limb (2003).
45 See cf 5.8.14.
46 See O'Donnell (1992b), 305.
47 *Et ecce cognosco alia Romae fieri, quae non patiebar in Africa.* cf 5.12.22 (CCSL 27.69).
48 cf 5.13.23.
49 Ross (2016), 27. For an introduction to Ammianus Marcellinus, see Wallace-Hadrill (1986), 13–35. According to Markus, "'Rome' was the head, centre and sum of the 'world'; the 'world' was only the expanded version of the City". Markus (1970), 26.
50 In *Rerum Gestarum* 14.6.2, Ammianus admitted that readers may feel that he "tell of nothing save dissensions, taverns, and other similar vulgarities" (*quae Romae geruntur, nihil praeter seditiones narratur et tabernas et uilitates harum similis alias*) in his description of current events at Rome. Substantiating this account, Ammianus summed up the vanities of the Romans in 14.7.26 which suggests that they are not worthy of the reputation of their city: *Haec similiaque memorabile nihil uel serium agi Romae permittunt* (Rolfe 36–37, 52); see also 28.4.1–35.
51 In *Rerum Gestarum*, the city of Rome was presented in such glowing terms as *uirtutum omnium domicilium Roma* (14.6.21) and the *urbem aeternam/aeternae urbis/urbis aeternae* (14.6.1; 15.7.1;15.7.10; 16.10.14; 19.10.1), the *augustissima omnium sede* (16.10.20) that will "live so long as men shall exist", *uictura dum erunt homines Roma* (14.6.3); (Rolfe 36–37, 48, 158, 164, 250). On how his depressing experience of contemporary Rome could not "overthrow the ideal in his mind", see O'Daly (1999b), 11–14. For an assessment of his account, which was asserted to be "fundamental to modern understanding and interpretation of the fourth century", see Barnes (1998); Drijvers (1999).

and empire" as well as "a link between the fortune of the empire and that of the city of Rome".[52] Unlike Jerome, who probably read Ammianus[53] and whose reaction to the sack of Rome was certainly more "Roma-centric"[54] than Augustine, Augustine neither displayed any knowledge of, nor engaged with, Ammianus's *Res Gestae*. Augustine was more concerned with "history of the Republic"[55] in the *De civitate Dei* while the emperors of late antiquity are the main focus of Ammianus's narrative. But crucially, Augustine had also witnessed the changing religious landscape in Rome and he will be aware of its cultural and socio-political implications on the prevalent "Roma-centric" ideology.

Besides, the traditional Roman cultic sentiment that Ammianus conveyed in his *Res Gestae*[56] was resonated by Symmachus, the prefect of Rome who endorsed Augustine for his new job in Milan. In the *Relatio* 3 that he wrote in 384,[57] Symmachus petitioned emperor Valentinian II to return the Altar of Victory to the Roman Senate House which was removed at the order of Gratian in 382. Dedicated by emperor Augustus on 28 August, 29 BCE, senators would offer some frankincense and a libation to the

---

52 See Harrison (1999), 163. As Wallace-Hadrill asserted, "The years during which his histories took shape, the late 380s and perhaps early 390s, were ones of acute religious and ideological conflict, in which the interpretation of the past, and particularly of the immediate past, was an integral part of the controversy". Wallace-Hadrill (1986), 19–20. On the various arguments regarding the date of publication of Ammianus's work, see Maenchen-Helfen (1955); Rohrbacher (2006); A. Cameron (2012).

53 On how Jerome may be an early reader of Ammianus's *Res Gestae*, see Maenchen-Helfen (1955); Rohrbacher (2006). On how he may knew Ammianus's books he wrote his *Aduersus Jouinianum* in spring 393, see A. Cameron (2012). On the view that Jerome had an identical theme with Ammianus's *Historia Augusta*, see Syme (1968), 80–83.

54 For a comparison of the reaction of Jerome, Socrates Scholasticus, Sozomen and Augustine to the fall of Rome, see Pelikan (1982). On how Augustine "passes over the *pax Romana* in a single subordinate clause, and carefully refrains from embroidering its theological significance" in his *De civitate Dei*, see Markus (1970), 52.

55 Observing that the prose writers from the time of the Emperors, compared with the great authors of the late Republic and Augustan age, were of little interest to Augustine, Hagendahl asserts that "there is nothing to indicate that either Tacitus or Suetonius or Ammianus Marcellinus, his own contemporary, were known to him". See Hagendahl (1967), 637, 667–69, 694. On why this historical period interested Augustine, see Burns (1999), 105–44, particularly 108 where we see the probable reasons that modern scholarship suggested.

56 According to Barnes, "Ammianus has a fundamentally consistent metaphysical scheme, which he applies to his evaluation of historical events and historical actions". Barnes (1998), 167. While he was eager to depict the magnificent sights of Rome which reveals his "own enthusiasm for the Eternal City", Wallace-Hadrill pointed out how Ammianus "fails to mention among these sights the Christian churches of Constantine, notably his Basilica, let alone record the controversial removal of the Altar of Victory from the Senate". See Wallace-Hadrill (1986), 450. On the debate whether his approach was secular or religious, see chapter 5 of Davies (2004), where Davies also asserted that Ammianus "uses all the erudite tools of his trade to undermine Christianity and enhance traditional rites". On the rhetorical shift from a totalizing discourse which stressed the "otherness" to a rhetoric of assimilation to marginalize Christianity before his period, see Hargis (1999).

57 According to Sogno, the word *relatio* specifically signifies an official report which eventually "became the technical term used for the detailed report addressed to the emperor by a judge whose decision was subject to an appeal to the imperial court". Sogno (2006), 32.

statue of Victory upon entering the senate house and take their vows of allegiance to the emperor at the Altar of the Victory.[58] As removing this Altar would renounce the traditional pagan religion of Rome and cut the state's funding of the cult,[59] Symmachus penned a carefully worded appeal for toleration and reversal of the decision where he invoked upon Romans' traditional religious beliefs.[60] Considering that he was Symmachus's protégé, and seeing how his passion to learn the trick of the trade led him to hear Ambrose in the first place (cf 5.13.23; 6.6.9), the aspiring Augustine — then still a Manichean "hearer" who could be alarmed by the growing influence of the Catholic church — would properly understand the religious sentiment behind Symmachus's *Relatio*.[61]

Augustine's move to the city of Milan as professor of rhetoric would also give him privileged access to politics of the emperor's court. Brown remarked that a rhetorician could serve like "Minister of Propaganda" and would give the official panegyrics on the Emperor and on the consuls of the year that "would have been carefully tuned to publicizing the programmes of the court".[62] Augustine, who "delivered at least two panegyrics at the court of Valentinian II",[63] would have known a lot about emperors to depict him in a good light and glossed over his weaknesses.[64] In short, we can say that Augustine had exposure to policy-makers in the Senate and the intellectual circles who would determine the "propaganda machinery" of the Roman empire at the highest level and he should be well aware of the cultural assumptions behind the myth of the city of Rome. Though mostly unrevealed in the *Confessiones*, Augustine's impression of the power play between Roman senators and the imperial court in Milan need to be considered when examining his method as he deconstructs the myth of Rome in the *De civitate Dei*. After all, between his high expectation of, and the reality in, Rome which make the "upstart" Augustine prefer to work in Milan, we can feel an aura of his critique of the ideology that Rome is the eternal city.

---

58 See Pohlsander (1969), 588–97.
59 See *Relatio* 3.11–15; on the three main implications of the removal of the altar, see Sogno (2006), 45.
60 Symmachus wrote: *repetimus igitur religionum statum, qui reip diu profit … uarios custodes urbibus cultus mens diuina distribuit … hic cultus in leges meas orbem redegit, haec sacra hannibalem a moenibus, a Capitolio Senonas reppulerunt … faueant clementiae uestrae sectarum omnium arcana praesidia et haec maxime, quae maiores uestros aliquando iuuerunt. uos defendant, a nobis colantur. Relatio* 3 (Seeck 281–83). For an assessment of Symmachus's petition, see O'Daly (1999b), 1–26. On the notion that Symmachus was not a bitter opponent of Christianity who championed paganism, as he was historically regarded, see Cameron (2011). But, on how "this dichotomy is a false one", see Salzman (2011), xxxiv.
61 On how he probably read and admired "the style of Symmachus' famous appeal for toleration", see Brown (2000), 60; on how there are curious echoes of Symmachus's *Relatio* in him, see O'Donnell (1992b), 321.
62 See Brown (2000), 58–60.
63 Gillett (2012), 267.
64 In his own words: *cum pararem recitare imperatori laudes, quibus plura mentirer, et mentienti faueretur ab scientibus.* cf 6.6.9 (CCSL 27.79). See also Pet 3.25.30 for the other instance. McLynn argued that in his presentation of the emperor Valentinian II in the *De civitate Dei*, "Augustine continued to see the boy he remembered from his encounter in Milan". McLynn (1999b), 32.

3. Of Heroes and Martyrs, Guardians and Sanctuaries: Interrogating Rome via Milan

The sack of Rome was "a tragedy of major proportions", not only to pagan aristocrats and intellectuals but also for optimistic Christians who considered the city as a "New Rome" and "in some sense a Christian city".[65] Christians "lost their earthly riches in the sack"; they were tortured "to make them surrender their goods" and "laid low by the protracted famine". Beyond the loss of their material goods, "many Christians were slaughtered" and "consumed by a great variety of dreadful deaths". Some will not get a proper burial because of the greatness of the massacre. Many Christians were led into captivity, where not only "married women and maidens" but "consecrated virgins" had been violated by their captors. Augustine had to address why Christians suffered these tragedies badly as their "adversaries" mocked the Christians on these grounds.[66]

Again, Augustine drew his responses to these allegations from familiar instances:[67] history of the Roman wars and invasions, and of heroes who were tortured and who committed suicide because their modesty had been violated. In spite of the "carnage"[68] in the sacking of Rome, Augustine was eager to point out how things were different from the "custom of war" (*bellorum morem*) to the "Christian era" (*christianis temporibus/ hoc tribuere temporibus christianis*) where Romans, who sought refuge in "the shrines of the martyrs and the churches of the apostles" and who "feigned to be servants of Christ themselves", were spared by the cruel barbarians in the name of Christ.[69] In record of wars (*bella gesta conscripta*) fought before and after the rise of Rome to imperial power, no one who sought refuge in the temples of their gods were spared by their enemies. And asserting from specific instances that it was the gods that need protection from invaders and not the other way around,[70] Augustine deduced that "the only cause of [Rome] perishing was that she chose to have guardians who could themselves perish".[71] It was therefore absurd and ironic that those who now mocked and blasphemed the name of Christ due to the sack of Rome are those "pagans" whom the cruel barbarians[72] spared because they took refuge in Christ's name.

---

65 According to Pelikan, "That identification of Old Rome as destined to stand as long as the earth became the common property of Christians in the first four centuries". On how the "imperial Old Rome" was replaced by Constantinople as the Christian's "New Rome" according to Socrates and Sozomen, see Pelikan (1982), 86–89. On how "Christians had even colluded with" the talisman "myth", see Brown (2000), 287.
66 See ci 1.10–12; 1.14; 1.16 (Dyson 16–21, 23, 26).
67 *Neque enim grauius uel grauiora dicimus auctoribus eorum et stilo et otio multum impares; quibus tamen ediscendis et ipsi elaborauerunt et filios suos elaborare compellunt.* ci 3.17 (CCSL 47.82).
68 This includes *uastationis trucidationis depraedationis concremationis.* ci 1.7 (CCSL 47.6).
69 See ci 1.1 (CCSL 47.2; Dyson 4–5).
70 *deorum suorum templa confugisse ... enim homines a simulacro, sed simulacrum ab hominibus seruabatur.* ci 1.2 (CCSL 47.2–3).
71 See ci 1.2–3 (CCSL 47.2–3; Dyson 5–7).
72 His description of the barbarians and their act of self-restrain was ironic: *cruentus saeuiebat inimicus ... trucidatoris furor ... et tota feriendi refrenabatur inmanitas et captiuandi cupiditas frangebatur.* ci 1.1 (CCSL 47.1–2).

Apart from the written records of wars and legendary figures that Augustine alluded to in his refutation of "our adversaries", the background to his contention can be traced back again and related to what he had experienced in, and after, Milan when he came under the influence of Bishop Ambrose. Ambrose "had enjoyed all the advantages of an upper-class education in Rome itself" and "could parade all the great 'names' and their opinions, only to dismiss them with contempt".[73] Augustine was greatly impressed by Ambrose's ability to connect his preaching with Platonic philosophy, as philosophy had "enchanted" him ever since he had read Cicero's *Hortensius*. Although Augustine invoked the authority of Ambrose only later when he vied for orthodoxy against Pelagius, Ambrose was considered to be one of the most influential figures upon Augustine's theological formation.[74] So, we will briefly look at the *Confessiones*, and Ambrose's letters to Marcellina and his refutation of Symmachus's *Relatio* to see how Augustine's arguments in *De civitate Dei* had corresponding "elements" with them.

Ambrose had an aristocratic background although it has been asserted that he actually belonged to "the margins of aristocratic society at Rome" and that his *Romanitas* itself was probably "more acquired than innate". His family's influence in Christian circles in Rome derived from their "privileged claim upon the memory and the grave" of their "ancestor" Soteris,[75] a martyr who had died in the Great Persecution of Diocletian. Following the "noble virgin" Soteris, Ambrose's sister Marcellina was also consecrated a virgin by pope Liberius in c. 353.[76] Though Ambrose was initially reluctant in his appointment to be the Bishop of Milan in 374 when he was still serving as a provincial governor of Aemilia and Liguria,[77] the vivid glorification of martyrdom in his accounts when he became a bishop, of which we shall see more below, may be inherent due to his devout upbringing.

Within a few years of his appointment as bishop, Ambrose had been "victorious over heretics and pagans, two of the three enemies of catholic Christianity" while his main engagement with the remaining one, the Jews, would happen later.[78] Crucially, during his struggle against the "Arian" and his claim to power as the Bishop of Milan when he had to defy the emperor's mother Justina,[79] Ambrose discovered the bodies of the martyrs Protasius and Gervasius in 386. The ensuing miracles when Ambrose moved these relics into his new basilica gave him vital impetus.[80] In his extant works,

---

73 Brown (2000), 74. His rhetorical skill was evident from his epp 17–18 in his reply to Symmachus's *Relatio*.
74 See chapter three above, particularly section 2.
75 McLynn (1994), 31–35; whether McLynn may be "excessively sceptical", see Liebeschuetz (2011), 57.
76 Moorhead pointed out that the social standing of Ambrose's family may be reflected by the involvement of the pope. Moorhead (2013), 21.
77 On Ambrose's governorship and his initial reluctance to be a bishop, see chapter three, n. 22 above.
78 Moorhead (2013), 128.
79 On his struggle with Justina and against the influence of the Arians, see Ramsey (1997), 25–27.
80 In reporting the dramatic event to Marcellina, Ambrose stated: "We are hard-pressed by the royal edicts, but we are strengthened by the words of Scripture". See Ambrose's ep 20.17 (Beyenka 370).

Augustine referred four times to the martyrs Protasius and Gervasius, and three times to the miracles occurring through their relics in Milan.[81]

These miracles reflected the world view of late antiquity when it was believed that a firm barrier existed between the earth and the stars that could be crossed with death. Death, as Peter Brown asserted, is the separation of the soul "from a body compounded of earthly dregs" to regain "a place intimately congruent with its true nature in the palpable, clear light that hung so tantalizingly close above the earth in the heavy clusters of the Milky Way". In line with this world view, Christians believe that "tombs, fragments of bodies or, even, physical objects that had made contact with these bodies — were privileged places, where the contrasted poles of Heaven and Earth met".[82] Therefore, we can see that the miracles connected with the relics of the martyrs Protasius and Gervasius were within the horizon of expectation of late antiquity Christians.

However, Brown maintains that there was a break between the pagan cult of heroes and Christian cult of the martyr though they are rooted in the same cultural setting:

> [For the Christians], the martyrs, precisely because they had died as human beings, enjoyed close intimacy with God. Their intimacy with God was the *sine qua non* of their ability to intercede for and, so, to protect their fellow mortals ... Thus, in Christian belief, the grave, the memory of the dead, and the religious ceremonial that might surround this memory were placed within a totally different structure of relations between God, the dead, and the living.[83]

Considering this background, we can see how moving the bodies of the martyrs to Ambrose's new basilica was ingenious, especially when "martyrdom" became Ambrose's rallying cry. Describing the impressive impact of this event to Marcellina, Ambrose wrote:

> They now cause the Church at Milan, barren of martyrs, now the mother of many children, to rejoice in the glory and examples of their suffering ... Thanks be to you, O Lord Jesus, for having aroused the spirit of the martyrs at this time when Your Church needs greater protection.[84]

And in his earlier letter to Marcellina, Ambrose described his standoff with the emperor who demanded "a speedy surrender of the basilica" since "all property was under his jurisdiction". Ambrose replied that "sacred objects are not subject to the jurisdiction even of the emperor" and that he "will more gladly be sacrificed before the altars". And when Calligonus, the grand chamberlain, threatened to kill Ambrose for treating the emperor Valentinian with contempt, Ambrose replied, "May God grant you to fulfil what you threaten, for I shall suffer what bishops suffer, and you

---

81 See cf 9.7.15–16; s 286.4; s 318.1 and ci 22.8.
82 Brown (1981), 2–3.
83 Brown (1981), 5–6.
84 ep 22.7 (Beyenka 378).

will act as eunuchs act".⁸⁵ Still more, in his treatise *De virginibus*, Ambrose exhorted Marcellina by reminding her of "the presence of a martyr in your background" and referred to how Saint Soteris endured torture until "she found the sword that she was searching for".⁸⁶

Ambrose's languages, in his defiance of the emperor and his exhortation to Marcellina, will make more sense when we consider how the notion of self-sacrifice was deeply rooted in the cultural values of the day. Martyrdom was "a spectacle played on the terms of Graeco-Roman society", which the Christian communities invaded by turning the violent spectacles, much like the public games, to their own purposes.⁸⁷ Martyrdom was also asserted to be in line with "the classical honor code and its ideal of the good death ... A martyr's feelings of control over death and torture — the voluntary, even eager acceptance of condemnation — transformed the sordid ordeals one suffered into a most honorable vindication".⁸⁸ In fact, Origen exhorted "most God-fearing" Ambrose to welcome "affliction upon affliction ... like a noble athlete" so that he will enjoy "hope upon hope ... shortly after the affliction upon affliction" and "to remember in all your present contest the great reward laid up in heaven".⁸⁹

This rationale had been reflected in Ambrose's sermon — when he was drawing upon the story of Job as the ideal "afflicted" believer and praised his patience and virtue as a model for his congregants — as the basilica was under siege:

> I mounted the pulpit to praise one man, Job; I have found all of you to be Jobs ... In each of you Job has lived again, in each the patience and virtue of that holy man has shone again ... It befits Christians to hope for the tranquility of peace and not to check the steadfastness of faith and truth when faced with danger of death. The Lord is our Head who will save those who hope in Him.⁹⁰

At this stage, we can draw corresponding elements between these episodes in Milan and Augustine's arguments in the *De civitate Dei* and see how Augustine implicitly invoked upon and addressed the prevalent sensibilities of his days. It is striking that Romans who sought refuge in "the shrines of the martyrs and the churches of the apostles" were spared by the cruel barbarians in the name of Christ. Considering the "cruel custom of war" (*bellorum morem truculenti*) before the Christian times (*christianis temporibus*), the absurdity of those who blamed and mocked the Christians in their tragedies was rhetorically highlighted: those who shamelessly insulted the servant of Christ "would not have escaped that ruin and disaster had they not feigned to be servants of Christ themselves"⁹¹ and sought refuge in sacred places. As histories clearly bore witness to the cruel customs of war, crediting their survival "to their own

---

85 ep 20.28 (Beyenka 375). On how martyrs should die rather than sin (*morere, ne pecces*), see ci 13.4.
86 *De virginibus* 7.37–38 (Ramsey 116).
87 Young (2001), 12–13.
88 Straw (2002), 40.
89 Origen, Εἰς Μαρτύριον Προτρεπτικός (*An Exhortation to Martyrdom*) 1.4 (Greer 41–43).
90 See ep 20.14 (Beyenka 369).
91 See ci 1.1 (CCSL 47.2; Dyson 5).

fate" and failing to acknowledge the act of clemency in Christ's name in the sack of Rome would amount to blindness, ungratefulness and even madness.[92]

Simultaneously addressing why, supposing that martyrs' shrines and churches offer refuge,[93] "the good" were still inflicted with temporal evils, Augustine asserted that divine providence often "tests the righteous and praiseworthy" with afflictions for a higher purpose.[94] He took the cases of Job, Daniel and the more contemporary Paulinus of Nola who had endured loss and suffering in the name of religion.[95] For those Christians who were slaughtered and "consumed by a great variety of dreadful deaths", Augustine asserted that "Death is not to be deemed an evil when a good life precedes it; nor is death made an evil except by what follows death".[96] We can see how the notion of death as an "honourable vindication" in Christianity, particularly in the case of martyrdom, was alluded to and was contrasted with the "vanities" of Marcus Regulus and Lucretia who valiantly approached death in the face of humiliation.[97]

Looking at past kingdoms and the Roman empire, Augustine asked if, and which of, the gods aided the rise and expansion of the Roman empire. Deducing that the "great number of false gods" were not responsible for the greatness and endurance of the Roman empire, Augustine considered the spirit of self-sacrifice that the Romans exhibited for the sake of the common good behind their worldly success. This spirit of sacrifice was driven by love of liberty and the desire for human praise.[98] And though there may be a hidden cause unknown to human beings behind why God aided the Roman empire in her achievements, ultimately, "the one true and just God aided the Romans in achieving the glory of so great an empire; for they were good men according to the lights of the earthly city".[99]

These notions of suffering in hope and perseverance, and death as an honourable vindication that Augustine alluded was the essence of Ambrose's arguments in his letter to the emperor Valentinian that was written as a reply to Symmachus's *Relatio*. Making "Rome", herself, to give a counter-testimony, Ambrose refuted the points that Symmachus made in his appeal[100] by contending that the rise and security of

---

92 *Hoc Christi nomini, hoc christiano tempori tribuendum quisquis non uidet, caecus, quisquis uidet nec laudat, ingratus, quisquis laudanti reluctatur, insanus est.* ci 1.7 (CCSL 47.6).
93 Observing how the sack of the "invulnerable city" had caused "much ideological chaos", O'Daly asserted that "Confusion was caused by the latent or overt paganism of many Romans, not least among the governing class, but also by the adoption of ideas of divine protection taken over by Christians from their pagan forerunners". O'Daly (1986–1994b), 971.
94 ci 1.1.
95 ci 1.9–10.
96 *multi etiam christiani interfecti sunt, multi multarum mortium foeda uarietate consumpti … mala mors putanda non est, quam bona uita praecesserit. neque enim facit malam mortem, nisi quod sequitur mortem.* ci 1.11 (CCSL 47.13; Dyson 19); on how the good turned death, an evil in itself (*quamuis sit mors malum*), to good, see ci 13.5 (CCSL 48.389).
97 See ci 1.15; 1.19.
98 See ci 5.15; 5.17; 5.18.
99 ci 5.19 (Dyson 225).
100 According to Ambrose, "I am responding by this note to the statements in the appeal … I have responded to those who are provoking me without being provocative myself, for my concern was to rebut the appeal and not to expose the superstition". ep 18.2; 18.39 (Ramsey 184, 194).

the Roman empire could not be ascribed to her traditional gods[101] but to human's determination and ingenuity.[102] Contrasting the decline of the favoured and patronized traditional Roman cults with the ascension of the church through adversities, Ambrose presented the "triumph" of Christianity as a progress that even "Rome" acknowledged:

> Never did they bestow on us more than when they ordered Christians to be beaten and proscribed and slain. What faithlessness considered to be torture, religion turned into profit. Look at them in their magnanimity! We thrived through insult, through want and through torture, but they do not believe that their ceremonies can survive without cash.

> The earth in former times knew nothing of agriculture. Later, when the diligent husbandman began to exercise control over his fields and to clothe the rude soil with vines, it laid aside its wild disposition, having been softened by homely cultivation ... Hence too the faith of souls is our harvest; the grace of the Church is our vintage of merits, which from the foundation of the world flourished in the saints but in this last age has been spread out among the peoples.[103]

Considering these vital corresponding elements, Augustine's disputations in the *De civitate Dei* will make more sense when read in the light of the *Confessiones* which centred around his experiences in Milan.[104] In fact, these dramatic events involving Ambrose in Milan overlapped with, and resonated, Augustine's spiritual "emergence": he was inspired by the story of the decorated Roman senator Victorinus[105] who renounced his long-cherished "pagan" ways to make a public confession of his Christian faith.[106] Then, Ponticianus told Augustine the story of his friends, an *agentes in rebus* who, after reading *Vita Antonii*, decided to leave their high offices under the emperor for the

---

101 "Hannibal for a long time mocked the Roman rites and, although the gods were contending against him, came as a conqueror up to the very walls of the city". ep 18.4 (Ramsey 185).
102 Ambrose stated thus: "The trophies of victory are found not in the entrails of cattle but in the strength of warriors. I [Rome] subdued the world by other techniques ... Why do you offer me the examples of the ancients? I [Rome] hate the rites of the Neros ... the ceremonies which promised victory were deceptive. If the old rites were pleasing, why did the same Rome give way to foreign rites? ... they believed that victory was a goddess. In fact, it is a gift and not a power; thanks to the army and not by the power of religion it is bestowed, but it does not rule". ep 18.7; 18.30 (Ramsey 185, 192).
103 See ep 18.11; 18.25; 18.29. Markus observed how it is peculiar "that at no time do men seem to have been as ready to speak of an ageing world, or of Rome in her old age, as in the last decades of the fourth century and the early years of the fifth". Markus (1970), 26.
104 As mentioned in chapter three, it constituted thirty eight percent of the first nine books of the *Confessiones*.
105 *doctor tot nobilium senatorum, qui etiam ob insigne praeclari magisterii, quod ciues huius mundi eximium putant, statuam Romano foro meruerat et acceperat.* cf 8.2.3 (CCSL 27.115).
106 According to Augustine, *pronuntiauit ille fidem ueracem praeclara fiducia ... sed ubi mihi homo tuus Simplicianus de Victorino ista narrauit, exarsi ad imitandum.* cf 8.2.5; 8.5.10 (CCSL 27.116; 27.119). We can also see how he inserted his critique of the traditional Roman gods here: *usque ad illam aetatem uenerator idolorum sacrorumque sacrilegorum particeps, quibus tunc tota fere Romana nobilitas inflata spirabat populi Pelusiam et "omnigenum deum monstra et Anubem latratorem, quae aliquando contra Neptunum et Venerem contraque Mineruam tela" tenuerant et a se uictis iam Roma supplicabat, quae iste senex Victorinus tot annos ore terricrepo defensit au erat.* cf 8.2.3 (CCSL 27.115).

service of God.¹⁰⁷ This culminated in Augustine's own renunciation of his profession as rhetor in Milan and getting baptized by Ambrose in that very same church where he resisted the emperor's edict to surrender his basilica,¹⁰⁸ and Augustine's resolve to return to Africa.¹⁰⁹ Again, Augustine's own "historical" account in the *Confessiones* could be read as a "subversive" discourse — a critique of the Roman religions and of the power-symbolism that Rome and Milan represented in the Roman empire, a temporal earthly city which stands in contrast to the eternal "City of God".

4. What is Time?¹¹⁰ Discerning the Authority of Scripture in the *De civitate Dei*

So far, we have argued that the credibility of Augustine's refutations on the various pagans' allegations in his *De civitate Dei* should not be assessed merely on the basis of his "handling" of the written historical traditions of Rome. In hindsight, his expectations of, and actual experiences in, Rome and Milan would determine his reckoning of these external sources and give legitimacy to his readings. Likewise, his subsequent experiences as the Bishop of Hippo and his changing conviction as he gets more acquainted with, and interprets, the Scriptures ultimately determined his stances toward the Roman empire and provided the theological core of the *De civitate Dei*. What had changed in Augustine's stance toward the Roman empire and how did he align his theology in the light of this changing conviction?

Once back in Africa, Augustine at first shared the optimism of Eusebius and Ambrose¹¹¹ who considered the drastic change in the Roman empire more as an evolution and prophetic fulfilment than a revolution. Resonating Ambrose's rhetoric that Rome had been "converted along with the whole world in [her] old age [as] it is not too late at any age to learn",¹¹² Augustine even asserted that

---

107 Augustine can still recollect their remarkable testimony: *maiorne esse poterit spes nostra in palatio, quam ut amici imperatoris simus? ... amicus autem dei, si uoluero, ecce nunc fio.* cf 8.6.15 (CCSL 27.122–23).
108 See cf 9.2.2–4; 9.6.14–9.7.16.
109 *Simul eramus simul habitaturi placito sancto. quaerebamus quisnam locus nos utilius haberet seruientes tibi: pariter remeabamus in Africam.* cf 9.8.17 (CCSL 27.143).
110 What we will see here is based on what we say about time further back in the previous chapters. In the introduction, we have asserted that Augustine's concept of the authority of Scripture was intertwined with his notion of an historical time which is the realm where divine revelation discloses the meaning of sacred history. His preoccupation with the notion of time was rooted in the tension between the already and the not yet that permeated the entire New Testament theological outlook. Basing upon his understanding of time, Augustine asserted against the Manicheans that the Old Testament complemented the New Testament. Against the Platonist's method of philosophical ascent, he stressed the implications of time which the Christ-event set in motion in history. Against the Donatists, he maintained that it is "not yet" the time to insist upon "purity" of the church. Now we are going to look at it yet again but recasting it in a precise way that relates it to the *De civitate Dei*.
111 On Eusebius's "theology of the Empire" that had been adopted by Ambrose and Jerome, and the prevalent theological tradition regarding the significance of the Roman Empire for the universal mission of the Apostles, see Markus (1963), 341–46, and (1970), 52; see also Pelikan (1982), 86–89.
112 See Ambrose's ep 18.7 (Ramsey 186).

"the frightful enmities of the many nations and mighty peoples" were "now brought almost totally under Christian dominion".[113] Although he ascribed this transformation upon the authority of Scripture in the context of the Manicheans' refutation, the underlying optimism of the *tempora christiana* that he expressed here was also in line with his writings around the years 399–400. These writings clearly reflect his association of the Roman empire with a Christian order which the Scriptures foretold.[114]

But the religious context of Africa, where many Christians were still grappling with the hangover of the Diocletian persecution, presented another reality. Discord between Christians in Africa regarding the question of authenticity[115] was deeply embedded in the cultural and social-political reality and was thus more passionate than the infighting Augustine witnessed in Milan.[116] Indeed, the fifth-century Christians who were under Romans' influence had been struggling to discern a working relationship between the church and the larger society in the light of the notion of *consummatio saeculi* that Jesus and his disciples envisaged. Particularly in North Africa, Christians who cherished their legacies of martyrdom[117] strived to assert and negotiate their identity in the more tolerant and patronizing Roman empire.

From his subsequent experiences in these changing contexts, Augustine gradually altered his optimistic endorsement of a legal, institutional enforcement of Christianity against pagans and heretics until the sack of Rome forced him to reconsider his stance even more radically. Already losing his "enthusiasm for the alliance between the Roman Empire and the Catholic Church, at just the time when it had become effectively cemented",[118] Augustine expressed the new stance that he adopted toward the Roman empire in the *De civitate Dei*. Theologically, this has been forged between

---

113 *Quae in illis libris fundata persistens non tantum paucissimorum Manichaeorum calumniosas argutias, uerum etiam gentilium tot tantorumque populorum horrendas inimicitias diuino iure contemnit, quos paene iam totos a nefaria superstitione simulacrorum ad unius dei ueri cultum christiano imperio subiugauit edomito orbe terrarum non uiolentia bellici certaminis, sed inuictae potential ueritatis.* Fau 22.60 (CSEL 25.1.656; Teske 340). This has been resonated in ci 11.1.
114 See Markus (1970), particularly chapter two for a thorough treatment of Augustine's association of the Roman empire with a Christian order during this period; also Markus (2000) for a "revisit" of this theme.
115 "The Donatists ... thought of themselves as the authentic Christian church in Africa: public opinion, traditional views of the church, not legal documents, were the mainstay of their case". Brown (2000), 331.
116 Frend even asserted that the questions that divided the "Donatists" from the "Catholics" were "not of doctrine" but "those of discipline and politics". See Frend (1953), 14.
117 Augustine was still close to "the time of persecutions" that the ideal of martyrdom lingers in his mind, largely due to the memory of Christians "who remained engrossed by the martyrs' struggles and to the liturgy that commemorated their anniversaries and venerated their relics" while the Donatists' "self-conception as the 'Church of the Martyrs' was central to their identity and ideology". Pinckaers (2016), 109; Gaddis (2005), 41.
118 Brown (2000), 338. According to Markus, Augustine's "working life coincided, almost exactly, with the legal establishment of Christian orthodoxy as the empire's official religion". While Augustine thought that "good and bad prophecies" are being equally fulfilled, "it is the euphoria about the official Christianisation that is gone". Markus (2000), 199, 211.

two opposing stances, the triumphalist Rome-Eusebius theology and the apocalyptic tradition more favoured by the Donatist.[119] Instead of giving prominence to the political ascension of Constantine, Augustine "began to invoke the incarnation of Christ as a decisive moment in God's action in human history".[120] Augustine also asserted that the realization of God's purposes neither depend upon the fate of Rome nor of any earthly society.[121] The apocalyptic prophecies refer to the final ending and not to any particular historical catastrophe.[122]

If the first ten books of the *De civitate Dei* primarily delineated the complex middle path which Augustine charted "to disassociate Rome's historical destiny from that of Christianity",[123] the focus in the rest of the books shifted to "the origin, progress and merited ends of the two cities".[124] The topics which he brought up now, unlike the themes in the first ten books of the *De civitate Dei* that had received scant treatment in his other works, embraced theological stances that Augustine previously held and refined into a more coherent structure.[125] If Augustine initially answered the question "what is time?" in relation to the *tempora christiana* that the pagans scathingly attacked due to the sack of Rome, he now depicted a Christian vision of time in relation to the "City of God" basing upon his readings of the Scriptures.[126] As Markus asserted, this notion of time is marked by the removal of "highly particularised moment" in contemporary history where Christianity "triumph" over paganism. "Augustine had come to see 'sacred history' as confined to the history to be found within the scriptural canon, and he came to deny this status to any other interpretations of historical events".[127] Therefore, as he looked at histories and made sense of contemporary

---

119   See Markus (1970), 53, 56.
120   Burns (1999), 108.
121   In ci 4.7, Augustine argued: *Quamquam Romanum imperium adflictum est potius quam mutatum, quod et aliis ante Christi nomen temporibus ei contigit et ab illa est adflictione recreatum, quod nec istis temporidus desperandum est. Quis enim de hac re nouit uoluntatem dei?* (CCSL 47.104).
122   See Markus (1970), 53; also ci 20.11.
123   O'Daly (1986–1994b), 972.
124   Augustine stated thus: *in decem istis libris ... satisfecimus refutando contradictiones impiorum ... de duarum ciuitatum ... exortu et procursu et debitis finibus.* ci 10.32 (CCSL 47.313–14; Dyson 447–48).
125   As O'Daly observed, "The ostensible unifying thread may be the two cities theme, but one has the impression that Augustine is essentially providing a review of his interpretation of fundamental theological issues, to instruct and inform Christian or potentially Christian readers. The polemical content is minimal". O'Daly (1986–1994b), 990. At the same time, *De civitate Dei* "should never be treated as though it were a static, complete photograph of Augustine's thought", and though it "has a real and intense unity", it is "a series rather than a unit". See Brown (1995), 17; Hardy (1955), 259.
126   *Ciuitatem dei dicimus, cuius ea scriptura testis est, quae non fortuitis motibus animorum, sed plane summae dispositione prouidentiae super omnes omnium gentium litteras omnia sibi genera ingeniorum humanorum diuina excellens auctoritate subiecit.* ci 11.1 (CCSL 48.321).
127   Markus (1970), 43; Markus (2000), 202. According to R. R. Williams, sacred history is "the view that a certain series of events, in other ways part of the whole series of events which make up the story of human happenings, are, and have been seen to be, of special significance in connection with the revelation of God. Williams (1950), 25. As Augustine asserted: *quod autem Porphyrius uniuersalem uiam animae liberandae nondum in suam notitiam historiali cognitione dicit esse perlatam: quid hac historia uel inlustrius inueniri potest, quae uniuersum orbem tanto apice auctoritatis obtinuit.* ci 10.32 (CCSL 47.312–13); cf. ci 11.3 regarding "*canonica*".

events in the light of Scripture, we can see Augustine expressing his understanding of the nature and authority of Scripture.

This "privileging" of the scriptural canon which Augustine asserted in the *De civitate Dei* developed in his mind over a long period of time. In the preceding chapters, we had seen his changing approaches to scriptural interpretation as he abandoned the Manicheans' materialistic reading to adopt Ambrose's spiritual reading that gave him new insights into the nature of Truth. And soon in Hippo where the Donatists were the dominant party, "a former Manichean turned marginal cleric" Augustine needed to assert himself as a reputable expositor of the Scriptures. Through his correspondence with Jerome, Augustine realized the challenges posed by the poor Latin translations of the Scriptures and the complexities involved in the translation process. As Augustine immersed himself in scriptural exposition, his move beyond the influence of the Neo-Platonists who could not fathom Christ as the incarnate Word[128] as well as his refutation of the Manicheans led him to the question of creation[129] and time, and again and again to the book of Genesis.

As early as 388/89, Augustine wrote the *De Genesi contra Manichaeos*, and a little later in 393, he wrote the *De Genesi ad litteram imperfectus*. Moreover, the last three books of Augustine's *Confessiones*, written around 397–401, were an exposition of the beginning of Genesis. Then, he laboured for about fifteen years to produce the *De Genesi ad litteram*. Finally, he again turned to the beginning of the book of Genesis in book eleven of the *De civitate Dei*. As seen in the last chapter, Augustine's expositions of Genesis which span his whole ministry exhibit a dynamic interplay between different factors. His exposition of *paradisus* in *De civitate Dei* also bears witness to this dynamism.[130]

Paradisus comes from the Hebrew word *pardes* through the Late-Babylonian term *pardisu* that is a derivative of the Avestan word *pairi-daēza/apiri-daēza* meaning "enclosed park", "orchard surrounded by a wall". The Septuagint used παράδεισος to translate both *pardes* and the more classic Hebrew word for garden, *gan* and gave this term a religious meaning, from where the term *paradisus* entered the Vulgate.[131] After delineating his epistemology concerning things visible and invisible to the human senses, Augustine introduced the theme of *paradisus* in relation to the "original" condition of human as created being in Book 11.

---

128 See cf 7.9.13–14. In ci 10.24, Augustine asserted, *hunc ille Platonicus non cognouit esse principium ... neque enim caro principium est aut anima humana, sed uerbum per quod facta sunt omnia* (CCSL 47.297).

129 "In dealing with Creation", Hardy remarked, "St Augustine has occasion to defend the reality of history. The world does not revolve in eternal cycles but moves onward to a divine goal". Hardy (1955), 268; cf. ci 12.10–15.

130 In the *De civitate Dei*, we see *paradisus* in its variant forms fifty times, while it occurs around 919 times in all of his extant writings (these numbers were collected using the cag-online.net database). Augustine mentioned this subject in Books 11, 13, 14, 15, 16, 20, 21 and 22 of the *De civitate Dei*, which constitutes around six percent of all usages in his extant works.

131 See Filoramo (2014), 3:66; Delumeau (2000), 4. On the question regarding "garden *in* Eden" or "garden *of* Eden", see Walton (2003), 202.

In his early work on Genesis, Augustine adopted a figurative interpretation of *paradisus* like Ambrose[132] and considered it a blissful state where Adam enjoyed spiritual delights.[133] But in *De Genesi ad litteram*, he denounced those who understood Paradise only figuratively while accepting "the authority of these writings" and insisted that Paradise should be understood according to the proper literal sense.[134] Augustine reconciled what was said about Paradise with what was written about the third and the six days of creation. According to this scheme, the trees laid out in Paradise are of the same varieties which the earth still went on producing in their proper time while the seed-bearing fodder contains "the things that were going to spring up over the earth from that generative power which the earth had already received".[135] Although the tree of life in the middle of Paradise and the tree of knowledge of discerning good and evil (Gen 2:9) "were themselves bodily realities", in its "forward reference that was figurative ... the tree of life also was Christ".[136]

Reiterating this argument in the *De civitate Dei*, Augustine maintained that although *paradisus* can be interpreted allegorically, one should also believe in "the truth of that story as presented to us in a most faithful narrative of events".[137] As *paradisus* was "rooted" in historical reality, the historical fact of "the Fall" in paradise which the Scriptures recorded had perpetual effect upon humanity.[138] This assertion,

---

132 Ambrose, who stated that the topic should not "be treated lightly" (*non uilem ... hunc paradisum*) regarded paradise as "a land of fertility that is to say, a soul which is fertile planted in Eden, that is, in a certain delightful or well-tilled land in which the soul finds pleasure" (*Est ergo paradisus terra quaedam fertilis, hoc est anima fecunda, in Edem plantata, hoc est in uoluptate quadam uel exercitata terra, in qua animae sit delectation*). de Paradiso 1.1; 3.12 (CSEL 32.1.266; 32.1.272; Savage 288, 294). Thus, paradise is "an aspect of the higher part of our nature". Savage (1961), ix. On how Ambrose relied upon Philo for his allegorical interpretation of paradise, see Benjamin (1999), 158–60.

133 *omnes istas figuras ... spiritales deliciae quas habet beata uita figurate explicantur.* Gn Ma 2.2.3; 2.9.12 (CSEL 91.121; 91.132). Later referring to them, Augustine stated: *quid figurate significarent, ea quae ad litteram inuenire non potui ... extimarem etiam per me posse secundum propriam, non secundum allegoricam locutionem haec scripta esse monstrari.* Gn li 8.2.5 (CSEL 28.1.232).

134 *qui auctoritatem harum litterarum sequuntur.* Gn li 8.1.4 (CSEL 28.1.231; Hill 347). Hill remarked that for Augustine, "to relativize the historical character of the paradise story was ... to relativize also the truths of faith that were closely bound up with the account". Hill (2002), 161.

135 *Sed cum ex his generibus sint ista ligna instituta in paradiso, quae iam terra tertio die produxerat, adhuc ea produxit in tempore suo ... quae super terram exortura erant ex illa uirtute generandi, quam terra iam acceperat.* Gn li 8.3.6–7 (CSEL 28.1.234–35; Hill 350).

136 *Aliud quam erant illa omnia significauerunt, sed tamen etiam ipsa corporaliter fuerunt. et quando a narrante commemorata sunt, non erat illa figurata locutio, sed earum expressa narratio, quarum erat figurata praecessio. erat ergo et lignum uitae quemadmodum petra Christus.* Gn li 8.4.8 (CSEL 28.1.235–36; Hill 351); see also Gn li 8.5.9.

137 *Quasi propterea non potuerit esse paradisus corporalis, quia potest etiam spiritalis intellegi; tamquam ideo non fuerint duae mulieres, Agar et Sarra, et ex eis duo filii Abrahae, unus de ancilla, alius de libera, quia duo testamenta in eis figurata dicit apostolus ... haec et si qua alia commodius dici possunt de intellegendo spiritaliter paradiso nemine prohibente dicantur, dum tamen et illius historiae ueritas fidelissima rerum gestarum narratione commendata credatur.* ci 13.21 (CCSL 48.404; Dyson 568–69).

138 *Ex uno quippe homine, quem primum deus condidit, humanum genus sumpsit exordium secundum sanctae scripturae fidem ... sed eosdem primos peccatores ita fuisse morte multatos, ut etiam quidquid de eorum stirpe esset exortum eadem poena teneretur obnoxium.* ci 12.9; 13.3 (CCSL 48.364; 48.386).

which also amounted to the beginning of the two cities in the human race,[139] was a distinctive feature of Augustine's theology which was largely based upon his reading of Paul in the light of Genesis.[140] What his predecessors regarded as God's greatest gift to humankind in Paradise like free will, liberty, autonomy and self-government was characterized by Augustine as being at the root of human bondage to sin.[141] Against their insistence that Paradise had been regained and "could be entered by entering into the Church" so as to live the "life that Adam lived before the Fall", he maintained that true happiness is unattainable in this present life,[142] thereby turning "the story of paradise into the story of the Fall".[143] The theological implications of his "historically-based" arguments became evident when Augustine defended his understanding of grace against Pelagius who was "concerned chiefly with Christian practices and its basis in free choice and human nature".[144]

Not only do we see the "privileging" of the scriptural canon as the crucible of sacred history whose historical truth needs to be asserted, we also see Augustine's privileging of the LXX in the *De civitate Dei*. Augustine's attempt to reconcile the inevitable differences between his preferred Latin text/s based on the LXX, which he referred to as "our own versions",[145] with that of Jerome's translation based on the Hebrew also displayed his notion of the authority of Scripture. We can take two passages as example. In Book 15.7, Augustine was expounding Gen 4:6–7 which was about Cain's anger over his brother Abel because God looked with favour on (*respiciens*) his sacrifice, while his own sacrifice was despised/overlooked (*despiciens*). According to the LXX, before he murdered Abel, God rebuked Cain by saying, "If your sacrifice is rightly offered, but not rightly divided

---

139 *in hoc homine, qui primitus factus est ... exortas fuisse existimemus in genere humano societates tamquam ciuitates duas.* ci 12.28 (CCSL 48.385); see also ci 14.1.
140 In fact, his arguments from ci 12.23 onwards heavily depended upon Pauline letters that have been intertwined with Genesis. We had also stressed this in the previous chapter.
141 See Pagels (1995), 381. According to Augustine: *Iam quippe anima libertate in peruersum propria delectata et deo dedignata seruire pristino corporis seruitio destituebatur ... ac per hoc a liberi arbitrii malo usu series calamitatis huius exorta est, quae humanum genus origine deprauata, uelut radice corrupta, usque ad secundae mortis exitium, quae non habet finem.* ci 13.13–14 (CCSL 48.395–96).
142 *Sed etiam ipse iustus non uiuet ut uult, nisi eo peruenerit, ubi mori falli offendi omnino non possit eique sit certum ita semper futurum. hoc enim natura expetit, nec plene atque perfecte beata erit nisi adepta quod expetit. nunc uero quis hominum potest ut uult uiuere, quando ipsum uiuere non est in potestate? uiuere enim uult, mori cogitur.* ci 14.25 (CCSL 48.448).
143 Benjamin (1999), 153–54, 167.
144 TeSelle (1999), 633. The basic teachings of Pelagius and Coelestius, his disciple was summarized by Augustine as follows: *Adam mortalem factum, qui siue peccaret siue non peccaret, moriturus esset. Quoniam peccatum Adae ipsum solum laeserit et non genus humanum. Quoniam lex sic mittit ad regnum quemadmodum euangelium. Quoniam ante aduentum Christi fuerunt homines sine peccato. Quoniam infantes nuper nati in illo statu sint, in quo Adam fuit ante praeuaricationem. Quoniam neque per mortem uel praeuaricationem Adae omne genus hominum moriatur neque per resurrectionem Christi omne genus hominum resurgat.* gest 23 (CSEL 42.76); see also hae 88.
145 See ci 15.10; 15.11; 15.14; 15.20 where he explicitly referred to the LXX as *nostros codices* and *secundum codices enim nostros*. We have partly dealt with the issue of the LXX and the *Vetus Latina* in chapter two above.

(*recte offeras recte autem non dividas*), have you not sinned?" In explaining this passage, Augustine remarked that it is an "obscure" passage that has given rise to many interpretations.¹⁴⁶

Jerome, who picked on these verses when he discussed problem texts in his *Quaestiones Hebraicae in Genesim* written around 391/2, was one such interpretation. He pointed out that the meaning in Hebrew differed drastically from the LXX: the Hebrew says, "If you do well, shall your sin be not forgiven?" But the LXX, in transposing the gender of the Hebrew word for "sin", missed this meaning.¹⁴⁷ For Jerome, the "obscurity" of the LXX rendering seems to lie mainly in one's ignorance of this correct Hebrew text.

When Augustine explained this passage in his *Contra Faustum Manichaeum* around 403, he saw the "obscurity" as a matter of "prophetic allegory". Even in the *De civitate Dei*, he still refused to conform with Jerome's explication because he believes there is some truth behind the "obscurity" of the passage in the LXX. For Augustine, Cain "allegorically" represented those people/societies who live "according to man" (*qui secundum hominem*), which is an antithesis of those who live "according to God" (*qui secundum Deum uiuunt*) as represented by Abel. Cain's story also epitomised how the wicked have acted against the good from the very beginning of "history".¹⁴⁸ Hence, this passage is a good example of how Augustine, in quoting the Scriptures, preferred the familiar LXX, even if in this case he know it deviated from the Hebrew.

And as Augustine set to defend the "historical truth"¹⁴⁹ of Scripture, he touched upon the credibility of longevity of human life as asserted in the Scriptures in Genesis 5. He then accounts for the differences between the LXX and the Masoretic Text's rendering of the ages of the first eight generations. For the first seven of these, Augustine does not consider it a serious problem. It is a matter of scribal errors because the total numbers of years agree in each of them in the end. The numerical discrepancy between the two versions was more severe when it comes to Methuselah's age. According to the LXX version, Methuselah would have lived fourteen years beyond the Flood which would contradict the assertion that only eight escape destruction of the Flood in the Ark and Methuselah was not one of them.¹⁵⁰ Since both versions cannot be true to the facts — and following the Hebrew version would avoid the awkward problem of Methuselah's survival of the Flood — Augustine concluded that the translated

---

146 In ci 15.7, he stated: *quia non elucet cur vel unde sit dictum, multos sensus peperit eius obscuritas, cum divinarum scripturam quisque tractator secundum fidei regulam id conatur exponere* (CCSL 48.460).
147 In *Quaestiones Hebraicae in Genesim* 4.6–7, Jerome asserted: *Quod autem in LXX interpretibus fecit errorem, illud est, quia peccatum, id est hatath, in hebraeo generis masculini est, in graeco femini, et qui interpretati sunt, masculino illud, ut erat in hebraeo, genere transtulerunt* (CCSL 72.7). Here, the Greek form ἥμαρτες is actually masculine gender while the Hebrew *hatath* חַטָּאת is feminine form. The lack of agreement in gender of the feminine subject חַטָּאת and the masculine predicate make this text difficult. See Abraham Tal (2015), 87*; also Hayward (1995), 121–22.
148 See ci 15.7; Fau 12.9.
149 In ci 15.8, he stated: *Nunc autem defendenda mihi videtur historia* (CCSL 48.462).
150 ci 15.11. In *Quaestiones Hebraicae in Genesim* 5.25–27, Jerome asked, *et quo modo uerum est quod octo tantum animae in arca saluae factae sunt?* (CCSL 72.8). See also 1 Pet 3:20.

version must conform to the original Hebrew version.¹⁵¹ Behind this admission was the larger theoretical supposition that there could not be a real contradiction in scriptural text as the text is from God.¹⁵² The other implication, which is an offshoot of this assumption is that the Hebrew version is a uniquely correct text while any contradiction with it will be an error of the translated version. So, discrepancy in one case highlighted by Jerome could be ignored, but in another had to be acted upon.

Augustine's exposition of Genesis in the *De civitate Dei* therefore signalled some changes in his approach to the LXX, particularly given his staunch "preference" for the *Itala*. In general, Augustine seems to resist Jerome's attempt to base his new translation on Hebrew if it was only on the ground of philology or the literary form, especially if he saw allegorical value. But when an alteration of the content had theological significances (Scripture as internally consistent, for example, as in the case of Methuselah's age), he was willing to make concessions to the authority of the Hebrew version. Ironically, it was also in the *De civitate Dei* where Augustine reaffirmed the status of the LXX as an inspired translation.¹⁵³ Despite his knowledge of the problems, these were not sufficient to make him deviate from his strong attachment to the LXX.

After Augustine described the historical course of the two cities from Genesis to the end of the Old Testament prophets, and stressed how the superficial inconsistencies between the LXX and the truth of Hebrew text can be reconciled by right understanding,¹⁵⁴ he asserted that "Christ was born in Bethlehem of Judah, in accordance with the prophecy given long before".¹⁵⁵ Although prophecies regarding Christ may not be necessarily limited to the Jews, Augustine denied that "this was granted to anyone unless he had received a divine revelation" of Christ, which again gives priority to the Jewish Scriptures.¹⁵⁶ Then describing the growth of the Church of Christ throughout the world, Augustine asserted that "many reprobates are mingled in the Church with the good" at this time.¹⁵⁷ As for Christians who had endured persecutions and asserted that "the Church will suffer no further persecutions ... until the time of the Antichrist", Augustine maintained that "no limit can be set to the number of persecutions which the Church must endure for her training".¹⁵⁸ As for the time of "that final persecution",

---

151 In ci 15.13, Augustine stated: *recte fieri nullo modo dubitauerim, ut, cum diuersum aliquid in utrisque codicibus inuenitur, quando quidem ad fidem rerum gestarum utrumque esse non potest uerum, ei linguae potius credatur, unde est in aliam per interpretes facta translatio* (CCSL 48.472).
152 O'Loughlin (1995), 184.
153 See ci 18.43.
154 *Hebraica ueritate putantur septuaginta interpretes discrepare et bene intellecti inueniuntur esse concordes.* ci 18.44 (CCSL 48.641).
155 *natus est Christus secundum praecedentem prophetiam in Bethleem Iudae ...* ci 18.46 (CCSL 48.643; Dyson 891).
156 *Quod nemini concessum fuisse credendum est, nisi cui diuinitus reuelatus est unus mediator dei et hominum, homo Christus Iesus.* ci 18.47 (CCSL 48.645; Dyson 893–94).
157 *multi reprobi miscentur bonis et utrique ...* ci 18.49 (CCSL 48.647; Dyson 896).
158 *non amplius ecclesiam passuram persecutiones usque ad tempus antichristi ... haec atque huius modi mihi cogitanti non uidetur esse definiendus numerus persecutionum, quibus exerceri oportet ecclesiam.* ci 18.52 (CCSL 48.650–52; Dyson 900–02).

and the "number of years that remain for this world", or for "the length of time for which the Christian religion is to endure",[159] Augustine asserted that "time" is in the hand of God. Until the end of "time", then, the two cities "intermingled":

> Both cities alike make use of the good things, or are afflicted with the evils, of this temporal state; but they do so with a different faith, a different hope, a different love, until they are separated by the final judgment, and each receives its own end, to which is no end.[160]

Concluding Remarks

De civitate Dei can be seen as an outcome of Augustine's meditation upon the theological meaning of time. Set against the background of the sack of Rome, Augustine initially refuted the allegation that this "catastrophic event" was due to the adoption of Christianity at the expense of the Roman traditional cults by "invoking authorities recognized by his opponents, who did not recognize the authority of Scripture".[161] Against what he considered to be an unsubstantiated and oversimplified charge made by the "pagans", Augustine listed diverse calamities from Roman history that had fallen upon the city before the establishment of Christianity. Deconstructing the myth of Rome as the eternal city, Augustine then related, located and incorporated this history within the larger rhetorical plan of the "City of God" that he had drawn from the Scriptures. Although his theological arguments had already taken shape in, and interrelated to, his previous works, it is in the *De civitate Dei* that Augustine exhaustively formulated his conviction that history is the manifestation of God's salvation within the realm of time.

Moreover, it was this conviction which defined Augustine's understanding of the authority of Scripture. In Scripture, the incarnated Word revealed the way back to God for human being. Augustine stated thus:

> [In] order that the mind walk more confidently towards the truth, the Truth itself, God, God's son, assuming humanity without putting aside His Godhood, established and founded this faith, that man might find a way to man's God though God made man.[162]

For Augustine, the authority of Scripture is therefore not propositional but relational,[163] a knowing in fellowship where the eternal Word addresses humanity's deepest

---

159 ci 18.53 (Dyson 903).
160 *Ambae tamen temporalibus uel bonis pariter utuntur uel malis pariter affliguntur, diuersa fide, diuersa spe, diuerso amore, donec ultimo iudicio separentur, et percipiat unaquaeque suum finem, cuius nullus est finis.* ci 18.54 (CCSL 48.656; Dyson 907–08).
161 Clark (2010), 167.
162 *In qua ut fidentius ambularet ad ueritatem, ipsa ueritas, deus dei filius, homine adsumpto, non deo consumpto, eandem constituit et fundauit fidem, ut ad hominis deum iter esset homini per hominem deum.* ci 11.2 (CCSL 48.322; Dyson 451).
163 On how Christian belief is relational, particularly in the early church and also in Augustine, see chapter one, n. 59 and chapter three, n. 72 above.

need — the "restless heart". Conversely, negating the veracity of scriptural accounts regarding God's salvific outworking would amount to shaking the foundation of scriptural authority.[164]

In order to substantiate this insight, Augustine goes back to the question of creation and time and the book of Genesis and then, the whole "Jewish" Scriptures. Augustine negates the "pagans'" notion of the evolution of the human race and the origin of the world and their rendering of history as well as the philosophers' notion of cyclic time. He then invokes scriptural accounts where the birth, death and resurrection of Christ, which has been foretold in prophecies, sets history in motion toward a specific end (ci 7.32; 12.10–14). And as Augustine mediates the beginning and the end of time which the Scriptures revealed, he also grappled with the enigma of time that had permeated the entire New Testament's outlook where the "Christ-event" actuates a sense of tension between the "already" and the "not yet".

For Augustine, this tension can be represented by the conundrum of the "two cities". Since the two cities "intermingled" at the present, believers are "already" in the realm where they should take confidence in divine providence. But it is "not yet" the time to insist upon "purity" or the final triumph of the church and the believers. In this way, Augustine also mediated between the contrasting apocalyptic and triumphalist understanding of the "last day", the *consummatio saeculi* which largely centred upon the destiny of the city of Rome and the imperial policy of the Roman empire (ci 12.53; 20.5).

As the "Christ-event" ushered in the decisive "last day", i.e., the resurrection of souls that will find its fulfilment in the resurrection of body and the last judgment, Augustine exhorted his readers to redeem the time (ci 20.6; 20.8–9) amidst the "inconstant age" (*temporali mobilitate*, ci prol 1). For Augustine, prophecies that has been foretold in the Scriptures were fulfilled in Christ's salvific work — the incarnation being the locus and the centre of salvation history. Basing upon this fact, prophecies and promises for the future will be fulfilled again. This assurance had established the authority of Scripture.[165] In other words, even in the uncertainty of the times surrounding the sack of Rome, Augustine sought meaning and purpose in Scripture. And the authority of Scripture which discloses the course of God's salvific plan in the realm of time from its inception to its ultimate goal gives him the assurance to say *bene uiuamus, et bona sunt tempora*.[166]

---

164 On the assertion that western Christianity developed a doctrine of Scripture's infallibility due to Augustine, see n. 33 in the *Introductory* chapter above.
165 "The incarnation of Christ ... and the everlasting reign of the most glorious City of God in endless enjoyment of the vision of God: all these things were foretold and promised in the Scriptures of this way. As we see so many of these promises fulfilled that we righteously and piously trust that the rest will also be fulfilled in time to come". ci 10.32 (Dyson 447).
166 s 80.8 (PL 38.498).

CHAPTER 8

Not "Perfection" but "Progress towards the Better"[1]

The Retractationes *as the Epitome of* Crede ut Intellegas

This work explores the significance of time in Augustine's understanding of the authority of Scripture. Asserting that authority is the natural outcome of being in a relationship, we have seen how *auctoritas*, which basically denotes the ability to have persistent influence long after an "event" actually occurred, was adapted for a distinct theological concept as "the authority of Scripture". For Augustine, the incarnation of the Word of God is an actual event in time which reveals God who is beyond time. The Scriptures records the overall pattern of God's salvific outworking that centres upon the "Christ-event" which, if appropriated with faith, becomes God's communication to human beings to restore their broken relationship with the Divine.

However, the "appropriation" of God's communication can be obscured by the "medium" in the process of "retrieval" since it is embedded in the mutability of the temporal human condition which has been determined by internal and external factors. The works of Augustine that we have studied depicts how he attempted to navigate through these sweeping factors of temporal life to hear the eternal Word of God speaking in the Scriptures. Since Augustine reflected upon this "odyssey" and brought his own thoughts to conclusion with the *Retractationes*, we shall conclude our survey of his works with the *Retractationes*. There we would see how the two seams of time and the authority of Scripture are finally interwoven in Augustine's mind.

Although Augustine partially completed the *Retractationes* around 427,[2] he had already expressed his wish, in his letter to Marcellinus in 412, to "collect and point out in some work drawn up for that purpose everything that, with the best of reasons, displeases me in all my books".[3] These dates itself were crucial when we consider that the last twenty years (410–430) of the elderly Augustine saw the decadence of the Roman empire and the political uncertainty engulfing the whole empire after the sack of Rome. Possidius even asserted that the last part of his life that Augustine endured was "the bitterest and saddest of his old age". But in spite of the uncertainty of the times, Augustine "always intended" that the library of the church "containing

---

1   *Ego mihi hanc perfectionem nec nunc arrogo cum iam sim senex … sed in melius proficientem.* re prol 2–3 (CCSL 57.6).
2   In his letter to Quodvultdeus written in 427/8, Augustine had mentioned this work thus: *et duo iam uolumina absolueram retractatis omnibus libris meis.* ep 224.2 (CSEL 57.453).
3   *Si enim mihi deus, quod uolo, praestiterit, ut omnium librorum meorum quaecumque mihi rectissime displicent, opere aliquo ad hoc ipsum instituto colligam atque demonstrem.* ep 143.2 (CSEL 44.251–52; Parsons 151). On how it was only partially completed, see the prologue and epilogue of the *Retractationes*.

his own books and discourses and those of other holy men ... should be carefully preserved for posterity".[4]

A "reconsideration" of his literary output "for posterity" in that challenging time therefore reflects Augustine's belief in the expansive future and his vision for the future horizon. Conversely, this stance also negated the prevalent apocalyptic worldview that had anticipated an imminent *Parousia*, where the political turmoil was seen as symbolic of "the end time". Aligning Augustine's "vision" with his statement that time itself is good if we live well,[5] we can assert that his outlook is more complex than simply being other-worldly or pessimistic. As a thinker, Augustine would like to "see the bigger picture" and takes the "metaphysical" into consideration, and this attitude has been reflected in his literary output.

Indeed, Augustine was also acutely aware of his own "finitude"[6] and, as evident from his preface to the *Retractationes*, his impending accountability. In order not to "be judged by the Lord" (1 Cor 11:31), Augustine wanted to judge his own works. As he will "give a reckoning on the day of judgment (Mt 12:36)" and that teachers in the church "are incurring a more severe judgment (Jas 3:1)",[7] Augustine wanted to avoid anything "unnecessary" in his works. With a sense of urgency,[8] he thus "reconsidered" his works "from an uncompromisingly critical perspective" so as "to single out for censure" what he disapproved of.[9]

This is a crucial avowal since his self-criticisms in the *Retractationes* had shown that his writings "were not for him accomplishments of the past, but living testimonies to faith that were just as subject to change and improvement as he was".[10] Anticipating the influence of his works upon his readers, Augustine would like to be imitated not in the errors that he had made but in his "progress towards the better".[11]

This scheme of a movement "towards the better" was espoused by the information Augustine had given regarding the time of composition of his works, arranged chronologically. Augustine broadly divided the *Retractationes* into two books which corresponded with his works before and after he became a bishop. The first book, which consisted of twenty-six works, is considerably more extensive than the second book where he discussed sixty-seven works. This suggested that Augustine considered his earlier works as needing a "much greater explication and correction than his later ones".[12]

---

4 O'Connell (1988), 129–30. On how Augustine's works were later circulated, see Weidmann (2012), 431–49.
5 See s 80.8. This statement is part of his sermon around 410 when the city of Rome was sacked.
6 Possidius noted that amid all the turmoil, Augustine was encouraged by the saying of Plotinus (in *Enneads* 1.4.7): "No one is great who is amazed that wood and stone collapse and mortals die". See O'Connell (1988), 113–14.
7 re *prol* 2 (Ramsey 20).
8 *differendum esse non arbitror* ... re *prol* 1 (CCSL 57.5; Ramsey 20).
9 re *prol* 1 (Ramsey 20).
10 Fitzgerald (1999b), 723.
11 re *prol* 3 (Ramsey 22).
12 Brachtendorf (2017), 225.

It has been remarked that "the *Confessiones* contains the history of Augustine's heart [or life]; the *Retractationes*, of his mind [or work]".[13] And we had mentioned that his personal narratives in the *Confessiones* have been eclipsed by the acknowledgement of God's authority whose eternal Word speaks through the Scriptures. Now, as Augustine reconsidered his previous writings, the *Retractationes* gives us a glimpse of how he dealt with issues regarding the authority of Scripture. We can make some crucial observations in this respect:

1. The Indispensability of the Scriptures

Augustine's earliest works as a Christian were directed against the Academics and the Manicheans (re 1.1; cf 5.14.25). Initially lacking a deep reflection on the Scriptures, these works were largely inspired by Augustine's reading of "certain books of the Platonist" (cf 7.9.13), which ultimately proved insufficient (cf 7.9.14). As Augustine was musing upon these works, he was eager to show that he could avoid some of the terms he had used and improved how he had articulated his earlier arguments[14] if he was already instructed sufficiently in "ecclesiastical writings" and "the sacred Scripture".[15] From the outset of the *Retractationes*, he was therefore eager to show the indispensability of the Scriptures where "Truth himself" speaks.[16] Seeing the Scriptures as a "benchmark" in the quest for truth[17] also reflects how Augustine acknowledges scriptural authority.

If the Scriptures is indispensable, what constituted this sacred Scripture for Augustine? In *De doctrina Christiana*, Augustine gives a list of the "complete canon of Scripture" and named "forty-four books" that form the "authoritative Old Testament" while the New Testament consists of twenty-seven books.[18] Prior to this assertion, Augustine maintained the harmony of the Old Testament and the New Testament

---

13   Eller (1949), 172; Pollmann (2011), 410. On the significance of the *Confessiones* for Augustine's theology of Scripture, see Bright (2006), 41–44.
14   Some examples of this are: I regret that I called upon fortune so frequently (*non mihi placet totiens me appellasse fortunam* (re 1.1.2; CCSL 57.7); I would have spoken more safely had I said "to go" (*iturus*) rather than "to return" (*rediturus*) (re 1.1.3; CCSL 57.9); when I said of the Father and the Son, "He who begets and he whom he begets is one", (*unum est*) it should have been said "are one" (*unum sunt*) (re 1.4.3; CCSL 57.14); [It] would have been better [to say] "sincere" rather than "complete" (*sincera quam plena*) (re 1.7.4; CCSL 57.19).
15   *litteris ecclesiasticis eruditi; litteris sacris ita eruditus* ... re 1.3.2; 1.5.2 (CCSL 57.13; 57.16).
16   Augustine stated, "And when I said of the Father and the Son, 'He who begets and he whom he begets is one', it should have been said 'are one', as Truth himself clearly says when he states, 'I and the Father are one' (Jn 10:30). *Et ubi dixi de patre et filio: qui gignit et quem gignit unum est, dicendum fuit: unum sunt, sicut aperte ipsa ueritas loquitur dicens: "ego et pater unum sumus"*. re 1.4.3 (CCSL 57.14; Ramsey 33). This can be contrasted with the Prologue where he equated "error" with adding one's own ideas (re *prol* 2) which is similar to the change he levelled against Jerome in his ep 28.
17   "I have not seen how I could be persuaded [that this world is ensouled] by the authority of the divine scriptures". re 1.11.4 (Ramsey 56); see also re 1.15.7. On how both Augustine and Pelagius shared "the evolving consensus among Christians" that Scripture is authoritative, see O'Donnell (2006), 277–78.
18   do 2.13.26; 2.13.29.

against Adimantus and stated that "there are no divine precepts and promises, however lofty, which are found in the gospels and in the apostolic teaching that are missing from those ancient books".[19]

In hindsight, Augustine still justifies his statement against Adimantus if the Old Testament is seen as figurative and as prophecies about Christ that have been fulfilled and will eventually be fulfilled. But if considered literally, since there are certain precepts which are "not found in the Old Testament but in the New", Augustine asserts that "it would have been more cautious and moderate to say that there are 'almost no' rather than 'no' [precepts] in the latter that are not also in the former".[20] Augustine also clarifies that when he used the term "the Old Testament" in the *De doctrina Christiana*, he "referred to the Old Testament according to the Church's customary way of speaking. The Apostle [Paul], however, seems to refer only to what was given on Mount Sinai as the Old Testament".[21]

These comments in the *Retractationes* show how much "progress" Augustine has made towards understanding the nature of the Scriptures. At the same time, the "shift" from an allegorical interpretation to a literal "consideration"[22] has been congruent with Augustine's reading of Paul, whose "theology" determines Augustine's interpretative postures in the *Retractationes*.[23] Furthermore, we can affirm that Augustine's view of the Scriptures is reflected in the way he actually uses it in exegesis.

2. The Human Aspects of the Scriptures

When Augustine set to defend the teachings of the Catholic church in his earlier works, he was not yet accustomed to the Scriptures so that the faultiness of his codex misled him. As he was not aware that there are more accurate versions of the same passage which he had provided as a proof text, Augustine feels that he "did not show the harmony of the Old and the New Testaments that [he] wanted to show" against the Manicheans.[24] On reconsideration, Augustine asserts that the LXX should be used to correct the Latin translations of the Scriptures.[25] Regarding the *De Genesi contra Manichaeos* which was published very explicitly against the Manicheans "in defense

---

19 re 1.22.2 (Ramsey 88).
20 re 1.22.2 (Ramsey 88).
21 re 2.4.2 (Ramsey 112).
22 On how scriptural passages should not be taken "exclusively in an allegorical sense", see re 1.10.2; 1.22.2; also 1.18; 2.24.1.
23 According to the "Index of Scripture" prepared by Michael T. Dolan (see "Index" in Ramsey [2010], 221–23), 183 passages from the Scriptures have been quoted in the *Retractationes*. While 45 passages are from the Old Testament, and 41 passages are from the Gospels, 33 passages are from Paul's Epistle to the Romans and 22 passages are from the Paul's first Epistle to the Corinthians. This shows the centrality of Paul's theology in the mature Augustine. O'Donnell even asserts that for Augustine, "everything Paul said add up to one systematic and true body of doctrine". O'Donnell (2006), 274.
24 re 1.7.2–3 (Ramsey 38).
25 *Hoc esse uerius Greci libri indicant … in multis quidem codicibus legi, sed hoc Grecus non habet.* re 1.7.2–3 (CCSL 57.18–19).

of the Old Law", Augustine realized that there are codices "with a better translation" and that what he referred as "prophetic words" was not to be considered as such.²⁶

In another instance, Augustine accused a Donatist, on the question of baptism, of deleting "from the Book of Ecclesiasticus words from the middle of a sentence that were pertinent to the matter". But he realized that the quotation was based on actual manuscripts predating the Donatist controversy. "If I had known this at the time", Augustine admitted, "I would not have been so outspoken against him as a thief and violator of divine Scripture".²⁷

So, although Augustine speaks appreciatively of the Scriptures and corrected his works in the light of the "better" readings, he conversely specifies the human agency in translating, copying and transmitting the Scriptures, thereby accentuating the enormous "progress" he had made towards realizing these aspects, which ultimately gives more credibility to his exegesis.

3. *Retractationes*²⁸ as the Epitome of *Crede ut Intellegas*²⁹ — The Theological Basis and Implications of "Progress towards the Better" in Augustine's Scriptural Odyssey

As Augustine stands back and reflects upon his works, he introduces a crucial theological concern: that perfection could not be acquired in this mortal life.³⁰ Just as the issues regarding this insight occupied him most at the later part of his ministry, it seems to permeate his entire *Retractationes* too. When Augustine countered the Manicheans "who deny that the origin of evil proceeds from the free choice of the will", he was not making sufficient reference to the grace of God "as though it were the object of the discussion".³¹ In fact, he initially reacted when he "was unable to bear in

---

26 re 1.10.1; 1.10.3 (Ramsey 50, 52); In re 1.19.4, he stated: "We also understood better afterwards what is written ... For the Greek [codices] do not have *without cause*, as appears here" (Ramsey 80); see also re 2.17; 2.24.2.
27 re 1.21.3.
28 On how this word connotes "retreatment" and "revision" to align his works in the light of a deeper insights rather than to "retract" or "recant" them, see Eller (1946), xvi–xvii.
29 "Believe in order to understand" (Jo 29.6; s 43.9; 118.1) is a characteristic Augustinian principle that is based upon Vetus Latina translation of Is 7:9, *nisi credideritis, non intellegetis*. He quoted Is 7:9 explicitly 42 times in his extant writings (these numbers were collected using the cag-online. net database). It was first used in lib 1.4, (Indeed, we are well aware that this is to take the course prescribed by the prophet Isaiah, who says: "Unless you believe you shall not understand" [*praescriptum enim per prophetam gradum, qui ait: "nisi credideritis, non intellegetis", tenere nos bene nobis conscii sumus*] CSEL 74.6; King 5), a book he defended at length against the Pelagians. This principle was also implicit in his reflection on *De Libero Arbitrio* in re 1.9.1: "[our deliberation] would bring to our understanding [*intellegentiam nostrum*] ... what we who were subject to divine authority already believed about this matter [*id quod de hac re diuinae auctoritati subditi credebamus*]" (CCSL 57.23; Ramsey 42). For a comprehensive treatment of the concept, see TeSelle (1986–1994), 116–19.
30 *Ego mihi hanc perfectionem nec nunc arrogo, cum iam sim senex*. re prol 2 (CCSL 57.6); see also re 1.7.5; 1.23.1.
31 re 1.9.2 (Ramsey 43).

silence the boasting of the Manicheans about their false and fallacious continence, or abstinence, by means of which, in order to deceive the ignorant, they put themselves above true Christians".[32] On the issue of "how a human ought to live",[33] Augustine arduously argued that the "two commandments" of love which the "two testaments" advocated[34] is the real defining factor of Christian morality, and not merely chastity and abstinence which the Manicheans boasted to observed.[35]

In hindsight, Augustine was too eager to refute the Manicheans' claim of "high morality" so that he had exaggerated the "degree" of love that true Christians can achieve in this life.[36] In negating "the error" of the Manicheans' "impiousness" (*impietatis errorem*) that is rooted in their dualistic cosmogony, Augustine's argument from "the free choice of will" had acknowledged the grace of God — the agent of love — only "in passing but not defended with careful reasoning".[37] And the Pelagians, who stressed "the free choice of will to such a degree that they leave no place for God's grace" took advantage of Augustine's argument to substantiate their stance.[38] Therefore, Augustine emphasized that "the grace of God frees a person from the wretchedness that is most justly inflicted on sinners", and of one's own accord — that is, by free choice — one could fall "and not also rise".[39]

Augustine insisted that while he initially directed his argument on free choice of will against the Manicheans who rejected "the holy scriptures" as deliberately corrupted, he now needed to defend "what both scriptures speak of" from the Pelagians who professed to accept the same Scriptures as Augustine.[40] The irony is that one of the principal theological concerns of Pelagius was and remained "the combating of Manichaean fatalism".[41] It has been asserted that Pelagius was concerned about the lax ethical standards among Christians in the *tempora christiana*.[42] Hoping to develop their conduct by his teachings, Pelagius rejected Augustine's assertion that sin is the outcome of human weakness which has been rooted in "original sin".[43] Stressing that God made human beings free to choose between good and evil, Pelagius asserted

---

32   re 1.7.1 (Ramsey 37); see also mor 1.1.2.
33   mor 1.2.4 (Teske 32); see also mor 1.3.6; 1.4.6; 2.3.5; 2.9.15.
34   mor 1.28.57; 1.32.69.
35   mor 1.31.65; 1.33.73.
36   In re 1.7.5, he stated, "The ardor of charity ... can indeed be born and increase in this life. Yet that does not mean that, because it is born, it can be perfect, such that no vice dwells in a person" (Ramsey 39).
37   re 1.9.2 (Ramsey 43). See also chapter four, n. 85 above for Augustine's previous stance.
38   re 1.9.3 (Ramsey 43); see also re 1.7.5.
39   re 1.9.6 (Ramsey 49).
40   re 1.9.6 (Ramsey 49). On his refutations of the Manicheans' claim, see also Fau 11.2; on how his arguments against the Manicheans prepared the ground for his arguments against the Pelagians, see chapter six, n. 162 above; on how Augustine and Pelagius had a shared conviction regarding Scripture, see also n. 17 above.
41   Evans (1968), 22.
42   As Bonner remarked, "the soul of Pelagianism is not to be sought in theological propositions but in a particular outlook, a desire to be a true Christian in the superficially-Christianized society of the Fifth century Roman Empire". Bonner (1972), 10.
43   On "original sin", see re 1.9.6; 1.10.3; 1.13.4; 1.14.4; 1.19.5; 2.62.

that sin is a voluntary act committed by a person against God's law.[44] And though the Pelagians even find endorsement in Augustine's refutation of the Manicheans,[45] Augustine branded Pelagius's stance as "a new heresy" and the Pelagians as "heretics".[46]

Interestingly, Augustine started to work on *De haeresibus ad Quodvultdeum* where he looked at 88 different heresies around the time that he wrote the *Retractationes*.[47] There, he asserted that Pelagius and his disciple Caelestius "are enemies of the grace of God" who hold that "a human being can observe all of God's commandments without it". Subordinating grace to free choice, they taught that human beings could fulfil God's commands "without grace, though with greater difficulty". While accepting that "God gives us knowledge which dispels ignorance", they reject that God "gives us the charity by which one lives a good life". For Augustine, the Pelagians believe that "the knowledge, which without charity causes pride, is a gift of God, but that the charity which does not cause pride, as knowledge does, but edification, is not a gift of God".[48]

In the light of the *De haeresibus ad Quodvultdeum*, we can see how Augustine considered both the Manicheans and the Pelagians as "heretics". While the Manicheans differed with Augustine regarding the origin and nature of evil to deny the scriptural account of the original sin, the Pelagians differed with Augustine regarding the impact of the original sin on the human nature to deny the teaching of Scripture on the indispensability of grace.[49] Therefore, the Manicheans were "heretics" who deny the reliability of the Scriptures while the Pelagians were heretics who misrepresented the teachings of the Scriptures.

Without further elaborating upon their specific arguments, we can say that Augustine and Pelagius's positions were, *inter alia*, the outcome of the enigma of time where the tension between the "already" and the "not yet" still shapes Christian identity. We have already asserted that the Christian Scriptures documented the different dimensions of the tension of time in the formative stage and well into the time of Augustine. Pelagius and Augustine mutually drew their postures from the scriptures and their theological and practical concerns reveal how orthodoxy intertwined with orthopraxis in their minds. Orthodoxy is not sought for its own sake but for the sake

---

44 For a summary of Pelagius's teaching, see chapter seven, n. 144 above and hae 88.
45 Augustine thus stated, "The Pelagians could think that I said that this perfection could be acquired in this mortal life [in mor 1.30.64]. But they should not think this". re 1.7.5 (Ramsey 39). See also re 1.10.2.
46 He first mentioned Pelagius in re 1.9.3 and the Pelagians in re 1.7.5 and referred to them as "the recent heretics" (*noui heretici Pelagiani*) in re 1.9.3 (see also 1.10.2 and 2.53) and mentioned the "Pelagian heresy" in re 1.9.6; 1.23.1; 2.50. On how Augustine use the "heretic" label against the Donatists, see chapter four, n. 8 and 9 above. On the two images of heresy and orthodoxy in Christian antiquity, see Markus (1989), 214–34; see also chapter five, n. 34 above.
47 *dispono ... quod poscis, incipere simul agens utrumque et hoc scilicet et illud de retractatione opusculorum meorum nocturnis et diurnis temporibus in singula distributis*. ep 224.2 (CSEL 57.453). On his request to Jerome to publish a "revised" work on all the false doctrine of the heretics (*omnium haereticorum peruersa dogmata*), see ep 40.9 (CSEL 34.2.80).
48 hae 88.1–3 (Teske 56).
49 For an assessment of Pelagius's stance on grace, see Bonner (1972); Evans (1968), 66–121 and the more recent works in TeSelle (1999), 633–40 and Teselle (2014), 1–13.

of morality, to be in a right relationship with God. The underlying issue is how we can stand in a right relationship with God in the interim period. This is the period when we know that the "Christ-event" ushered in the "last day" but does not yet find its consummation in the *Parousia*. While faith, understanding and morality is a continuum in the quest for being "true Christians" in this *tempora christiana*, what is the believer's role and potential to achieve that quest?

As Augustine grapples with this question in his scriptural exegesis, he established the argument that what inspires this morality is love, which is solely "the gift of the Holy Spirit, through whom charity has been poured forth in our hearts (Rom 5:5)".[50] Not only that, "even faith itself is among God's gifts that are given in the same Spirit (1 Cor 12:9)".[51] For Augustine, individual Christians and the church are "work in progress" whose conformation in the image of God[52] is a lifelong process while Pelagius argues that "this perfection could be acquired in this mortal life".[53] Thus, the "tension" of the "already and not yet" regarding the moral perfection of believers at the present life determined the distinct theological approaches of Augustine and Pelagius.

Augustine expressed this "tension" with the Pauline imagery of "the law fighting against the law of our mind" (re 1.19.1; see also 2.7.3; 2.53.1) and "spiritual [person] already living under grace" (re 1.26; 1.23.1). This personal/individual struggle[54] finds "collective expression" in the church that is not yet without "spot or wrinkle" (re 1.19.9; also 2.18). For Augustine:

> since the whole Church says as long as it is here, *Forgive us our debts* (Mt 6:12), it is certainly not here without spot or wrinkle or anything of the sort. But, from what she accepts here, she is brought to that glory and perfection which does not exist here.[55]

What we can ultimately deduce from these "assured" accounts of Augustine, as he progresses "toward the better" in contrast to the "heretical" Pelagians, is how the

---

50 re 1.23.1 (Ramsey 90); later, he said, "'For believing and willing are ours, but it is his to give to those who believe and who will the ability to do good through the Holy Spirit, by whom charity is poured forth in our hearts'. But by this same rule, however, both are his, because it is he who readies the will, and both are ours, because nothing is done unless we will it". re 1.23.3 (Ramsey 93).
51 re 1.23.2 (Ramsey 92).
52 Augustine introduce the *imagine dei* in re 1.13.8, which is based upon Gen 1:26 (re 1.18). He extensively dealt with *imago dei* in re 1.26, on the fifty-first and sixty-seventh of the "Eighty-Three Questions" that he looked at. See also re 2.24.2 on the effect of Adam's sin on the image of God.
53 *possunt putare Pelagiani istam perfectionem in hac mortali uita me dixisse posse contingere.* re 1.7.5 (CCSL 57.20; Ramsey 39).
54 On the possible meaning of the "conflict" in Romans 7, viz. autobiographically (as implying Paul himself), or psychologically (as implying human experience in general), or objectively (as relating a real situation which does not necessarily correspond with personal experience), TeSelle asserted that "Augustine always understood the chapter experientially". TeSelle (2002b), 111.
55 re 1.7.5 (Ramsey 39); see also re 1.19.3; 2.18. We can juxtapose this with Bonner's observation: "The ecclesiology of Donatism and Pelagianism had remarkable affinities. Both contended for a pure Church, the one by external separation, the other by an internal migration". Bonner (1972), 36.

Scriptures formed the narrative structure of his arguments. From acknowledging the indispensability, and accepting the authority, of Scripture, Augustine drew an all-encompassing theological vision which he revised and corroborated against his interlocutors in a logical and coherent way. Therefore, in his attempt to align his past works in the light of a deeper insight into the Scriptures, we have seen how the *Retractationes* epitomised *crede ut intellegas* for Augustine.

4. Beyond Time, Beyond "the Authority of Scripture"

We have mentioned that for Augustine, Scripture is a "temporal dispensation" and a "word uttered in time" while only Christ is the eternal Word of God.[56] It is the vulnerability of human nature through "original sin" which makes the Scriptures an existential need. But while the tentativeness of the human moral condition makes grace indispensable, grace also inspires love that has implications beyond the temporal realm and which also transcends the authority of Scripture, the temporal dispensation. This stance has been reflected in the *Retractationes* when Augustine maintained that our love for God can never be "complete" in this life:

> But what I said, "The very one whom we wish to know"—that is, God —"we must first love with a complete charity", would have been better said by using "sincere" rather than "complete", lest perhaps it be thought that our charity for God will not be greater when we shall see face to face (1 Cor 13:12). That, indeed, is how it should be taken, as though "complete" is being said in terms of that which cannot be greater as long as we are walking by faith, for it will be complete — no! most complete — but by vision.[57]

In other words, Scripture is authoritative so long as it facilitates our relationship with God, by faith and not by sight. With nothing to hinder our relationship when we come "face to face" with God, then we shall no longer need the Scriptures to mediate the will of God. There, "the restless heart"[58] shall find "the eternal rest".[59]

Conclusions

This book reassesses the notion of "the authority of Scripture" — often equated with the "authority" of stable texts which were mass-produced as "the Bible" after the Sixteenth Century and later epitomised by the watchword *sola scriptura* — by appealing to the insights of Augustine. Discerning that the experience of time is

---

56 See the *Introduction* and chapter three above where this insight has been treated.
57 re 1.7.4 (Ramsey 38); see also re 1.14.2.
58 cf 1.1.1.
59 Augustine puts this most eloquently in the closing passage of his epic *De civitate Dei*: "There we shall rest and see, and see and love, and love and praise". *Ibi uacabimus et uidebimus, uidebimus et amabimus, amabimus et laudabimus.* ci 22.30 (CCSL 48.866; Dyson 1182).

always momentous and stimulating to Augustine's theological reflection, the book asserts that Augustine's notion of the authority of Scripture was also embedded in his awareness of time.

This notion of time was rooted in the tension between the "already" and "not yet" of the "last days" that permeated the entire New Testament theological outlook. This transpired as the temporal tension between an achieved victory of the incarnated Christ over the powers of evil and its apocalyptic fulfilment until the *Parousia*, so that the interim period becomes the arena of apocalyptic activity. As we explore how Augustine and his contemporaries grappled with the existential implications of this tension in time, we can see that the authority of Scripture is not the authority of "the Book" in the modern sense but is related to more complicated sources of authority that are linked to this specific notion of time.

While this does not mean that it is reflections on time that is the determining feature of a particular complex debate, or the origin of a particular work in Augustine's corpus, this book specifically affirms and delineates how Augustine's experience of time as a living, ongoing and creative tension critically determined his theological stances towards scriptural authority. As we explore the implications of this insight, we have seen how Augustine's awareness of this temporal tension was roused by the acceptance of his own temporality and creaturehood which brings to the fore the importance of the incarnate Christ.

And though Augustine reflected upon different aspects of the human experience of time, this interiorized sense of human temporality largely determined his notion of historical time that has been incorporated into the grander divine economy. Augustine's concept of the authority of Scripture was therefore intertwined with his notion of an historical time which is the realm where divine revelation discloses the meaning of sacred history. This book accordingly made a fundamental link between revelation, time, and the authority of the documents that Christians read. And acknowledging how the temporal tension shapes Augustine's theological postures will ascertain how his concept of the authority of Scripture is ultimately different from our modern notion of *sola scriptura*.

In tandem with his evolving understanding of time, Augustine asserted against the Manicheans — who maintained that Paul's writings disagree with the teaching of the Old Testament — that the entire Scripture is a work of divine eloquence. Against the Manicheans reading of Paul which endorse their radical dualism, their moral determinism and their docetic Christology, Augustine draw imagery particularly from Genesis and established that Genesis is in line with Paul. Similarly, the Old Testament complemented the New Testament while Christ determined and opened the deeper meaning to Scripture. The distinction between Old and New Testaments is broken down so that Christ as the Word is active within the whole of sacred history.

This insight partially negated Jerome's insistence on *Hebraica veritas* which endorsed working "backwards" toward scriptural text to arrive at its meaning. It also negated Jerome's attempt to portray himself, following Eusebius's view of history, as standing at the pinnacle of Christian literary tradition. For Augustine, because God does not fail to communicate to human beings, it is the frailty of the human mind that obscure the divine messages, though knowledge of the original languages can be a partial remedy. But unlike Jerome, Augustine advocated working "forwards" towards the sense of the Scriptures which pointed to Christ as the fulfilment as well as the definite point of departure in scriptural expositions and Christian literary reflections.

Against the Platonist's method of philosophical ascent, Augustine stressed the implications of time which the incarnation of the eternal Word set in motion in history so that history is the confluence of time and eternity. The Platonist insisted that "there are many ways to so great a mystery" while the natural divinity of the human soul nullifies the necessity of the incarnation for salvation and the resurrection of the body. And while they downplayed the significance of the temporal order, Augustine stressed the reality of time and history in the larger divine economy without either conforming to Eusebian triumphalism and Donatist apocalypticism.

While Augustine needs to assert the harmony of Christian Scriptures against the Manicheans, as well as defending the particularity of the Christian view of salvation history, he also needs to discern the correct signification of Scripture in the *tempora christiana* against the Donatists and the Pelagians. Against the Donatists whose vision of the church as a "mixed body" and its implications diverges, Augustine maintained that it is "not yet" the time to insist upon "purity" of the church. Against Pelagius who argues that Christian perfection "could be acquired in this mortal life", Augustine stressed that individual Christians and the church are "work in progress" whose conformation in the image of God is a lifelong process.

In retrospect, we can see that Augustine's responses to his interlocutors, and the theological stances emerging out of these engagements, can be roughly categorized into two distinct but overlapping framework of temporality: the theological implications of the "already" and the "not yet" of the "last days". Particularly against those who negated the historical reality of the incarnation and its salvific decisiveness, Augustine stressed that "now" is already the "last days" which the Scriptures bear living witness, whereby God addresses human being through the eternal Word in this temporal realm. Against those who insisted upon the perfection of the church and her members "now", Augustine stressed the "not yet" aspect of the "last days".

This "already and not yet"-ness of our temporal human experience has been epitomized by Augustine's notion of the "restless heart" that anticipated the eternal rest of the Sabbath. And it was this "restless heart" of fallen humanity that interweaved the two seams of time and the authority of Scripture in Augustine's understanding. Until that day when we achieve this everlasting rest and time shall be no more (cf 13.35.50), Scripture is the channel and the reliable witness of the eternal Word.

Bibliography

1. Ancient Sources

Ambrose, *De bono mortis: Death as a Good* (M. P. McHugh, 1972, Washington, DC, FOTC, 65).
———. *De paradiso* (C. Schenkl ed, 1896, CSEL 32.1.275–366); *Paradise* (J. J. Savage, 1961, New York, NY, FOTC, 42).
———. *De virginibus*: "On Virgins", in *Ambrose, Early Church Fathers* (B. Ramsey, 1997, London, 71–116).
———. *Epistularum liber decimus* (M. Zelzer ed, 1982, CSEL 82.3.1–140); *Letters* (M. M. Beyenka, 1954, New York, NY, FOTC, 26); "The Letters pertaining to the Altar of Victory Controversy", in *Ambrose* (Early Church Fathers), (B. Ramsey, 1997, London, 175–94).
Ammianus Marcellinus, *Rerum gestarum*: *History*, Vol. I, Books 14–19 (J. Rolfe, 1936, Cambridge, MA, LCL 300).
Anon, *Res gestae divi Augusti: The Achievements of the Divine Augustus* (P. A. Brunt and J. M. Moore, 1967, Oxford); (A. E. Cooley, 2009, Cambridge).
Augustine, *Ad Simplicianum de diuersis quaestionibus* (A. Mutzenbecher ed, 1970, CCSL 44.7–91); *Miscellany of Questions in Response to Simplician* (R. Canning, ed, B. Ramsey, intro, trans and notes, 2008, New York, NY, WSA 1/12).
———. *Confessiones* (L. Verheijen ed, 1981, CCSL 27.1–273); *Confessions* (T. Williams, trans with intro and notes, 2019, Indianapolis, IN).
———. *Contra Adimantum Manichaei discipulum* (J. Zycha ed, 1891, CSEL 25.1.115–90); *Answer to Adimantus, a disciple of Mani* (B. Ramsey, ed, R. Teske, intro, trans and notes, 2006, New York, NY, WSA 1/19).
———. *Contra duas epistulas Pelagianorum* (K. F. Vrba, J. Zycha eds, 1913, CSEL 60.423–570); *Answer to the Two Letters of the Pelagians* (J. E. Rotelle, ed, R. Teske, intro, trans and notes, 1998, New York, NY, WSA 1/24).
———. *Contra epistulam Manichaei quam uocant fundamenti* (J. Zycha ed, 1891, CSEL 25.1.193–248); *Answer to the Letter of Mani known as the Foundation* (B. Ramsey, ed, R. Teske, intro, trans and notes, 2006, New York, NY, WSA 1/19).
———. *Contra epistulam Parmeniani* (M. Petschenig ed, 1908, CSEL 51.19–141).
———. *Contra Faustum Manichaeum* (J. Zycha ed, 1891, CSEL 25.1.251–797); *Answer to Faustus, a Manichean* (B. Ramsey, ed, R. Teske, trans 2007, New York, NY, WSA 1/20).
———. *Contra Felicem Manichaeum* (J. Zycha ed, 1892, CSEL 25.2.801–52); *Answer to Felix, a Manichean* (B. Ramsey, ed, R. Teske, intro, trans and notes, 2006, New York, WSA 1/19).
———. *Contra Fortunatum Manicheum* (J. Zycha ed, 1891, CSEL 25.1.83–112); *A Debate with Fortunatus, a Manichean* (B. Ramsey, ed, R. Teske, intro, trans and notes, 2006, New York, NY, WSA 1/19).

——. *Contra Iulianum* (J. P. Migne ed, 1845, PL 44.641–874).

——. *Contra Iulianum opus imperfectum* 1–3 (M. Zelzer ed, 1974, CSEL 85.1.3–506).

——. *Contra litteras Petiliani* (M. Petschenig ed, 1909, CSEL 52.3–227).

——. *De beata uita* (V. M. Green, K. D. Daur eds, 1970, CCSL 29.65–85).

——. *De ciuitate dei* (B. Dombart, A. Kalb eds, 1955, CCSL 47.1–314; 48.321–866); *The City of God against the Pagans* (R. Dyson, 1998, Cambridge); *Concerning the City of God against the Pagans* (H. Bettenson, 1972, London).

——. *De consensu euangelistarum* (F. Weihrich ed, 1904, CSEL 43.1–61, 81–418); *The Harmony of the Gospels* (P. Schaff, ed, S. D. F. Salmond, trans, 1892, Edinburgh, NPNF Series 1/6).

——. *De diuersis quaestionibus octoginta tribus* (A. Mutzenbecher ed, 1975, CCSL 44A.11–249); *Miscellany of Eighty-Three Questions* (R. Canning, ed, B. Ramsey, intro, trans and notes, 2008, New York, NY, WSA 1/12).

——. *De doctrina Christiana* (W. M. Green ed, 1963, CSEL 80.3–169); *De Doctrina Christiana* (R. P. H. Green, 1995, Oxford).

——. *De dono perseuerantiae* (J. P. Migne ed, 1865, PL 45.993–1034); *The Gift of Perseverance* (J. E. Rotelle, ed, R. Teske, intro, trans and notes, 1999, New York, NY, WSA 1/26).

——. *De duabus animabus* (J. Zycha ed, 1891, CSEL 25.1.51–80); *The Two Souls* (B. Ramsey, ed, R. Teske, intro, trans and notes, 2006, New York, NY, WSA 1/19).

——. *De fide et symbolo* (J. Zycha ed, 1900, CSEL 41.3–32).

——. *De Genesi ad litteram* (J. Zycha ed, 1894, CSEL 28.1.3–435); *The Literal Meaning of Genesis* (J. E. Rotelle, ed, E. Hill, trans and notes, 2002, New York, NY, WSA, 1/13).

——. *De Genesi ad litteram imperfectus* (J. Zycha ed, 1894, CSEL 28.1.459–503) *Unfinished Literal Commentary on Genesis* (J. E. Rotelle, ed, E. Hill, trans and notes, 2002, New York, NY, WSA, 1/13).

——. *De Genesi contra Manichaeos* (D. Weber ed, 1998, CSEL 91.67–172); *On Genesis: A Refutation of the Manichees* (J. E. Rotelle, ed, E. Hill, trans and notes, 2002, New York, NY, WSA, 1/13).

——. *De gestis Pelagii* (K. F. Vrba, J. Zycha eds, 1902, CSEL 42.51–122); *The Deeds of Pelagius* (J. E. Rotelle, ed, R. Teske, into., trans, and notes, 1997, New York, NY, WSA, 1/23).

——. *De haeresibus ad Quoduultdeum* (R. Vander Plaetse, C. Beukers eds, 1969, CCSL 46.286–345); *Heresies* (J. E. Rotelle, ed, R. Teske, intro, trans, and notes, 1995, New York, NY, WSA, 1/18).

——. *De libero arbitrio* (W. M. Green ed, 1956, CSEL 74.3–154); *On the Free Choice of the Will* (Peter King, ed and trans, 2010, Cambridge).

——. *De mendacio* (J. Zycha ed, 1900, CSEL 41.413–66).

——. *De moribus ecclesiae catholicae et de moribus Manicheorum* (J. B. Bauer ed, 1992, CSEL 90.3–156); *The Catholic Way of Life and the Manichean Way of Life* (B. Ramsey, ed, R. Teske, intro, trans and notes, 2006, New York, NY, WSA 1/19).

——. *De peccatorum meritis et remissione et de baptismo paruulorum ad Marcellinum* (K. F. Vrba, J. Zycha eds, 1913, CSEL 60.3–151); *The Punishment and Forgiveness of Sins and the Baptism of Little Ones* (J. E. Rotelle, ed, R. Teske, intro, trans, and notes, 1997, New York, NY, WSA 1/23).

——. *De spiritu et littera ad Marcellinum* (K. F. Vrba, J. Zycha eds, 1913, CSEL 60.155–229); *The Spirit and the Letter* (J. E. Rotelle, ed, R. Teske, intro, trans, and notes, 1997, New York, NY, WSA 1/23).

———. *De uera religione* (K.-D. Daur ed, 1962, CCSL 32.187–260).

———. *Enarrationes in Psalmos*, 51–100 (E. Dekkers, J. Fraipont eds, 1956, CCSL 39.623–1417).

———. *Enarrationes in Psalmos*, 101–50 (E. Dekkers, J. Fraipont eds, 1956, CCSL 40.1425–2196).

———. *Enchiridion ad Laurentium, seu de fide, spe et caritate* (E. Evans ed, 1969, CCSL 46.49–114).

———. *Epistulae* (A. Goldbacher ed, 1895, CSEL 34.1&2.1–123); (A. Goldbacher ed, 1904, CSEL 44.124–84); (A. Goldbacher ed, 1911, CSEL 57.185–269); (J. Divjak ed, 1981, CSEL 88); *The Correspondence (394–419) between Jerome and Augustine of Hippo* (C. White, 1990, New York, NY); *Letters*, Vol. 1–5 (W. Parsons, 1951–1956, New York, NY, FOTC 12, 18, 20, 30, 32).

———. *Epistulae ad Romanos inchoata expositio* (J. Divjak ed, 1971, CSEL 84.145–81); *Unfinished Commentary on Romans* (https://sites.google.com/site/aquinasstudybible/home/romans/augustine-on-romans).

———. *Expositio epistulae ad Galatas* (J. Divjak ed, 1971, CSEL 84.55–141); *Augustine's Commentary on Galatians* (E. Plumer, Intro, text, trans and notes, 2003, New York, NY).

———. *Expositio quarundam propositionum ex epistula apostoli ad Romanos* (J. Divjak ed, 1971, CSEL 84.3–52); *Two Questions About the Epistle to the Romans* (https://sites.google.com/site/aquinasstudybible/home/romans/augustine-of-hippo-two-question-about-the-epistle-to-the-romans).

———. *In Iohannis euangelium tractatus CXXIV*, (R. Willems ed, 1954, CCSL 36.1–688); *Homilies on the Gospel of John (1–40)* (A. Fitzgerald, B. Ramsey, eds, E. Hill, trans, 2009, New York, NY, WSA 3/12).

———. *Quaestionum in Heptateuchum libri VII* (D. De Bruyne ed, 1958, CCSL 33.1–377).

———. *Retractationes* (A. Mutzenbecher ed, 1984, CCSL 57.5–143); *Revisions* (B. Ramsey, ed, R. Teske, ed, B. Ramsey, trans, notes and intro, 2010, New York, NY, WSA 1/2).

———. *Sermones* (CCSL 41.1961–2016, 5 Vols); (PL 38.24–1484). There are numerous editions of Augustine's sermons, the vast majority in Latin are found within this edition. For all other additional Latin editions referred to in this work, E. Rebillard (1999), "Sermones" in Allan D. Fitzgerald (ed), *ATA*, Grand Rapids, MI, 773–92; *Sermons* (John E. Rotelle, ed, E. Hill, trans and notes, 1991, New York, NY, WSA III/3).

Clement of Alexandria, Στρωματέων (J. P. Migne ed, 1847, PG 8.685–1382); *Stromateis, Books 1–3* (J. Ferguson, 1991, Washington, DC, FOTC 85).

Jerome, *Commentarii in epistulam ad Galatas* (J. P. Migne ed, 1845, PL 26.307–438); *Commentary on Galatians* (A. Cain, 2010, Washington, DC, FOTC 121); *St Jerome's commentaries on Galatians, Titus, and Philemon* (T. P. Scheck, 2010, Notre Dame, IN).

———. *De uiris illustribus: Gli Uomini Illustri* (Aldo Ceresa-Gastaldo ed, 1988); *On Illustrious Men* (T. P. Halton, 1999, Washington, DC, FOTC 100).

———. *Epistulae, 1–70* (I. Hilberg ed, 1910, CSEL 54).

———. *Epistulae, 71–120* (I. Hilberg ed, 1912, CSEL 55).

———. *Prologus* (Incipit Prologus Santi Hieronymi in Libro Regum/ Prologus in libris Salomonis) *Vulgata* (Stuttgart, 1969, 364–66, 957); *Jerome: The Principal Works of St Jerome* (P. Schaff, ed, W. H. Fremantle, trans, 1892, Edinburgh, NPNF Series 2/6).

———. *Quaestiones hebraicae in libro Geneseos* (P. de Lagarde ed, 1959, CCSL 72.1–56); *Saint Jerome's Hebrew Questions on Genesis* (C. Hayward, 1995, Oxford).

Marius Victorinus, *Commentarii in Epistulam Pauli Apostoli ad Galatas*: *Commentary on Galatians* (S. A. Cooper, 2005, Oxford).

Origen, Εἰς Μαρτύριον Προτρεπτικός: *An Exhortation to Martyrdom* (R. A. Greer, 1979, New York, NY).

Optatus, *De Schismate Donatistarum/ Contra Parmenianum Donastitam*: *Against the Donatists* (M. Edwards, 1997, Liverpool).

Symmachus, *Relatio 3* (O. Seeck, 1883, *Q. Aurelii Symmachi Quae supersunt*, Berlin, Weidman); *The letters of Symmachus*, Book 1, (M. R. Salzman, 2011, Atlanta, GA).

Tyconius, *In Apocalypsin*: *Exposition of the Apocalypse* (F. X. Gumerlock, 2017, Washington, DC, FOTC 134).

———. *Liber regularum*: *The Book of Rules of Tyconius*: An Introduction and Translation with Commentary (D. L. Anderson, 1974, Louisville, KY); *Le Livre Des Règles* (J.-M. Vercruysse, 2004, Paris).

2. Modern Authors

Aitken, E. B. (2000) "The Cologne Mani Codex", in Richard Valantasis (ed), *Religions of Late Antiquity in Practice*, Princeton, NJ, 161–76.

Aitken, J. K. (2015) *The T&T Clark Companion to the Septuagint*, London.

Alexander, J. S. (1986–1994) "Donatistae", in Cornelius Mayer (ed), *AL*, Vol. 2, Basel, 622–38.

Allen, P.L. (2012) *Theological Method: A Guide for the Perplexed*, London.

Allison, J. D. (2013) "The Old Testament in the New Testament", in James C. Paget, Joachim Schaper (eds), *NCHB*, Vol. 1, From the Beginnings to 600, Cambridge, 479–502.

Ames, C. (2007) "Roman Religion in the Vision of Tertullian", in Jörg Rüpke (ed), *A Companion to Roman Religion*, Malden, MA, 457–71.

Anderson, C. R. (2009) "Phenomenology of Time", in H. James Birx (ed), *ET*, Vol. 3, New Delhi, 1296–98.

Angus, S. (1906) *The Sources of the First Ten Books of Augustine's De Civitate Dei: A Thesis Presented to the Faculty of Princeton University for the Degree of Doctor of Philosophy*, Princeton, NJ.

Aune, D. (1992) "Eschatology (Early Christian)", in David Noel Freedman (ed), *ABD*, Vol. 2, New York, NY, 594–609.

Ayres, L. (2006) "Patristic and Medieval Theologies of Scripture", in Stephen Westerholm (ed), *Christian Theologies of Scripture: A Comparative Introduction*, New York, NY, 11–20.

———. (2011) "Augustine", in Justin S. Holcomb (ed), *The Blackwell Companion to Paul*, First Edition, Oxford, 345–60.

Babcock, W. S. (1979) "Augustine's interpretation of Romans (A.D. 394–396)", in *AS*, 10, 55–74.

———. (1982) "Augustine and Tyconius: A Study in the Latin Appropriation of Paul", in *SP*, 17 (3), 1209–15.

Baird, W. (1992) "Biblical Criticism", in David Noel Freedman (ed), *ABD*, Vol. 1, New York, NY, 725–36.
Bammel, C. (1993) "Pauline Exegesis, Manichaeism and Philosophy in the early Augustine", in Caroline P H Bammel, Lionel R Wickham (eds), *Christian Faith and Greek Philosophy in Late Antiquity*, Leiden, 1–25.
Bar-Ilan, M. (1990) "Scribes and Books in the Late Second Commonwealth and Rabbinic Period", in Martin Jan Mulder (ed), *Mikra: Text, Translation, Reading and Interpretation of the Hebrew Bible in Ancient Judaism and Early Christianity*, Minneapolis, MN, 21–38.
Bardon, A. (2013) *A Brief History of the Philosophy of Time*, New York, NY.
Barnes, T. D. (1998) *Ammianus Marcellinus and the Representation of Historical Reality*, New York, NY.
Barton, J. (2013) "The Old Testament canons", in Joachim Schaper, James Carleton Paget (eds), *NCHB*, Vol. 1, From the Beginnings to 600, Cambridge, 145–65.
Bate, H. (1922) "Some technical terms of Greek Exegesis", in *JTS*, 24 (93), 59–66.
BeDuhn, J. (2001) "The Metabolism of Salvation, Manichaean Concepts of Human Physiology", in Paul Mirecki and Jason BeDuhn (eds), *The Light and the Darkness: Studies in Manichaeism and its World*, Leiden, 5–37.
——. (2009) *New light on Manichaeism, Papers from the Sixth International Congress on Manichaeism*, Leiden.
——. (2011) "Did Augustine Win His Debate with Fortunatus?", in Jacob Albert van den Berg, et al., *In Search of Truth, Augustine, Manichaeism and other Gnosticism*, Leiden, 463–79.
——. (2013) "'Not to Depart from Christ', Augustine between 'Manichaean' and 'Catholic' Christianity", in Johannes van Oort (ed), *Augustine and Manichaean Christianity*, Leiden, 1–18.
Beetham, D. (2004) "Political Legitimacy", in Kate Nash and Alan Scott (eds), *The Blackwell Companion to Political Sociology*, Oxford, 107–16.
Benjamin, H. (1999) "Paradisiacal Life, The Story of Paradise in the Early Church", in Gerard P. Luttikhuizen (ed), *Paradise Interpreted, Representations of Biblical Paradise in Judaism and Christianity*, Leiden, 153–67.
Berardino, A. D. (1999) "Milan", in Allan D. Fitzgerald (ed), *ATA*, Grand Rapids, MI, 561–62.
Berchman, R. M. (2005) *Porphyry Against the Christians*, Leiden.
Betz, H. D. (1979) *Galatians: A Commentary on Paul's Letter to the Churches in Galatia*, Philadelphia, PA.
——. (1994) *Paulinische Studien, Gesammelte Aufsatze III*, Tubingen.
Birx, J.H. (2009) "Introduction", in H. James Birx (ed), *ET*, Vol. 1, New Delhi, xxix–xxxiv.
Bogaert, P.-M. (2012) "The Latin Bible, c. 600 to c. 900", in Richard Marsden, E. Ann Matter (eds), *NCHB*, Vol. 2, From 600 to 1450, Cambridge, 69–92.
——. (2013) "The Latin Bible", in James C. Paget, Joachim Schaper (eds), *NCHB*, Vol. 1, From the Beginnings to 600, Cambridge, 505–26.
Boniface, R. (1999) "De Mendacio/ Contra Mendacium", in Allan D. Fitzgerald (ed), *ATA*, Grand Rapids, MI, 555–57.
Bonner, G. (1970) "Augustine as Biblical Scholar", in C. F. Evans, P. R. Ackroyd (eds), *The Cambridge History of the Bible*, Vol. 1, From the Beginnings to Jerome, Cambridge, 541–63.

———. (1972) *Augustine and Modern Research on Pelagianism*, Villanova, PA.
———. (1986) *St Augustine of Hippo: Life and Controversies* (rev), Norwich.
———. (1989) "Augustine and millenarianism", in Rowan Williams (ed), *The making of Orthodoxy: Essays in honour of Henry Chadwick*, Cambridge, 235–54.
Boone, M. J. (2015) "The Role of Platonism in Augustine's Conversion to Christ", in *RC*, 9 (5), 151–61.
Bourke, V. J. (1973) "Socio-Religious Issues in Augustine's Day", in *AS*, 4, 205–12.
Brachtendorf, J. (2012) "The Reception of Augustine in Modern Philosophy", in Mark Vessey (ed), *A Companion to Augustine*, Oxford, 478–91.
———. (2017) "Augustine's Reception of Himself", in Tarmo Toom (ed), *Augustine in Context*, Cambridge, 221–29.
Bright, P. (1988) *The book of Rules of Tyconius: Its Purpose and Inner Logic*, Notre Dame, IN.
———. (1999a) "Donatist Bishops", in Allan D. Fitzgerald (ed), *ATA*, Grand Rapids, MI, 281–84.
———. (1999b) "'The Prepondering Infuence of Augustine', A Study of the Epitomes of the Book of Rules of the Donatist Tyconius", in Pamela Bright (ed and trans), *Augustine and the Bible*, Notre Dame, IN, 109–28.
———. (1999c) "Introduction", in Pamela Bright (ed and trans), *Augustine and the Bible*, Notre Dame, IN, xiii–xvi.
———. (2006) "St Augustine", in Justin S. Holcomb (ed), *Christian Theologies of Scripture: A Comparative Introduction*, New York, NY, 39–55.
Brown, P. (1981) *The Cult of the Saints: Its Rise and Function in Latin Christianity*, Chicago, IL.
———. (1992) *Power and persuasion in Late Antiquity: Towards a Christian Empire*, Chicago, IL.
———. (1995) "Saint Augustine and Political Society", in Dorothy F. Donnelly (ed), *The City of God: A Collection of Critical Essays*, New York, NY, 17–35.
———. (2000) *Augustine of Hippo: A Biography*, Berkeley and Los Angeles, CA.
Brown, S. J. (2006) "Introduction", in Stewart J. Brown and Timothy Tackett (eds), *The Cambridge History of Christianity: Enlightenment, Reawakening and Revolution 1660–1815*, Cambridge, 1–11.
Bruce, F. (1988) *The Canon of Scripture*, Glasgow.
Burchill-Limb, K. (2003) "'Philokalia' in Augustine's 'De Pulchro et Apto'", in *Augustiniana*, 53, (1), 69–75.
Burges, J. and Amy Elias (2016) *Time: A Vocabulary of the Present*, New York, NY.
Burns, J. P. (1990) "Ambrose Preaching to Augustine, The Shaping of Faith", in Joseph C. Schnaubelt and Frederick Van Fleteren (eds), *Collectanea Augustiniana: Augustine "Second Founder of the Faith"*, New York, NY, 373–86.
Burns, P. C. (1999) "Augustine's use of Sallust in the City of God: The Role of the Grammatical Tradition", in Karla Pollmann, Allan D. Fitzgerald, Mark Vessey (eds), *History, Apocalypse, and the Secular Imagination: New Essays on Augustine's City of God*, Bowling Green, OH, 105–14.
Burton, P. (2000) *The Old Latin Gospels: A study of their texts and language*, Oxford.
———. (2007) *Language in the Confessions of Augustine*, Oxford.

Cain, A. (2009) *The Letters of Jerome: Asceticism, Biblical Exegesis, and the Construction of Christian Authority in Late Antiquity*, Oxford.
———. (2011) "Jerome's Pauline Commentaries between East and West, Tradition and Innovation in the Commentary on Galatians", in Josef Lössl and John W. Watt (eds), *Interpreting the Bible and Aristotle in Late Antiquity: The Alexandrian Commentary Tradition between Rome and Baghdad*, Surrey, 91–110.
Callahan, J.F. (1948) *Four Views Of Time In Ancient Philosophy*, Cambridge, MA.
Calvin, J. (1559) "Institutio Christianae" in E. Cunitz, G. Baum, E. Reuss (eds), *Religionis Joannis Calvini opera quae supersunt omnia*, CR 30.2, Braunschweig.
Cameron, A. (2011) *The Last Pagans of Rome*, Oxford.
———. (2012) "Nichomachus Flavianus and the Date of Ammianus's Last Books", in *Athenaeum*, 100, 337–58.
Cameron, M. (1999) "The Christological Substructure of Augustine's Figurative Exegesis", in Pamela Bright (ed and trans), *Augustine and the Bible*, Notre Dame, IN, 74–103.
———. (2012a) "Augustine and Scripture", in Mark Vessey (ed), *A companion to Augustine*, Oxford, 200–14.
———. (2012b) *Christ Meets Me Everywhere: Augustine's Early Figurative Exegesis*, Oxford.
Canty, A. (2013) "Saint Paul in Augustine", in Steven R. Cartwright (ed), *A Companion to St Paul in the Middle Ages*, Leiden, 115–42.
Carrigan Jr., H.L. (2004) "Bible," in Hans J. Hillerbrand (ed), *The Encyclopedia of Protestantism*, Vol.1, New York, NY, 364–72.
Cary, P. (2000) *Augustine's Invention of the Inner Self: The Legacy of a Christian Platonist*, Oxford.
———. (2003) "Book Seven, Inner Vision as the Goal of Augustine's Life", in Kim Paffenroth and Robert P. Kennedy (eds), *A Reader's Companion to Augustine's Confessions*, Louisville, KY, 107–26.
Cavadini, J. C. (2018) "*Creatio ex nihilo* in the Thought of Saint Augustine", in Gary A. Anderson and Markus Bockmuehl (eds), *Creation ex nihilo: Origins, Development, Contemporary Challenges*, Notre Dame, IN, 151–71.
Chadwick, H. (1986) *Augustine: A Very Short Introduction*, Oxford.
———. (2009) *Augustine of Hippo: A Life*, Oxford.
Chapman, M. (2008) "Authority", in Gerard Mannion and Lewis S. Mudge (eds), *The Routledge Companion to the Christian Church*, New York, NY, 497–510.
Childs, B. S. (1979) *Introduction to the Old Testament as Scripture*, Philadelphia, PA.
Christian, W. A. (1955) "The creation of the world", in Roy W. Battenhouse (ed), *A Companion to the study of St Augustine*, Grand Rapids, MI, 315–42.
Cimosa, M. (2014) "Holy Scripture (Ancient Version)", in Angelo Di Berardino (ed), *Encyclopedia of Ancient Christianity*, Second English Edition, 3 Vols, Downers Grove, IL, 3:514–20.
Clark, E. A. (1992) *The Origenist Controversy: The Cultural Construction of an Early Christian Debate*, Princeton, NJ.
Clark, G. (2010) "Paradise for pagans? Augustine on Virgil, Cicero, and Plato", in Markus Bockmuehl and Guy G. Stroumsa (eds), *Paradise in Antiquity: Jewish and Christian Views*, Cambridge, 166–78.

Cohen, W. (2017) *A History of European Literature: The West and the World from Antiquity to the Present*, Oxford.
Cole-Turner, R. S. (1980) "Anti-Heretical Issues and the Debate over Galatian 2:11–14 in the Letters of St Augustine to St Jerome", in *AS*, 11, 155–66.
Colish, M.L. (2006) *Studies in Scholasticism*, Hampshire.
Conybeare, C. (1999) "Terrarum Orbi Documentum: Augustine, Camillus, and Learning from History", in Karla Pollmann, and Allan D. Fitzgerald, Mark Vessey (eds), *History, Apocalypse, and the Secular Imagination*: New Essays on Augustine's City of God, Bowling Green, OH, 59–74.
———. (2016) *The Routledge guidebook to Augustine's Confessions*, Oxford.
Cooley, A. E. (2012) *The Cambridge manual of Latin Epigraphy*, Cambridge.
Copleston, F. (1993) *A history of Philosophy*, Vol. 2, New York, NY.
Costello, C. J. (1930) *St Augustine's Doctrine on the Inspiration and Canonicity of Scripture*, Washington, DC
Coyle, J. K. (1999a) "Anti-Pelagian Works", in Allan D. Fitzgerald (ed), *ATA*, Grand Rapids, MI, 39–41.
———. (1999b) "Contra Secundinum Manicheum", in Allan D. Fitzgerald (ed), *ATA*, Grand Rapids, MI, 759–60.
———. (1999c) "De moribus ecclesiae Catholicae et de moribus Manicheorum", in Allan D. Fitzgerald (ed), *ATA*, Grand Rapids, MI, 571.
———. (2009) *Manichaeism and its legacy*, Leiden.
Cullmann, O. (1962) Floyd V. Filson (trans), *Christ and Time: The Primitive Christian Conception of Time and History*, Revised Edition, London.
Danielou, J. (1958) Nigel Abercrombie (trans) *The Lord of History: Reflections on the Inner Meaning of History*, London.
Davies, J. P. (2004) *Rome's Religious History: Livy, Tacitus and Ammianus on their Gods*, New York, NY.
Dawson, D. (1999) "Figure, Allegory", in Allan D. Fitzgerald (ed), *ATA*, Grand Rapids, MI, 365–68.
de Jong, A. (2015) "The Cologne Mani Codex and the Life of Zarathustra", in Geoffrey Herman (ed), *Jews, Christians and Zoroastrians: Religious Dynamics in a Sasanian Context*, Piscataway, NJ, 129–247.
de Ste. Croix, G. (2006) "Aspects of the 'Great' Persecution", in Michael Whitby and Joseph Streeter (eds), *Christian Persecution, Martyrdom, and Orthodoxy*, Oxford, 35–78.
DeWeese, G. (2002) "Atemporal, Semipiternal, or Omnitemporal: God's Temporal Mode of Being", in Gregory E. Ganssle and David M. Woodruf (eds), *God and Time: Essays on the Divine Nature*, Oxford, 49–61.
Dearn, A. (2016) "Donatist Martyrs, Stories and Attitudes", in Richard Miles (ed), *The Donatist Schism, Controversy and Contexts*, Liverpool, 70–100.
Delumeau, J. (2000) Matthew O'Connell (trans), *History of Paradise: The Garden of Eden in Myth and Tradition*, Urbana and Chicago, IL.
Dillistone, F. W. (1979) "The Anti-Donatist Writings", in Roy W. Battenhouse (ed), *A Companion to the Study of St Augustine* (reprinted), Grand Rapids, MI, 175–202.

Dimitrov, D. Y. (2014) "Neoplatonism and Christianity in the East, Philosophical and Theological challenges for Bishops", in Pauliina Remes and Svetla Slaveva-Griffin (eds), *The Routledge Handbook of Neoplatonism*, London, 525–40.

Dorival, G. (2013) "Origen", in James Carleton Paget and Joachim Schaper (eds), *NCHB*, Vol. 1, From the Beginnings to 600, Cambridge, 605–28.

Drijvers, J. W. (1999) *The Late Roman World and its Historian, Interpreting Ammianus Marcellinus*, London.

Drobner, H. R. (2000) "Studying Augustine, An overview of recent research", in Robert Dodaro and George Lawless (eds), *Augustine and his critics: Essays in honour of Gerald Bonner*, London, 17–33.

Dyke, H. and Adrian Bardon (2013) 'Introduction', in Heather Dyke and Adrian Bardon (eds), A Companion to the Philosophy of Time, Oxford, 1–6.

Ebbeler, J. (2012) *Disciplining Christians: Correction and Community in Augustine's Letters*, New York, NY.

Eck, W. (2007) *The Age of Augustus*, Second Edition, Malden, MA.

Eder, W. (2005) "Augustus and the Power of Tradition", in Karl Galinsky (ed), *The Cambridge Companion to the Age of Augustus*, Cambridge, 13–32.

Edward, M. (2012) "Augustine and his Christian predecessors", in Mark Vessey (ed), *A Companion to Augustine*, Oxford, 215–26.

——. (2013) "Figurative readings, Their scope and justification", in James C. Paget and Joachim Schaper (eds), *NCHB*, Vol. 1, From the Beginnings to 600, Cambridge, 714–33.

——. (2016) "The Donatist Schism and Theology", in Richard Miles (ed), *The Donatist Schism: Controversy and Contexts*, Liverpool, 101–19.

Eller, M. F. (1946) *The Retractationes of Saint Augustine*, Boston, MA.

——. (1949) "The 'Retractationes' of Saint Augustine", in *CH*, 18 (3), 172–83.

Eno, R. (1976) "Some Nuances in the Ecclesiology of the Donatists", in *SP*, 14, 417–21.

——. (1999) "Epistulae", in Allan D. Fitzgerald (ed), *ATA*, Grand Rapids, MI, 298–310.

Evans, C. A. (2006) "The Life and Teaching of Jesus and the Rise of Christianity", in J. W. Rogerson and Judith M. Lieu (eds), *The Oxford Handbook of Biblical Studies*, Oxford, 301–16.

Evans, G. (2003) "Introduction", in Henry Bettenson (trans), *St Augustine: Concerning the City of God against the Pagans* (reissued) London, ix–lvii.

Evans, R. F. (1968) *Pelagius, Inquiries and Reappraisals*, London.

Ever, A. (2012) "Augustine on the Church (Against the Donatists)", in Mark Vessey (ed), *A companion to Augustine*, Oxford, 375–85.

Everson, D. L. (2012) "The Vetus Latina and the Vulgate of the Book of Genesis", in Craig A. Evans, Joel N. Lohr and David L. Petersen (eds), *The Book of Genesis, Composition, Reception, and Interpretation*, Leiden, 519–36.

Feeney, D. (2007) *Caesars Calendar, Ancient Time and the Beginnings of History*, Berkeley and Los Angeles, CA.

Ferguson, E. (2002) "Factors Leading to the Selection and Closure of the New Testament Canon", in Lee Martin McDonald and James A. Sanders (eds), *The Canon Debate: On the origins and formation of the Bible*, Peabody, MA, 295–320.

Ferrari, L. (1992) "Beyond Augustine's Conversion Scene", in Joanne McWilliam (ed), *Augustine: From Rhetor to Theologian*, Waterloo, Ontario, 97–107.

Fiedrowicz, M. (2006) "General Introduction", in John E. Rotelle (ed), *On Genesis*, (2nd Printing), New York, NY, 13–22.
Filice, C. (2009) "Eternity", in H. James Birx (ed), *ET*, Vol. 1, New Delhi, 437–41.
Filoramo, G. and I. Ramelli (2014) "Paradise", in Angelo Di Berardino (ed), *Encyclopedia of Ancient Christianity*, Second English Edition, 3 Vols, Downers Grove, IL, 3:65–68.
Fischer, B. (1951) *Vetus Latina, Die Reste der Altlateinischen Bibel, 2, Genesis*, Freiburg.
Fitzgerald, A. D. (1999a) "Alypius", in Allan D. Fitzgerald (ed), *ATA*, Grand Rapids, MI, 16.
——. (1999b) "Retractationes", in Allan D. Fitzgerald (ed), *ATA*, Grand Rapids, MI, 723–24.
Flores, R. (1984) *The Rhetoric of Doubtful Authority*, London.
Foerster, W. (1964) "ἐξουσία", in W. Gerhard Kittel (ed and trans), *TDNT*, Vol. 2, Grand Rapids, MI, 562–75.
Forsyth, P. (1912) *The Principle of Authority in Relation to Certainty, Sanctity and Society: An Essay in the Philosophy of Experimental Religion*, New York, NY.
Fortin, E. L. (1980) "Augustine and Roman Civil Religion: Some Critical Reflections", in *REA*, 26 (3–4), 238–56.
Frankfurter, D. (1997) "Apocalypses Real and Alleged in the Mani Codex", in *Numen*, 44 (1), 60–73.
——. (2006) "Traditional Cult", in David S. Potter (ed), *A Companion to the Roman Empire*, Malden, MA, 543–64.
Frede, H. J. (1995) *Kirchenschriftsteller, Verzeichnis und Sigel (Vetus Latina, Die Reste der Altlateinischen Bibel 1/1)*, Freiburg.
Fredriksen, P. (1988) "Beyond the body-soul dichotomy: Augustine on Paul against the Manichees and the Pelagians", in *RA*, 23, 87–114.
——. (1999a) "Tyconius", in Allan D. Fitzgerald (ed), *ATA*, Grand Rapids, MI, 853–55.
——. (1999b) "Massa", in Allan D. Fitzgerald (ed), *ATA*, Grand Rapids, MI, 345–47.
——. (2010) *Augustine and the Jews: A Christian Defense of Jews and Judaism*, New Haven, CT.
——. (2012) "The Confessions as Autobiography", in Mark Vessey (ed), *A Companion to Augustine*, Oxford, 87–98.
Frend, W. H. (1951) *The Donatist Church, A Movement of Protest in Roman North Africa* (reprinted 2003), New York, NY.
——. (1953) "The Gnostic-Manichaean Tradition in Roman North Africa", in *JEH*, 4 (1), 13–26.
——. (2006) "Persecutions, Genesis and Legacy", in Margaret M. Mitchell and Francis M. Young (eds), *The Cambridge History of Christianity*, Vol. I, Origins to Constantine, New York, NY, 503–23.
Friedrich, C. J. (1972) *Tradition and Authority*, London.
Froehlich, K. (1984) *Biblical Interpretation in the Early Church*, Philadelphia, PA.
Fuhrer, T. (2012) "Conversationalist and Consultant, Augustine in Dialogue", in Mark Vessey (ed), *A companion to Augustine*, Oxford, 270–83.
Gadamer, H.-G. (2004) Joel Weinsheimer and Donald G. Marshall (rev and trans), *Truth and Method*, Second Revised Edition, London.
Gaddis, M. (2005) *There Is No Crime for Those Who Have Christ: Religious Violence in the Christian Roman Empire*, Los Angeles, CA.
Galinsky, K. (2007) "Continuity and Change, Religion in the Augustan Semi-Century", in Jörg Rüpke (ed), *A Companion to Roman Religion*, Malden, MA, 71–82.

——. (2011) "The Cult of the Roman Emperor: Uniter or Divider?", in Jeffrey Brodd and Jonathan l. Reed (eds), *Rome and Religion: A Cross-disciplinary Dialogue on the Imperial Cult*, Atlanta, GA, 1–21.

Gallagher, E. L. (2012) *Hebrew Scripture in Patristic Biblical Theory: Canon, Language, Text*, Leiden.

——. (2016) "Augustine on the Hebrew Bible", in *JTS*, 67 (1), 97–114.

——. (2017) *The Biblical Canon Lists from Early Christianity: Texts and Analysis*, Oxford.

Gamble, H. Y. (1995) *Books and Readers in the Early Church: A History of early Christian texts*, New Haven, CT.

Ganssle, G. E. (2002) *God and Time: Essays on the Divine Nature*, New York, NY.

George, T. (2005) "St. Augustine and the Mystery of Time", in Harry Lee Poe and J. Stanley Mattson (eds), *What God knows: Time, Eternity, and Divine Knowledge*, Texas, TX, 27–46.

Gersh, S. (1986) *Middle Platonism and Neoplatonism: The Latin Tradition*, 2 Vols, Notre Dame, IN.

Gerson, L. P. (1994) *Plotinus*, London

——. (1999) "Introduction", in Lloyd P. Gerson (ed), *The Cambridge Companion to Plotinus*, Cambridge, 1–9.

——. (2004) *Neoplatonic Philosophy: Introductory Readings*, Indianapolis, IN.

Gillett, A. (2012) "Epic Panegyric and Political Communication in the Fifth-Century West", in Gavin Kelly Lucy Grig (eds), *Two Romes: Rome and Constantinople in Late Antiquity*, Oxford, 265–90.

Gilson, É. (1967) L. E. M. Lynch (trans), *The Christian Philosophy of Saint Augustine*, New York, NY.

Glare, P. G. W. (1968) *Oxford Latin Dictionary*, Oxford.

Goldingay, J. (2007) "Authority of scripture", in Stanley E Porter (ed), *Dictionary of Biblical Criticism and Interpretation*, Abingdon, 30–32.

Goshen-Gottstein, M. (1992) "Scriptural Authority, Biblical Authority in Judaism", in David Noel Freedman (ed), *ABD*, Vol. 5, New York, NY, 1017–21.

Grebe, S. (2004) "Augustus" Divine Authority and Vergil's *Aeneid*', in *Vergilius*, 50, 35–62.

Green, L. (2005) "Authority", in Edward Craig (ed), *The Shorter Routledge Encyclopedia of Philosophy*, Abingdon, 75.

——. (n.d.) "Authority", in *Routledge Encyclopedia of Philosophy*, retrieved from https://www.rep.routledge.com/articles/thematic/authority/v-1.

Gribomont, J. (2014) "Holy Scripture", in Angelo Di Berardino (ed), *Encyclopedia of Ancient Christianity*, Second English Edition, 3 Vols, Downers Grove, IL, 3:511–14.

Güven, S. (1998) "Displaying the *Res Gestae* of Augustus: A Monument of Imperial Image for All", in *JSAH*, 57 (1), 30–45.

Hagendahl, H. (1967) *Augustine and the Latin Classics*, Vol. 1: Testimonia, Göteborg.

Häkkinen, S. (2005) "Ebionites", in Antti Marjanen and Petri Luomanen (eds), *A Companion to Second-century Christian "Heretics"*, Leiden, 247–78.

Hardy, J. E. (1955) "The City of God", in Roy W. Battenhouse (ed), *A Companion to the Study of St Augustine*, Grand Rapids, MI, 257–83.

Hargis, J. W. (1999) *Against the Christians: The rise of early anti-Christian Polemic*, New York, NY.

Harmless, W. (2010) *Augustine in his own words*, Washington, DC
Harris, H. A. (1998) *Fundamentalism and Evangelicals*, Oxford.
Harrison, C. (2005) 'Augustine', in Kevin J. Vanhoozer (gen ed), *Dictionary for Theological Interpretation of the Bible*, Grand Rapids, MI, 76–78.
——. (2006) *Rethinking Augustine's Early Theology: An Argument for Continuity*, Oxford.
——. (2013) "Augustine", in James C. Paget and Joachim Schaper (eds), *NCHB*, Vol. 1, From the Beginnings to 600, Cambridge, 676–96.
Harrison, J. (2004) "In Quest of the Third Heaven: Paul and his Apocalyptic Imitators", in *VC*, 58, 24–55.
Harrison, L., Adrian Little and Edward Lock (2015) *Politics: The Key Concepts*, Oxford.
Harrison, S. (1999) "Truth", in Allan D. Fitzgerald (ed), *ATA*, Grand Rapids, MI, 852–53.
Harrison, T. (1999) "Templum mundi totius: Ammianus and a religious ideal of Rome", in Jan Willem Drijvers and David Hunt (eds), *The Late Roman World and its Historian: Interpreting Ammianus Marcellinus*, London, 158–68.
Hassard, J. (1990) *The Sociology of Time*, New York, NY.
Heidegger, M. (1924) William McNeill (trans), *Der Begriff der Zeit: The Concept of Time*, Warwick.
Heine, R. E. (2004) "The beginnings of Latin Christian Literature", in Frances Young, Lewis Ayres and Andrew Louth (eds), *The Cambridge History of Early Christian Literature*, Cambridge, 131–41.
Heinze, R. (1925) "Auctoritas", in *Hermes*, 60 (3), 348–66.
Hengel, M. (2002) *The Septuagint as Christian Scripture*, Edinburgh.
Henrichs, A. (1973) "Mani and the Babylonian Baptists: A Historical Confrontation", in *HSCP*, 77, 23–59.
——. (1979) "The Cologne Mani Codex Reconsidered", in *HSCP*, 83, 339–67.
——. (1981) "Literary Criticism of the Cologne Mani Codex", in Bentley Layton (ed), *The Rediscovery of Gnosticism*, Vol. 2, Sethian Gnosticism, Leiden, 724–33.
——. (2019) "The timing of supernatural events in the Cologne Mani Codex", in Harvey Yunis (ed), *Greek Myth and Religion*: Collected Papers II, Berlin, 569–90.
Hoek, A. V. (2007) "Allegorical Interpretation", in Stanley E Porter (ed), *Dictionary of Biblical Criticism and Interpretation*, Oxford, 9–12.
Hoeveler, J. J. (1974) "The New Humanism, Christianity, and the Problem of Modern Man", in *JAAR*, 42 (4), 658–72.
Holder, R.W. (2012) "Revelation and Scripture", in David M. Whitford (ed), *T&T Clark Companion to Reformation Theology*, London, 32–56.
Hopkins, K. (2018) "Conquest by Book", in Christopher Kelly (ed), *Sociological Studies in Roman History*, Cambridge, 363–90.
Houghton, H. A. G. (2008) *Augustine's text of John: Patristic Citations and Latin Gospel Manuscripts*, Oxford.
——. (2016) *The Latin New Testament: A Guide to its Early History, Texts, and Manuscripts*, Oxford.
Hurtado, L. W. (2013) "Writing and book production in the Hellenistic and Roman periods", in James C. Paget and Joachim Schaper (eds), *NCHB*, Vol. 1, From the Beginnings to 600, Cambridge, 63–80.

Ierodiakonou, K. and George Zografidis (2010) "Early Byzantine Philosophy", in Lloyd P. Gerson (ed), *The Cambridge History of Philosophy in Late Antiquity*, Vol. 2, Cambridge, 843–68.
Jenson, R. (1997) *Systematic Theology*, Vol. 1, The Triune God, New York, NY.
Kamesar, A. (1993) *Jerome, Greek Scholarship, and the Hebrew Bible: A Study of the Quaestionaes Hebraicae in Genesim*, Oxford.
——. (2013) "Jerome", in James Carleton Paget and Joachim Schaper (eds), *NCHB*, Vol. 1, From the Beginnings to 600, Cambridge, 653–75.
Kannengiesser, C. (1995) "The Interrupted De doctrina christiana", in Duane W. H. Arnord and Pamela Bright (eds), *De doctrina christiana: A Classic of Western Culture*, Notre Dame, IN.
——. (1999) "Augustine and Tyconius: A conflict of Christian Hermeneutics in Roman Africa", in Pamela Bright (ed and trans), *Augustine and the Bible*, Notre Dame, IN, 149–77.
Kaster, R. A. (1983) "Notes on 'Primary' and 'Secondary' Schools in Late Antiquity", in *TAPA*, 113, 323–46.
Kato, T. (2017) "Greek or Hebrew? Augustine and Jerome on Biblical Translation", in *SP*, 24, 9–19.
Kedar, B. (1990) "The Latin Translations", in Martin Jan Mulder (ed), *Mikra: Text, Translation, Reading and Interpretation of the Hebrew Bible in Ancient Judaism and Early Christianity*, Minneapolis, MN, 299–338.
Kelly, J. (1975) *Jerome: His Life, Writings, and Controversies*, London.
King, P. (March 2005) "Augustine's encounter with Neoplatonism", in *MSch*, 82 (3), 213–26.
Koenen, L. (1978) "Augustine and Manichaeism in Light of the Cologne Mani Codex", in *ICS*, 3, 154–95.
Koselleck, R. (1985) Keith Tribe (trans), *Futures Past: On the Semantics of Historical Time*, Massachusetts, MA.
Kotze, A. (2004) *Augustine's Confessions: Communicative Purpose and Audience*, Leiden.
Kugler, R. A. (1999) "Tyconuis's Mystic Rules and the Rules of Augustine", in Pamela Bright (ed and trans), *Augustine and the Bible*, Notre Dame, IN, 129–48.
Kulikowski, M. (2007) *Rome's Gothic Wars: From the Third Century to Alaric*, Cambridge.
La Bonnardière, A.-M. (1999) "Augustine's Biblical initiation", in Pamela Bright (ed and trans), *Augustine and the Bible*, Notre Dame, IN, 5–25.
Lamb, M. (2018) "Beyond Pessimism: A Structure of Encouragement in Augustine's City of God", in *Rev. Politics*, 80 (4), 591–624.
Lamb, R. (2009) "Linear Time," in H. James Birx (ed), *ET*, Vol. 3, New Delhi, 1273–74.
Leadbetter, B. (2009) *Galerius and the Will of Diocletian*, Oxford.
Liebeschuetz, J. (2011) *Ambrose and John Chrysostom: Clerics between Desert and Empire*, Oxford.
Lienhard, J. T. (1999) "Canon of Sacred Scripture, Septuagint", in Allan D. Fitzgerald (ed), *ATA*, Grand Rapids, MI, 121.
Lieu, S. N. (1994) *Manichaeism in Mesopotamia and the Roman East*, Leiden.
Lincoln, B. (1994) *Authority Construction and Corrosion*, Chicago, IL.

Lohr, W. (2013) "Gnostic and Manichaean interpretation", in James C. Paget and Joachim Schaper (eds), *NCHB*, Vol. 1, From the Beginnings to 600, Cambridge, 584–604.
Löschke, J. (2015) "Authority in Relationships", in *IJPS*, 23 (2), 187–204.
Lossl, J. (2017) "Latin Christian Literature I (Polemical and Theological Writings)", in Tarmo Toom (ed), *Augustine in Context*, Cambridge, 94–101.
Lutcke, K.-H. (1986–1994) "Auctoritas", in Cornelius Mayer (ed), *AL*, Vol. 1, Basel, 498–510
Lyotard, J. (2000) Richard Beardsworth (trans), *The Confession of Augustine*, California, CA.
Maenchen-Helfen, O. J. (1955) "The Date of Ammianus Marcellinus' Last Books', in *AJP*, 76 (4), 384–99.
Maher, J. P. (1979) "Saint Augustine and Manichean Cosmogony", in *AS*, 10, 91–104.
Marion, J.-L. (2012) Jeffrey L. Kosky (trans), *In the Self's Place: The Approach of Saint Augustine*, Stanford, CA.
Markus, R. A. (1963) "The Roman Empire in Early Christian Historiography", in *DRev*, 81, 340–54.
——. (1965) "Two Conceptions of Political Authority: Augustine, De Civitate Dei, XIX. 14–15, and some Thirteenth-Century Interpretations", in *JTS*, 16 (1), 68–100.
——. (1970) *Saeculum: History and Society in the Theology of St Augustine*, Cambridge.
——. (1989) "The legacy of Pelagius: Orthodoxy, heresy and conciliation", in Rowan Williams (ed) *The making of Orthodoxy: Essays in honour of Henry Chadwick*, Cambridge, 214–34.
——. (1991) "Augustine's 'Confessions' and the Controversy with Julian of Eclanum: Manicheism Revisited", in *Augustiniana*, 41, (1), 913–25.
——. (1999) "Donatus, Donatism", in Allan D. Fitzgerald (ed), *ATA*, Grand Rapids, MI, 284–87.
——. (2000) "'Tempora Christiana' Revisited", in Robert Dodaro and George Lawless (eds), *Augustine and his critics*, London, 199–211.
Martin, T. F. (2003) "Book Twelve, Exegesis and Confessio", in Kim Paffenroth and Robert P. Kennedy (eds), *A Reader's Companion to Augustine's Confessions*, Louisville, KY, 185–206.
Mathison, K.A. (2001) *The Shape of Sola Scriptura*, Idaho, ID.
May, G. (1994) A. S. Worrall (trans) *Creatio ex nihilo: The Doctrine of "Creation out of Nothing" in Early Christian Thought*, London.
McDonald, L. M. (2002) *The Canon Debate: On the origins and formation of the Bible*, Peabody, MA.
——. (2016) "Critical Issues in the Formation of the Hebrew Bible", in Craig A. Evans, Jacob Neusner Alan J. Avery-Peck (eds), *Earliest Christianity within the Boundaries of Judaism*, Boston, MA, 49–84.
McDonald, L. M. and S.E. Porter (2000) *Early Christianity and its sacred literature*, Peabody, MA.
McGrath, A.E. (2013) *Historical Theology: An Introduction to the History of Christian Thought*, Second Edition, Oxford.
McKim, D. K. (1992) "Biblical Authority and the Protestant Reformation", in David Noel Freedman (ed), *ABD*, Vol. 5, New York, NY, 1032–35.
McLaughlin, P. (2007) *Anarchism and Authority: A philosophical Introduction to Classical Anarchism*, Hamshire.

McLynn, N.B. (1994) *Ambrose of Milan: Church and court in a Christian Capital*, Berkeley, Los Angeles, CA.
——. (1999a) "Ambrose of Milan", in Allan D. Fitzgerald (ed), *ATA*, Grand Rapids, MI, 17–19.
——. (1999b) "Augustine's Roman Empire", in Karla Pollmann, Allan D. Fitzgerald, Mark Vessey (eds), *History, Apocalypse, and the Secular Imagination*: New Essays on Augustine's City of God, Bowling Green, OH, 29–44.
Meconi, D.V. (2021) "Introduction," in *The Cambridge Companion to the City of God*, Cambridge, 1–18.
——. (2021) "Book 1: The Crumbling and Consecration of Rome," in *The Cambridge Companion to the City of God*, Cambridge, 19–38.
Metzger, B. M. (1977) *The Early Versions of the New Testament: Their Origin, Transmission, and Limitations*, Oxford.
——. (1987) *The Canon of the New Testament: It's Origin, Development, and Significance*, Oxford.
——. (2001) *The Bible in Translation : Ancient and English Versions*, Grand Rapids, MI.
Meyer, R. (1985) "Prophetes: Judaism in the Hellenistic-Roman Period", in Geoffrey W. Bromiley (trans), *TDNT, Abridged in One Volume*, Grand Rapids, MI, 957–60.
Middleton, P. (2006) *Radical Martyrdom and Cosmic Conflict in Early Christianity*, London.
Miles, R. (2016) "The Donatist Controversy: Parallel Histories, Multiple Narratives", in Richard Miles (ed), *The Donatist Schism: Controversy and Contexts*, Liverpool, 1–12.
Miller, C. (2008) "Authority", in Antonio Marturano and Jonathan Gosling (eds), *Leadership: The Key Concepts*, London, 7–11.
Mirecki, P. A. and Jason BeDuhn (2001) "Introduction", in Paul Allan Mirecki and Jason BeDuhn (eds), *Light and the Darkness: Studies in Manichaeism and its World*, Leiden, 1–4.
Momigliano, A. (1977) *Essays in Ancient and Modern Historiography*, Oxford.
——. (1990) *The Classical Foundations of Modern Historiography*, Los Angeles, CA.
Moorhead, J. (2013) *Ambrose: Church and Society in the Late Roman World*, Oxford.
Moran, D. (2014) "Neoplatonism and Christianity in the West", in Paulina Remes and Svetla Slaveva-Griffin (eds), *The Routledge Handbook of Neoplatonism*, London, 508–24.
Mulder, M. J. (1990) "The Transmission of the Biblical Text", in Martin Jan Mulder (ed), *Mikra: Text, Translation, Reading and Interpretation of the Hebrew Bible in Ancient Judaism and Early Christianity*, Minneapolis, MN, 87–135.
Muller, M. (1996) *The First Bible of the Church: A plea for the Septuagint*, Sheffield.
Murphy, A. R. (2005) "Augustine and the Rhetoric of Roman Decline", in *HPT*, 26 (4), 586–606.
Myllykoski, M. (2005) "Cerinthus", in Antti Marjanen and Petri Luomanen (eds), *A Companion to Second-century Christian "Heretics"*, Leiden, 213–46.
Nightingale, A. (2011) *Once Out of Nature: Augustine on Time and the Body*, Chicago, IL.
Nock, A. D. (1988) *Conversion: The Old and the New in Religion from Alexander the Great to Augustine of Hippo* (reprint), London.
O'Connell, M. (1988) *Possidius: The Life of Saint Augustine*, Villanova, PA.
O'Daly, G. (1986–1994a) "Aeternitas", in Cornelius Mayer (ed), *AL*, Vol. 1, Basel, 159–64.
——. (1986–1994b) "De Ciuitate Dei", in Cornelius Mayer (ed), *AL*, Vol. 1, Basel, 969–1010.
——. (1999a) "Augustine", in David Furley (ed), *Routledge History of Philosophy*, Vol. 2: From Aristotle to Augustine, London, 389–429.

———. (1999b) *Augustine's City of God: A Reader's Guide*, Oxford.
O'Donnell, J. J. (1980) "Augustine's Classical Readings", in *RA*, 15, 144–75.
———. (1992a) *Augustine: Confessions I — Introduction and Texts*, Oxford.
———. (1992b) *Augustine: Confessions II — Commentary on Books 1–7*, Oxford.
———. (1992c) *Augustine: Confessions III — Commentary on Books 8–13*, Oxford.
———. (1999) "Bible", in Allan D. Fitzgerald (ed), *ATA*, Grand Rapids, MI, 99–103.
———. (2001) "Augustine: His time and lives", in Eleonore Stump and Norman Kretzmann (eds), *The Cambridge Companion to Augustine*, Cambridge, 8–25.
———. (2006) *Augustine: A New Biography*, New York, NY.
O'Loughlin, T. (1995) "The Controversy over Methuselah's death: Proto-Chronology and the origins of the Western concept of Inerrancy", in *RTAM*, 62, 182–225.
———. (1999) *Teachers and Code-Breakers: The Latin Genesis Tradition*, Turnhout, 430–800.
———. (2012) "Latina Veritas! — Language a guarantor of truth?", in *The Furrow*, 63, (7/8), 343–47.
———. (2014) "The Structure of the Collections that Make Up the Scriptures: The Influence of Augustine on Cassiodorus", in *RB*, 124 (1), 48–64.
———. (2015) "The Prefaces De La Bible Latine after a Century", in Donatien De Bruyne, *Prefaces to the Latin Bible*, Turnhout, xi–xv.
O'Meara, J. (1961) *Charter of Christendom: The Significance of the City of God*, Dublin.
———. (1992) "Augustine's Confessions: Elements of Fiction", in Joanne McWilliam (ed), *Augustine: From Rhetor to Theologian*, Waterloo, Ontario, 77–96.
Ortiz, J. (2016) *"You Made Us for Yourself": Creation in St Augustine's Confessions*, Minneapolis, MN.
Paddison, A. (2009) *Scripture: A Very Theological Proposal*, London.
Pagels, E. H. (1975) *The Gnostic Paul: Gnostic Exegesis of the Pauline Letters*, Philadelphia, PA.
———. (1995) "The Politics of Paradise", in Dorothy F. Donnelly (ed), *The City of God: A Collection of Critical Essays*, New York, NY, 373–402.
Parker, D. C. (1997) *The living text of the Gospels*, New York, NY.
Parsons, T. (1954) *Essays in Sociological Theory* (rev ed), Glencoe, IL.
Pasquale, P. (2013) "Time", in Karla Pollmann (ed), *OGHRA*, Vol. 3, Oxford, 1810–1815.
Patte, D. and Eugene TeSelle (eds) (2002) *Engaging Augustine on Romans: Self, Context, and Theology in Interpretation*, Harrisburg, PA.
Pelikan, J. (1982) "The Two Cities: The Decline and Fall of Rome as Historical Paradigm", in *Daedalus*, 111 (3), 85–91.
———. (2005) *Whose Bible is it: A history of the Scriptures through the Ages*, New York, NY.
Perczel, I. (2015) "Dionysius the Areopagite", in Ken Parry (ed), *The Wiley Blackwell Companion to Patristics*, Oxford, 211–25.
Pinckaers, S. (2016) Patrick M. Clark and Annie Hounsokou (trans) *The Spirituality of Martyrdom to the Limits of Love*, Washington, DC
Ployd, A. (2015) *Augustine, the Trinity, and the Church: A Reading of the Anti-Donatist Sermons*, New York, NY.
Pohlsander, H. A. (1969) "Victory: The Story of a Statue", in *Historia*, 18, 588–97.
Pollmann, K. (2005) "Augustine's Hermeneutics as a Universal Discipline!?", in Mark Vessey, Karla Pollmann (eds), *Augustine and the Disciplines: From Cassiciacum to Confessions*, Oxford, 206–31.

———. (2009) "Nullus quippe credit aliquid, nisi prius cogitaverit esse credendum: Augustine as Apologist", in Jörg Ulrich, David Brakke, Anders-Christian Jacobsen (eds), *Critique and Apologetics: Jews, Christians and Pagans in Antiquity*, Frankfurt, 303–27.
———. (2011) "Alium sub meo nominee: Augustine between His Own Self-Fashioning and His Later Reception", in *ZAC*, 14 (2), 409–24.
———. (2014) "Christianity and Authority in Late Antiquity: The Transformation of the Concept of Auctoritas", in Caroline Humfress, Isabella Sandwell, Carol Harrison (eds) *Being Christian in Late Antiquity: A Festschrift for Gillian Clark*, Oxford, 156–74.
Portalié, E. (1975) *A guide to the thought of Saint Augustine* (reprinted), Westport, CT.
Pose, E. R. (2014) "Donatism", in Angelo Di Berardino (ed), *Encyclopedia of Ancient Christianity*, Second English Edition, 3 Vols, Downers Grove, IL, 1: 735–41.
Power, S.E. (2021) *Philosophy of Time: A Contemporary Introduction*, New York, NY.
Pranger, M.B. (2006) "Politics and Finitude: The Temporal Status of Augustine's Civitas Permixta," in Hent de Vries and Lawrence E. Sullivan (eds), *Political Theologies: Public Religion in a Post–Secular World*, New York, NY, 113–21.
Pratt, K. J. (1965) "Rome as Eternal", in *JHI*, 26 (1), 25–44.
Quinn, J. M. (1992) "Four faces of time in St Augustine", in *RA*, 26, 181–231.
———. (1999) "Time", in Allan D. Fitzgerald (ed), *ATA*, Grand Rapids, MI, 832–38.
Rabb, T. K. (1975) *The Struggle for Stability in Early Modern Europe*, New York, NY.
Ramsey, B. (1997) *Ambrose* (Early Church Fathers), London.
Rapp, C. (2005) *Holy Bishops in Late Antiquity: The Nature of Christian Leadership in an Age of Transition*, Berkeley and Los Angeles, CA.
Raspanti, G. (2009) "The Significance of Jerome's Commentary on Galatians in his exegetical Production", in Andrew Cain and Josef Lössl (eds), *Jerome of Stridon: His Life, Writings and Legacy*, Surrey, 163–71.
Raz, J. (1979) *The Authority of Law: Essays on Law and Morality*, Oxford.
Rebenich, S. (2002) *Jerome*, London.
Reis, H. T. and S. Sprecher (2009) *Encyclopedia of Human Relationships*, Los Angeles, CA.
Riches, J. (2013) *Galatians through the Centuries*, Oxford.
Ricoeur, P. (1984) Kathleen McLaughlin and David Pellauer (trans), *Time and Narrative*, Vol. 1, Chicago, IL.
Ridley, R. T. (2003) *The Emperor's Retrospect: Augustus' Res Gestae in Epigraphy, Historiography and Commentary*, Leuven.
Rist, J. (1996) "Plotinus and Christian philosophy", in Lloyd P. Gerson (ed), *The Cambridge Companion to Plotinus*, Cambridge, 386–413.
Ritcher, M. (1995) *The History of Political and Social Concepts: A Critical Introduction*, New York, NY.
Rohrbacher, D. (2006) "Jerome, An Early Reader of Ammianus Marcellinus", in *Latomus*, 65 (2), 422–24.
Ross, A. J. (2016) *Ammianus' Julian: Narrative and Genre in the Res Gestae*, Oxford.
Rummel, E. (2008) *Biblical Humanism and Scholasticism in the age of Erasmus*, Leiden.
Rüpke, J. (2011) David M. B. Richardson (trans) *The Roman Calendar from Numa to Constantine: Time, History and the Fasti*, First Edition, Oxford.
———. (2014) David M. B. Richardson (trans) *From Jupiter to Christ: On the History of Religion in the Roman Imperial Period*, Oxford.

Saebo, M. (2006) "שָׁלַט", in Helmer Ringgren, Heinz-Josef Fabry, G. Johannes Botterweck (eds), *TDOT*, Vol. 15, Grand Rapids, MI, 83–88.

Salzman, M. R. (2011) *The Letters of Symmachus*, Book 1, Atlanta, GA.

———. (2013) "Religion in Rome and Italy: Late Republic through Late Antiquity", in Michele Renee Salzman and Marvin A. Sweeney (eds), *The Cambridge History of Religions in the Ancient World, From the Hellenistic Age to Late Antiquity*, New York, NY, 371–97.

SanPietro, I. (2017) "The making of a Christian Intellectual Tradition in Jerome's *De Viris Illustribus*", in *Memoirs of the American Academy in Rome*, 62, 231–60.

Scanlon, L. (1994) *Narrative, authority, and power: The medieval exemplum and the Chaucerian tradition*, Cambridge.

Scheid, J. (2009) "To Honour the Princeps and Venerate the Gods: Public Cult, Neighbourhood Cults, and Imperial Cult in Augustan Rome", in Jonathan Edmondson (ed), *Augustus*, Edinburgh, 275–99.

Schleiermacher, F. (1988) Richard Crouter (trans and ed), *On Religion: Speeches to Its Cultured Despisers*, Cambridge.

Sears, G. (2017) "Augustine in Roman North Africa (Thagaste, Carthage)", in Tarmo Toom (ed), *Augustine in Context*, New York, NY, 37–43.

Shagan, E. H. (2018) *The Birth of Modern Belief: Faith and Judgment from the Middle Ages to the Enlightenment*, Princeton, NJ.

Shanzer, D. (2012) "Augustine and the Latin Classics", in Mark Vessey (ed), *A companion to Augustine*, Oxford, 161–74.

Shaw, B. D. (2011) *Sacred Violence: African Christians and Sectarian Hatred in the age of Augustine*, Cambridge.

Simmons, M. B. (1995) *Arnobius of Sicca: Religious Conflict and Competition in the Age of Diocletian*, Oxford.

———. (2015) *Universal Salvation in Late Antiquity: Porphyry of Tyre and the Pagan-Christian Debate*, New York, NY.

Skarsaune, O. (1996) "The Development of Scriptural Interpretation in the Second and Third Centuries — except Clement and Origen", in Magne Saebo (ed), *Hebrew Bible — Old Testament: The History of its Interpretation*, Vol. I, Gottingen, 373–450.

Smith, C.S. and LiChing Hung (2009) "Bible and Time," in H. James Birx (ed), *ET*, Vol. 1, New Delhi, 87–90.

Sogno, C. (2006) *Q. Aurelius Symmachus: A Political Biography*, Ann Arbor, MI.

Sorabji, R. (1983) *Time, Creation and the Continuum: Theories in Antiquity and the Early Middle Ages*, London.

Soskice, J. (2018) "Why *Creatio ex nihilo* for Theology Today?", in Gary A. Anderson and Markus Bockmuehl (eds), *Creation ex nihilo: Origins, Development, Contemporary Challenges*, Notre Dame, IN, 37–54.

Spat, E. (2004) "The 'Teachers' of Mani in the Acta Archelai and Simon Magus", in *VC*, 58, 1–23.

Stambaugh, J. (1974) "Time, Finitude, and Finality", in *PEW*, 24 (2), 129–135.

Starnes, C. (1990) *Augustine's Conversion: A Guide to the argument of Confessions I–IX*, Waterloo, Ontario.

Steinhauser, K. B. (1992) "The Literary Unity of the Confessions", in Joanne McWilliam (ed), *Augustine: From Rhetor to Theologian*, Waterloo, Ontario, 15–30.

Stern, S. (2012) *Calendars in Antiquity: Empires, States, and Societies*, Oxford.
Stock, B. (1996) *Augustine the reader: Meditation, self-knowledge, and the ethics of interpretation*, Cambridge.
——. (2010) *Augustine's inner dialogue: The philosophical soliloquy in late Antiquity*, Cambridge.
Straw, C. (2002) "'A Very Special Death': Christian Martyrdom in Its Classical Context", in Margaret Cormack (ed), *Sacrificing the Self: Perspectives in Martyrdom and Religion*, New York, NY, 39–57.
Streeter, J. (2006) "Introduction: de Ste. Croix on Persecution", in Michael Whitby and Joseph Streeter (eds), *Christian Persecution, Martyrdom, and Orthodoxy*, Oxford, 3–34.
Streigh, G. W. (2005) "Authority", in M. C. Horowitz (ed), *New Dictionary of the History of Ideas*, Vol. 1, Detroit, MI, 181–83.
Strugnell, A. (2013) "Authority, Government, and Power," in Michel Delon (ed), *Encyclopedia of the Enlightenment*, Oxford, 127–30.
Sutcliffe, E. F. (1948) "The Name 'Vulgate'", in *Biblica*, 29 (4), 345–52.
Swedberg, R. and Ola Agevall (2005) "Domination (Herrschaft)", in *The Max Weber Dictionary: Key Words and Central Concepts*, Stanford, CA, 88–91.
Syme, R. (1968) *Ammianus and the Historia Augusta*, Oxford.
Tal, A. (2015) *BHQ: Introduction and Commentaries on Genesis*, Stuttgart.
Tardieu, M. (2008) M. B. DeBevoise (trans) *Manichaeism*, Urbana and Chicago, IL.
TeSelle, E. (1970) *Augustine the Theologian*, London.
——. (1986–1994) "Crede ut intellegas", in Cornelius Mayer (ed), *AL*, Vol. 2, Basel, 116–19.
——. (1999) "Pelagius, Pelagianism", in Allan D. Fitzgerald (ed), *ATA*, Grand Rapids, MI, 633–40.
——. (2002a) "Engaging Scripture, Patristic Interpretation of the Bible", in Daniel Patte and Eugene TeSelle (eds), *Engaging Augustine on Romans: Self, Context, and Theology in Interpretation*, Harrisburg, PA, 1–62.
——. (2002b) "Exploring the Inner Conflict, Augustine's Sermons on Romans 7 and 8", in Daniel Patte and Eugene TeSelle (eds), *Engaging Augustine on Romans: Self, Context, and Theology in Interpretation*, Harrisburg, PA, 111–28.
——. (2014) "The Background, Augustine and the Pelagian Controversy", in Brian J. Matz and Augustine Casiday, Y. Hwang (eds), *Grace for Grace: The debates after Augustine and Pelagius*, Washington, DC, 1–13.
Teske, R.J. (1996) *Paradoxes of Time in Saint Augustine*, Milwaukee, WI.
——. (1999) "De Genesi ad litteram liber", in Allan D. Fitzgerald (ed), *ATA*, Grand Rapids, MI, 376–77.
——. (2009) *Augustine of Hippo: Philosopher, Exegete, and Theologian* (A second collection of essays), Milwaukee, WI.
Thiselton, A.C. (2015) *Systematic Theology*, Grand Rapids, MI.
Tilley, M. A. (1996) *Donatist Martyr Stories: The Church in Conflict in Roman North Africa*, Liverpool.
——. (1999) "Contra Epistulam Parmeniani", in Allan D. Fitzgerald (ed), *ATA*, Grand Rapids, MI, 312.
Toom, T. (2013) "Augustine on Scripture", in C. C. Pecknold and Tarmo Toom (eds), *T&T Clark Companion to Augustine and Modern Theology*, London, 75–90.

Torchia, N. J. (1999) *Creatio ex nihilo and the Theology of St Augustine: The Anti-Manichean Polemic and Beyond*, New York, NY.

Tribe, K. (2019) *Max Weber: Economy and Society, A new translation*, Cambridge, MA.

Ulrich, E. (2002) "The Notion and Definition of Canon", in Lee Martin McDonald and James A. Sanders (eds), *The Canon Debate: On the origins and formation of the Bible*, Peabody, MA, 21–35.

———. (2015) *The Dead Sea Scrolls and the Developmental Composition of the Bible*, Leiden.

van den Belt, H. (2008) *The Authority of Scripture in Reformed Theology: Truth and Trust*, Leiden.

———. (2018) "The Problematic Character of Sola Scriptura," in Hans Burger, Arnold Huijgen and Eric Peels (eds), *Sola Scriptura: Biblical and Theological Perspectives on Scripture, Authority, and Hermeneutics*, Leiden, 38–55.

van den Berg, J. A. (2010) *Biblical argument in Manichaean missionary practice: The case of Adimantus and Augustine*, Leiden.

———. (2013) "Biblical Quotations in Faustus' Capitula", in Johannes van Oort (ed), *Augustine and Manichaean Christianity*, Leiden, 19–36.

van Dusen, D. (2014) *The Space of Time: A Sensualist Interpretation of Time in Augustine, Confessions X to XII*, Leiden.

Van Fleteren, F. (2013) "De Doctrina Christiana", in Karla Pollmann (ed), *OGHRA*, Vol. 1, Oxford, 285–91.

van Gaans, G. M. (2013) "The Manichaean Bishop Faustus: The State of Research After a Century of Scholarship", in Johannes van Oort (ed), *Augustine and Manichaean Christianity*, Leiden, 199–227.

van Oort, J. (2001) "Secundini Manichaei Epistula: Roman Manichaean 'Biblical' Argument in the Age of Augustine", in Johannes van Oort, et al, *Augustine and Manichaeism in the Latin West*, Leiden, 161–73.

———. (2004) "The Paraclete Mani as the Apostle of Jesus Christ and the Origins of a New Church", in A. Hilhorst (ed), *The Apostolic age in Patristic Thought*, Leiden, 139–57.

———. (2012) "Augustine and the Books of the Manicheans", in Mark Vessey (ed), *A Companion to Augustine*, Malden, MA, 188–99.

———. (2013) "Augustine and Manichaean Christianity: A Testimony to a Paradigm Shift in Augustinian Studies?", in Johannes van Oort (ed), *Augustine and Manichaean Christianity*, Leiden, ix–xv.

Vaught, C. G. (2003) *The Journey toward God in Augustine's Confessions, Books I–VI*, Albany, NY.

———. (2004) *Encounters with God in Augustine's Confessions, Books VII–IX*, Albany, NY.

Veltri, G. (2006) *Libraries, Translations, and "Canonic" Texts: The Septuagint, Aquila and Ben Sira in the Jewish and Christian Traditions*, Leiden.

Verhey, A. (1986) "Bible in Christian Ethics," in John Macquarrie and James Childress (eds), *A New Dictionary of Christian Ethics*, London, 57–61.

Vessey, M. (1993) "Conference and Confession: Literary Pragmatics in Augustine's 'Apologia contra Hieronymum'", in *JECS*, 1 (2), 175–213.

———. (1999) "The Great Conference: Augustine and His Fellow Readers", in Pamela Bright (ed and trans) *Augustine and the Bible*, Notre Dame, IN, 52–72.

———. (2004) "Jerome and Rufinus", in Andrew Louth, Frances Young and Lewis Ayres (eds), *The Cambridge History of Early Christian Literature*, Cambridge, 318–27.
———. (2012) "Augustine among the Writers of the Church", in Mark Vessey (ed), *A Companion to Augustine*, Oxford, 240–54.
———. (2015) "Literary History: A Fourth-Century Roman Invention?", in Lieve Van Hoof and Peter Van Nuffelen (eds), *Literature and Society in the Fourth Century AD: Performing Paideia, Constructing the Present, Presenting the Self*, Leiden, 16–30.
Vessey, M., Karla Pollmann and Allan D. Fitzgerald (eds) (1999) *History, Apocalypse and the Secular Imagination: New Essays on Augustine's City of God*, Bowling Green, OH.
Wallace-Hadrill, A. (1986) Walter Hamilton (trans) "Introduction Note and Notes on the Text", in *The Later Roman Empire (A.D. 354–378): Ammianus Marcellinus*, Middlesex, 13–35, 445–75.
Walton, J. (2003) "Garden of Eden", in David W. Baker, T. Desmond Alexander (eds), *Dictionary of the Old Testament: Pentateuch*, Downers Grove, IL, 202–07.
Ward-Perkins, B. (2005) *The Fall of Rome And the End of Civilization*, New York, NY.
Wasserstein, A. and David J. Wasserstein (2006) *The Legend of the Septuagint: From Classical Antiquity to Today*, Cambridge.
Watson, A. (1999) *Aurelian and the Third Century*, London.
Weidmann, C. (2012) "Augustine's Works in Circulation", in Mark Vessey (ed), *A Companion to Augustine*, Oxford, 431–49.
Wetzel, J. (2012) *Augustine' City of God: A Critical Guide*, Cambridge.
Wilken, R. L. (2003) *The Christians as the Romans Saw Them*, Second Edition, New Haven, CT.
Williams, D. H. (1995) *Ambrose of Milan and the end of the Arian-Nicene Conflicts*, Oxford.
Williams, M. S. (2012) "Augustine as a Reader of His Christian Contemporaries", in Mark Vessey (ed), *A companion to Augustine*, Oxford, 227–39.
———. (2017) *The Politics of Heresy in Ambrose of Milan: Community and Consensus in Late Antique Christianity*, Cambridge.
Williams, R. R. (1950) *Authority in the Apostolic Age*, London.
Williams, T. (2019) *Confessions*, Indianapolis, IN.
———. (ed) (1965) *Authority and the Church*, London.
Wills, G. (2011) *Augustine's Confessions: A Biography*, Princeton, NJ.
———. (2012) *Font of life: Ambrose, Augustine and the mystery of baptism*, Oxford.
Wisse, M. (2013) "Hermeneutics: From 1500–2000", in Karla Pollmann and Willemien Otten (eds), *OGHRA*, Oxford, 1130–35.
Withers, C. W. (2007) *Placing the Enlightenment: Thinking Geographically about the Age of Reason*, Chicago, IL.
Wolf, P. (2001) "Authority, Delegation", in Neil J. Smelser and Paul B. Baltes (eds), *International Encyclopedia of Social and Behavioral Sciences*, Amsterdam, 972–78.
Young, R. D. (2001) *In procession before the world: Martyrdom as public liturgy in early Christianity*, Milwaukee, WI.
Zambrano, E. (2001) "Social Theories of Authority," in Neil J. Smelser and Paul B. Baltes (eds), *International Encyclopedia of Social and Behavioral Sciences*, Amsterdam, 978–82.
Ziegler, P.G. (2004) "Authority" in Hans J. Hillerbrand (ed), *The Encyclopedia of Protestantism*, Vol.1, New York, NY, 225–30.

Indices

1. Index of Scriptures

Genesis
1	132, 135
1:1	126, 135
1:1–5	130, 132
1:2	129
1:4	130
1:6–8	139
1:26	176
1:26–27	127
1:27	130
1:28	127
1–3	125
1–6	18
2:2–3	127
2:5–6	19
2:7	127–28, 134
2:9	139, 162
2:16–17	134–35
2:17	133–34
2:18–20	130
2:22	131
2:24	132, 138
3:5	135
3:6	133–35
3:19	129, 133–34
4:6–7	163
4:7	136
5	164
12:3	131
16:1–3	131
21:9–10	131
26:4	136

Psalms
10	90

Proverbs
3:27	57
19:17	57

Isaiah
7:9	76, 124, 137, 173
7:14	52
45:7	125

Daniel
2:29, 39	37
3:27	37
4:14	37–38
4:22–23, 29	37
5:7, 16, 21	37
6:25	37

Matthew
6:12	176
7:29	38
9:8	38
10:31	125
12:36	170
15:11	125
19:3–9, 29	130
22:37, 39	126
28:18–20	39

Mark
1:15	38
2:1–12	38
2:10	38
3:15	38
10:29–30	130
13:26–32	39

Luke

2:14	125
4:16–29	38
6:11	38
12:11	38
16	76
16:16	112
18:29–30	130
19:17	38
20:20	38
23:7	38
24:25–27	56

John

1:1, 14	132
1:10	130, 132
1:14	43, 132
1:16–17	112
5:17	127
5:18	112
5:39	56
8:36	125
8:47	124
10:30	171
15:22	129

Acts of the Apostles

1:7, 8	39
1:17	43
2:14–36	56
4:20	39
5:4	38
9:14	38
10:10–12	139

Romans

1:2, 3, 4	132
1:17	137
1:21, 22	124, 135
3:20	132
3:21	136
4:11–12	137
5:5	176
5:15	136
5:19	129
7	176
7:7–25	134
7:11	133
7:18, 19	124
7:21	134
7:23–25	122, 129
7:25	127
8	133
8:2	129
8:7	122, 129, 133
8:19–23	133
8:26	127
9:6–8	136
9:20	122
9:20, 21	134
9:32	136
10:3, 4	136
11:36	124, 130
13:1	38
13:10	127
13:13	75
13:14	125
14:1–15:3	125
14:21	125

1 Corinthians

1:1	120
1:24	124, 127
2:11	127
3:1	127
3:17	124
6:3	124
7:4	131
7:12, 15	130
8:4–13	125
10:6, 10	137
10:11	138
10:19–25	125
10:28–11:1	125
11:7–12	127
11:12	124
11:17	130
11:19	127
11:31	170
12:9	176

13:2, 8	127	5:22, 25	130
13:9	122	5:31–32	127, 136
13:12	127, 177	5:32–33	130
13:13	93		
15:21	129	Philippians	
15:24	38, 127	2:5–8	122
15:45	128	2:6–7	136
15:46	127	2:7	127
15:50	122	4:3	120

2 Corinthians		Colossians	
1:1	120	1:1	120
1:20	136	1:15–16	130
2:11	127	1:16	38
3:3	127	3:9, 10	127
3:6	69		
3:12	127	1 Thessalonians	
6:14	130	5:1	39
11:2–3	127		
11:3	127	1 Timothy	
12:2–4	139	1:5	93, 126
12:17	127	1:13	124
		1:20	127
Galatians		4:4	129
2	108, 114	5:6	127
2:11–14	97-98, 102–04, 107–08	6:10	124
2:13	107		
2:14	109	2 Timothy	
2:16	131	2:25	127
3:6, 8	137	4:4	127
3:16	136		
4:4	43, 131	Titus	
5:13	125, 129	1:1–2	126
5:17	122, 124, 129		
5:24	127	James	
6:14	122, 129	3:1	170

Ephesians		1 Peter	
1:21	38	3:20	164
2:1–18	122	3:22	38
2:2	38, 127		
2:3	124	Apocalypse [Revelation]	
4:22, 24	127	4:4–10	60
5:6	129	17:22	38

2. Index of the Works of Augustine

Augustine
  Contra Adimantum
  1 — 121, 130
  3.1–3.3 — 130
  3.3 — 130
  12.1–5 — 121
  14.1–3 — 121
  16.1–3, 25 — 121

  de duabus animabus
  7.9 — 124

  Confessiones
  1 — 148
  1.1.1 — 20, 78, 177
  1.8.13 — 64
  1.9.14 — 148
  1.10.16 — 64
  1.11.18 — 64
  1.13.20 — 148
  1.13.20–14.23 — 148
  1.13.21–22 — 148
  1.14.23 — 148
  1.16.25, 26 — 148
  1.17.27 — 148
  1.18.28 — 148
  2.3.5 — 64, 149
  2.5.11 — 148
  2.6.13 — 64
  2.8.16 — 64
  3.1.1 — 64, 149
  3.2.4 — 64
  3.4.7 — 64
  3.5.9 — 61, 64–65, 70, 123
  3.6.10 — 64–65
  3.6.11 — 64
  3.7.12 — 64, 126
  3.7.12–13 — 61, 64
  3.8.15 — 126–27
  3.12.21 — 126, 128
  4.2.2 — 149
  4.3.6 — 65
  4.12.18 — 64
  4.13.20–14.23 — 149
  5 — 67
  5.3.3 — 64
  5.3.4 — 64
  5.3.6 — 65
  5.5.8 — 65
  5.7.13 — 19, 65
  5.8.14 — 149
  5.10.19 — 65
  5.10.20 — 71
  5.11.21 — 64
  5.12.22 — 149
  5.12.23 — 67
  5.13.23 — 64–65, 67, 70, 149, 151
  5.14.24 — 69–70, 123
  5.14.25 — 123, 171
  6 — 71
  6.1.1 — 64
  6.2.2 — 67
  6.3.3 — 64
  6.3.4 — 65
  6.3.4–5.8 — 70
  6.4.6 — 69, 76
  6.5.8 — 69, 75–76, 94
  6.6.9 — 64, 151
  6.10.17 — 64
  6.11.18 — 19, 65, 67–68
  7 — 70–71, 74
  7.5.7 — 71
  7.8.12 — 75
  7.9.13 — 71–72, 74, 123, 161, 171
  7.9.14 — 72, 161, 171
  7.10.16 — 71, 123
  7.11.17 — 73
  7.18.24 — 70–71, 74, 94
  7.19.25 — 72, 74
  7.20.26 — 71
  7.21.27 — 72, 74, 117, 123
  8 — 70, 74
  8.1.1 — 76
  8.1.2 — 72

8.2.2	67	1.9–10	156
8.2.3	71, 157	1.10–12	152
8.2.5	157	1.11	156
8.5.10	157	1.14	18, 152
8.6.14	117	1.15	156
8.6.15	158	1.16	152
8.11.25	75	1.19	156
8.11.29	75	2.3	147
8.12.26	65	3.2	148
8.12.28, 29	135	3.9	144
9.2.2–4	158	3.12	146
9.4.7	123	3.17	152
9.5.13	87	3.30	145
9.6.14	67	4.1	146–47
9.6.14–9.7.16	158	4.2	144
9.7.15–16	67, 154	4.7	160
9.8.17	158	4.26	148
10.6.9	59	5.15	156
10.29.40	77	5.17–19	156
10.37.61	127	7.32	167
10.42.67	74	10.24	161
10.43.68	74	10.32	160, 167
11	15, 22–23, 29	11.1	24, 159–60
11.2.2	68	11.2	166
11.3.5	76	11.3	160
11.5.7	73	11.6	15–16
11.6.8	16, 59	12.9	162
11.7.9	73	12.10–14	17, 167
11.14.17	15, 29, 45	12.10–15	161
11.23.30	16	12.16	16–17
11.29.39	20	12.21	42
12.17.25	72–73	12.23, 28	163
12.22.31	72–73	12.53	167
12.25.35	127	13.3	162
12.31.42	76	13.4	155
13.24.36	127	13.5	156
13.35.50	78, 179	13.13–14	163
13.37.52	78	13.21	162
		13.24	134
De ciuitate Dei		14.1	163
prol 1	143, 167	14.11	134
1.1	152, 155–56,	14.25	163
1.2	152	15.1	24
1.2–3	152	15.7	164
1.7	152, 156	15.8	18, 164

15.10	163	1.43.93	113
15.11	163–64	2.7.10	20
15.13	47, 165	2.8.15	48
15.14	163	2.10.18	127
15.20	163	2.12.25	54
15.23	59	2.13.26	47, 171
16.10	48	2.13.29	48, 171
18.29	87	2.14.30	76
18.42–43	48	2.16.34	49, 53, 93
18.43	51, 53–54, 165	2.16.36	61
18.44	165	2.19.43	49
18.46–47	165	2.22.53	48
18.49	165	2.22.55	54
18.52	165	2.22.56	61
18.53	39, 166	2.25.64	127
18.54	166	2.28.71	48
20.5–6	167	2.35.88	48
20.8–9	167	2.58.139	114
20.11	160	2.59.141	115
20.23	44	2.59.142	48
21.8	148	3.1.1	88
21.12	135	3.35.78	91
22.8	154	3.42.92	80, 83
22.30	177	3.42.93	90–91
25.23	24	3.43.97	80
		3.45.100	90
		3.46.103–05	90
		3.51.120	48
		3.56.133	90
		4.15.48	93

De utilitate credendi
1.2	19

De doctrina Christiana
prol 1.1	89, 93
prol 3.6	89
prol 5.11	102
prol 8.17	78
prol 9.18	114
1.1.1	88
1.11.23	94
1.12.25	91
1.15.33	94
1.21.41	127
1.27.57	127
1.34.73	48
1.38.81–39.85	16, 59
1.39.85	88
1.40.86–44.95	93
1.42.92–43.93	91

Enchiridion
27	135

Epistulae
21.4	87, 128
28	97–98, 108, 111, 113, 171
28.1	98
28.2	48, 50–51, 53, 87, 105
28.3	102, 111
28.3–4	109
28.3–5	103
28.4	105, 108, 111, 113, 130
28.5	109
28.6	98, 111

28.9–11	111
36.32	67
40	97–98, 108
40.2	103
40.4	108, 112
40.4–6	110
40.4–7	103
40.7	102
40.9	103, 113, 175
41.2	89
54.3	67
71	97
71.4	50–51, 54
71.5	53
71.6	53–54
73	104
73.1–2	106
73.3	113
73.9	106, 113
82	97, 108
82.3	47, 110–11
82.4, 7, 10	111
82.5	54
82.6	54, 111, 130
82.8	112
82.9–11	111
82.13	108, 112
82.14	108
82.15	112
82.16	108
82.22	113
82.35	50–51
93.43–44	83
102.30–31	18
102.33, 38	18
118.21	42
143.2	169
167.6.21	116
190.9	135
194.14	135
224.2	169, 175

De consensu euangelistarum

1.51	44
1.54	60

Contra Faustum Manichaeum

11.2	176
12.1, 3–6, 8–9	138
12.9	164
12.25	138
12.30, 37	137
12.46–48	137
22.60	161
30.4	122

Contra Felicem Manichaeum

1.8	122
1.9	122
1.13	122

Contra Fortunatum Manichaeum disputatio

1	129
7	122
12	129
13	129
16	122
15	129
19	122, 129, 132
20	129
21	122
22	129
23	129
25	129
26	122

Contra epistulam Manichaei quam uocant fundamenti

5.6	41

Epistulae ad Galatas expositionis

15	103, 107–09, 131

De gestis Pelagii

23	163

De Genesi ad litteram imperfectus

2.5	18
4.13	130
5.23	130
16.61	130

De Genesi ad litteram

1.1.1	134, 138
1.21.41	77
3.22.34	134
6.1.1	134
6.3.4	134
6.5.8	134
6.6.11	134
6.9.16	134
6.11.19	134
6.12.21	134
6.13.23	134
7.5.8	134
7.6.9	134
8.1.2	18
8.1.4	138, 162
8.2.5	138, 162
8.3.6–7	162
8.3.7	139
8.4.8	139, 162
8.5.9	139, 162
12	139
12.2.5	139
12.24.51	139
12.34.67	139
12.35.68	139

De Genesi contra Manichaeos

1.1.1	128
1.1.1–2	114, 125
1.1.2	126
1.2.3	117, 125–26
1.2.4	126
1.17.27	127
1.20.31	127
1.22.33	127
1.23.35–40	133
1.23.40	127
1.25.43	127
2	127
2.1	134
2.1.1	18
2.2.3	138, 162
2.5	19
2.8, 9	134
2.9.12	138, 162
2.23.36	127
2.24.37	132
2.27.41	127
2.37	134

Quaestionum in Heptateuchum

2.73	55

De haeresibus ad Quoduultdeum

7	148
88	163, 175
88.1–3	175

In Iohannis euangelium tractatus

29.6	173

Contra Iulianum

6.2	135

Contra Iulianum opus imperfectum

1.141	135
2.178	134

De libero arbitrio

1	124, 135
1.4	173
3	124, 135
3.9.28	124
3.11.33	124
3.14.40	124
3.17.48	124
3.18.51	124
3.19.54	124
3.24.72	124, 135

De mendacio

3.3	109
21.43	109

De moribus ecclesiae Catholicae et de moribus Manicheorum

1.1.2	124, 174
1.2.4	124, 174
1.3.6	124, 174

1.4.6	124, 174	*Enarrationes in Psalmos*	
1.8.13	124, 127	89.3	134
1.9.14	124, 127	118.18.2	134
1.10.16	125		
1.11.18	124, 127	*De diuersis quaestionibus octoginta tribus*	
1.16.26	124		
1.16.29	127	66–74	131
1.17.30	125	67.3	133–34
1.17.31	127	68.2	134
1.21.39	124, 127	68.3	135
1.25.46	127		
1.28.57	124–25, 127, 174	*Ad Simplicianum de diuersis quaestionibus*	
1.30.62	124		
1.30.64	175	1.1.2, 4	134
1.31.65	125, 174	1.1.13, 16	134
1.32.69	125, 127, 174	1.2.16, 19	135
1.33.73	125, 174	1.2.20	134
1.34.75	128		
2.2.2	125, 127	*Retractationes*	
2.3.5	124, 174	*prol* 1	170
2.7.9, 10	125	*prol* 2	170–71, 173
2.9.15	124, 174	*prol* 2–3	169
2.10.19	125	*prol* 3	170
2.11.22	125	1.1	171
2.12.26–13.27	128	1.1.2	171
2.13.28	125	1.1.3	17, 171
2.14.31	125	1.3.2	171
2.14.32–34	125	1.4.3	171
2.17.60	128	1.5.2	171
		1.7.1	174
Contra epistulam Parmeniani		1.7.2	128
1.1.1	80	1.7.2–3	47, 49, 172
		1.7.4	171, 177
De peccatorum meritis et remissione et de baptismo paruulorum ad Marcellinum		1.7.5	173–76
		1.9.1	173
		1.9.2	173–74
1.4	134	1.9.3	174–75
		1.9.6	174–75
Contra duas epistulas Pelagianorum		1.10.1	173
4.11.31	69	1.10.1–3	49
		1.10.2	172, 175
Contra litteras Petiliani		1.10.3	128, 173–74
3.25.30	151	1.11.4	171
		1.13.4	174
De dono perseuerantiae		1.13.8	176
53	77	1.14.2	177

1.14.4	174	*Expositio quarundam propositionum ex epistola ad Romanos*	
1.15.7	171		
1.18	172, 176	1, 59	132
1.19.1, 3	176	13–18	133
1.19.4	49, 173	39, 49, 53	133
1.19.5	174		
1.19.9	176	*Epistolae ad Romanos inchoata expositio*	
1.21.3	173		
1.22.2	172	4, 5	132
1.23.1	132, 173, 175–76	15–16	118
1.23.2, 3	176		
1.25.1	132	*Sermones*	
1.26	176	43.9	173
2.4.1	88	80.8	15, 167, 170
2.4.2	172	81.7	42
2.7.1	135	118.1	173
2.7.3	176	286.4	154
2.17	173	318.1	154
2.17.43	88		
2.18	176	*Sermones M. Denis*	
2.24.1	172	24.11.13	42
2.24.2	173, 176		
2.43.1	143–44	*Sermones Dolbeau*	
2.50	175	6.12.13	42
2.53	175–76		
2.62	174	*De Spiritu et littera*	
		18	55
De uera religione			
7.13	16	*De fide et symbolo*	
12.24	127	4.8	16
46.86	127		
		De Beata uita	
		1.4	19, 71

3. Index of Other Ancient Authors

Ambrose		*Epistularum liber decimus*	
De paradiso		11.17–18	66
1.1	162	17–18	153
3.12	162	18.2, 39	156
De virginibus		18.4	157
7.37–38	155	18.7	157–58

18.11, 25, 29	157
18.30	157
20.14	155
20.17	153
20.28	155
22.7	154
40.6	66
41.28	66

Ammianus Marcellinus
Rerum gestarum

14.6.1–3	149
14.6.21	149
14.7.26	149
15.7.1, 10	149
16.10.14, 20	149
19.10.1	149
28.4.1–35	149

Cassiodorus
Institutiones

1.1–9	47

Clement of Alexandria
Στρωματέων

2.6.28, 29	57
3.6.54	57

Jerome
Commentarii in epistulam ad Galatas

prol 1	99, 101–02, 105, 115
prol 3	100
1.1	101
1.2	102, 105, 109, 112–13
2.3	101
De uiris illustribus	97–98, 100–101, 103, 106, 111, 113–16

Epistulae

20.2	105
27.1	101
102.1	104
102.2	103–05
105.1–4	104
105.2	103
105.3	103, 105
105.4	104
105.5	103, 105
112.1	103
112.4	104, 109
112.4–5	110
112.5	104
112.5–6	110
112.6	104, 106
112.6–11	110
112.7–10	111
112.7–14	112
112.8	104
112.13	104, 109–10
112.14	112
112.14–16	110
112.16	104
112.19	105
112.20	50, 105
112.22	104–06

Prologus : Vulgata	52, 58, 60
Quaestiones hebraicae in libro Geneseos	52, 104, 164

Origen

Εἰς Μαρτύριον Προτρεπτικός

1.4	155

Secundinus
Epistula

894.9	122

Symmachus
Relatio

	149–151, 153, 156

Tyconius
In Apocalypsin

	80
Liber regularum	80, 83, 86, 88–89, 92, 117

4. Index of Modern Authors

Aitken, E. B.   119
Aitken, J. K.   48, 50
Alexander, J. S.   81
Allison, J. D.   55
Ames, C.   143
Anderson, C. R.   22
Anderson, D. L.   80, 83, 87–90, 92–93
Angus, S.   148
Aune, D.   39
Ayres, L.   86, 122
Babcock, W. S.   92–93, 128, 131
Baird, W.   48
Bammel, C.   117, 119
Bardon, A.   23
Bar-Ilan, M.   58
Barnes, T. D.   149–50
Barton, J.   51, 58
Bate, H.   69
BeDuhn, J. D.   18, 73, 117, 119
Beetham, D.   30–31
Benjamin, H.   162–63
Berardino, A. D.   66
Berchman, R. M.   81
Betz, H. D.   121–22, 131
Birx, J.H.   21, 26, 45
Bogaert, P.-M.   48–50, 53, 106
Boniface, R.   109
Bonner, G.   17, 43, 79, 84, 92, 118, 174–76
Boone, M. J.   123
Bourke, V. J.   84–85
Brachtendorf, J.   15, 170
Bright, P.   77, 80–83, 86–91, 94, 114, 171
Brown, P.   63–64, 66–67, 71, 77, 79, 85–87, 92–93, 119, 151–54, 159–60
Brown, S. J.   44
Bruce, F.   50, 57
Burchill-Limb, K.   149
Burges, J.   21
Burns, J. P.   18, 65, 69, 71
Burns, P. C.   150, 160
Burton, P.   48–49, 70
Cain, A.   98, 99, 100–01, 103–06, 108, 115

Callahan, J.F.   23
Calvin, J.   41
Cameron, A.   150–51
Cameron, M.   16, 19–20, 64, 70–71, 76, 90, 117, 137, 141
Canty, A.   133
Carrigan Jr., H.L.   26
Cary, P.   70–71
Cavadini, J. C.   24, 74
Chadwick, H.   64, 66, 70, 148–49
Chapman, M.   31–32, 34, 37, 40–41, 63
Childs, B. S.   48
Christian, W. A.   15–18
Cimosa, M.   48
Clark, E. A.   104
Clark, G.   166
Cohen, W.   112
Cole-Turner, R. S.   108, 113
Colish, M.L.   21
Conybeare, C.   76, 146,
Cooley, A. E.   34–36, 145
Copleston, F.   73–74
Costello, C. J.   20
Coyle, J. K.   17, 118, 121–22, 124
Cullmann, O.   26, 39–40
Danielou, J.   17, 24
Davies, J. P.   150
Dawson, D.   70–71
Dearn, A.   82
de Jong, A.   86
Delumeau, J.   161
de Ste. Croix, G.   81, 84
DeWeese, G.   16
Dillistone, F. W.   82
Dimitrov, D. Y.   73
Dorival, G.   53
Drijvers, J. W.   149
Drobner, H. R.   65
Dyke, H.   21
Ebbeler, J.   97, 103, 105
Eck, W.   145
Eder, W.   33, 35–36
Edward, M.   55, 68–69, 81–82, 84–85

Eller, M. F.   171, 173
Eno, R.   84, 97
Evans, C. A.   39
Evans, G.   146
Evans, R. F.   174–75
Ever, A.   81, 86
Everson, D. L.   49
Feeney, D.   17, 146
Ferguson, E.   40, 55–57
Ferrari, L.   65
Fiedrowicz, M.   16
Filice, C.   16
Filoramo, G.   161
Fischer, B.   49–50
Fitzgerald, A. D.   97, 170
Flores, R.   76
Foerster, W.   37–38, 55
Forsyth, P.   30–31
Fortin, E. L.   147
Frankfurter, D.   122, 143
Frede, H. J.   13, 15
Fredriksen, P.   67, 74–78, 80, 83, 87, 89, 93, 112, 124, 130, 133, 135
Frend, W. H.   79, 81–82, 86, 117–19, 159
Friedrich, C. J.   29
Froehlich, K.   86
Fuhrer, T.   97
Gadamer, H.-G.   20, 26, 41–42
Gaddis, M.   42, 81–82, 159
Galinsky, K.   144–45
Gallagher, E. L.   54, 59, 61
Gamble, H. Y.   58
Ganssle, G. E.   15
George, T.   22, 24
Gersh, S.   73
Gerson, L. P.   70, 72
Gillett, A.   151
Gilson, É.   17
Glare, P. G. W.   33–34, 69, 75
Goldingay, J.   60
Goshen-Gottstein, M.   52
Grebe, S.   36
Green, L.   31
Green, R.P.H   89
Gribomont, J.   61

Güven, S.   35
Hagendahl, H.   147, 150
Häkkinen, S.   104
Hardy, J. E.   160–61
Hargis, J. W.   150
Harmless, W.   69
Harris, H. A.   60
Harrison, C.   20, 49, 69, 86, 117
Harrison, J.   119, 121
Harrison, L.   31
Harrison, S.   64
Harrison, T.   150
Hassard, J.   21–22, 32
Heidegger, M.   16, 22, 26
Heine, R. E.   48
Heinze, R.   33–34
Hengel, M.   48, 51–52, 58
Henrichs, A.   17, 86, 119–20
Hoek, A. V.   69
Hoeveler, J. J.   45
Holder, R.W.   25
Hopkins, K.   40–42
Houghton, H. A. G.   47–49, 58
Hurtado, L. W.   58
Ierodiakonou, K.   74
Jenson, R.   25
Kamesar, A.   49, 52–53, 101, 106, 109
Kannengiesser, C.   79–80, 88–91
Kaster, R. A.   148
Kato, T.   54
Kedar, B.   50, 54–55
Kelly, J.   98, 100–01, 104, 106
King, P.   73
Koenen, L.   119–23, 132–33
Koselleck, R.   24
Kotze, A.   65, 67
Kugler, R. A.   87, 91
Kulikowski, M.   144, 146
La Bonnardière, A.-M.   59, 64, 87
Lamb, M.   147
Lamb, R.   25
Leadbetter, B.   81
Liebeschuetz, J.   66, 153
Lienhard, J. T.   47
Lieu, S. N.   70–71

Lincoln, B.   29–30, 36–37
Lohr, W.   57
Löschke, J.   30
Lossl, J.   66
Lutcke, K.-H.   37, 63
Lyotard, J.   22
MaenchenHelfen, O. J.   150
Maher, J. P.   121
Marion, J.-L.   15
Markus, R. A.   17–18, 26, 42, 69, 81–82, 84, 114, 143, 146–47, 149–50, 157–60, 175
Martin, T. F.   64, 68
Mathison, K.A.   25
May, G.   73
McDonald, L. M.   50–52, 54, 56, 60
McGrath, A.E.   21
McKim, D. K.   60
McLaughlin, P.   31
McLynn, N.B.   66–67, 148, 151, 153
Meconi, D.V.   24
Metzger, B. M.   49–52, 56–57, 61, 118
Meyer, R.   55
Middleton, P.   82
Miles, R.   84, 95
Miller, C.   31
Mirecki, P. A.   17
Momigliano, A.   21, 24–25, 44–45
Moorhead, J.   66, 69, 153
Moran, D.   72–73, 77
Mulder, M. J.   52
Muller, M.   48, 50, 52–53
Murphy, A. R.   45
Myllykoski, M.   104
Nightingale, A.   22
Nock, A. D.   70
O'Connell, M.   170
O'Daly, G.   16, 74–77, 147, 149, 151, 156, 160
O'Donnell, J. J.   20, 42, 47–49, 53, 65–76, 79–80, 82, 85, 98, 118, 123, 147–49, 151, 171–72
O'Loughlin, T.   18, 36, 47, 49, 51, 56, 59–60, 91, 97, 138, 165
O'Meara, J.   23–24, 65, 67
Ortiz, J.   72, 74

Paddison, A.   25
Pagels, E. H.   92, 163
Parker, D. C.   47
Parsons, T.   31
Pasquale, P.   15
Patte, D.   141
Pelikan, J.   44, 55–56, 60–61, 150, 152, 158
Perczel, I.   21
Pinckaers, S.   159
Ployd, A.   84
Pohlsander, H. A.   151
Pollmann, K.   31–32, 37, 41, 63, 70, 86, 88, 171
Portalié, E.   85
Pose, E. R.   81–82, 84–85
Power, S.E.   21, 23
Pranger, M.B.   23
Pratt, K. J.   146
Quinn, J. M.   15–18, 22
Rabb, T. K.   45
Ramsey, B.   66–67, 153
Rapp, C.   66
Raspanti, G.   54, 101
Raz, J.   31
Rebenich, S.   101
Reis, H. T.   30
Riches, J.   109
Ricoeur, P.   15, 22, 26
Ridley, R. T.   33–35
Rist, J.   66, 73–74
Ritcher, M.   29–30
Rohrbacher, D.   150
Ross, A. J.   149
Rummel, E.   60
Rüpke, J.   145–46
Saebo, M.   38
Salzman, M. R.   145, 151
SanPietro, I.   59
Scanlon, L.   30, 76
Scheid, J.   144–45
Schleiermacher, F.   44
Sears, G.   149
Shagan, E. H.   45
Shanzer, D.   147

Shaw, B. D.   80
Simmons, M. B.   81, 99
Skarsaune, O.   58
Smith, C.S.   24
Sogno, C.   150–51
Sorabji, R.   15, 17, 23
Soskice, J.   72
Spat, E.   118, 128
Stambaugh, J.   22
Starnes, C.   65
Steinhauser, K. B.   64
Stern, S.   145
Stock, B.   68, 90
Straw, C.   155
Streeter, J.   81, 84
Streigh, G. W.   29, 31–32
Strugnell, A.   32
Sutcliffe, E. F.   49
Swedberg, R.   30
Syme, R.   150
Tal, A.   164
Tardieu, M.   73
TeSelle, E.   19, 65, 89, 93, 97, 113, 127, 141, 163, 173, 175–76
Teske, R. J.   19, 23, 65, 116, 135, 138
Thiselton, A.C.   21
Tilley, M. A.   80–82, 85, 88
Toom, T.   20, 59
Torchia, N. J.   19, 118
Tribe, K.   30
Ulrich, E.   51–52, 58

van den Belt, H.   25
van den Berg, J. A.   118–19, 122
van Dusen, D.   22
Van Fleteren, F.   88
van Gaans, G. M.   122
van Oort, J.   19, 117, 119–22
Vaught, C. G.   70, 135
Veltri, G.   41
Verhey, A.   25
Vessey, M.   50, 93, 100, 104, 114–15, 147–48
Wallace-Hadrill, A.   149–50
Walton, J.   161
Ward-Perkins, B.   146
Wasserstein, A.   50–51
Watson, A.   145
Weidmann, C.   170
Wetzel, J.   24
Wilken, R. L.   95
Williams, D. H.   66
Williams, M. S.   66, 68, 89, 93, 110–11
Williams, R. R.   37–38, 40, 45, 56, 160
Williams, T.   64, 76
Wills, G.   64, 66–67, 78
Wisse, M.   26
Withers, C. W.   44
Wolf, P.   30–31
Young, R. D.   155
Zambrano, E.   30–32
Ziegler, P.G.   4